Public Administration in the United States

A Reader

Public Administration in the United States

A Reader

John C. Koritansky
Hiram College

FOCUS PUBLISHING
R PULLINS AND COMPANY

TABLE OF CONTENTS

Introduction

Public Administration and American Liberal Democracy

In the United States, the study of public administration needs to overcome a certain prejudice against the subject matter itself. Americans tend to have a jaundiced attitude towards government and also towards bureaucracy, in all its forms. It may be useful to reflect on the reasons for this, since it bears on many of the problems that constitute public administration as an academic discipline.

With regard to government, Americans' attitudes tend to derive from that body of social and political philosophy usually indicated by the term "Liberalism" as set forth in crystalline outline in the Declaration of Independence. Government, it is attested, derives its legitimate powers only from the consent of the governed. Individuals give their consent in order to render more secure their unalienable rights, with which they are endowed by nature. Not only do the formal strictures of the law depend on that foundation, but so do the rhetorical terms and limits that the general public sets for its political and legal talk. This was the fact that Louis Hartz perceived and brought to the surface already well into the twentieth century; and while Hartz's thesis has undergone subsequent refinement and modification since, his basic point remains firm. It is true, to be sure, that contemporary Americans are probably too agnostic to repeat with confidence the Declaration's assertion that there are truths that are "self-evident." For the same reason they may abjure saying that their personal rights are "unalienable' or that they are an endowment from a "Creator" who is "nature's god." This, though, only confirms the point that it is Liberalism that roots and limits their thought and speech. For anything but the agnosticism spoken of here would be rejected as being in bad taste, perhaps even uncivilized, because it is *illiberal*.

This near paradox is caused by the fact that, outside the terms of what individuals consent to, Liberalism allows to each person the right to such doctrines or beliefs as he or she finds suitable as part of one's pursuit of one's own happiness. Therefore Liberalism is, so to speak, shy about its own status as a doctrine. This is true especially in the absence of really threatening alternatives. Americans consider themselves "open", and in some senses this is accurate, but there is not and cannot be complete openness on certain fundamentals. After all, is there anyone who doubts, at least publicly, that rights do belong to individuals as such; or does anyone think that the foundation for legitimate authority is anything other than consent? Americans, whatever their position on their political spectrum, tend to believe genuinely in the value of freedom, even to love it. Nor do they differ as to its meaning. The freedom that Americans love is not Kant's conformity to the moral law within, or Thomas Aquinas' conformity to natural and divine law. American freedom means the limited license for an individual to do as he or she pleases. It cannot be doubted that the spirited love of freedom, in this sense, is what has made it possible for America to pull together and to sustain heroic acts of patriotism; to play its role in recent history of the world.

America is a Liberal country; and yet, relatedly to the rhetorical paradox spoken of above, Liberalism is not a sort of creed that can unite Americans in mind and feeling except perhaps in times of crisis. It would be permissible to say that Americans are united by Liberalism only if one adds at once that they are also divided by it. Almost from its founding, and to the bitter disappointment of many of the founders, America has exhibited partisan division. In the twentieth century that division has been roughly describable as an opposition between left and right. Those on the left, who today enjoy the name "liberal", are deeply imbued with the notion of the equal natural right of all persons at birth to freedom. Recognizing, then, the actual constraints upon freedom that derive from the complexity and interdependency of modern society, "liberals" are given to think about how to enlist the powers of government to alleviate these constraints—to overcome through cooperation, organization, and government the things that impede the individual. In this respect, contemporary "liberals" are similar to those who called themselves "progressives" a hundred years ago; in fact they are of the same lineage. Probably it would make sense to use the term "progressive" even today so as to avoid the clumsiness of trying to distinguish "big L" versus "little l" liberals. Opposed to the contemporary progressives are an array of "conservatives," some "neo" and others more traditional, all of whom share the concern that when government is employed to reengineer society, as the progressives are eager to do, government itself is likely to become the chief danger to individual freedom. Concessions to government's power should always be made warily; and wherever possible it is safer to trust to the impersonal mechanism of the market and to the effect of traditional morality to maintain a decent social order.

Abstractly considered, there is of course a certain plausibility in both sides of the opposition. The reason it persists, intractably, as an *opposition* is that each side is far more clear sighted in identifying the shortcomings of its opponent than it is its own. Progressives and conservatives are really accusing each other of a kind of apostasy, i.e. of refusing to go along with a necessary emendation of Liberalism in order to preserve its essential value—freedom. For conservatives, active, positive government is the most important impediment to individual freedom. They tend therefore not to be drawn to the study of government, especially not to public administration. The social sciences that are more appealing to them are economics, or perhaps history. Progressives, of course, think of the conservative attitude as quaint and unrealistic. And yet, while progressives are far less wary of governmental power than conservatives, they do have a problem, perhaps "embarrassment" would be a more precise word, with the *authority* that government necessarily claims when it does employ power. For some people to be bossing others around is, well, discomforting. To be sure, the Liberal doctrine holds that all governmental authority is derived, ultimately, from the consent of the governed. Skeptical of abstractions and formalities as they are, however, the progressives would like to condition the exercise of governmental authority on an actual consent of those most immediately affected by government's activity. Thus, when these people study public policy and public administration they tend to stress principles of representativeness and popular involvement, often to the detriment of efficiency, effectiveness, and justice.[1] The contemporary currency of a term like "representative bureaucracy" is obviously a measure of the progressive influence on the field.

The fact that progressive liberals and conservative liberals see each other's difficulties better than they do their own is not surprising or strange once we understand that each camp is wrestling with the same problem, a problem of Liberalism, but in inverse ways. The fundamental problem lies in the postulation of freedom, in the limited sense of the absence of restraint, as a substantive value and as the end or aim of government as such. For one cannot escape the incoherence of thinking that government is an instrument of a purpose which is in turn expressible only as a restriction on the use of that same instrument. Thoreau's anarchism is in fact the more rigorous, if less practical, conclusion from the idealization of freedom. His joke at the expense of the more conventional thinkers of his time, and our own, is apt. "If government is indeed 'best which governs least,' why not one still better, which does not govern at all?" It ought not be considered political heresy to recognize Liberalism's shortcoming thus. In some way or other, nearly all Americans realize it. Probably there is truth in Tocqueville's dictum that every political society depends upon some principles which, if they were driven to their ultimate practical conclusion, would spell destruction. But are we not moved by an understanding of just this, to embrace what moderating statesmanship we can to forestall, perhaps indefinitely, such an outcome?

The American attitude towards bureaucracy is as deeply rooted as that towards government; indeed it is a part of the same broad stream. For one thing, it is felt that bureaucracy depersonalizes us. We may agree to become a member of a bureaucratic organization through an exercise of our power of consent, but once in the bureaucracy we are required to behave as elemental parts of something like a machine; and our essentially human prerogative is put on hold. It may be feared that we will be beguiled into forgetting ourselves and so become victims of repression within the bureaucracy. Of this fear there may be no more eloquent spokesman than Thoreau, or at least none who resonates with more automatic sympathy among Americans. In the second place, Americans dislike bureaucracy because it is inherently undemocratic. Even where it is formally a tool to serve the dictates of electoral majorities, it remains the case that its own structure is hierarchical. The sociologist Roberto Michels' famous statement that "He who speaks organization speaks oligarchy," was meant to chill the hearts of the friends of democracy and it succeeds particularly well among Americans.

Adverse as they are, though, to both government and to bureaucracy, Americans also pride themselves on a practical sort of common sense which saves them from being drawn to extremes. Anarchism is an isolated phenomenon; most are troubled or embarrassed by it. There are some things that government must do and more that it can do best. Even Milton Friedman, an

---

[1]   The ill-fated Community Action Program, as chronicled, for example, by Daniel Patrick Moynihan and Theodore Lowi, illustrates this point. So massive was the embarrassment of contemporary progressivism by the failure of this approach to welfare reform that it dogs the movement and undermines its *elan* even today.

economist widely regarded as a leader of the conservative wing of his discipline, in his delineation of indispensable governmental activities includes several so called "positive" as well as merely regulative functions.[2] We are simply not being serious if we express concern only for less government. Our
concern must be for good government, and that includes government's having the capacity to carry out its necessary tasks effectively and efficiently. We
want, and in fact demand, competence in public administration. If we have a
problem in achieving that, it is because public administration is a tool, the
material of which is human. But American Liberalism and democracy do not
tend to produce the best sort of human material to serve the purpose. Such
material would be men and women who aspire to government, while not
being driven by ambition to elective office. To whatever satisfaction they attained in the successful performance of their duties would have to be added a
measure of pride in their station as public servants. People like that are always going to be the exception among citizens who tend to enjoy and honor
most a private life.

A good statement of the sort of public administration that democracy
needs is provided by Joseph Schumpeter in his classic, *Capitalism, Socialism,
and Democracy*. He writes,

> … democratic government in industrial society must be able to
> command, for all purposes the sphere of public activity is to include—
> no matter whether this be much or little, the services of a well trained
> bureaucracy of good standing and tradition, endowed with a strong
> sense of duty and a no less strong *esprit de corps*.

And then, in his characteristically tough and insistent tone, Schumpeter
continues,

> It is not enough that the bureaucracy should be efficient in cur-
> rent administration and competent to give advice. It must also be
> strong enough to guide and, if need be, to instruct the politicians who
> head the ministries. In order to be able to do this it must be in a posi-
> tion to evolve principles of its own and sufficiently independent to
> assert them. It must be a power in its own right. [3]

Schumpeter thinks that whether modern democracies *will* tend actually
to produce the sort of public administration that he describes as necessary is
at best an open question, a fact which enters into his general iconoclastic style
and his repudiation of the comforts of optimism. Schumpeter's statement helps
sharpen the question: is there an education that can tend towards producing
the "corps" of loyal and competent civil servants that is needed? What, in
particular, might schools do?

By and large, the contemporary study of administration, in business
schools and in graduate programs in sociology and organizational psychology, do not speak to the sort of educational requirements for public administrators that Schumpeter helps us recognize. This is a challenge for the study of
public administration, to the extent that the professionalization of the Ameri-

[2]   Milton Friedman, *Capitalism and Freedom*, (Chicago: The University of Chicago
      Press, 1962) ch.2
[3]   Joseph A. Schumpeter, *Capitalism, Socialism and Democracy*, (New York: Harper &
      Row, Publishers, 1950), pp. 293. The whole three-paragraph passage should be
      considered carefully.

can civil service, and the still significant effects of the politics/administration distinction, have caused academic programs in public administration to be dominated by those same approaches.

An education appropriate to a public career ought to be not only complemented but rooted in a study of government and politics. One may even hope, reasonably, that if the study of administration were developed in the direction of being a more essentially political subject, there would be a gain in sophistication and intellectual coherence that is still being sought for the field. To this point more material will be provided later on in this text. For the present, this much may be observed. Ever since the discovery, or rediscovery, of the necessity for dealing with the "human element" in the management of individuals in organization, the study of administration has looked to an understanding of human organization in which individuals' various needs, including psychological needs, would be effectively satisfied by way of cooperation and contribution to the organization as a whole. Unfortunately, the contemporary science fails to accord the appropriate privileged cognitive status to that peculiar instance of organization which is, or at least aims at being, comprehensive in fact, i.e. the sovereign political organization. Abstracting from the political dimension of human life, much contemporary study of administration seeks its theoretical foundation in a sort of "psychology" that delineates a scale of human needs. However this psychology is embarrassingly crude and question-begging.[4] Nor it is surprising that this same a-political approach to administration should have proved sensitive to the charge of being irrationally biased in favor of the organization, and hence exploitative and manipulative.

Whatever one may think of the current status of organization theory and administrative science in general, however, few will quarrel with the suggestion that an education to *public* administration ought to include some study of government and politics. Moreover, there is probably considerable agreement as to what should be the primary elements of such study. One would naturally recommend the basic regime-defining documents: the Declaration of Independence, the Constitution, selected episodes and legal cases that have augmented the Constitution, and ideally some expression of the social and political philosophy which explains the rationale for the structural features of the regime. Fortunately, with respect to the American Constitution, there are the *Federalist Papers*, which are without parallel or peer as a set of explanatory defenses of the Constitutional system. If there is a problem with political education, it is not so much in knowing where or with what materials to begin. Perhaps there is a difficulty in setting limits, i.e. in keeping the study within reasonable proportions. We can not, after all, be thinking in terms of an indoc-

---

4   The psychologist whose name is invariably mentioned as being at the fountainhead of the modern, "human relations" approach to organization theory is Abraham Maslow. It was he who "postulated" a hiearchy of human psychological needs of which the highest, or last, is "self fufillment". Organizations, it was then concluded, could be successful insofar as they allowed for the satisfaction of the needs of their human members, including this last one. In view of the hopeless vagueness of the term "self-fufillment", at least as Maslow used the term, however, it is amazing that his work should still be relied on so uncritically today. One may well wonder, is he really a foundation, or rather a convenient prop for some obvious prejudices of Liberal democratic ideology?

PUBLIC ADMINISTRATION IN THE UNITED STATES

trination of a set of principles that are fixed and finite. Such a notion would be whimsical if not actually dangerous. One cannot take seriously the image of a civil service whose special preserve would be an American political orthodoxy. The features of the regime are indeed "given", by law; which is to say that they are the products of deliberation and judgment that are continually subject to review and revision. Who can read the *Federalist Papers*, for example, with real interest and understanding, and not enter into the argument with their authors about the whys and wherefores of the Constitution's provisions? Perhaps subsequent experience may even have shed new light on their issues. Does not any reader of the *Federalist Papers* not want to question whether James Madison really has sufficient grounds for establishing barriers to what he calls a "factious" majority? To take up their arguments in a serious way, one would even have to reexamine thinkers on whom the *Federalists Papers* rely as authorities: "the celebrated Montesquieu", Locke, and beyond. When one comes within range of the philosophical dimension of the study of government and politics, one risks being taken up into a field whose expanse is so vast that one may postpone indefinitely whatever practical concerns may have drawn one there.[5]

To be sure, all sciences have their philosophical foundations. Nevertheless, the philosophy of science is not the same thing as, say, chemistry, and we do not require that the chemist constantly call into question the presuppositions of his activity. Political science is different because it cannot help but direct attention to fundamental considerations insofar as these are at least latent within political talk and action. One may be discomforted with this situation at times; but surely a more proper, wiser posture is one of modesty, combined with gratitude for the way that "our" political and legal system offers access to the rich and sophisticated tradition of political philosophy in which it is rooted. Such gratitude naturally induces one to preserve the political and legal system as consonant with a level of intellectual freedom and humane decency that is still rare in the world. If political science were to imbue this sort of virtue, it would obviously prove its benefit, especially for an education specifically intended for civil servants.

And yet, while this point is important, it still leaves us with the question about how to structure a political science that would pay its necessary and proper homage to tradition and philosophy, but which would at the same time be useful in a direct way—one whose possession would make one competent. When we pose the question in this way, it is noteworthy that we are returning to the general consideration, or mood, of people like Frank Goodnow

---

5   John Rohr has suggested that the education of today's civil servants could be enriched by what he aims to show would be the right kind of study of significant cases at Constitutional law. He has in mind a Constitutional law course of instruction that would guide students from immediate practical issues towards the fundamental questions of regime politics. Rohr's attention to this whole issue is extremely thoughtful, and his writing is very measured. Still, in view of what Rohr himself is forced to contend against as the wrong treatment of the cases, reinforcing certain contemporary prejudices rather than subjecting them to genuine criticism, one wonders whether what one is able to take away from such a study is not critically and obviously derivative from what one brings to it. If this is so, must we not press harder in the direction of fundamentals, i.e. of philosophical underpinnings, albeit still in a way that is appropriate for a practical life and career? Cf. John Rohr, *Ethics for Bureaucrats*, (New York: Marcel Dekker, 1978).

or especially Woodrow Wilson, which caused them to launch the study of public administration roughly a century ago. Wilson sensed that the political science of his day, which he saw as a popularized edition of Constitutional philosophy, though important, remained somehow excessively formal and abstract from political reality and from the emerging needs of political life. He offered the suggestion that Americans pay attention to European thinkers who were developing a science of practical *administration*, albeit outside the American system with its central concern for individual liberty. The study of administration, he ventured, needed to be developed here, too, and come to have a vital part of our political science. Have we not, a hundred years later, come back to a situation where we might take up Wilson's challenge once more, with renewed energy and understanding? Of course, we must be wary of retracing the dead-end logic of the "politics/administration" distinction for which Wilson and the other early proponents of a science of administration do bear responsibility. In seeking to articulate a science of public administration we need to be guided by a twofold proposition. The study of the conditions of efficient and effective administration of the public's business has a contribution to make to the broad science of politics; and the study of public administration cannot come into its own unless it aims towards making such a contribution, weighing its recommendations against other politically relevant considerations. One can, in fact, find support for both of these propositions in Wilson; however it is the second of them which needs renewed stress today.

The selection and organization of the readings in this text is intended for an introductory course in public administration that, it may be argued, belongs in an American political science curriculum, at the undergraduate level. We begin with a brief outline of the principles that governed the staffing of the civil service in the early years of the regime, showing the difficulties that attended the various attempts to reconcile the requirement for excellence in the bureaucracy under the conditions of Liberalism and democracy. Next comes reference to the Pendleton Act, which brought about the merit system, and a setting forth of its fundamental idea of the distinction between politics and administration. Woodrow Wilson' classic statement of 1883 is presented along with Herbert J. Storing's remarkably insightful and thorough treatment of the career of Leonard White, who was probably the dean of students of public administration during the years of its most intensive struggle for a distinct identity as an academic discipline. Parts III and IV offer selections that deal with two sets of political problems that have attended the merit system: the problem of responsibility and control, and the problem of coordination and coherence of administrative policy. The last two parts offer foundational materials from which to launch a critique of the attempts to develop a science of administration and organization that is separate and independent of political science. Part V includes a debate over "planning, programming, budgetary systems" since this budgetary technique exemplifies an attempt to put into actual practice the sort of administrative rationality that has been promoted in the work of Herbert Simon. Part VI contains materials that are foundational to the attempt to develop a science of human organization, from which various influences upon contemporary personnel administration have been derived. The reader is encouraged to treat these materials in the way one studies important Constitutional and other legal cases in the administration of law and justice. That is to say, one ought to enter into the arguments, criticizing the logic and the premises as measured against the "intentions of the framers", and be open at the same time to the possibility that those same "intentions" may be subject to suspension or correction in the light of new considerations and requirements, particularly administrative requirements.

PART 1

Founding Principles and Democratic Reforms: America's First Century

I. HAMILTON

Does the American system of government have the capacity for the effective administration of the public's wishes and needs? The question has been well worn. It has been at or near the center of the professional study of political science and public administration in the United States for the better part of this past century. Progressives especially used to like to ask whether the government that succeeds in frustrating a majority faction's domination of policy does not end up being a government that succeeds in not being able to *do* much of anything.[1] American governmental bureaucracy is a far cry from a model of an efficient administrative machine, where lines of responsibility and jurisdiction are clear and where unambiguous standards of performance are effectively enforced. The basic reason for this is the Constitution itself, in the scheme of checks and balances among three coordinate but largely independent branches of government that James Madison eloquently defended as setting "interest against interest and ambition against ambition".[2] Whatever unity and cohesion the American governmental bureaucracy does exhibit is derived from the president in the role of administrative chief; but that role is limited insofar as each bureau and agency owes its specific authorization and its budgetary appropriation to a set of committees in a legislature that is itself fragmented and politically independent.

The question of our government's effectiveness remains central for us. However, in continuing to pursue it today, we are informed by the modest success that students of government have had towards improving the capacity of government for action, short of scrapping and replacing the basic constitutional framework. We are also informed by having witnessed new forms of tyranny in the twentieth century, or at least new guises for it, which cause us to have renewed concern for the preservation of personal freedom.

In revisiting the thought of the framers, with particular regard for the issue of the effectiveness of American government, it is necessary to pay clos-

---

[1] James MacGregor Burns, *The Deadlock of Democracy*, (Englewood Cliffs: Prentice-Hall, Inc. 1963).

[2] James Madison, *Federalist #51*, in Clinton Rossiter ed., *The Federalist Papers*, (New York: The New American Library, Inc. 1961), p. 322.

est attention to the features of the regime that are described by Alexander Hamilton. As one of the two principal contributors to *The Federalist Papers*, which is *the* text of explanation for the Constitution, Hamilton supplements James Madison's arguments concerning representation and federalism with his own discussion of the executive and administrative side of the picture. It is also more than just a supplement. Without suggesting any contradiction between them, it can be said that when Hamilton's account of the executive power is developed, the system takes on a different hue from what is suggested by a reading of Madison's *Federalist Papers* alone. One can detect already in these early statements by the two men the seeds of what would later become a full-blown partisan opposition, whereby Madison would join Thomas Jefferson's accusation against Hamilton as being an apologist for "monocracy", or even "monarchy," and that he was therefore willing to sacrifice an essential part of what the American War for Independence had been about. Whether this is a fair charge obviously depends on whether, in his *Federalist Papers*, Hamilton shows successfully that his proposals regarding executive power are compatible with genuinely republican government, and, if so, whether Hamilton remained true to those principles throughout his later career.

The common ground on which Hamilton joins Madison, and nearly all the members of his generation, is his acceptance of the classical Liberal definition of the natural foundation and purpose of government. Thus, the fundamental standard of government is legitimacy, and that was to be satisfied by the consent of the governed. The distinguishing features of Hamilton's thought derive from his keen desire to use government to accomplish certain social and economic aims. He perceived that the structured pursuit of self-interest in a free society is only an *imitation* of natural competition, not simply an extension of it, and that it therefore requires a positive governmental policy to bring it about and to maintain it. In his early paper, *The Continentalist*, Hamilton marked out his views that those who endorsed the *laissez faire* approach to public policy were naive. And in *The Federalist Papers*, Hamilton repeats his ridicule of those who believed that the natural harmony of productive arts would, if left undisturbed, produce economic and social harmony.[3]

The positive policies that Hamilton had in mind were those necessary to promote a large and commercial republic. They are exemplified in the legislative program of the Washington administration.[4] That program included: i) full funding of the public debt, at par, and therewith the vigorous use of the taxing power and the sale of new federal bonds; ii) the establishment of a national bank under federal charter; iii) protective tariffs for nascent industries; and iv) a program of public roads and canals. For all of this, Hamilton looked to the executive department to provide the leadership and management of this legislative program. With Washington as president, Hamilton had the example of the sort of executive leadership that he had argued for.

---

[3] Alexander Hamilton, *Federalist #'s* 6, 11, 15 especially. Gerald Stourzh provides an excellent discussion of the difference between Hamilton and many of his contemporaries on the question of whether commerce tends by its own nature towards peace. Cf. Stourzh, *Alexander Hamilton and the Idea of Republican Government*, (Stanford: Stanford University Press, 1970), pp. 126-170.

[4] Hamilton, *Papers on Public Credit, Commerce, and Finance*, Samuel McKee, Jr. ed. (New York: The Bobbs-Merrill Company, Inc. , 1957).

Why, though, *executive* leadership? Could Congress not direct the government of the new nation? In *The Federalist Papers* Hamilton argued that the key feature whereby the executive has and deserves its preeminence is the mere fact of its unity. It is easy to see how the executive, being one, will have an advantage of dispatch over Congress. When emergencies arise that require a direct and immediate response, the president is the only officer who is in a position to make that response. Moreover, the president is the principal source of energy in government. This is simply because he does not need to spend nearly as much energy as does Congress in bringing about unanimity among contending forces.

That a primarily executive officer, that is, one who is charged to put into execution directives from a formally superior authority, should be equipped to direct the government itself is an arrangement that did not make sense to Hamilton's political opponents. It can be thought to make sense only on the basis of a Hamiltonian estimation of the status of administrative rationality in the world of practical affairs. Hamilton himself summarizes his view of this beautifully in his qualified agreement with the poet Alexander Pope, who said,

> For forms of government let fools contest—
> That which is best administered is best—

While Hamilton does accuse Pope of political "heresy" for underrating the importance of "forms", he does agree that ". . .the true test of government is its aptitude and tendency to produce a good administration."[5] The point that Hamilton preserves is that the relatively pedestrian standards of efficiency and effectiveness are the operationally relevant standards for government as a whole. Ends or aims, it would seem, take care of themselves.

As for responsibility, or representativeness, even here Hamilton thought that the same feature of the executive office that made it an engine of effective government was also the sufficient condition for the president's being held to account. Hamilton stressed that only where a single officer had ultimate authority for the execution of public policy could government avoid the problem of a conspiracy among rulers to hide their responsibility from the people. This is always a fundamental problem, the wish on the part of those who govern to be able to commit crimes or even simply errors with impunity. And the answer to it is, again, unity in the character of the office. Thus the standards of representativeness and the capacity for action tend to blur in Hamilton's thought into a single requirement for executive unity.[6]

Hamilton's understanding of the role of the executive in the American Constitutional framework is extended and amplified by his argument concerning the indefinite reeligibility of the president. He would doubtless have considered the 22nd Amendment, limiting a president to two terms, to be a major blot on the original text. His considerations are reducible to three: first, he appeals to the notion of the wisdom of experience and the general sense that it is unwise to "change horses in mid-stream;" second, the executive who is constitutionally ineligible for reelection is without the necessary motive to serve well and also lacks the power to do so—he is a "lame duck," in American parlance; third, a former executive who is ineligible to be returned to that

---

[5] Hamilton, *Federalist # 68*, p. 414.
[6] John C. Koritansky, "Alexander Hamilton's Philosophy of Government and Administration," *Publius*, vol. 9, #2, spring 1979, pp. 111-114.

high office by any legitimate means poses the danger of illegitimate ambition and is a possible focal point of seditious unrest.[7] In sum, a wise people would probably want to reward a competent executive with a life tenure through periodic reelection, and the Constitution ought to permit it. In the light of Hamilton's defense of the president's indefinite reeligibility, it is easy to surmise that he expected President Washington to capitalize on the advantages of his incumbency and to serve for life. Had that happened, and the precedent been maintained by a successor younger than Washington, it would have made more obvious the monarchical character of the American regime which Jefferson feared Hamilton was working to bring about. Even as it was and is, however, it is permissible to say that from the perspective formed by Hamilton's writing, America is a republic only in a rarefied sense of the word. It might be more readily understood as an elective monarchy—perhaps not so different after all from the explicitly monarchical plan that Hamilton had proposed to the Constitutional Convention in Philadelphia and which was rejected out of hand. Hamilton himself appears not to have considered the terms "monarchy" and "republic" to be mutually exclusive and, in fact, it appears that the American system is both. The major part of his effort was in securing the advantages of the monarchical element in what would always appear to most citizens to be a more emphatically republican frame.

Against the backdrop of this quasi-monarchical plan for government we can understand the whole idea of government service that Hamilton's Federalist Party employed in staffing the civil service. In his still-authoritative study of the history of the American civil service, Leonard White reports that President Washington was guided by a "rule of fitness" for making bureaucratic appointments. This was important especially since the new federal government was in competition with the states for the allegiance of the American people. The plan of the Federalists was that the federal governmental officers would make up in competence and high moral character what they lacked in proximity and familiarity. But what exactly did "fitness" mean? What would be the specific criteria of selection? There were some considerations that excluded a candidate, for example nepotism or indolence or a penchant for strong drink. But beyond this it is not easy to say exactly what Hamilton or Washington meant by such expressions as "fitness of character" or "the first characters of the union" by which they described those thought worthy of national office. Terms like these are hard to define and are therefore subject to abuse; nevertheless, that in itself does not mean that they are empty or that they can be dispensed with without cost. The Federalists frankly wanted to erect a political nobility to staff their government. They thought it was necessary because they thought that genuine responsibility requires a level of moral character that is above that of the general run of mankind to whom responsibility is ultimately owed. There may be a subtlety here, but one that would not be lost on someone well versed in practical affairs on a broad scale. If in our day we tend to downplay the importance of nobility in public service, it may likely be due more to wishful thinking than to tough-mindedness.

An issue related to the president's power of appointment was that of the power to remove executive officers. This important matter was, interestingly, not addressed in the Constitution itself; but the First Congress answered it in

---

[7]   Hamilton, *Federalist* # 72.

what has come to be termed "the decision of 1789." In connection with the establishment of the Department of Foreign Affairs, the question came up as to how the Secretary was to be removed. In the original draft of the legislation, the wording had seemed to suggest that Congress was *granting* the power to remove to the president; and this implication was objected to by some members on the argument that the president should be understood *already to have* the exclusive power to remove his own appointments, by direct implication of the Constitution. As a result of this objection, the bill was redrafted in language that indicates a recognition rather than a grant of power to the president to remove the officer. Years later, in the 1925 case *Myers v. United States*, the Supreme Court confirmed the significance of the "decision of 1789" as a matter of Constitutional law. There are some important exceptions to the president's removal power, but generally speaking the powers of appointment and removal make the president the actual chief of the federal administration.

The preservation of the unitary character of administration necessitated the president's exclusive power over removals; by the same token the president would have to employ that power sparingly. It was to be expected that executive appointees would enjoy a long tenure, and this for two reasons: first, as was argued in connection with the president himself, there is a certain competence that comes from experience. Second, and probably as important, public office had to be considered a high station in society if it were to appeal to persons of noble character and provide satisfaction to their legitimate ambition.

In many respects this vision of government by a republican political nobility, responsible to its own character even more deeply than it would be responsible to a democratic electorate, is appealing. It should not be dismissed today as quaint or unrealistic, nor need it be. It is true, to be sure, that it does not correspond to the subsequent actual development of America, development that intensified the democratic character of the regime more than was imagined by the framers, Hamilton in particular. Yet it remains to be determined whether Americans can find a substitute for the sort of public servant that suited Hamilton. Can modern liberal government satisfy the requirements for effective administration and coherent policy, but in a way that smacks less of monarchy and the rule of nobility?

II. THE JEFFERSONIAN "REVOLUTION"[8]

Thomas Jefferson called his electoral victory and ascension to the presidency in 1800 a "revolution", and while that term may have been even deliberately hyperbolic, it is not misleading. What Jefferson meant was that he and his Republican party were returning the country to the true, original principles of its founding, i.e. to the true meaning of the nation's independent existence. That meaning, he thought, had been compromised and even sabotaged by the Federalist Party's veer towards "monarchism" or "monocraticism," which Jefferson believed to be Hamilton's real aim. Jefferson might well

---

[8] The following account is derived largely from Lynton Caldwell, *The Administrative Theories of Hamilton and Jefferson*, (New York: Russell & Russell, Inc., 1964) and from Leonard White, *The Jeffersonians*, (New York: The Macmillan Company, 1951). I am also heavily indebted to Harvey Mansfield Jr. for his article on Jefferson in Frisch and Stevens, eds. *American Political Thought, the Philosophical Dimension of American Statesmanship*, (Dubuque: Kendall Hunt Publishing Company, 1976).

have felt this way, since he really did ride the crest of a wave whose sources were deep and whose effects would be lasting. After 1800 the Federalist Party would never again mount a serious challenge for the presidency, which is to say they would never come close to winning another *national* election. The Federalists survived as an effective party only in the New England states.

Jefferson's intention was to return the country to a more genuinely republican, and also agrarian, model. The agrarianism was essential because Jefferson was sure that republican forms depended upon virtues that reposed reliably only among the landed yeomanry. In his book written in 1781, *Notes On Virginia,* Jefferson explains his belief in the simple, stolid virtues of the American yeomen, and the comparative evil of life in cities, where men live within shouting distance of their mutually dependant and often discontented neighbors. Country people are more self-reliant. They are dependent on things like the weather, i.e. on nature; but this dependence brings with it a sensitivity to and appreciation of the beneficence of nature, with its regular cycles: rain following a dry spell, spring following the winter. Urbanites, it may be conceded, are likely to be more acute, but the country folk are, more importantly, calmer and tougher. The words of a demagogue that speak to the neediness and anger of city people are far less moving in rural areas. There the response is more likely to be a wary suspicion, turning very easily into cold hostility. Country folk are not, however, incapable of cooperating. Jefferson saw that first hand. But they will cooperate only where it is fairly easy to see just what mutual benefit is to be attained. That is a benefit for genuinely republican government, "genuinely" in the sense that governing initiatives come from the people themselves, reflected and deliberated by representatives in a spirit of fidelity to the wishes and needs of their electors. Essentially, the virtue of the landed yeomanry is a deep, shared, moral conservatism. This serves republicanism because it allows people to trust one another, while it relieves them of the need to trust each other very far.

Today most Americans still tend to credit Jefferson as the member of the founding generation who articulated the deepest and purest strain of American liberalism and republicanism. His star has, it must be admitted, been tarnished somewhat insofar as the issue of his slave holding has drawn more attention. Jefferson's thoughts about his own personal involvement in the institution of slavery is a subject that probably needs further examination, as does his thoughts concerning slavery as it existed in Virginia and the other Southern states during the nation's early years. Would Jefferson have had a response, for example, to Lincoln's subsequent statement that "a house divided against itself permanently. . . cannot stand"? If so, what might that response have been? (cf. his *Notes on the State of Virginia,* where he excoriates the moral and political evils of slavery as a violation of the equal rights of all men, Blacks included, while at the same time he expresses doubts regarding the equal capacities of the Blacks.) Even if we cannot find in Jefferson a satisfactory answer to such vexing questions, it remains beyond doubt that Jefferson held slavery to be a violation of the equal rights of *all* human beings to liberty. It was a crime against nature. In fact, the repudiation of slavery is articulated by Jefferson in pretty much the same terms in which contemporary Americans would express it. There is no divergence here. On the other hand, there is a respect in which Jefferson's ideals do diverge from what many Americans take for granted, and this does impose a burden of criticism and self-criticism on us precisely because Jefferson is so much the spokesman for fundamental American political ideals. Jefferson was decidedly not an egalitarian in the full sense. He was profoundly impressed with the differences among people's capacities; one may turn to his discussion of his proposal for public education in his *Notes on Virginia* for a perfectly unambiguous illustration of this point and its most important consequences. Moreover, Jefferson accepted as a necessary fact of civilized life a high degree of social inequality. As much as any Federalist, Jefferson was convinced that there exists a "natural aristocracy"; and along with Madison he could identify "the leveling spirit" as a principal danger that needed to be avoided by the friends of popular government. There will always be the rich and the poor. As an agrarian, Jefferson did not seek to mitigate or excuse this fact by appealing to a high degree of social mobility, such as might be hoped for by the friends of commercialism and urbanism. Rather, what was important for a healthy and good society was that the vast majority be economically independent and that the rich be a true gentry. That is, the rich should reflect and amplify the virtues of the independent yeomen. They would strengthen such a society by gracing it. Superior in learning, they would be aware of vain philosophies and doctrinaire confusions which might corrupt the manners of republican citizens; and in their continued preference for the charms of rustic life they would provide personal testimony against such corruptions. In short, Jefferson was soberly impressed with the fact that although the principles of the Declaration of Independence were universally true, they were, sadly, far from being universally acknowledged or known. His vision of a healthy society was not simply a matter of aesthetic taste. Rather, it derived from his thoughtful judgment about what sort of life and what sort of character would preserve the appreciation of those principles, sensing from afar sources of danger and corruption and providing, in his famous phrase, that "eternal vigilance" which is liberty's price.

There were several specific features of Jefferson's program; today we might speak of them as "planks" of the Republican platform. Foremostly, Jefferson's social policy was pro-agrarian. This did not mean that there would be a vigorous employment of national power on behalf of rural economic activity. Rather it meant that Jefferson would call for a sparing use of the commerce power. In contrast to the sorts of pro-business and commerce measures that Hamilton had promoted, for example in the *Report on Manufactures* that he wrote as Washington's Secretary of the Treasury, Jefferson's administration would pursue a more *laissez-faire* economic policy. He was not a doctrinaire free-marketeer; it was just that the sort of economic activity that Jefferson thought was best for the country did not need protection or elaborate commercial regulation—or so he presumed. Secondly, and consonant with his view of the modest need for governmental activity, Jefferson stood for strict Constitutional construction of the federal government's authority, and for the protection of the residual sovereignty of the states. The *Kentucky Resolutions*, which Jefferson authored, illustrate this point. It was, Jefferson held, the ongoing responsibility of the states to be the watchdogs that would declare when the federal government had exceeded its Constitutional authority, as he asserted it had in enacting the Alien and Sedition Acts. While stopping short of the later doctrine of nullification, the *Kentucky Resolutions* did already point in that direction. As regards the broad issue of the separation between national and state power, Jefferson's principal antagonist was Washington's appointee, Chief Justice John Marshall. Short of impeaching Marshall, however, there was little that Jefferson, or his Republican successors, could do to oppose the Court's expansionary, nationalistic reading of the commerce power and the necessary and proper clause, culminating in the *McCulloch v. Maryland* case. For his own part, Jefferson even expressed his opinion derogating the whole notion of judicial review; but the force of that opinion could not rebut the precedent, once established. Thirdly, with respect to foreign policy, Jefferson and the Republicans stood for peace. They recognized the wisdom of keeping the young nation clear of embroilment with Europe, especially as regards the war between France and England. Republican sympathies may have been with France; but their policy was neutrality. For Jefferson himself this was more than a matter of strategic calculation. Peace was the condition necessary to agrarianism and republicanism. The passions of war and the practical requirements of war both worked to the advantage of "monarchism"; that was the great danger. In fact, Jefferson was consistent in opposing the assertion of executive prerogative in the field of foreign policy even where it might be employed for purposes he approved. Thus, while in Washington's cabinet, Secretary of State Jefferson repudiated Washington's "Proclamation of Neutrality" on the grounds that the President lacked Constitutional authority to issue such a statement unilaterally. Jefferson then charged Madison, as the more astute Constitutional scholar, to write the *Helevidius* Papers challenging Washington's act.

The overarching aims of Jefferson's presidency and of the Republican party were clear and coherent. Nevertheless there were on a practical level certain tensions between what might be required to serve those aims in the immediate circumstances *versus* what Jefferson felt was a sound principle of Constitutional precedent or of political morality. Thus, for example, while Jefferson would decline to use the powers of the federal government to promote business and industry, he did not even conceive of using those same powers to curb their development. In fact, it is hard to imagine any such curbs that would not be, manifestly, an arbitrary violation of private liberty and the rights of property. The problem was that by 1800, although the American economy was still largely agrarian, the seeds of business and industry had already taken root. They would grow and prosper under the Republicans' modest use of the power to regulate commerce.

Jefferson's principle of strict Consitutional constructionism also ran into a practical problem, dramatically, in connection with his Purchase of the Louisiana Territory. This episode illustrated with a vengeance Hamilton's argument in *Federalist 35* that the contingencies that govenment may have to meet are impossible to circumscribe *a priori*, and therefore formal limits on government's powers are always exercises in wishful thinking. Jefferson was convinced that he lacked the authority as President to enter into a treaty of purchase on his own. But he was also convinced that he could not afford to let slip away the opportunity to acquire the new territory. So, rather than seek to find Constitutional warrant for his action, as Madison urged him to do, Jefferson deliberately violated his own reading of the Constitution, offering only the excuse that there was a critical advantage for the nation to be served![9] In other words, in order to preserve his strict reading of the letter of the Constitution, and the *textual* limits on executive power in particular, Jefferson showed an amazing willingness to establish a precedent of executive lawless-

---

[9]   Cf. Morton J. Frisch, *The Hamilton-Madison-Jefferson Triangle*, (Ashland: John M. Ashbrook Center for Public Affairs, 1992).

ness that would go beyond what any American president has ever explicitly articulated, before or since.

Finally, the area of foreign relations provides another example of the practical tension between Jefferson's actual policies and his broader Constitutional and political principles. In this case it was the policy that compromised the principles. During Jefferson's second term, America was experiencing measures at the hands of the English that could not be tolerated, such as the seizure of American ships and their cargoes and the restriction of American trade. Jefferson's response was to sponsor measures that were designed to bring England to terms while preserving America's neutrality. He secured the enactment first of a "Non-intercourse Act", and when this proved ineffective, he succeeded it with the infamous "Embargo Act" of 1807. The legislation was completely ineffective of its purpose; it suceeded only in ruining the foreign trade for American merchants and severely hampering the whole of American commerce. Understandably, it proved to be the most bitterly opposed element of the Republican program. Still Jefferson stubbornly defied the opposition. He stuck to the policy even though it stood in glaring contrast to his general aversion to the vigorous use of the federal commmerce power, and even though it tarnished the vision of a nation made whole through the triumph of Republican sentiments.

The tension between Jefferson's broad aims and the means he needed to employ to serve them is exemplified not only in these isolated instances of policy. It is a general characteristic of Jefferson's whole approach to the presidency, that is, of his "Republicanism." It can be seen directly in his words and actions regarding his political party. To be sure, Jefferson's election is the first instance in which an American president was chosen on the basis of a contest between two parties asserting divergent policies and pointing the nation in different directions. But no more than his Federalist opponents did Jefferson concede that such partisan opposition and electioneering was a good thing, or that it would be a permanent feature of American politics.

Quite the contrary. In fact Jefferson hated party politics; and part of his animus against the Federalists was precisely that their brand of politics was responsible for the growing bane of partisanship. His election was going to reverse that. He intended, as Harvey Mansfield Jr. has put it, "to put his party in the service of trans-partisanship." Of course the problem with all such hopes for rising above partisanship is, what to do with those who continue to oppose your approach to trans-partisanship? In some form it must be met by any party that wins an election. Wounds must be bound; one's own victorious party must make the claim to be the party of inclusivity; but the cancer—if there is a cancer—must be isolated and neutralized. What is distinctive about Jefferson is that he thought that the need for such sophistry was extra-ordinary, because Republicanism really was, as he saw it, the movement that represented what was deepest and truest about America. It really did transcend any possible, legitimate partisan divergence. Thus Jefferson says in his First Inaugural, "We are all Federalists; and we are all Republicans," and in these words he means to seal the Republican victory. Today, as we reread that sentence, we are naturally prompted to a wry smile; and yet are we not aware at the same time that we are compelled in some way to share the wish that we find amusing?

While Jefferson himself was in the driver's seat, his trans-partisanship could be a source of frustration for the hopes and the ambitions of his fellow

Republican party members. At issue were Jefferson's appointments to the federal bureaucracy. He naturally considered it unconscionable to purge the bureaucracy of Federalist office-holders. For one thing, there had by 1800 already developed a claim to competence and a sense of established procedures among civil servants, and Jefferson had too much regard for these advantages to abandon them to partisan considerations. More importantly, Jefferson was horrified by the prospect of electoral contests fought among partisans whose passions were inflamed by a prize of appointive office. His presidency was to have the significance of forestalling just such a corruption. A closely related consideration is that Jefferson did not want to contribute to the strengthening of the executive branch through such a partisan employment of the appointment and removal power.

The patronage system was a temptation that strong Republican statesmanship needed to resist.

Unfortunately, when Jefferson acceded to the presidency he found himself confronted with a federal bureaucracy that was staffed almost entirely with members of the party that had opposed him. To his credit, Jefferson did not engage in a wholesale purge, despite the obvious pressures to do so. He declared publicly that "Those who have acted well have nothing to fear."

Only some "midnight appointments" that his Federalist predecessor, Adams, had made in the closing days of his administration were removed for partisan considerations; those and a scarce few who voiced their opposition to the Republicans stridently and publicly. For the rest, Jefferson resolved to wait for the natural processes of death and resignation to provide opportunities to redress the imbalance among bureaucratic offices by appointing Republicans. But, as Jefferson was said to confide his annoyance to an associate, "Few die; none resign."

Because of the tensions connected with Jefferson's Republicanism, the lasting significance of his presidency is that it served as a transition (that is, *only* a transition) from the high-toned sort of government of the Federalist party, which one may go so far as to call a political aristocracy, as Tocqueville does, to the more simple and frankly democratic alternative that would not be fully present until Andrew Jackson was elected president. Jefferson himself continues to believe in the necessity of the rule of the best— "best" meaning those not only competent to perform the tasks of their offices, but who also had some share of the Republican statesmanlike virtue that rises above pettiness and venality. In sharp contrast to the Federalists, especially to Hamilton, Jefferson's aristocracy would not be characterized by an ambition to rule. On the contrary, their freedom from that passion would be chief among their distinguishing virtues. Whereas for Hamilton the ambition to rule is a leading feature defining "the first characters of the union," for Jefferson that same passion is close to being the root of all evil. In this Jefferson may have felt that he was holding closer to the most sublime element of Liberalism, namely the notion of government is to faciliate the exercise of private rights, and that it is for the sake of the private realm that the public realm may legitimately exist. Rule cannot itself be the prize, the Liberal statesman cannot find happiness there; rather, rule is to be understood as a duty, to be borne nobly, for the sake of a better happiness. It is a beautiful sentiment to be sure; one which probably still stirs Americans. It is not exclusively American, or Liberal, though. Does not Socrates say that the philosopher king would be characterized precisely by the disdain for rule, such that one would have to be forced to the task? In Jefferson, Liberalism is beautiful because it has this share of Socraticism—popularized Socraticism. This comparison, though, also helps us see the problem with Jefferson in the broadest terms. Will the best be "forced to rule"? Is it likely that the people wll scramble over themselves, so to speak, to drop the mantle of responsibility on the shoulders of the statesman, while he or she looks the other way? The answer is "maybe", in some rare cases, probably in the case of Jefferson own election; but it can hardly be the norm. In the real world the best will have to arrange to accept their responsibility. The question then is, what will motivate them to do so? If we cannot honor ambition and offer government as its legitimate field, there is no answer to this question. A government of the gracefully reluctant, accepted as a *noblesse oblige*, is a rare, fortunate accident, not to be counted on.

The fate of Jefferson's party in the years following his administration is a demonstration of the fundamental flaw of his Republicanism. His successors, Madison and Monroe, were little more than "caretaker" presidents. Real direction tended to be provided by Congressional leaders, among whom Henry Clay formulated a "New Republicanism" that all but abandoned the agarianism that was so close to the heart of Jefferson's vision of American society. All that was left was an anti-executive, legislative supremacist bias. In 1820 the New Republicans secured passage of the Tenure of Office Act, limiting the tenure of certain executive officers to four years. This was intended by them as a way of providing Congress more opportunity for control over the executive branch, through its "advise and consent" power regarding appointments. Writing from his retirement at Monticello, Jefferson condemned the act on the basis of his abiding principles. By forcing the termination of honest public servants and opening a large number of places, the act would, he predicted, serve more sordid motives by legitimating the notion of appointive office as a prize of electoral victory. But Jefferson's high sentiments were paid little heed. With his own great, philosophic temper no longer at the helm, his party had given way to petty jealousy of executive power, and had interpreted that to be its legacy.

III. THE JACKSONIAN REFORM AND THE "SPOILS SYSTEM"[10]

America had been at its founding a "democratic republic," as James Madison had termed it in the *Federalist*. In describing it as "democratic" Madison had meant to identify the principal dangers that the new order faced and the limits within which the Constitutional remedies for those dangers would have to operate. That is, in all democacies the danger is that of the tyranny of the majority, which is distinguished from non-tyrannical majorities because it is animated by a "leveling spirit" hostile to the security of private rights. The Constitution is designed to meet this danger through its complicated scheme of checks and balances, but without compromising the essentially democratic base. The election of Andrew Jackson in 1828 marks a dramatic change in the character of American political life. "Democracy" is no longer a basic but prob-

---

[10] The following summary of President Jackson's approach to administration is derived from Leonard White, *The Jacksonians* (New York: The Macmillan Company, 1954), and from E. S. Corwin, *The President, Office and Powers* (New York: New York University Press, 1957), esp. pp. 20-22, 64, 83-85.

lematical fact; it is a term of pride by which to praise the country. In Jacksonian America Alexis de Tocqueville could observe that the "love of equality" dominated political and social life. This passion burst forth in the form of an anti-government populism which, like a wave, bore Jackson into the White House. The demands were for the extension of the franchise and the opening of the Western Territories; and Jackson was the champion. His was the first presidential candidacy to have a popular, not a Congressional, base. Thereafter, the activity of narrowing down the range of choices among policies and candidacies to be presented to the electorate required organization among the electorate itself. Patronage came to be recognized as a tool for the organization of the democratic electorate into popular political parties; and as such it was seen as a practical necessity for democratic politics. This popularization of American politics achieved its first stage when, in 1836, presidential candidates were nominated to national party "tickets" in popular conventions.

Jackson used his political independence and popularity to reassert the powers of the presidency—as a sort of tribune for the people. For example, in his Bank Veto Message of July 10, 1832, Jackson argued that it was his right and his duty as president to veto legislation on his own opinion of its unconstitutionality, despite earlier Supreme Court rulings that similar legislation was within the Constitutional powers of Congress. The difficult question raised by Jackson's Message, one that alarmed many of his contemporaries, was: who is the final authority for the interpretation of the Constitution—the Supreme Court or the President? Jackson had not actually defied a Court ruling, but he had made statements that might have been construed to sanction such defiance. On the substantive issue of the powers of Congress, Jackson presented himself as a champion of the cause of strict construction of the Constitution and, with that, strictly limited government; but it was a form of championship that threatened the ultimate authority of the rule of law. This strange combination caused Tocqueville to find in Jackson an incarnation of the evil form of leadership that democracy is all too likely to cast up—a partisan of limited and lawful government by calculation, a populist despot by disposition.[11]

As a result of Jackson's willingness to use powers of a tribune-president to champion the cause of democracy and limited government, we have from this period a precedent that illustrates the limits of the president's power to control the administration, one that is especially noteworthy for students of public administration. The case is *Kendall v. Stokes*. Jackson had ordered his Postmaster General, Kendall, to disobey a direct mandate from Congress to pay a sum of money to one Stokes, owed to him as back salary. Kendall obeyed his president and disobeyed Congress. The case was tried by the Supreme Court, and the Court ruled in favor of Stokes. The rule is that the President has no power to dispense the legitimate expression of legislative power, and Congress does have the ability to charge administrative officers with specific responsibilities derivative from its power to create the office itself and to define its duties in general law.

Jackson was the first president to purge the federal bureaucracy of political opponents— Leonard White estimates the number was in the thousands. Included among these was Secretary of the Treasury Duane, whose firing represented the unprecedented and, to most, shocking instance of a cabinet of-

---

[11] Alexis de Tocqueville, *Democracy in America*, transl. George Lawrence, (New York: Harper and Row, Publishers, 1966), pp. 359-61.

ficer being dismissed for the explicit reason of partisan policy differences. Duane had refused to remove government deposits from the national bank on Jackson's order, thinking that such an act would require Congressional authorization. Duane surely thought that he had both the authority and the duty to resist Jackson in this way. Congress had, after all, created the bank as the place where government revenues were to be held, and Jackson was clearly trying to destroy the bank in violation of Congress's intent. Moreover, ever since Alexander Hamilton himself had held the position of Secretary of the Treasury, that office had enjoyed a special relationship with and responsibility to Congress, deriving ultimately from Congress's power over taxation and appropriations. In Jackson's mind Duane was guilty of bald insubordination for refusing to carry out his explicit order. If there was an issue here, the dismissal settled it. The appointment *and removal* power were instruments to be used to guarantee partisan discipline within the ranks of the administration.

The consequences of Jackson's new approach to the power of appointment and removal have been called the "spoils system," suggesting that an election is in some ways similar to a war in which the spoils naturally belong to the victor. Some of Jackson's near contemporaries defended the extended use of patronage in just those terms; but for Jackson himself the defense was different. He did not exactly intend to inaugurate a spoils system; rather, his idea was to promote equality of opportunity for employment in the federal government service, and also to create a more democratically representative bureaucracy by a continual *rotation* in office. His First Annual Message to Congress makes this rather clear:

> In a country where offices are created solely for the benefit of the people no man has any more intrinsic right to official station than another. Offices were not established to give support to particular men at the public expense. No individual wrong is, therefore, done by removal since neither appointment to nor continuance in office is a matter of right. The incumbent became an officer with a view to public benefits, and when these require his removal they are not to be sacrificed to private interests. It is the people, and they alone, who have a right to complain when a bad officer is substituted for a good one. He who is removed has the same means of obtaining a living that are enjoyed by the millions who never held office. The proposed limitation would destroy the idea of property now so generally connected with official station, and although individual distress may be sometimes produced, it would, by promoting that rotation which constitutes a leading principle in the republican creed, give healthful action to the system.[12]

Jackson's sentiments can be applauded as being, perhaps, nobler than the "spoils" apology for the extended use of patronage; but whatever the sentiment, Jackson did pave the way for the spoils system in practice. Subsequent presidents followed his example, if not his defense, so that Martin Van Buren, and then the even more frankly Whig president William Henry Harrison, openly condoned the idea that to the victor belong the spoils as their rule in appointment and removal. Indeed, what Jackson's reform had to mean in practice is best illustrated by the predicament of his party's oppo-

---

[12] White, *The Jacksonians*, p. 318.

nents, the Whigs. On an ideological level, the Whigs opposed the idea of spoils as part of their general bias against executive power; and they expressed their intention to refrain from using it if and when they succeeded in capturing the presidency from their Democratic rivals. Yet the Whig Administrations of Harrison (1836) and Taylor (1840) found themselves unable to resist using patronage to reward their own in order to play the game of popular party politics by the new rules of the spoils system. Once the tradition of a career in office had been overturned by the Jacksonian reform, the intentions of presidents not to treat appointive offices as prizes was too much in conflict with nearly universal expectations among partisans to be effective.

Contemporary historians, who are able to look back on the spoils system with the benefit of hindsight, but who may also be sheltered from actually feeling its most pernicious effects, reflect a certain ambiguity in their judgment. For example, Carl Fish[13] and even Leonard White acknowledge its consistency with democratic theory and with the practical requirements of managing democratic politics. For one thing, the idea of a new president carrying into effect the mandate of an electoral victory by bringing in a whole new platoon of bureaucratic officers has some cogency. Moreover, friends of democracy usually acknowledge that party structures are a necessity in democratic politics, in order to narrow the range of choice among policies and candidates so that the electorate can be presented with and informed about a manageable issue. Patronage is a highly useful means of enforcing some degree of party discipline so that members can be relied on to perform their necessary functions. Nevertheless, despite these sophisticated defenses, in practice the spoils system produced a disastrous situation in the federal government service. The primary requirement for competent administration was the one that suffered. White reports that the costs of the system were severe by each of four measures: 1) a loss of administrative efficiency, 2) a loss of prestige for the government service and for government altogether, 3) an increase in the political obligations among office holders which compromised their legal duty, and 4) a scandalous decline of political morality and public service ethics, affecting not only the bureaucracy itself but also infecting the general citizenry.

So serious were the embarrassments to the nation from the spoils system that the cry for civil service reform was begun almost as soon as the spoils system took effect. What ultimately would be called the "civil service reform movement" was driven by an impulse that linked high statesmanship and common morality from the start. From the broadest point of view, the whole, as yet new, American experiment in republican democracy might be thought to hang in the balance of the attempt to purge government of both the ruinous incompetence and petty moral corruption that Jackson's reforms had wrought. In fact, among the political effects directly expressive of a concern for the fundamental soundness of American social and political order and the health of its collective soul throughout its history, the civil service reform movement ranks only behind the abolition of slavery. It would dominate the domestic political scene following the Civil War and Reconstruction. Third place probably belongs to Prohibition.

---

[13] Carl R. Fish, *The Civil Service and the Patronage*, (New York: Longmans, Green and Co., 1905), pp. 155-57.

PART

Meritocracy and the "Politics/Administration" Distinction

In 1883, in a wave of emotion that was partly generated by the assassination of the much admired President James A. Garfield two years before, Congress passed the Pendleton Act, otherwise known as the Civil Service Reform Act. The essential feature of this law is the establishment of a system of competitive examinations for appointment to the civil service. The exams are intended to test for a candidate's competence to perform the job with no regard to party connection. Anticipating the later Hatch Act, the law also attached specific sanctions to the use of appointive office for partisan activity. To administer the law, a Civil Service Commission was created. The Commission would consist of three persons, to be appointed and removed by the president.

The reformers who had designed and pushed for the Pendleton Act had studied the English system of organizing and staffing the civil service and had adopted it as their model. Nevertheless there were some important differences. In the American system, civil servants would be appointed on the basis of politically neutral merit; but it goes too far to say that the civil service would be a *meritocracy*. That word suggests an arrangement that is more thoroughly English: a limited sort of aristocracy of technical competence, with a high level of *esprit de corps* among careerists who share a fairly similar background and formal education, a large part of which points up the nobility of such public service. In America there was no such formal educational system to train up a class of civil servants; and naturally the competitive examinations put comparatively little stress on whatever might be gained thereby. Relatedly, there existed from the beginning in America a more open competition for positions, in contrast with the English norm of bottom-level entry and promotion from within the bureaucracy.[1] Both systems honor the idea of *merit*. The reason for the difference is that Americans understand competition for merit in a way that does not compromise democracy—indeed they understand the two ideas as fully compatible and even implying one another. Bot-

---

[1] In these respects the English system is more closely approximated by the American foreign service than the rest of the bureaucracy. Perhaps the job of administering and preserving a steady and sound foreign policy requires something more quasi-aristocratic than other governmental activities. And perhaps Americans are more willing to tolerate a qualification or suspension of their democratic principles in the administration of the relations with foreigners than they are among themselves.

tom-level entry and promotion from within would seem hostile to the equality of opportunity that any American ought to have to compete for a government job, regardless of previous status. Beneath that, there remains a Jacksonian hostility to public service being anything so exclusive as a profession or
vocation. Public service may call for a variety of professional competencies or
forms of merit; but the thing itself, serving the public, is still something for
amateurs. The civil service too is to be "of" and "by" the people. A final difference between the English and the American civil service system is provided
by the important structural distinctiveness of the American Constitution. That
is, the president retains a nearly unilateral power over removal from appointive office. The "Decision of 1789," to which we referred in the previous chapter, remains in force. The broad values of cohesion, coherence—in a word,
"unity"— depend in America more, or at least more obviously, on the institution of the executive than is the case in England or in fact in any contemporary
democratic republic.

The Pendleton Act had been enacted in order to purge the civil service of
corrupt personal and partisan favoritism. It was not until afterwards, although
shortly afterwards, that a certain notion that was probably latent within the
civil service reform movement from the beginning came to the fore. This was
the notion of a dichotomy between "politics" and "administration," such that
one might think of two distinct institutional arrangements, each structured
according to its own principles. Frank Goodnow's textbook of 1900 established
the metaphor, which he meant as more than merely a metaphor, of two "pyramids," joined at their apexes. The consideration governing the political pyramid was that the public's true will be sounded and translated into governing
mandates, the chief problem being to reduce the corruption of special interests. The administrative pyramid was to be governed by the considerations of
efficiency and effectiveness; the problem to be warded off was the undermining of these virtues by the effects of allowing "political" considerations into
administration where they did not belong. Goodnow's text was to be a primer
in the science of administration as such. Three years earlier, in the *Political
Science Quarterly*, Woodrow Wilson had published a now classic statement
along the same lines. Wilson had argued that America had succeeded marvel-
ously well, that it might be the envy of the world, with regard to the basic
issues of Constitutional structure and the overarching aim of securing personal liberty, but that America still had much to learn regarding the requirements of the efficient and effective administration of the public's will. He suggested that we might turn to Europe, to Germany in particular, to find useful
lessons and models that might be appropriated to an American context. Wilson argued unabashedly that America could profit from European examples
of administrative practices and arrangements even though those political systems were less democratic and less liberal than America's. This can be so because, he insisted, "politics" and "administration" have as dichotomous a relationship as an agent and a tool. A knife, for example, should be hard and
sharp; whether the agent who wields it intends to cut bread or a throat is
another matter.

In this section Wilson's 1887 article is presented. Following that, and
completing the section, is Herbert J. Storing's outline of the career of Leonard
White, longtime professor of public administration at the University of Chicago in the middle decades of the twentieth century. With deftness and preci-

sion, Storing traces and explains the movement of White's thought, as reflected in the subtle changes among the various editions of his authoritative
textbook. Throughout his professional life, White was committed to the development of the study of public administration, hoping and expecting that it
would, someday, rise to the rank of a genuine science. But why *public* administration? Why would the science White hoped for not be a science of administration *per se*? Storing shows that White gradually came to recognize explicitly that the field of public administration depends for its principles decisively on what may be called regime politics questions; and, as a corollary,
that the issue of the best political constitution has to be informed by the requirements of efficient and effective administration. That is to say, Wilson's
and Goodnow's dichotomy would have to be abandoned. Together, these two
statements set the stage for a reconsideration of the seminal statements and
issues that have been the field of public administration in America.

THE STUDY OF ADMINISTRATION

Woodrow Wilson

[Reprinted with permission from the *Political Science Quarterly*, Vol. II , June
1887, pp. 198-201, 209-214, 217-222. Footnotes deleted.]

ONE

The science of administration is the latest fruit of that study of the science of politics which was begun some twenty-two hundred years ago. It is a
birth of our own century, almost of our own generation. Why was it so late in
coming? Why did it wait till this too busy century of ours to demand attention for itself? Administration is the most obvious part of government; it is
government in action; it is the executive, the operative, the most visible side
of government, and is of course as old as government itself. It is government
in action, and one might very naturally expect to find that government in
action had arrested the attention and provoked the scrutiny of writers of politics very early in the history of systematic thought.

But such was not the case. No one wrote systematically of administration as a branch of the science of government until the present century had
passed its first youth and had begun to put forth its characteristic flower of
systematic knowledge. Up to our own day all the political writers whom we
now read had thought, argued, dogmatized only about the constitution of
government; about the nature of the state, the essence and seat of sovereignty,
popular power and kingly prerogative; about the greatest meanings lying at
the heart of government, and the high ends set before the purpose of government by man's nature and man's aims. The central field of controversy was
that great field of theory in which monarchy rode tilt against democracy, in
which oligarchy would have built for itself strongholds of privilege, and in
which tyranny sought opportunity to make good its claim to receive submis-
sion from all competitors. Amidst this high warfare of principles, administration could command no pause for its own consideration. The question was
always: Who shall make law, and what shall that law be? The other question,
how law should be administered with enlightenment, with equity, with speed,

and without friction, was put aside as "practical detail" which clerks could arrange after doctors had agreed upon principles.

That political philosophy took this direction was of course no accident, no chance preference or perverse whim of political philosophers. The philosophy of any time is, as Hegel says, "nothing but the spirit of that time expressed in abstract thought"; and political philosophy, like philosophy of every other kind, has only held up the mirror to contemporary affairs. The trouble in early times was almost altogether about the constitution of government; and consequently that was what engrossed men's thoughts. There was little or no trouble about administration—at least little that was heeded by administrators. The functions of government were simple, because life itself was simple. Government went about imperatively and compelled men, without thought of consulting their wishes. There was no complex system of public revenues and public debts to puzzle financiers; there were, consequently, no financiers to be puzzled. No one who possessed power was long at a loss how to use it. The great and only question was: Who shall possess it? Populations were of manageable numbers; property was of simple sorts. There were plenty of farms, but no stocks and bonds: more cattle than vested interests....

This is the reason why administrative tasks have nowadays to be so studiously and systematically adjusted to carefully tested standards of policy, the reason why we are having now what we never had before, a science of administration. The weightier debates of constitutional principle are even yet by no means concluded; they are no longer of more immediate practical moment than questions of administration. It is getting to be harder to run a constitution than to frame one....

There is scarcely a single duty of government which was once simple which is not now complex; government once had but a few masters; it now has scores of masters. Majorities formerly only underwent government; they now conduct government. Where government once might follow the whims of a court, it must now follow the views of a nation.

And those views are steadily widening to new conceptions of state duty; so that, at the same time that the functions of government are every day becoming more complex and difficult, they are also vastly multiplying in number. Administration is everywhere putting its hands to new undertakings. The utility, cheapness, and success of the government's postal service, for instance, point towards the early establishment of governmental control of the telegraph system. Or, even if our government is not to follow the lead of governments of Europe in buying or building both telegraph and railroad lines, no one can doubt that in some way it must make itself master of masterful corporations. The creation of national commissioners of railroads, in addition to the older state commissions, involves a very important and delicate extension of administrative functions. Whatever hold of authority state or federal governments are to take upon corporations, there must follow cares and responsibilities which will require not a little wisdom, knowledge, and experience. Such things must be studied in order to be well done. And these, as I have said, are only a few of the doors which are being opened to offices of government. The idea of the state and the consequent ideal of its duty are undergoing noteworthy change; and "the idea of the state is the conscience of administration." Seeing every day new things which the state ought to do, the next thing is to see clearly how it ought to do them.

This is why there should be a science of administration which shall seek to straighten the paths of government, to make its business less unbusinesslike, to strengthen and purify its organization, and to crown its duties with dutifulness. This is one reason why there is such a science.

TWO

The field of administration is a field of business. It is removed from the hurry and strife of politics; it at most points stands apart even from the debatable ground of constitutional study. It is a part of political life only as the methods of the counting-house are a part of the life of society; only as machinery is part of the manufactured product. But it is, at the same time, raised very far above the dull level of mere technical detail by the fact that through its greater principles it is directly connected with the lasting maxims of political wisdom, the permanent truths of political progress.

The object of administrative study is to rescue executive methods from the confusion and costliness of empirical experiment and set them upon foundations laid deep in stable principle.

It is for this reason that we must regard civil-service reform in its present stages as but a prelude to a fuller administrative reform. We are now rectifying methods of appointment; we must go on to adjust executive functions *more* fitly and to prescribe better methods of executive organization and action. Civil-service reform is thus but a moral preparation for what is to follow. It is clearing the moral atmosphere of official life by establishing the sanctity of the public office as a public trust, and, by making the service unpartisan, it is opening the way for making it businesslike. By sweetening its motives it is rendering it capable of improving its methods of work.

Let me expand a little what I have said of the province of administration. Most important to be observed is the truth already so much and so fortunately insisted upon by our civil-service reformers; namely, that administration lies outside the sphere of *politics*. Administrative questions are not political questions. Although politics sets the task for administration, it should not be suffered to manipulate its offices.

This is a distinction of high authority; eminent German writers insist upon it as a matter of course. Bluntschli, for instance, bids us separate administration alike from politics and from law: Politics, he says is state activity, "in things great and universal," while "administration on the other hand," is "the activity of the state in individual and small things. Politics is thus the special province of the statesman, administration of the technical official." "Policy does nothing without the aid of administration"; but administration is not therefore politics. But we do not require German authority for this position; this discrimination between administration and politics is now, happily, too obvious to need further discussion.

There is another distinction which must be worked into our conclusions, which, though but another side of that between administration and politics, is not quite so easy to keep sight of: I mean the distinction between *constitutional* and administrative questions, between those governmental adjustments which are essential to constitutional principle and those which are merely incidental to the possible changing purposes of a wisely adapting convenience.

One cannot easily make clear to everyone just where administration resides in the various departments of any practicable government without entering upon particulars so numerous as to confuse the distinctions so minute as to distract. No lines of demarcation, setting apart administrative from non-administrative functions, can be run between this and that department of government without being run up hill and down dale, over dizzy heights of distinction and through dense jungles of statutory enactment, hither and thither around "ifs" and "buts," "whens" and "howevers," until they become altogether lost to the common eye not accustomed to this sort of surveying, and consequently not acquainted with the use of the theodolits of logical discernment. A great deal of administration goes about *incognito* to most of the world, being confounded now with political "management," and again with constitutional principle.

Perhaps this ease of confusion may explain such utterances as that of Niebuhr's: "Liberty," he says, "depends incomparably more upon administration than upon constitution." At first sight this appears to be largely true. Apparently facility in the actual exercise of liberty does depend more upon administrative arrangements than upon constitutional guarantees; although constitutional guarantees alone secure the existence of liberty. But—upon second thought—is even so much as this true? Liberty no more consists in easy functional movement than intelligence consists in the ease and vigor with which the limbs of a strong man move. The principles that rule within the man, or the constitution, are the vital springs of liberty or servitude. Because dependence and subjection are without chains, are lightened by every easy-working device of considerate, paternal government, they are not thereby transformed into liberty. Liberty cannot live apart from constitutional principle; and no administration, however perfect and liberal its methods, can give men more than a poor counterfeit of liberty if it rest upon illiberal principles of government.

A clear view of the difference between the province of constitutional law and the province of administrative function ought to leave no room for misconception; and it is possible to name some roughly definite criteria upon which such a view can be built. Public administration is detailed and systematic execution of public law. Every particular application of general law is an act of administration. The assessment and raising of taxes, for instance, the hanging of a criminal, the transportation and delivery of the mails, the equipment and recruiting of the army and navy, etc., are all obviously acts of administration; but the general laws which direct these things to be done are as obviously outside of and above administration. The broad plans of governmental action are not administrative; the detailed execution of such plans is administrative. Constitutions, therefore, properly concern themselves only with those instrumentalities of government which are to control general law. Our federal constitution observes this principle in saying nothing of even the greatest of the purely executive offices, and speaking only of that President of the Union who was to share the legislative and policy making functions of government, only of those judges of highest jurisdiction who were to interpret and guard its principles, and not of those who were merely to give utterance to them....

There is, indeed, one point at which administrative studies trench on constitutional ground—or at least upon what seems constitutional ground. The study of administration, philosophically viewed, is closely connected with the study of the proper distribution of constitutional authority. To be efficient it must discover the simplest arrangements by which responsibility can be unmistakably fixed upon officials; the best way of dividing authority without hampering it, and responsibility without obscuring it. And this question of the distribution of authority, when taken into the sphere of the higher, the originating functions of government, is obviously a central constitutional question. If administrative study can discover the best principles upon which to base such distribution, it will have done constitutional study an invaluable service. Montesquieu did not, I am convinced, say the last word on this head.

To discover the best principles for the distribution of authority is of greater importance, possibly, under a democratic system, where officials serve many masters, than under others where they serve but a few. All sovereigns are suspicious of their servants, and the sovereign people is no exception to the rule; but how is its suspicion to be allayed by knowledge? If that suspicion could be clarified into wise vigilance, it would be altogether salutary; if that vigilance could be aided by the unmistakable placing of responsibility, it would be altogether beneficent. Suspicion in itself is never healthful either in the private or in the public mind. Trust is strength in all relations of life; and, as it is the office of the constitutional reformer to create conditions of trustfulness, so it is the office of the administrative organizer to fit administration with conditions of clear-cut responsibility which shall insure trustworthiness.

And let me say that large powers and unhampered discretion seem to me the indispensable conditions of responsibility. Public attention must be easily directed, in each case of good or bad administration, to just the man deserving of praise or blame. There is no danger in power, if only it be not irresponsible. If it be divided, dealt out in shares to many, it is obscured; and if it be obscured, it is made irresponsible. But if it be centered in heads of the service and in heads of branches of the service, it is easily watched and brought to book. If to keep his office a man must achieve open and honest success, and if at the same time he feels himself intrusted with large freedom of discretion, the greater his power the less likely is he to abuse it, the more is he nerved and sobered and elevated by it. The less his power, the more safely obscure and unnoticed does he feel his position to be, and the more readily does he relapse into remissness.

THREE

...Government is so near us, so much a thing of our daily familiar handling, that we can with difficulty see the need of any philosophical study of it, or the exact point of such study, should it be undertaken. We have been on our feet too long to study now the art of walking. We are a practical people, made so apt, so adept in self government by centuries of experimental drill that we are scarcely any longer capable of perceiving the awkwardness of the particular system we may be using, just because it is so easy for us to use any system. We do not study the art of governing: we govern. But mere unschooled genius for affairs will not save us from sad blunders in administration. Though democrats by long inheritance and repeated choice, we are still rather crude democrats. Old as democracy is, its organization on a basis of modern ideas and conditions is still an unaccomplished work. The democratic state has yet to be equipped for carrying those enormous burdens of administration which the needs of this industrial and trading age are so fast accumulating. Without comparative studies in government we cannot rid ourselves of the misconception that administration stands upon an essentially different basis in a democratic state from that on which it stands in a non-democratic state.

After such study we could grant democracy the sufficient honor of ultimately determining by debate all essential questions affecting the public weal, or basing all structures of policy upon the major will; but we would have found but one rule of good administration for all governments alike. So far as administrative functions are concerned, all governments have a strong structural likeness; more than that, if they are to be uniformly useful and efficient, they must have a strong structural likeness. A free man has the same bodily organs, the same executive parts, as the slave, however different may be his motives, his services, his energies. Monarchies and democracies, radically different as they are in other respects, have in reality much the same business to look to.

It is abundantly safe nowadays to insist upon this actual likeness of all governments, because these are days when abuses of power are easily exposed and arrested, in countries like our own, by a bold, alert, inquisitive, detective public thought and a sturdy popular self-dependence such as never existed before. We are slow to appreciate this; but it is easy to appreciate it. Try to imagine personal government in the United States. It is like trying to imagine a national worship of Zeus. Our imaginations are too modern for the feat.

But, besides being safe, it is necessary to see that for all governments alike the legitimate ends of administration are the same, in order not to be frightened at the idea of looking into foreign systems of administration for instruction and suggestion; in order to get rid of the apprehension that we might perchance blindly borrow something incompatible with our principles....

We can borrow the science of administration with safety and profit if only we read all fundamental differences of condition into its essential tenets. We have only to filter it through our constitutions, only to put it over a slow fire of criticism and distill away its foreign gases....

Let it be noted that it is the distinction already drawn between administration and politics which makes the comparative method so safe in the field of administration. When we study the administrative systems of France and Germany, knowing that we are not in search of political principles, we need not care a peppercorn for the constitutional or political reasons which Frenchmen or Germans give for their practices when explaining them to us. If I see a murderous fellow sharpening a knife cleverly, I can borrow his way of sharpening the knife without borrowing his probable intention to commit murder with it; and so, if I see a monarchist dyed in the wool managing a public bureau well, I can learn his business methods without changing one of my republican spots. He may serve his king; I will continue to serve the people; but I should like to serve my sovereign as well as he serves his. By keeping this distinction in view—that is, by studying administration as a means of putting our own politics into convenient practice, as a means of making what is democratically politic towards all administratively possible towards each—we are on perfectly safe ground, and can learn without error what foreign systems have to teach us. We thus devise an adjusting weight for our comparative method of study. We can thus scrutinize the anatomy of foreign governments without fear of getting any of their diseases into our veins; dissect alien systems without apprehension of blood-poisoning.

Our own politics must be the touchstone for all theories. The principles on which to base a science of administration for America must be principles which have democratic policy very much at heart. And, to suit American habit, all general theories must, as theories, keep modestly in the background, not in open argument only, but even in our own minds—lest opinions satisfactory only to the standards of the library should be dogmatically used, as if they must be quite as satisfactory to the standards of practical politics as well. Doctrinaire devices must be postponed to tested practices. Arrangements not only sanctioned by conclusive experience elsewhere but also congenial to American habit must be preferred without hesitation to theoretical perfection. In a word, steady, practical statesmanship must come first, closet doctrine second. The cosmopolitan what to-do must always be commanded by the American how-to-do-it. Our duty is, to supply the best possible life to a federal organization, to systems within systems; to make town, city, county, state, and federal governments live with a like strength and an equally assured healthfulness, keeping each unquestionably its own master and yet making all interdependent and co-operative, combining independence with mutual helpfulness. The task is great and important enough to attract the best minds. This interlacing of local self-government with federal self-government is quite a modern conception. It is not like the arrangements of imperial federation in Germany. There local government is not yet, fully, local self-government. The bureaucrat is everywhere busy. His efficiency springs out of esprit de corps, out of care to make ingratiating obeisance to the authority of a superior, or, at best, out of the soil of a sensitive conscience. He serves, not the public, but an irresponsible minister. The question for us is, how shall our series of governments within governments be so administered that it shall always be to the interest of the public officer to serve, not his superior alone but the community also, with the best efforts of his talents and the soberest service of his conscience? How shall such service be made to his commonest interest by contributing abundantly to his sustenance, to his dearest interest by furthering his ambition, and to his highest interest by advancing his honor and establishing his character? And how shall this be done alike for the local part and for the national whole?

If we solve this problem we shall again pilot the world. There is a tendency—is there not?—a tendency as yet dim, but already steadily impulsive and clearly destined to prevail, towards, first the confederation of parts of empires like the British, and finally of great states themselves. Instead of centralization of power, there is to be wide union with tolerated divisions of prerogative. This is a tendency towards the American type—of governments joined with governments for the pursuit of common purposes, in honorary equality and honorable subordination. Like principles of civil liberty are everywhere fostering like methods of government; and if comparative studies of the ways and means of government should enable us to offer suggestions which will practicably combine openness and vigor in the administration of such governments with ready docility to all serious, well-sustained public criticism, they will have approved themselves worthy to be ranked among the highest and most fruitful of the great departments of political study. That they will issue in such suggestions I confidently hope.

LEONARD D. WHITE AND THE STUDY OF PUBLIC ADMINISTRATION

Herbert J. Storing

[From *Public Administration Review*, March 1965. Reprinted by permission of the American Society for Public Administration.]

Leonard D. White did not plant the seeds from which the field of public administration grew; but for four decades he tended that garden with unexcelled devotion. Carefully cultivating, pruning, and transplanting, he sought to understand and to make clear to others the plan of the whole and to articulate the details of the several parts. The vast majority of students of public administration today were shaped at least in part by their exposure to White. Many have seen no need to leave the paths that he laid out or improved. Others have found White's landscape too restrictive. Yet all must, in one way or another, come to terms with it as a vital part of coming to terms with their field of study.

INTRODUCTION

This essay is designed to assist and deepen that confrontation. No reference is made to White's universally acknowledged qualities as administrator, teacher, and gentleman, or to his numerous specific contributions to the study and practice of public administration.[2] Our concern is with his attempts to give definition to the whole. It will be argued here that throughout his career White was concerned with a fundamental contradiction that lay and still lies at the heart of the study of public administration, and that in the work of his later years he provided his best advice on the approach to that study. The focus will be on White's *Introduction to the Study of Public Administration*, the four editions of which appeared in 1926, 1939, 1948, and 1955, and particularly the introductory and more theoretical chapters.[3]

The first comprehensive text in public administration, the *Introduction* stood supreme even while an increasing number of texts appeared; it is still widely considered to be in a class by itself. To a degree unusual for a text, it was the focus and expressed the range and depth of its author's scholarly interests.[4] Admittedly, the Introduction *has* been criticized, at least in private, to an extent not entirely attributable to the hazards of preeminence. The generation of students after the Second World War, when memory of the reasons for the founding of the discipline had faded, often thought that White's conception of public administration avoided or obscured many of the important questions. In the third and fourth editions, it often seemed that problems had been cloaked in

---

[2] See John M. Gaus, "Leonard Dupee White—1891-1958," *Public Administration Review,* Summer 1958.

[3] Published by the Macmillan Company, New York; throughout this paper the Roman numeral citations are to edition, Arabic numbers refer to page.

[4] While an elaborate discussion of this contention is unnecessary, an attempt has been made to provide sufficient references at appropriate points for the convenience of the reader who may wish to satisfy himself, as the writer has done, that the thesis presented here finds support in White's other writings.

definition; vigorous criticism and prescription replaced by bland description; the driving force of reform transformed into a slow, methodical process of reorganization and rereorganization; and the confident and restless pursuit of scientific principles of administration encrusted with qualification and reservation. In this as in other respects White faithfully represented his discipline. Dissatisfaction with White's approach is dissatisfaction with the study of public administration itself, as it is still widely understood.

WHITE'S BASIC ASSUMPTIONS
1. ADMINISTRATION IS A SINGLE PROCESS

In the Preface to the first edition of the *Introduction* White wrote:

> The book rests on at least four assumptions. It assumes that administration is a single process, substantially uniform in its essential characteristics wherever observed, and therefore avoids the study of municipal administration, state administration, or federal administration as such. It assumes that the study of administration should start from the base of management rather than the foundation of law, and is therefore more absorbed in the affairs of the American Management Association than in the decisions of the courts. It assumes that administration is still primarily an art but attaches importance to the significant tendency to transform it into a science. It assumes that administration has become, and will continue to be the heart of the problem of modern government.[5]

These assumptions are still perhaps the best concise statement of the foundations of the discipline of public administration, despite the extraordinary development that the discipline has enjoyed since the words were written in 1926.

The most striking characteristic of these assumptions is that they all refer to *administration*, although the book is an introduction to Public administration. Thus the positive part of the first assumption—"that administration is a single process, substantially uniform in its essential characteristics wherever observed"—emphasizes the uniformity of administration; but the negative part warns against an unrealistic division, not of administration, but of public administration. White begins his first chapter with an emphatic statement of this point.

> There is an essential unity in the process of administration, whether it be observed in city, state, or federal governments, that precludes a "stratified" classification of the subject. To treat it in terms of municipal administration, state administration, or national administration, is to imply a distinction that in reality does not exist. The fundamental problems such as the development of personal initiative, the assurance of individual competence and integrity, responsibility, coordination, fiscal supervision, leadership, morale, are in fact the same; and most of the subjects of administration defy the political boundaries of local and state government.[6]

This inevitably suggests the question whether the essential unity in the process of administration also precludes a "stratified" classification of public administration and private administration. Is that also a distinction "that in

---

[5]　vii-viii; the preface is reprinted in all editions.

[6]　I, 1; cf. II, 7; III, 3; IV, 1.

reality does not exist"? White seems to be led, in principle, to answer this question affirmatively; but the very title and subject matter of his book imply a negative answer. He seeks to leave the question open. Public administration, he says, is "the management of men and materials in the accomplishment of the purposes of the state"; its objective is "the most efficient utilization of the resources at the disposal of officials and employees."[7] This definition "relates the conduct of government business to the conduct of the affairs of any other social organization ... in all of which good management is recognized as an element essential to success"; but it "leaves open the question to what extent the administration itself participates in formulating the purposes of the state, and avoids any controversy as to the precise nature of administrative action."[8] White avoids this controversy partly by providing no definition of administration, despite his emphasis on its essential homogeneity.[9]

In the second edition, public administration in its broadest sense is said to consist "of all those operations having for their purpose the fulfillment or enforcement of public policy as declared by the competent authorities."[10] It is a special case of the larger category of administration, "a process which is common to all organized human effort" or (in the third and fourth editions) "a process common to all group effort, public or private, civil or military, large scale or small scale."[11] "The art of administration is the direction, coordination, and control of many persons to achieve some purpose or objective." An administrator is one who exercises that art, and "there are administrators in all human activities except those capable of being executed by one person."[12]

It is possible to construct a definition of administration from the elements that White provides, and the result may suggest the reason for this curious omission: administration consists of all those operations aiming at the achievement of some purpose or objective shared by two or more people. It excludes, then, only those "operations" that are nonpurposive and those that concern only one person.

2. ADMINISTRATION HAS ITS BASE IN MANAGEMENT

"Despite great differences in culture and technology, the process of management throughout the centuries was inherently the same as that which now makes feasible great business enterprises, continental systems of government, and the beginnings of a world order."[13] Yet only comparatively recently has the process of management as such been subjected to systematic study. In the

---

[7] I, 2; II, 7.

[8] I, 2.

[9] In later editions White does define "the art of administration" and "an administrator." He also quotes in passing a well-known definition of administration by Brooks Adams in III, 4 and IV, 2, as well as a comment by Paul Appleby that might be called a definition in III, 8.

[10] II, 3. In italics in the original. Consistently with his broader, more "political" understanding of public administration in recent years, White repeats this definition in the third and fourth editions but omits "as declared by competent authorities," presumably in recognition of the participation of public administration in deciding, as well as fulfilling or enforcing, public policy. III, 3; IV, 1.

[11] II, 3-4; III, 3; IV, 1.

[12] III, 4; IV, 2; the definition of the art of administration is in italics in the original.

[13] III, 3; V, 1.

case of public administration, the late start can be attributed to an excessive preoccupation with law. White's second assumption is "that the study of administration should start from the base of management rather than the foundation of law, and is therefore more absorbed in the affairs of the American Management Association than in the decisions of the courts." This confirms what seemed to be an implication of the first assumption, that the unity in the process of administration precludes a distinction between public and private administration— as it precludes a distinction between federal, state, and municipal administrations. However, this proposition is the end of one of the paths along which White proceeded; the beginning was a declaration of independence from law.

Goodnow and the Relation to Law

White would have agreed with Frank Goodnow's statement written in 1905:

> The most striking if not the most important questions of public law and the first to demand solution are those to which the name "constitutional" is applied. To their solution the wisdom and political activity of the past have been devoted. The present age; however, is devoting itself primarily to questions which are generally referred to as "administrative." A function of government called "administration" is being differentiated from the general sphere of governmental activity, and the term "administrative law" is applied to the rules of law which regulate its discharge.[14]

White argues, however, that Goodnow's writings "do not make a clear distinction between administration and administrative law. This distinction is only now emerging in fact."[15] He adopts Goodnow's definition of administrative law: "that part of the public law which fixes the organization and determines the competence of the administrative authorities, and indicates to the individual remedies for the violation of his rights." This definition, White says, rightly emphasizes the major objective of administrative law, which is the protection of private rights. The objective of public administration, in contrast, is the efficient conduct of public business. "These two goals are not only different, but may at times conflict. Administration is of course bound by the rules of administrative law, as well as by the prescriptions of constitutional law; but within the boundaries thus set it seeks the most effective accomplishment of public purposes."[16] What Goodnow did not sufficiently recognize was that public administration and administrative law are related but distinct fields, governed by internal principles of their own. Thus White does not focus, as Goodnow does, on the rules of law regulating the discharge of the emerging function of "administration," but on the internal rules of the function. This helps to explain both the similarity and the differences between White's *Introduction* and Goodnow's *The Principles of the Administrative Law of the United States*. Viewed in a half-century perspective, the similarity is per-

---

[14] Frank J. Goodnow, *The Principles of the Administrative Law of the United States* (New York: G.P. Putnam's Sons, 1905), p.1.

[15] I, 2n. White refers here to Goodnow's writings on administrative law and not to his *Politics and Administration*(New York: Macmillan Co., 1900) which, although cited in the first edition, appears to have made little impression on White until later; cf. II, 12.

[16] I, 4-5, quoting Goodnow, *Comparative Administrative Law*, Vol. 1, pp. 8-9.

haps the more surprising. In every respect but one[17] the main outlines of White's book follow those of Goodnow's, occasionally chapter by chapter and even section by section. The frequency with which White's discussion parallels Goodnow's is almost as striking as the fact that White exhibits a very considerable concern with the decisions of the courts and scarcely any concern with the affairs of the American Management Association.

Several explanations can be suggested for this similarity between the first comprehensive statement of the new field of public administration and the then major work in the field from which public administration issued. Goodnow, while a teacher and scholar in the field of administrative law, was at the same time deliberately laying the ground for the study of public administration and is one of its acknowledged founders. It is not startling that White patterned himself after Goodnow, even after having set out on his independent way. Although White's second edition contains a new section on fiscal management (which finds no parallel in Goodnow), and further changes occur in subsequent editions, the basic organization remains the same. Goodnow and White were, after all, examining the same subject, if from different points of view. Thus, for example, while Goodnow treats "offices and officers," White deals with "the personnel problem"; for Goodnow the central problem is the law governing the official relation, for White it is morale.

This is more than a difference in point of view. For White, it was the difference between looking at the "boundaries" of a thing, and looking at the thing itself. However, in order to press deeper into White's conception of the study of public administration, it is important to see why this statement of the difference is problematical. The thing looked at, administration, is said to be a process. As process, it does not contain its own definition; it does not set its own boundaries or the end toward which it moves. Indeed, as process, administration seems to comprehend all human activity, except that which is entirely solitary. What, then, gives public administration its definition? It is law, as White admits. Law provides both the ends and the means of public administration.

White's definition of public administration does not deny its dependence on law, but "emphasizes the managerial phase of administration and minimizes its legalistic and formal aspect."[18] This is not sufficiently precise, however, for White emphasizes the managerial phase of public administration. This adjective again introduces "the foundation of law" as starting point for the study of public administration—contrary to White's second assumption. White attempts to surmount this difficulty by arguing that, while the ends and boundaries of public administration are set by law, public administration is management and, as such, no different from any other kind of administration. In that case, why study public administration at all? Is such study a purely arbitrary selection of a part of the ubiquitous process of administration, or is it based on some fundamental distinction that cuts through "process as process"?

Wilson and Subordination to Law

The question of the basis of the study of public administration is most directly considered in the second edition, the only one to contain a chapter

---

[17] One of Goodnow's major sections deals with "Local Administration" to which there is nothing comparable in White. Many of White's individual chapters are, however, arranged on the basis of the federal-state-municipal distinction.

[18] I, 2.

called "Scope and Nature of Public Administration," and the only one to make use of Woodrow Wilson's definition of public administration as "detailed and systematic execution of public law."[19] "Law," White says, "provides the immediate framework within which public administration operates," defining its tasks, establishing its major structure, providing it with funds, and setting forth rules or procedure. "Public administration is embedded in law, and the student of the subject will often be with the statutes."[20] Nevertheless, White contends that an almost exclusive concern with law has blinded American students and civil servants to the essential unity of the process of administration and the internal non-legal principles governing it. One practical result is that American public administration displays "an exaggeration of legal correctness, and in consequence an accentuation of the lawyer in administration...."[21]

By Wilson's definition of public administration, "every particular application of general law is an act of administration." To deal with administration in such terms, White says, "would require analysis of the military as well as the judicial and civil arms of government, and would lead into each of the many activities supported by the modern state...." He proposes to deal with "only a part of the entire field" and proceeds to set some limits.[22]

White is not concerned with "operations peculiar to the special fields of administration," such as techniques of preventing soil erosion or identifying suspected criminals. These are highly particularized procedures, best left to specialists. "They are, however, the primary substantive functions of administration and from one point of view it is artificial to describe public administration apart from these major functions." It would be "feasible" to approach public administration starting from the substantive activities toward which all official work is directed, but "for practical as well as technical reasons ... it is necessary to stop short of describing all human problems and public policies in an effort to clear one path through the field of public administration." Clearing "one path" is possible and desirable, because, underlying the particular substantive functions, "there are certain common procedures and problems characteristic of modern administration under any political system and in any field of government activity.... These aspects of administration are broadly managerial in nature. They comprise the content of this volume."

---

[19] II, 4. The definition is given in a footnote in I, 2, and is taken from Wilson's essay on "The Study of Administration," *Political Science Quarterly*, June 1887.

[20] II, 11.

[21] II, 32. "Legality therefore becomes a primary consideration of administrators, and legal advisors acquire an importance which far outweighs their strictly administrative contribution." II, 11. For White's views on lawyers as administrators see his *Government Career Service* (Chicago: University of Chicago Press, 1953), pp. 45-47; and his essay on "The Public Service of the Future" in the volume of essays in honor of Charles E. Merriam which White edited, *The Future of Government in the United States* (Chicago: University of Chicago Press, 1942), pp. 205-206.

[22] II, 4; the quotations in the following three paragraphs are taken from II, 5-7. It is unnecessary to deal with White's discussion of the exclusion of military administration. It appears, indeed, to be a misapprehension to think that Wilson's definition of public administration requires the inclusion of military administration, which does not have as its end the detailed and systematic execution of public law. The army is not characteristically a law enforcement agency but acts in an area and seeks to accomplish ends that the law cannot reach. Whatever the difficulty in excluding military administration, it arises from White's definition of public administration, not Wilson's.

These "managerial" procedures and problems are not, evidently, merely "aspects" of administration, for White goes on to say that this study "concentrates on the *central core of* the total complex of administration."[23] He is concerned with "process as process," and he seeks to expose and to treat the "essential unity in the process of administration." It is unnecessary to restate the whole series of questions and counter-questions to which this argument gives rise; but it is notable that while White concludes that "the study of the content of public policy, on which all administration depends, is not necessary to the technical study of administrative procedures as such," he does not retract his earlier warning that a description of public administration apart from its substantive functions is somehow "artificial."

Judicial administration is also excluded from the Introduction, even though "the major purpose of the court is the same as that of the administration: to enforce and to implement public policy as declared in law."[24] It is "due to the specialized nature of law enforcement by judicial decision [that] the judges as administrators will not be given systematic consideration in this volume." What is it about this particular specialization that supports the exclusion of judicial administration from a text in public administration? Wilson's definition seems to imply that what the courts do is public administration *par excellence*; thus, the study of public administration would seem to be centrally, although not exclusively, concerned with what is called the administration of justice. But one of White's major objectives was to replace the judge as the central figure in public administration with, say, the city manager.[25] Wilson's definition, which leads back to the radical subordination of public administration to law, is abandoned in White's subsequent editions.[26]

3. ADMINISTRATION—AN ART, IN TRANSFORMATION TO A SCIENCE

The functioning of a modern administrative department "is a far cry from the Egyptian scribe who laboriously copied accounts on his roll of papyrus, but the natural history of administration connects its ancient and modern forms in an unbroken sequence of development…. What differentiates the modern public official from the scribe of antiquity is the marvelous material equipment with which he works, and the contribution which science has made, and continues to make, to his profession."[27] Thus, White's third assumption is that, while administration is still an art, there is a "significant tendency to

---

[23] Italics supplied.

[24] Cf. I, 40.

[25] White's book on the city manager was published the year after the first edition of the *Introduction* and gave expression to White's conviction of the significance of this "emerging technical-professional official in the development of a "new ideal of officialdom." The city manager, White thought, was "a forerunner of the type of official who must become the pattern of the next generation if the American government is to achieve its purpose, or even maintain its self respect." *The City Manager* (Chicago: University of Chicago Press, 1927), p. 287. In later years the city manager was replaced as the central figure in White's view of public administration by the Hamiltonian Chief Executive and the federal senior civil servant. But see below, p. 48 n. 57.

[26] It should be said that White nevertheless follows, to a very considerable degree, the lines set out in Wilson's essay as a whole. White's difficulty here reflects a difficulty in Wilson's essay itself.

[27] I, 4.

transform it into a science." Besides furnishing the tools with which modern administration works, science "is transforming the methods of administration (in the sense of management) from rule of thumb empiricism to ascertained principle." Scientific management, "with its quest for the one best way," has been the leader in this movement. Sufficient progress has been made so that "we are wholly justified in asserting that a science of management appears to be immediately before us."[28]

However, each succeeding edition of the *Introduction* contains fewer scientific "principles" of organization and management and more qualifications about those remaining. For example, discussing the allocation of responsibility and authority, White says in the first edition: "The principle to be observed here is simple enough; to define responsibility so precisely that each official will be specifically charged with definite duties, under such conditions that success or failure will depend upon his own diligence and wisdom, or the contrary." A "necessary corollary" is that each official should be vested with "adequate authority, both legal and financial, to enable him to discharge efficiently the duties pertaining to his office." White concedes that "the application of these principles is full of difficulty," but the principles themselves are clear.[29] In the second edition he adds "the rule of unity of command," to which he attaches "cardinal importance," and which "emphasizes the desirability of a single source of final authority in any organization, a reminder of the old saw, 'No man can serve two masters'." He repeats that "the location of authority, given unity of command, must be in the clearest terms" and that "power must be commensurate with responsibility."[30] In the third edition, these principles appear in a much more qualified form.[31] In a new section called "The Search for Principles" White says that "in the strictest sense of the term, principles in administration are still largely to be formulated. In the meaning of 'principles' that suggests only working rules of conduct which wide experience seems to have validated, a number can be stated."[32] He then shows, following Herbert Simon, that the traditional principles are often in conflict and invariably imprecise. White retains as "a sound working rule" the notion that authority should be allocated in clear and precise terms, especially at the bottom of the hierarchy; at the top, such allocation is difficult and perhaps even damaging. That authority must be commensurate with responsibility is now said to contain "an essential kernel of truth"; but it is a maxim "rarely if ever attained in practice, and ought perhaps to be reformulated in reverse: responsibility does not exceed the most effective use of authority and resources actually available."

Re-evaluating Scientific Management

White never abandoned the pursuit of principles of administration,[33] but he came to the view that what had formerly seemed to be solid principles (however difficult their application) were, rather, prudential rules of thumb, useful

---

[28] I, 15-16; cf. *The City Manager*, pp. 257-58.

[29] I, 59-60. See White's brief informative essay on "The Meaning of Principles in Public Administration," in the volume that he, Marshall E. Dimock, and John M. Gaus wrote in 1936, *The Frontiers of Public Administration* (Chicago: University of Chicago Press, 1936), esp. pp. 18, 22, 24-25.

[30] II, 45-46.

[31] III, 35-36

[32] III, 37-39.

[33] III, 39; IV, 42.

but far from genuinely scientific. He came also to the view that the goal was something less than the "transformation" of administration into a science.

This was no radical revision of opinion. Moderate in everything, White had always reserved his opinion as to how far the "transformation" might go. The very formulation of his third assumption indicates a reservation. So also, for example, does the discussion in the first edition, of methods to measure the efficiency of public administration. White claims that the measurement of so complex and elusive a subject will be the work of many years if, indeed, it can ever be achieved. "But practically we are constantly making judgments as to the success or failure of our institutions and their methods, and it is certainly in point to attempt to refine those judgments so far as possible.... From the scientific point of view, the search for tangible standards is of fundamental importance; and brief experience indicates that it has a practical value as well."[34]

White did not in his early years unreservedly assert that administrative practice could be wholly comprehended under scientific administrative theory, as he did not in his later years altogether abandon the search for scientific principles. But there was a cooling of his confidence in the scientific way, as may be seen in the later editions of the *Introduction* and in the direction of his later research interests. Even as late as the third edition of the *Introduction*, White wrote that "scientific management in principle is applicable to government as well as to industry."[35] But, in the last edition scientific management is assessed in different and more modest terms. White argues that the influence of the "underlying ideas of Taylorism" was not destroyed by "a more sophisticated skepticism" about the possibility of discovering "the one best way." "The very great influence of the scientific management movement in government has been due, not to its specialized procedures, but to the ideas that administration is subject to constant improvement, that some ways of organizing and operating are better than others, and that it is the duty of top management to find the best way for a given staff under given conditions of operation—all of which may change unpredictably."[36] There is little, according to this description, that is "scientific" in the contribution of scientific management. If White is correct, the main force of Taylorism appears to have been dissipated into the most general notions of continuous self-improvement.

In the last two editions, White chose to emphasize the problematical character of administrative science by calling the introductory chapter, "The Art of Administration."[37] In the last edition this chapter contains a section called "Administration— Science or Art" in which White much qualifies the earlier expectation of a "transformation" of administration from an art into a science.

---

[34] I, 76. In the same place White speaks of a technique of rating city services devised by the Colorado League of Municipalities. The technique would now be regarded as extremely crude, and White saw the difficulties; but at the same time he did not wish to discourage this kind of attempt. His criticism is a delightful model of his characteristic circumspection: "Consideration of this plan will reveal a number of assumptions which require careful consideration before too great reliance can be placed on the results. In general it may be said that it is easier to secure statistical material than to give it sound interpretation in evaluating the efficiency of city government."

[35] III, 18.

[36] IV, 21.

[37] The title in the first edition was "Administration and the Modern State" and in the second edition "Scope and Nature of Public Administration."

"Whether these promising attempts to reduce some part of the field of administration to propositions of general, if not universal, validity will transform the study and practice of administration is still an open question. The effort is eminently worth making.... Since administration is certainly in part an art, non-scientific writing will continue to hold an important place. It may, however, progressively become a science, or a science bounded by cultural differences...."[38]

"A science bounded by cultural differences"—bounded by what White calls "the form and spirit of public administration in the United States." These words reflect a significant change in emphasis or, perhaps more exactly, in perspective.

Each edition of the *Introduction* contains a chapter dealing with "technical problems of large-scale organization and management" or "pure theory" of organization—the subject matter of the science of administration, as White generally understood it.[39] In the last three editions this chapter deals systematically and more or less abstractly with such matters as the individual and his position, the formation of administrative units, hierarchy, authority, and coordination.[40] It presents "some of the characteristic elements of large and complex organizations, viewed for the moment merely as huge aggregations of people at work."[41] By the last edition, this chapter is "bounded," literally, by "cultural differences.' It opens with the distinctly political and constitutional question of the authority to determine organization.[42] And, to the otherwise unchanged conclusion, White adds this sentence:

> These generalities become more meaningful in the pages that follow, as they are translated in terms of the living experience of Presidents, Secretaries, staff advisers, and field agents, into what President John Tyler once described as "the complex, but at the same time beautiful, machinery of our system of government."[43]

Thus, generalities about organization become more meaningful as they are seen in terms of the living experience of American public administration. This statement stands in significant contrast to the main thrust of White's original intention, which was to give meaning to American public administration by seeing it in terms of generalizations about administration as a universal process.

---

[38]   IV, 9.

[39]   II, 38; III, 27; IV, 27. This chapter introduces the section of the book dealing with "structure and Organization." In the last edition White attempts to recast the whole discussion in terms of "Hamilton's doctrine of executive unity." IV, 44. Thus what began in the first edition as a discussion of the "Forms and Methods of Integration" became in the second and third editions a discussion of "The Chief Executive as General Manager" and in the fourth edition a discussion of "The Quest for Unity: The Chief Executive."

[40]   In the fourth edition, however, White proceeds "from the top of the hierarchy down through its principal levels" (IV, 29) rather than, as in the former editions, from the bottom up.

[41]   IV, 26.

[42]   This subject had also opened the comparable chapter in the first edition but had been dropped from the intervening ones, presumably on the ground that it was not appropriately dealt with in a chapter on the "pure theory" of organization.

[43]   IV, 43.

4. ADMINISTRATION—THE CENTRAL PROBLEM OF MODERN GOVERNMENT

The fourth assumption is "that administration has become, and will continue to be the heart of the problem of modern government." White begins the first edition, as writings on American government had ordinarily begun, with a discussion of the Constitutional separation of powers or functions, but he insists that the traditional assertion of the centrality of the legislative function misses the main characteristic of modern government.

In an earlier and simpler age, legislative bodies had the time to deal with the major issues, the character of which was suited to the deliberations of the lay mind; they were primarily problems involving judgments on important questions of political ethics, such as the enfranchisement of citizens by abolishing property qualifications, the disposition of the public land, the disestablishment of the Anglican Church, or the liberalization of a Monarchist state. The problems which crowd upon legislative bodies today are often entangled with, or become exclusively technical questions which the layman can handle only by utilizing the services of the expert. ...These (experts) are not merely useful to legislators overwhelmed by the increasing flood of bills; they are simply indispensable. They are the government. One may indeed suggest that the traditional assignment of the legislature as the pivotal agency in the governmental triumvirate is destined at no distant date to be replaced by a more realistic analysis which will establish government as the task of administration, operating within such areas as may be circumscribed by legislatures and courts.[44]

Nor is this merely a matter of the administration doing what legislatures (and courts) formerly did.[45] The work of government has changed, so that the experts now "are the government." More is involved here than an enormous increase in the complexity and technicality of the problems of modern government; for however indispensable the technician or the expert might become, he would remain, as technician, subordinate to those dealing with the non-technical, political problems. The point is that the political sphere, to which the technician is in principle subordinate, is no longer the place where the real problems arise. The great political questions are settled, and a form of government and distribution of powers appropriate when these questions were still unanswered is appropriate no longer.[46] This is the explanation of White's com-

---

[44] I, 6.

[45] But see pp. 48-9, *Public Administration Review*, March 1965.

[46] "Governmental problems have become intricate and ever more insistent. They call for solution with the aid of science, not with the wisdom of a ward politician." *The City Manager*, p. 295; cf. *Introduction*, I, 13, where White says that, "science has revealed the objects to be achieved...." In another study during this early period, White says of the old disputes over the dominance of power in the federal system that "the advent of a new society... took the issue boldly away from the Constitutional lawyers and the orators, settled it in broad outline by the pressure of events and vested the *modus vivendi* largely in the hands of administrators." *Trends in Public Administration* (New York: McGraw-Hill, 1933), p. 8; and see pp. 11, 235-256, 330-331; see in the same connection White's more recent essay on "The Public Service of the Future," in *The Future of Government in the United States*.

ment that, though the role of administration "in the logic of our governmental system is distinctly subordinate," yet "this should not conceal the fact . . . that the business of government in the twentieth century is fundamentally the business of administration."[47] On this ground it is possible to understand the culmination of White's four assumptions: that administration, itself essentially non-political, is the heart of the problem of modern government.

The Development of American Administration

Especially in the first edition, White takes care to describe how administration came to occupy this central position in modern government. The source is a new social philosophy, growing out of "the industrial revolution and its many social, economic, and political implications. . . ." "The industrial revolution has necessitated . . . a degree of social cooperation in which *laissez faire* has become impossible; and gradually the new environment is building up in men's minds a conception of the role of the state which approximates the function assigned it by the conditions of modern life. These new ideas involve the acceptance of the state as a great agency of social cooperation, as well as an agency of social regulation."[48] Again there is the inference that the fundamental political questions are closed. This analysis is carried forward, in the second edition, in a chapter entitled "Trends in the American Administrative System," in which White traces the development of the American administrative system—and by implication other advanced systems—from that appropriate to a simple rural civilization demanding little from government to that required by an urban, industrialized civilization dependent on government at every turn. As industrialization developed, "the relative equality of life in early America began to fade...and the line of separation between those who had much and those who had little became clearer and clearer." But political inequality had been largely extinguished; and the government, "responsive to the voting power of the masses," began to protect those harmed by unregulated industrial competition and to prevent the steady concentration of wealth in a few hands. "Here is one of the basic social changes which supports much modern administration."[49]

White did not press on with this broad inquiry, perhaps because the historical understanding from which it was derived came to seem doubtful, or, more likely, because by 1939 it seemed that what distinguished American government and administration from other modern administrative states was more significant than what it had in common with them—to say nothing of non-governmental administrations.[50]

---

[47] I, 24. "The legislature, although of all the organs of government the most representative, is forced by its own methods to stand at the greatest distance from the real business of governing." I, 339.

[48] I, 8; cf. I, 463-466.

[49] II, 22.

[50] See the prefaces to the third and fourth editions. There are in later editions expressions of the early view of the great march of history toward the modern administrative state where the problems are technical ones; but it is of some significance that more stress is laid on the political as distinguished from the economic and technological causes. See III, 5-6; IV, 3-4. Moreover, this view lost its former importance in White's over-all understanding.

The Form and Spirit of American Administration

As early as the second edition, White anticipates his later use of history, less as a way of understanding the rise of administration and administrative science, than as a way of understanding the political conditions and ends that give American public administration its special character. "As the result of well over a hundred years uninterrupted development, an administrative structure has been evolved with characteristics peculiar to it. It is different from the Dutch, the Japanese, the Argentinean or the English civil service; it is peculiarly American."[51]

The title of the comparable chapter in the third and fourth editions indicates a clarification of intention; the discussion now centers not upon "trends" but upon "The Form and Spirit of Public Administration in the United States" and consists of a more extensive and systematic statement of the foundations of the American system. Its significance lies in the effort to describe what distinguishes American public administration, not only from administration in general, but from systems of public administration elsewhere, to give the study of public administration that meaningfulness that comes from its connection with "the complex, but at the same time beautiful, machinery of our system of governments."

The complex organization that carries on the common business of the American people bears today the unmistakable marks of its evolution: the initial Federalist conception emphasizing energy and responsibility, the Jacksonian insistence upon democracy in administration, the appeal for integrity and decency launched by the moral reformers after the Civil War, and the influence of technology and management in a later day.

> The catastrophic forces of depression and war, the international tensions since 1945, and the mere magnitude of the administrative machine, at home and overseas, tend toward the dominance of the ideas of Alexander Hamilton rather than those of Andrew Jackson. The first half of the present century may indeed be called the new Hamiltonianism. The democratic ideal, nevertheless, has not lost strength even though the rule of rotation is circumscribed; and the power of moral standards in the public service is magnified, not lessened, by occasional personal failures.[52]

Originally, White's problem seemed to be to dispose of the political aspect of public administration, while acknowledging its importance in order to get down to the real work of studying administration proper.[53] This was thought to be consistent with the historical trend thrusting administration into preeminence. White never entirely abandoned this view, but increasingly a

---

51   II, 32.

52   IV, 22-23; cf. I, 475-476; III, 7.

53   "It ought to be possible in this country to separate politics from administration. Sound administration can develop and continue only if this separation can be achieved. For a century they have been confused, with evil results beyond measure. The [city] managers have an unparalleled opportunity and deep obligation to teach the American people by their precept and conduct that their job is to administer the affairs of the city with integrity and efficiency and loyalty to the council, without participating in or allowing their work to be affected by contending programs or partisans." *The City Manager*, p. 301. See generally the important discussion herein ch. 10, 11, 14. On politics and administration, cf. *Introduction*, II, 12-13; IV, 6-8.

different one made a strong claim upon his understanding. This was the view that the "political" element of public administration cannot be disposed of by the student of public administration, because it affects "administration" at every turn and is, therefore, an intrinsic, even fundamental, part of the study of public administration.[54]

White could still write in the fourth edition that "one day a philosopher-practitioner with a global experience may write a book that has as much meaning for Mexico as for Sweden, for the Indonesian Republic as for Israel."[55] But it is difficult to imagine, on the basis of this last edition, what such a book would include and even whether it would be a book about public administration; it is even more difficult to imagine White pursuing, or seriously urging the pursuit, of the common denominator among, not only these nations, but also, say, the Red Cross, General Motors, Dartmouth College, and the Egyptian scribe.

The Role of Administration in the United States

Inevitably, White's growing concern with the form and spirit of public administration in the United States, and his declining confidence in a science of administration, affected his view of the role of public administration and public administrators in the United States and other similar governments.

In the early years, he had argued that modern government is characterized by the replacement of the great old constitutional and political questions by what are essentially technical questions of administration or management—thus the paradox that the central problem of modern times is not a political problem. But in spite of all the emphasis on "management," there was always some reservation concerning the supposedly non-political nature of administration. In the first edition, White writes that the work of the administrative branch of the government involves judicial and legislative functions, as well as the executive functions to which the theory of the separation of powers would seem to confine it. As he put it in the next edition, "the essence of modern government is an obstinate intermingling of functions theoretically separate."[56] Much of the work formerly done by legislatures and courts is now performed by officials in that part of the government called "administration." In itself, this means only that certain legislative and judicial functions are performed by new agencies. Assuredly, this raises problems unsettled by the old separation of powers theory; but it does not necessarily follow that these new functions of the administration are any the less legislative or judicial, or that they should be performed according to any but the traditional legislative and judicial standards. Following this line of reasoning, it could be argued that administration is the heart of modern government in the sense that age-old political and constitutional problems now present themselves as problems of (or in) public administration.[57]

---

[54] See for example White's shifting interests as indicated by the chapter headings in the section of the *Introduction* dealing with public personnel administration. White's study of *Whitley Councils in the British Civil Service* (Chicago: University of Chicago Press, 1933) represents an early exploration of the kind of "personnel" question with which White was always (but especially in later years) concerned. See below, n. 66.

[55] IV, 11; cf. IV, viii.

[56] I, 5; II, 9.

[57] It is of some interest to note, bearing in mind White's second assumption, that this is the theme around which the discipline of administrative law turns, so far as it is concerned with more than legal technicalities.

More explicitly, this argument might be taken to imply that administration is the heart of modern government precisely to the extent that public administration in modern government is not mere administration, but the main field within which political and constitutional problems now move. This is, in fact, a secondary and subdued theme of White's *Introduction*; and although it never entirely displaces the emphasis on administrative management, it receives more emphatic statement in the later editions.[58]

> The initiation of public policy has escaped legislative halls and now rests principally with official agencies and with citizen groups. The latter necessarily represent special segments of opinion and interest. The former have the moral obligation to represent the interest of all, to seek the public good. Being somewhat less vulnerable to outside pressures, public servants may cultivate the general welfare with greater detachment, with a surer reliance on rational analysis, with a clearer appreciation of long run consequences, than representative bodies. This is not to say that their opinions should supersede the preferences of elected, representative bodies; it is merely to indicate the special values that are involved in the role which administration has now achieved.

This point of view suggests that statesmen are needed in the higher ranks of administration rather than technicians.[59]

On the one hand, then, "administration is process common to all group effort, public or private, civil or military, large scale or small scale."[63] On the other, "the role which administration has now achieved" in American government is not common to all groups or to all governments; and it seems to be in that uncommon role, not in the common process, that the heart of the problem of modern government is to be found. "The need, incessant and urgent, is for the administrative mind that can hold fast to the public interest and bind conflicting special interests to it by skillful contrivance, based on knowledge but exceeding mere *expertise*." Exceeding, that is to say, mere administration or management. "In the highest reaches the administrative art touches the political, but it grows out of different soil."[61]

White did not undertake the further reconstruction of the *Introduction* that this wise remark might be thought to call for. He did not consider whether a soil consisting of mere managerial expertise could nurture the highest form of the administrative art, or whether his original view of the way to study public administration—to search for principles of the uniform process of administration—was compatible with his later view of the governing reason for studying it—the urgent and incessant need for administrative statesmanship.

---

[58] Both themes are present in White's well known and still valuable, *Government Career Service* (1935), see especially pp. 23, 60-61, 89ff. Some readers may find interesting White's dialogue with the politician T. V. Smith, in their *Politics and the Public Service* (New York: Harper and Brothers, 1939). See *The Future of Government in the United States*, pp. 209-215. Finally should be mentioned White's undoubtedly influential membership on the committee that drew up the 1955 Hoover Commission Task Force *Report on Personnel and Civil Service*, with its proposal for a senior civil service of a more than technical competence and responsibility.

[59] III, 7-8; cf. II, 12-13; IV, 6-8.

[60] III, 3; IV, 1.

[61] III, 8; cf. IV, 521.

The True Foundations

White was confronted with two different guides to his subject. One urged the need to penetrate beneath the superficial differences between administrative systems and political orders to an investigation of the universal process of administration. The other persistently maintained the overriding importance of the difference between public and private administration and between the political conditions and ends of one administrative system and those of another.

In the early editions, the tension between these two guides is evident in White's struggle to define public administration and to set future lines of study. However often he fell back on the political guide to mark the boundaries of his subject, he still thought that the subject itself was the uniform process of administration. However, the theoretical problem—whether a mere process is worth studying and can be studied apart from what directs it—persisted. The conviction that such a study is possible and worthwhile was never abandoned, but it became much less marked. By the third edition, the conflicting claims of the "political" and the "administrative" guides to the study of public administration had been muted. The introductory chapter, considerably compressed, and with the theoretical problem smoothed over as far as possible, was followed by a pair of chapters in which the form and spirit of public administration in the United States and the pure theory of organization were given separate treatment. These warring approaches were not reconciled; but, under White's judicious superintendence, they were made to march together, quietly if not harmoniously, throughout the book.

The comment should be made, however, that the third and fourth editions represent less fully than the first two White's conception of public administration at the time he wrote them. In the third edition there is found a distinct indication that White had come to regard the *Introduction* as having been built on only a partial view of public administration.

> The study of public administration has advanced to an extraordinary degree since 1920. As an intellectual discipline the field of public administration still lacks much, including an account of its historical development, a comprehensive statement in general terms of its underlying principles, an exact definition of its central concepts, a penetrating analysis of its foundations in psychology and sociology, and an interpretative account of its role in the structure of government and of life. Further, it needs to be related to the broad generalizations of political theory concerned with such matters as justice, liberty, obedience, and the role of the state in human affairs.[62]

According to this statement, the discipline of public administration still lacked (among other important things) an account of its historical development and a comprehensive statement of its theoretical and political foundations. White's last works deal with the history. Why did he not choose what seems to be the greater of these tasks? Part of the answer may be that, while White saw the need he found himself unable to perceive the line of inquiry by which the true foundations might be exposed. He saw the merits, but also the limitations, of many different approaches. Characteristically, the suggestion for fundamental probing quoted above is replaced, in the fourth edition, by a list of useful approaches.

---

[62]   III, 10.

There are many ways to study the phenomena of public administration. The first systematic American approach was through law and was devoted to the legal organization of public authorities, their legal forms of action, and the limits of their powers... Subsequently came systematic writing primarily concerned with the nature of administrative institutions viewed as agencies of management, an approach related to the scientific management movement and reflecting the criterion of efficiency. More recently attention has been given to historical and biographical materials that reveal the evolution of administrative systems and trends in thinking about administration. The nature of administration has also been explored by sociologists, as one among many significant social structures. Most recently the sociological-psychological school of behaviorists has made important contributions to the understanding of why officials and public employees act as they do. All of these approaches are relevant and from all of them come wisdom and understanding.[63]

Missing here is an expression of White's earlier concern for a comprehensive theoretical examination, or re-examination, of the study of public administration.[64] Indeed, White seems to express that complacent, undiscriminating eclecticism which is all too common in this field—the view that public administration consists, somehow, of an aggregate of an almost infinite number of "perspectives," institutional, political, sociological, psychological, technical, historical. Yet this judgment is insufficient when the work that occupied White's last years is taken into account.

It is interesting to consider the order in which White presents these ways of studying public administration. It appears at first glance to be a simple progression—and so perhaps the behaviorists would argue; but there is reason to believe that White did not so regard it. Although he had a genuine respect for the contributions of sociology and the social-psychological school of behaviorists, and had made some early contributions himself along these lines,[65] he was not altogether comfortable with the ways in which they led. He observed a brash young science drive assumptions and principles, which he had been one of the first to state systematically, to extremes that were foreign and distasteful to him. He saw this science carry the pursuit of an underlying process to the point where it seemed to abandon a concern with public administration altogether—a direction in which he had also been pressed but which he had resisted, in practice if not always in principle. As the rest of the discipline became more scientific and more concerned with process as process, White became less so. As the most vigorous movements within the discipline shunted the political environment and ends of public administration more and more to the periphery, White brought them back to a prominent place.

---

[63] IV, 11.

[64] But see IV, viii.

[65] *The Prestige Value of Public Employment in Chicago: An Experimental Study* (Chicago: University of Chicago Press, 1929); *Further Contributions to the Prestige Value of Public Employment* (Chicago: University of Chicago Press, 1932). These were preceded by *Conditions of Municipal Employment in Chicago* (City of Chicago, 1925), which yields insight into the methodological assumptions of White's very early work and provides valuable information about Chicago city government in the 1920's.

It is misleading to regard White as having sought haven in the quiet eddy of history, while the rest of the discipline rushed by. Following what was in his case always a strong and sound instinct, he put aside as far as possible inherited theoretical apparatus and simply looked at public administration in the United States. He looked, it is true, at the public administration of yesterday, not today. The skill with which he described and the wisdom with which he interpreted what he saw have been almost universally acclaimed; and it is both likely and appropriate that his historical studies will be the most enduring products of a long and fruitful career. But the full significance of these books is missed if they are taken merely as history.

A thorough investigation of the importance of White's histories for the study of public administration would require another lengthy essay, but the essential point has been anticipated, and can be stated briefly. White entitled the histories: *The Federalists, The Jeffersonians, The Jacksonians, and The Republican Era.*[66] What was most important about public administration in the early years of the United States was not what it shared with all administration everywhere, but its character as *Federalist* administration. Federalist administrative theory and practice, best expressed in Hamilton's views of executive energy, Washington's conception of competence and the notion of administration by gentlemen were intrinsically connected with and subordinate to Federalist political and constitutional theory; and that, in the main, is the way White treats them. He did not choose arbitrarily, as one perspective among many, the middle way of historical study for his mature years. It was his way of looking at the field of public administration afresh, of seeking not merely one perspective, but the true perspective within which other partial perspectives find their focus. White's histories may be taken as an object lesson in the study of public administration: which aspects are primary and which secondary; which perspectives are narrow and which broad; which ways lead to the heart and which to some non-essential limb.

This vital lesson in the discipline's standards of relevance and significance was taught, as White thought best, by example rather than by systematic theoretical exposition. Some of the original assumptions—and the difficulties to which they give rise—are still present in the histories.[67] Theoretical

---

[66] Published in New York by the Macmillan Company in 1948, 1951, 1954, and 1958 respectively. White's reconsideration of federalism in *The States and the Nation* (Baton Rouge: Louisiana State University Press, 1953) is consistent with the interpretation here and should be compared with the earlier discussions in the first edition of the *Introduction* (ch. 4 and pp. 469-70) and in *Trends in Public Administration* (Part I, esp. Ch. 11). It is significant that during his last decade White chose as the subjects of his articles in the field of administration: "Strikes in the Public Service" (*Public Personnel Review,* January 1949); "The Loyalty Program of the United States Government" (*Bulletin of the Atomic Scientist December, 1951;* and "The Senior Civil Service" (*Public Administration Review*, Autumn 1955; *Personnel Administration*, January-February, 1956).

[67] Thus providing some ground for Dwight Waldo's criticism that "the dominant perspective in these volumes plainly is the POSDCORB perspective." *Perspectives on Administration* (University, Ala.: University of Alabama Press, 1956), p. 59. That the POSDCORB, or pure theory of organization, "perspective" is present is, indeed, plain, for example in White's numerous remarks on the state of the "administrative art" at different times. Whether, contrary to the argument here, this perspective is dominant, whether it provides the over-all orientation, the standards of relevance and importance, the reader will have to judge for himself by reading the histories and reflection on the relations between their parts and their whole.

precision is not to be expected. Although concerned with the theoretical problems of his discipline for most of his life, White's was not fundamentally a
theoretical mind. His true compass was his uncommonly good common sense,
which enabled him to make substantial contributions to the study of public
administration, even while leaving unresolved some of its most basic questions.

   This quality also led him to choose administrative history as his way of
beginning to relate the study to what he called, in the third edition of the
Introduction, "the broad generalizations of political theory concerned with such
matters as justice, liberty, obedience, and the role of the state in human affairs."[68] White would have been the first to insist that his histories do not
constitute a comprehensive "interpretative account" of the role of American
public administration "in the structure of government and of life." But it is
precisely White's breadth of concern—his concern with the relation between
public administration and matters such as justice, liberty, obedience, and the
role of the state in human affairs—that gives these books their special excellence and a great part of their value to present day students of public administration.

---

[68]   III, 10.

3

The Problem of Responsibility and Control of the Neutral Civil Service

Whatever the criticisms of the American civil service, and however much the "politics/administration" dichotomy may have been called into question by later theorists and practitioners, almost never does anyone go so far as to recommend the wholesale abolition of the merit system and a return to spoils. Generally speaking, the net result of the Civil Service Act has been very positive. The efficiency level of public service in the United States today, and the sheer capacity of government to provide services, is greatly enhanced over what was the case during the decades preceding the Civil War. Moreover, American politics is not generally perceived as the maelstrom of moral depravity in the way that it was then, even granting that a strong element of cynicism continues to be felt.

Still, questions do persist. This section begins with Herbert Kaufman's article from 1956 which provides a comprehensive sketch of issues and conflicts—he called them "emerging conflicts" at the time—that still describe much of the field of public administration. In the case of some of these conflicts one may hold out that further research could be useful. Probably the most commonly felt frustration with the merit system is the one eloquently stated by Robert Dince, namely, that it is cumbersome. It deprives the line officers of the necessary tools of personnel management by prescribing a heavy overlay of record-keeping and procedural requirements that compromise efficiency. Agency heads and bureau chiefs feel that they are prevented from using their own initiative in such normally routine matters as transfer and promotion of personnel, altering position classifications, or hiring and firing. The persistence of this problem leads Dince to complain that ". . .the original conception of the merit system has been stood on its head. Civil Service today is designed to insulate federal personnel practices from the claims of merit. You learn very rapidly in government that if you want to get, or hold on to, good people and avoid being stuck with the lemons, you must learn how to thwart the Civil Service Commission and its regulations." Crucial to addressing such problems, however, is the question of their source. More particularly, do problems such as Dince identifies derive ultimately from irremovable vagaries and conflicts within political life, or is it the case that the public character of public administration poses no necessary special impediment to administrative efficiency? The exchange between Herbert Simon, Donald Smithberg and Victor

Thompson vs. Donald Rowat lays out this issue and covers much of the ground for further reflection on it. Relevant especially to Professor Rowat's position is the difficulty in interpreting and providing for "responsibility" of public administrators. The classic argument waged between Herman Finer and Carl J. Friedrich exhibits this difficulty. To whom ought public administrators be held responsible and to what degree of exactitude? In what way, if any, should a responsible civil servant seek to influence the formulation of policy; and does responsibility imply resistance to policy that he or she may find incoherent or inconsistent with established policy? We seem to reach an impasse; but Herbert J. Storing's *Public Administration Review* article from1964 recasts this whole issue in a way that gets beyond it.

The remaining selections in this section all exemplify specific proposals for fine-tuning the merit system. Except for the last two, they derive from or bear directly upon reports from special Presidential commissions. These reports have themselves achieved the rank of classics in public administration literature. In thinking about the prospects for reform today, it behooves us to be aware of what reforms have been considered and recommended by these eminent and respectable authorities in the past and to consider the reasons that made for their limited success. The first of these reports came in 1937 from the "President's Commission on Administrative Management," also known as the "Brownlow Commission" after its illustrious chairman, Louis Brownlow. The report recommended abolishing the Civil Service Commission. Responsibility for personnel management would instead be assigned to a personnel director, serving in the president's immediate staff, while the guardianship of the merit system would be charged to a civil service board with advisory and investigatory powers but no administrative authority over such things as examinations, classification, enforcement, or internal operations. The view of the Brownlow Commission was that a single officer, close to the president and to the needs of the particular agencies, would be more apt to interpret his mission in terms of program accomplishments rather than in terms of technical compliance with regulations. Congress took no action as a result of the Brownlow Commission Report, although President Roosevelt was encouraged by it to appoint on his own initiative a special liaison officer between himself and the CSC; and in the following year the President issued an order that required each federal agency to install its own personnel officer to assist the agency head in relations with the CSC.

The Brownlow Commission had made "decentralization" into something of a battle cry for good government types, even though over-centralization was probably not the principal problem with federal personnel administration. As such things go, in 1947 another, more famous and influential commission was appointed to study and recommend improvements in the civil service. This was the first Hoover Commission. The Hoover Commission's recommendations were along the same line of what the Brownlow Commission had proposed but they were put in a somewhat less jolting form. The Civil Service Commission was to be preserved, but with a division of responsibility between its chairman, who would be charged with all administrative duties and who would report directly to the president, and the Commission sitting *en banc*, which would retain only the rule making and appellate duties. The Hoover Commission also recommended that the personnel administration of the agencies be decentralized to a considerable extent. Position classifications and examinations should be conducted at the agency level, with only supervisory review by the chairman of the CSC. Each of these recommendations required legislative action and they were all subsequently enacted into law.

Nothing is easier than to criticize the alterations of the CSC during this period as a series of compromise measures that preserve the essential problems of cumbersome procedure and especially presidential isolation. But is there a more radical response to the problem that does not put the whole idea of the merit system into jeopardy? Commissioner James K. Pollock's single dissenting report from the first Hoover Commission's study highlights this question because Pollock *did* take a more radical approach. In his view, the Hoover Commission reflected an "... unduly limited concept of personnel administration, viewing it as a procedural, mechanical process called personnel transactions." Pollock was much impressed with what he believed to be the developments in the "human relations" school of management and he wanted to liberate agency heads to use human relations techniques fully. To this end, Pollock recommended a complete abolition of the CSC and a full decentralization of all personnel management among the agencies. A new Civil Service Agency would be created that would have only limited staff and only general supervisory powers. This new agency would be charged to make human relations techniques known to agency heads. As for protection against the spoils system, Pollock suggested a simple law forbidding favoritism in the making of appointments and removals from office. The law would be enforced by the courts, in response to privately initiated suits.

Pollock's ringing dissent, and his counter-proposals, make the recommendations of the First Hoover Commission look pale by comparison. It is true that as long as general civil service regulations persist, and as long as a central commission can be appealed to by government employees or applicants against agency heads, the frustration with government red tape in personnel administration will be felt. Still it can be wondered whether Pollock's boldness is not due to his narrower and more simple definition of the whole problem that occupied the Commission's attention. For one thing, it seems doubtful that a science of human relations would be able to arm agency heads with answers to all the questions of employee incentive, morale, and especially responsibility such that we could depend on them almost exclusively for the faithful and efficient administration of public policy. As far as protecting the merit system goes, Pollock's proposal amounts to transferring this responsibility from the CSC to the courts; but why would the courts be able to discharge it in a fairer or less meddlesome way? Finally, Pollock's recommendations are devoted exclusively to the issue of the procedural costs of centralization. He appears to pay little attention to the problem of the isolation of the executive, with all of the corresponding problems of lack of overarching rationality and responsibility in governmental policy.

Even following Congress' enactment of the essential program recommended by the Hoover Commission, a nagging sense of dissatisfaction with American public administration continued. Further tinkering was on the agenda. Perhaps as a result of a renewed spirit of realism among students and professionals it came to be questioned whether the early civil service reformers were not naive; that the idea of cleaning up government by taking the politics out of it was insufficiently mindful of the irreducibly political character of government at all levels, in the execution as in the formation of public policy. Hence, in 1955, a Second Hoover Commission filed its report to Congress. As if one might have one's cake and eat it too, the newer commission acknowledged the propriety of advocacy and defensive explanations of particular policies in the administration, while at the same time it sought to preserve the fundamental idea of neutrality. To achieve both these aims, the commission urged a renewed precision in the definition of career public service so that career officers would not be responsible for advocating policy; then in addition there would be installed new political officers within the agencies, for whom advocacy would be the primary responsibility. Extending the same idea onto another plane, the Second Hoover Commission also recommended the creation of a new class of government servants who would make up a "senior civil service." The idea was that such persons would form a pool of experienced talent to assist the political executives by the benefit of their advice and counsel in the business of administration. The senior civil service would not be political appointees; they would be career officers whose appointment to a particular agency would be temporary and whose rank in the bureaucracy would attach to them personally, rather than to the office that they occupied at a given time.

The report of the Second Hoover Commission proved less successful than that of its predecessor. The idea of a senior civil service fell upon barren ground and was not acted upon. There were too many misgivings among career bureaucrats themselves about just how the "seniors" would operate. Moreover, the basic idea of rank attaching to persons rather than to office smacked of an elitism not easily consistent with the basic, democratic spirit of American politics. As for the recommendation for drawing a precise line between political and politically neutral officers and granting both a place in the administration, that was at least attempted. A number of political executives were appointed and attached to agencies. Whether that scheme has been successful in practice is difficult to assess. Insofar as the aim has been to relieve career officers of the job of advocating and defending policy, especially before Congressional committees for example, it may have been somewhat useful. If the aim, though, is to relieve career officers of responsibility for informed judgments regarding the soundness of the policies they administer, the reform is probably hopeless. It is to be expected and desired that seasoned career officers would have such judgments; but if that is true, should those judgments inform the business of policy formation and reformation, i.e. of government? The answer seems obvious; and yet it poses a challenge to the very heart of a system of public administration that is supposed to be competent but strictly neutral and subordinate to a democratic political process.

The most recent development in this ongoing process of tinkering with the administration of the merit system is the Civil Service Reform Act of 1978. By this law the Civil Service Commission has been dissolved, and is replaced by two new entities: the Office of Personnel Management and the Merit Systems Protection Board. The Office of Personnel Management is intended to be the President's own personnel arm. It is headed by a director who, along with the rest of the members, is appointed for a term of four years and who is personally responsible to the president. The duties of the Office are administrative; they include the enforcement of civil service rules, administration of the retirement program, and position classification. The Office will also assist the President in formulating new rules and regulations for the civil service.

The idea of decentralizing personnel administration is explicitly encouraged by the law; the Director of the Office is allowed to delegate to agency heads any personnel administrative function except the conduct of competitive examinations where the requirements are common to several agencies. The Office retains an oversight responsibility over the agencies in these matters. The Merit Systems Protection Board bears a somewhat closer resemblance to the old CSC. It has three members, no more than two of whom can belong to the same political party, appointed for a term of seven years. The main function of the board is to hear cases and adjudicate appeals brought by civil servants. The law notes explicitly that such appeals are subject to review by the courts. The Board is assisted in its work by a Special Counsel who is charged to lodge cases with the Board in behalf of plaintiffs.

The main thrust of the new law seems to be to make government more efficient by providing a closer measurement of performance coupled with greater flexibility in promotion, demotion, and firing, and also merit pay for performance. Agencies are specifically charged to establish stricter performance appraisal systems under the approval of the Office of Personnel Management and to rely on them in their personnel decisions. In the same vein, the law revives and enacts the idea of a senior executive service, whose appointment to any particular agency will be temporary and who will be expected to bring "management expertise" to "ensure that the executive management of the Government of the United States is responsive to the needs, policies, and goals of the Nation and otherwise is of the highest quality." In contrast to the Second Hoover Commission's recommendation for a senior civil service, the new senior executives' responsibilities are to be specific and definite, though alterable depending on the needs of the agency to which they are assigned. The head of the agency in question must develop a performance appraisal system to judge the effectiveness of the senior executive, and can make bonus pay awards of up to twenty percent of the senior executive's base salary. The new senior executive service represents an attempt to combine the advantages of a pool of top quality managers, recognized for their general talent for "getting things done" and available for a variety of appointments, with the insistence on specifically measurable performance on the job and merit reward. It remains to be seen whether these two sets of aims are compatible in practice. Abstractly, one may wonder whether there is not some likelihood of a conflict of authority between the agency heads and their senior executives whose work they are charged to appraise but to whom a more than ordinary measure of discretion would presumably have to be conceded.

The final exchange in this section deals with the specific issue of the right to strike by civil servants. The issue clearly should be included among a selection of readings that are devoted to the general theme of administrative responsibility. The question of a right to strike is of course only one of a number of questions regarding the whole matter of unionization and collective bargaining in the civil service, although in a sense it is the ultimate one. A useful supplement to these statements would be to review and consider assessments of the formal proceedures: fact finding, arbitration, etc. that are mandated by law.

EMERGING CONFLICTS IN THE DOCTRINES OF PUBLIC ADMINISTRATION

Herbert Kaufman

[From the *American Political Science Review*, Vol. 50, December 1956, pp. 1057-1073. Reprinted by permission of the American Political Science Association.]

As a self-conscious discipline among the cluster of specialties or "fields" encompassed by political science, public administration came late and grew fast. Its recent arrival and rapid growth sometimes obscure the fact that its origins are to be found in a process of experimentation with governmental structure that long preceded the appearance of public administration as a subject of systematic study and is likely to continue as long as the nation exists. This process of experimentation goes on vigorously today, and the development of new forms is generating discord more profound and far-reaching than any that has ever hitherto divided students of public administration. It is with the sources and significance of that discord that this paper is concerned.

I. THREE CORE VALUES

The central thesis of this paper is that an examination of the administrative institutions of this country suggests that they have been organized and operated in pursuit successively of three values, here designated representativeness, neutral competence, and executive leadership. Each of these values has been dominant (but not to the point of total suppression of the others) in different periods of our history; the shift from one to another generally appears to have occurred as a consequence of the difficulties encountered in the period preceding the change. Much of the early literature commonly identified as within the province of public administration was written during the transition from the first to the second of these values, and the great flood of materials produced after World War I often reflected both the second and third values when these for a time (and for reasons to be explained) pointed in the same direction for governmental improvement. Lately, however, the courses of action indicated by the second and third values have been not only different, but contradictory; the cleavage is becoming increasingly apparent in the doctrines of public administration. What the effects will be on the fraternity of practitioners and on their aspirations to professional status is difficult to say, but it seems clear that commitments to values that have become incompatible can produce only gulfs in the realm of ideas and confusion in proposals for governmental reform.

The Quest for Representativeness

The earliest[1] stress was placed on representativeness in government, the quest for which clearly had its roots in the colonial period, when colonial assemblies were struggling with royal governors for control of political life in the New World and "No taxation without representation" was a slogan that

---

[1] It is impossible to date any of the periods with precision, except arbitrarily, and it is probably unnecessary to do so for most purposes, but their origins can be identified, and so, roughly, their zeniths.

RESPONSIBILITY AND CONTROL OF THE NEUTRAL CIVIL SERVICE   49

expressed one of the principal interests and anxieties of the colonists. The legislatures thus became the champions of the indigenous population, or at least of the ruling elements in the colonies, against what was regarded in many quarters as executive oppression. When the Revolution drove the British out, the legislatures in the new states were, with but a couple of exceptions,[2] enthroned in positions of leadership of the new governments, and, although the franchise continued to be limited to a relatively small proportion of the people, it was through the legislatures that governmental policy was formulated and legitimated. Even in the states that continued to operate under their colonial charters in the post-Revolutionary years, the governors were reduced to figureheads with little influence in the making of governmental decisions. In ten of the states, the governors were elected by the legislatures, most of them for only one-year terms; in just one state did the governor have a veto, and even that was limited by present-day standards. Governors had few powers of appointment and removal, or of administrative supervision and control. They did not function as legislative leaders. Lacking in status and in constitutional and administrative strength, governors had no source of political strength, and they therefore remained subordinate to the legislatures in every respect; they had no leverage with which to exert influence even if they had been so inclined. Hence, the office was regarded as primarily ceremonial and a symbol of honor rather than as a seat of power, and it therefore rarely attracted men of distinction in the early days of the Republic. Consequently, as late as the opening years of the twentieth century, the governorship was a dead-end road. As one authority has remarked, they served their short terms and returned to private life with few accomplishments behind them and nothing before them but the pleasure of being called "Governor" for the rest of their days.[3] The legislatures ruled virtually unchallenged.

In local government, too, collegiate bodies were in charge. Whether they were truly "representative," and whether one ought to refer to the governing organ of a community that is not "sovereign" as a legislature, are questions we need not consider here. Suffice it to say that local executives labored under the same or perhaps greater handicaps than their state counterparts and therefore presented no more of a challenge to the local institutions corresponding to legislatures than did the governors to the state bodies.

The constitutional specifications for the Presidency constituted a countertrend to the apparent value system of governmental designers in early America. For the President was invested with greater authority than almost any other chief executive of the time. Yet even at the federal level, there were clearly widespread expectations that the Congress would provide the primary motive power for the government, a view shared, according to Binkley, even by many incumbents of the White House whose "Whig conception" of the presidency as subservient to the legislature may be contrasted with the "steward-

---

[2] New York and Massachusetts. These states provided important models for the federal executive, which ultimately was set up as an even stronger—and perhaps better—office than its prototypes.

[3] There were notable exceptions of course. Cleveland became President after serving as Governor of New York, Hayes and McKinley had both been Governors of Ohio before moving to the White House, and other governors became influential in national politics. As a general rule, however, the governorship was not a springboard to power or prominence.

ship theory" of independent presidential authority to be enunciated much later in history. While Washington and Jefferson fought to protect and extend executive power from the very first, it is probably not stretching the facts to argue that Presidents for a long time had an uphill struggle in this effort, and that many chose to yield to the sentiment of the day and the strength of the giants in Congress. Whether or not the legislatures were actually the most representative institutions need not be explored here; there is ample evidence that they were thought to be so.

The enthronement of the legislature was one of the two major tangible indications of the value placed on representativeness; the other was the rather uncritical faith in the electoral principle. It began with the extension of the franchise and a thrust toward universal adult suffrage. But the faith in elections also took the form of an increasing number of official positions filled by balloting. The first half of the Nineteenth Century saw the number of elective offices sharply increased, especially after the Jacksonian Revolution burst upon the country. The ballot grew in length until almost every public official from President down to dogcatcher came to power via the electoral route. Moreover, with the rise of the party organizations to new influence as a result, even those positions which were not made elective were filled by party faithful; the spoils system came into its own. By the time of the Civil War, voters found themselves confronted by hundreds of names on their ballots, and each change of party brought with it a change in virtually all government employees.

The Quest for Neutral Competence

As early as the middle of the Nineteenth Century, it had become clear to some people that legislative supremacy, the long ballot, and the spoils system did not in fact increase representativeness; as a matter of fact, they often seemed to have just the opposite effect. For one thing, they tended to confuse both voters and interest groups and thereby opened the way to power to political bosses who, while providing a measure of integration in the bewildering pullulation of government, often utilized their positions to advance their personal interests and the interests of the organizations they headed without regard for the interests of many of the governed. For another thing, legislators and administrators at every level of government proved themselves peculiarly vulnerable to the forces let loose by the burgeoning industrial system; corruption beset legislatures from county boards and city councils right up to Congress itself, and the venality and incompetence of many public officers and employers were common knowledge.

Disillusionment with existing governmental machinery was a result. State and local constitutions and charters grew longer and more detailed as reformers tried to reduce the discretion of legislative bodies. Limitations on the length and frequency of state legislative sessions were imposed to limit the amount of harm they could do. And at every level, reformers began to cast around for new governmental machinery that would provide a high level of responsible government service while avoiding the high costs of unalloyed representative mechanisms.

Thus began the quest for neutral competence in government officials, a quest which has continued to the present day. The core value of this search was ability to do the work of government expertly, and to do it according to explicit, objective standards rather than to personal or party or other obligations and loyalties.[4] The slogan of the neutral competence school became, "Take administration out of politics."

This school produced its own rationale and mechanisms for this purpose. The rationale was the now-familiar politics-administration dichotomy, according to which politics and administration are distinct and separable processes that should therefore be assigned to separate and distinct organs. The mechanisms were independent boards and commissions and the merit system, which were designed to insulate many public officials and public policies from political pressures.

The movement gathered momentum after the Civil War, although the first agitation for some of its objectives goes back even further. In local and state governments, library boards and park boards and police boards and boards of health and finance boards and utilities commissions and boards of education and boards of assessment and equalization and boards and commissions for a dozen other purposes mushroomed up all over the governmental landscape. At the federal level, the Interstate Commerce Commission came into being, to be followed in the twentieth century by a host of like bodies. These agencies, at every level, differed from each other in details, but had the same underlying structure: their members were appointed for overlapping terms supposedly on the basis of their reputations for general ability and character and specialized knowledge. They were granted wide discretion and secure tenure for substantial periods, and were expected to formulate policy on nonpolitical premises. Objectivity was reinforced in some instances by mandatory bipartisan membership on the boards The exigencies of the times made it necessary for legislatures to delegate power to administrative agencies; the advocates of neutral competence deflected delegation from the chief executives and the departments under their control to what was later to be branded "the headless fourth branch of government."

The merit system, peculiarly, made its greatest advances where boards and commissions were slowest to gain a foothold—the federal government. Pressure for the merit system began before the Civil War; its first fruit was the federal Civil Service Act of 1883. Initially, the objectives of the program were

---

[4] Proponents of this value generally did not demean representative institutions; on the contrary, they claimed their programs would strengthen those institutions by rationalizing governmental operations and improving their quality to such an extent that elected officials would be in a position to exert greater control over policy than they could ever hope to do in the prevailing political jungle. The case for neutral competence has normally been made not as an alternative to representativeness, but as a fulfillment of it.

The disillusionment of some was so thorough, however, that they lost faith completely in representativeness, in the capacity of a people to rule themselves, and returned to advocacy of leaders among the grandsons and great-grandsons of the "patricians" of the early days, among the "Old Whigs," and their sons, among those who had been enamored of, or grew up under, British or French or German institutions (for example, the Adamses, Godkin, Schur, Villard, Rosengarten), and among the urban mercantile and older businesses or professions rather than among the new industrialists. Distrust of the populace may still be observed in some modern writers and even in some current supporters of the neutral competence idea, but, for the most part, the concept of representation was so deeply ingrained in American thinking—and, indeed, in American emotions, for the word has become a revered one—that few dare to attack it openly whatever their beliefs may be.

confined principally to controlling the selection of government workers by taking the power to hire staff from the hands of executive heads (who were politicians) and lodging it with experts who, if they did not actually appoint personnel, at least could screen out all but those who could pass tests of one sort or another. This aspect of the program spread rapidly in the federal government; despite the subsequent growth of the federal service, about nine out of ten government employees today are under some form of merit appointment. But the process did not stop with the removal of the appointing power from politics; over the years, the Civil Service Commission extended its surveillance to dismissal, promotion, and position classification; eventually, with the aid of new legislation, the political activities of civil servants were reduced to little more than voting. A wall was erected between the government bureaucracy and the politicians, a wall policed by the Civil Service Commission.[5]

The quest for neutral competence, though it began about a century ago, has never waned. The training of civil servants became steadily more formal and systematic as time passed; courses, departments, and even schools of administration appeared in universities. Organization and methods analysis became a profession in itself. Boards and commissions are still common modes of handling administrative problems—witness, for example, the Atomic Energy Commission. Supporters of the merit system continue unabated their efforts to extend it "upward, outward, and downward." The desire to make government employment an attractive career was given new voice by the Commission of Inquiry on Public Service Personnel a generation ago, and by the Task Force on Personnel and Civil Service of the Second Hoover Commission more recently. The city manager plan—and even the town, county, and state manager plans—have continued to score successes. Neutral competence is still a living value among students of government, career civil servants, and, perhaps more significantly, among much of the general populace.

The Quest for Executive Leadership

Just as the excessive emphasis on representativeness brought with it bitterly disappointing difficulties unforeseen by its advocates, so too the great stress on neutral competence proved to be a mixed blessing. And just as the failures of the machinery established with an eye primarily to representativeness helped produce the reaction toward neutral competence, so too the weaknesses of the governmental arrangements devised by the latter school—or, more accurately, the weaknesses of government resulting from the work of both schools—gave impetus to the supporters of a third value: executive leadership.

For both earlier philosophies, and the mechanisms to which they gave rise, created a thrust toward fragmentation of government, toward the formation of highly independent islands of decision-making occupied by officials who went about their business without much reference to each other or to other organs of government. Neither elected administrative officials nor inde-

---

[5] The states and localities were slow to follow suit. By the turn of the century, only two states had enacted civil service legislation and only a few of the largest cities. Even today, the formal merit system still has a long way to go at these levels: states and localities remain the prime targets of the civil service reformers. But they have made some impressive gains during the last quarter-century, and the idea is still spreading.

pendent boards and commissions welcomed direction from the chief executives; the former were supported by constituencies in much the same way as governors and mayors, and their tenure was linked largely to their vote-getting prowess, while the latter generally remained in office longer than the chief executives and depended very little on them for support. Besides, as these officials and agencies became more accomplished in their respective areas of specialization, they tended to resent efforts of "laymen" and "amateurs" to intervene; this tendency revealed itself even in some civil servants nominally under the chief executives, who, though formally subject to dismissal, turned out in practice to have quite secure tenure, and who, by adept maneuvers in negotiating bureaucratic armistices ("memoranda of agreement") and in forming alliances with legislative committees and clientele groups, succeeded in carving out for themselves broad areas of discretion free of real supervision by their political chiefs.

The drive toward fragmentation could not be effectively countered by legislative bodies, despite their vast statute-making, financial, and investigative powers. Even Congress can exercise only a general and intermittent oversight over administrative agencies, and has had to confine itself to providing general standards guiding the exercise of administrative discretion and to occasional intervention to correct abuses or to force specific changes in policy. And state legislatures and city councils and county boards operate under still greater limitations; many of these bodies are in session for only brief periods out of each year (or biennium), and administrative officials conduct the business of government with great latitude in the long intervals between meetings. Moreover, even if legislatures met often enough and had enough technical assistance of their own to exert control over administration, their composition and procedures would render them incapable of providing integration; working through tens of committees, reaching decisions through processes of compromise and concession among representatives of small territorial units, functioning increasingly as reviewing bodies for proposals placed before them by executive and administrative agencies and by interest groups, they are generally too slow and too fragmented to perform this function effectively.

Neither have the courts been able to integrate the component elements of American government. They were not designed for this responsibility, and they are completely unable to discharge it. Limited to refereeing disputes between contending parties, formal in procedure and deliberate in method, they could not play this role even had they been willing. In fact, they have increasingly moved toward acceptance of findings of fact by administrative organizations and toward restriction of their own activities to review of questions of jurisdiction and procedure.

The centrifugal drives of the representativeness and neutral competence institutions thus found no important counter-force in the legislatures or in the courts. So the efforts to maximize these values brought with them the dispersion of governmental policy-making processes.

There were widespread criticisms of this fragmentation.[6] It bred chaos;

---

[6] Criticisms, that is to say, of the fragmentation "in general." When it came to the particular fragments over which they exerted their greatest influence, legislators, bureaucrats, party organizers, and interest groups were often defensive of their special positions and hostile to integrating remedies which might disturb their control.

agencies pursued contradictory policies in related fields. It fomented conflict; agencies engaged in bitter bureaucratic warfare to establish their spheres of jurisdiction. It opened gaps in the provision of service or of regulation; clienteles were sometimes denied benefits or escaped supervision because they fell between agencies. It was costly; many agencies maintained overhead organizations that could have been replaced more cheaply and effectively by a common organization, and citizens had to make their own way through bureaucratic labyrinths. And most important of all, it led to irresponsibility; no one quite knew how the pattern of organization and program came into existence or what could be done to alter it, each segment of the fragmented governments became a self-directing unit, the impact of elections on the conduct of government was minimized, and special interest groups often succeeded in virtually capturing control of individual agencies. No one seemed to be steering the governmental machinery, though everyone had a hand in it. At best, it seemed to be drifting (and just when the growth of the economic system appeared to make greater direction necessary), while at worst it showed signs of flying apart or grinding to a stop. These were among the forces that persuaded many students of government that chief executives had to be built up to take charge of the machinery.

The office of the chief executive became their hope because it furnished the only available means of achieving the end sought.[7] Movement toward strengthening chief executives began long before there was an explicit body of doctrine to explain and justify it. In the federal government, it took the form of struggles between Presidents and Congress for control of policy. Since the Presidency was set up with strong constitutional powers at the very start, the battle raged over the breadth of the powers conferred rather than over formal constitutional changes. Those powers were firmly defended, liberally interpreted, and gradually expanded under the strong Presidents from Washington. The governors, on the other hand, having been granted few powers at the start, gained strength slowly, largely through constitutional amendment, in the course of the nineteenth century. In the same period, many city executives developed from mere chairmen of councils to weak mayors and then to strong mayors, and there was even an occasional step in this direction among the rural units of government. These things were taking place even while the emphasis on representativeness was predominant; they continued after the pursuit of neutral competence became the order of the day; but the twentieth century was well on its way before executive leadership became a systematic quest supported by articulate theories, and before it really began to gather speed.

One of the first signs of the new emphasis was the rapid spread of the executive budget in government. For a long time, agency requests for funds were considered individually, and there was no central point at which total expenditures were reviewed and the competing claims balanced against each other in the light of the resources available; indeed, very often, the only way governments could figure out how much they were spending was to add up

---

[7]   Party bosses occasionally did serve this function, but *only* occasionally, for it must be remembered that our political parties are really congeries of smaller organizations in most places and therefore hardly equipped to provide governmental integration. Besides, they were phenomena from which governmental designers were seeking to deliver the political process.

the appropriation bills after they had been passed. The reformers turned to the chief executives to rationalize the spending process, and out of it came the now familiar phenomena of executive review and adjustment of agency requests, and the submittal of a comprehensive budget supposed to make it possible to see the overall spending pattern. The practice was often far short of ideal, but, for the first time, chief executives were given a powerful instrument with which to control administrative behavior; it was a major advance in striving to equip them to integrate American government. A few large cities and states adopted budgetary legislation during the first two decades of the twentieth century, and the Taft Commission on Efficiency and Economy in 1912 urged such a measure upon the federal government. By the middle of the third decade, many of the largest cities, virtually all of the states, and the federal government had budget laws on the books. Since then, in general, the tendency has been toward continued increase in the budgetary powers of chief executives, and toward adoption of the process by those jurisdictions in which it did not previously obtain. A large body of literature now backs up this practice, and, though the lack of a theory of budgeting (as contrasted with beliefs about the appropriate machinery for budgeting) has been pointed out, the executive-budget doctrine is widely accepted and rarely challenged.

Another indication of the concern with executive leadership is the administrative reorganization movement. It is frequently described as having begun in 1917, when Illinois adopted a sweeping change in its administrative structure, although such measures had been unsuccessfully urged in other states several years earlier. Under this plan, the number of agencies was reduced, and they were grouped into comparatively few departments headed by officials appointed by the governor; an administrative pyramid, with the governor standing at the apex, was the goal, and if it was rarely achieved completely, the extent to which it was approximated is indeed remarkable considering the degree of fragmentation prior to the changes. The number of elected administrative officials was sharply diminished, and ballots became correspondingly shorter. The appointing and removal power of the governor was also increased. In a single vast upheaval, the reorganizers sought to elevate him from an almost impotent exhorter to a powerful leader; if their efforts did not—as they could not—immediately produce the consequences sought, it was not very long before they began to bear fruit. Administratively and politically, the Illinois governor ascended to new eminence and influence. And more than half the states, some cities, and a few counties and towns followed Illinois' lead. All during the 'twenties and 'thirties, surveys of government machinery were commonplace, and they became even more so after World War II as the first federal Hoover Commission touched off a wave of "little Hoover Commissions" in the states and many cities. "Concentration of authority and responsibility," "functional integration," "direct lines of responsibility," "grouping of related services," "elimination of overlapping and duplication," and "need for coordination" echoed through state capitols, city and town halls, and even through some county courthouses as chief executives became the new center of governmental design.

At the federal level, there were occasional adjustments and readjustments in the machinery of government in the early part of the century, and the President was even invested with broad powers of reorganization during the emergencies of World War I and the depression. But it was not until the mushrooming agencies of the New Deal strained that machinery to its limits that the practices and supporting dogmas of the reorganizers made their appearance in strength in Washington. Few clearer statements of the executive leadership value than the Report of the President's Committee on Administrative Management have ever been published; with its recommendations on pulling the administrative functions of the independent regulatory commissions back under the President, on drawing the government corporations back into the hierarchy, on bringing personnel management under close direction by the President, on strengthening the White House staff, on getting the General Accounting Office out of the pre-auditing field and returning this operation to the executive branch, and in the tightly reasoned explanations of these recommendations (which were tied to the peg of the separation of powers), the Committee offered the classic presentation of the reorganization aspects of the executive leadership school.[8]

The Reorganization Act of 1939, which reversed one formal relationship of the President to Congress by conferring initiatory responsibility for reorganization plans on the former and authorizing the latter in effect to veto such proposals, reflected in practice the theory of the Report; even the frequent use of the legislative veto does not reduce the significance of this expansion of executive power, and the fierceness of the periodic battles over renewal of the Act suggests both Congressmen and Presidents are conscious of this significance. In the course of the years since the Report, without much fanfare, other recommendations of the Committee have been put into practice, too; the influence of the Committee continued to make itself felt for a long time.

The first Hoover Commission was considerably less emphatic about strengthening the chief executive than its predecessor, and the second Hoover Commission has displayed, if anything, some coldness (if not outright hostility) to the concept. It is conceivable, therefore, that the reorganization movement has for the time being run its course in the federal government. But it would probably be an error to write off entirely this phase of the quest for executive leadership.

A third index of this quest, an index related to, but distinguishable from, the developments in budgeting and administrative reorganization, is the increase in the size of executive staffs. The archetype is the Executive Office of the President with its hundreds of specialists providing the President with advice on every aspect of policy, reviewing legislative proposals to work out the Presidential attitude, studying administrative management from the President's point of view, planning, researching, furnishing legal counsel, serving as a source of information alternative and supplementary to the formal hierarchy, and studded with "the President's men," responsible and loyal to him and him alone. This is a far cry from the days when a President's secretariat consisted of a few aides who helped him with his official correspondence; it has helped to give the chief executive the means with which to direct the administration he heads and to formulate programs and press them into

---

[8]   To be sure, the Committee also advocated expansion of the merit system, and restated the argument that stronger executive leadership would mean greater popular control of government (i.e. representativeness), thus indicating how deep-seated these parallel values were. But this cannot obscure the basic premise of the Committee's Report, nor negate its general impact; it is overwhelmingly for executive leadership in sentiment.

statute and then into operation; it has helped make him a real center of political and administrative power. In like fashion, the executive offices of many of the governors have been transformed into instruments of leadership, and some local executives have been similarly equipped; at these levels, the evolution has been somewhat less dramatic, but not much less effective. The tendencies may be uneven in their fulfillment, but they are pronounced.

Doctrinally, the sharp conceptual cleavage between politics and administration, which gained currency during the years when neutral competence was ascendent, and which served as such a useful philosophical prop for the machinery favored in those years, became an impediment to the justification of executive leadership. For one thing, chief executives, in whom administrative responsibility and power were to be lodged, were also partisan politicians. Moreover, one of the main reasons advanced for seeking integration was elimination of the fragmentation resulting from acceptance of the idea of the separability of politics and administration. Gradually, therefore, the politics-administration dichotomy fell out of favor in public administration, and the doctrine of the continuity of the policy-formulating process, better suited to the aims of executive leadership, began to replace it. Before long, the traditional orthodoxy became old-fashioned and found few defenders.

By every measure then, the years from 1910 to 1950 were characterized by the rise of the quest for executive leadership to a place of pre-eminence in administrative thought and action.

The Concurrence of Values

For expository purposes, the quest for the three values has here been treated as sequential, and, to be sure, each had a different high point in time. Nevertheless, it is worth pausing to reiterate that at no point was any of them pursued to the complete exclusion of one or both of the others; evidence of interest in all three can be found at any stage of our history, sometimes in a single document by a single author. As has been observed, the defense of any one was often framed in terms of advancement of the others simultaneously. The story is thus one of changing balance among the values, not of total displacement.

II. THE COALITION

For many years, the proponents of neutral competence and the partisans of executive leadership were able to make common cause, and their alliance became so imbedded in their thinking that the differences between them were hardly recognized. The divisive factors beginning to emerge today then lay hidden beneath the mutual striving after a shared goal—a merit system to replace the spoils system.[9] Much of the standard literature of public administration was written during this honeymoon period and therefore embraced both values at once.

That the members of the neutral competence school should support the merit system as against the spoils system is not at all surprising; this reform

---

9 "Merit system" and "spoils system," as used in this section of this paper, include, but are not restricted to, personnel management. Patronage, it will be seen, is but one aspect—albeit the principal one—of spoils, which, includes contracts, purchases, and other "favors." The remedies of the reformers were aimed at every aspect.

lay at the core of their program for redesigning governmental organization. But it does require some explanation to account for the position of the executive leadership people, since spoils were allegedly one of the most effective devices through which executive influence could be exerted. There would seem to be a contradiction between advocacy of measures to strengthen executives on the one hand and endorsement of a system that appeared to reduce executive influence on the other.

The contradiction is more apparent than real. The spoils system had its uses for chief executives, but, as it operated in this country, it never really gave these officers control of the administrative hierarchy. As a source of inducements to persuade legislators to support executive-sponsored measures, it was quite helpful at times. It was also valuable in providing incentives to attract workers for the parties. But it never furnished the executives with loyal, enthusiastic, capable, disciplined administrative machines; it did not make them chief administrators.

Federal patronage, for example, about which more is known than has been revealed about patronage practices at any other level of government, was distributed largely through Senators and Representatives, hopefully in return for the legislators' votes on issues in which the Presidents were interested. But Congressmen ordinarily had to farm out their patronage to the party organizations in their states and districts, and even dissident wings of Presidential parties which did not give Presidential measures consistent support in the legislative chambers could often count on nominating some federal appointees. During election campaigns the Presidents needed the support of all segments of the parties and could not, therefore, afford to weaken them for their legislative defections. In short, the patronage system strengthened party leaders and legislators more than it did executives. Thus the appointing power of the Presidents was bargained away—shrewdly sometimes, to be sure, from the point of view of legislation and of political survival, but at some cost from the standpoint of administrative management. Moreover, if a President's own nomination was itself the result of bargaining in which he was the chosen rather than the chooser, then his appointing power was largely taken away at the start.

It was not just a matter of creating "ten enemies and one ingrate" with every appointment. Equally important, patronage tended to fragment the executive branch as much as did election of administrative officers. For the loyalty of appointees who owed their positions only formally to the appointing official, but in fact to the state and local party units that nominated them, lay with the nominating powers. In the exercise of their legal authorizations, the appointees tended to be as responsive to individual legislators, local and state party leaders, and local community pressures as to their nominal superiors in the hierarchy. Moreover, since their tenure was sure to be cut short as soon as the opposing party won an election, they tried to squeeze all they could out of their posts while they occupied them; their own personal interests, therefore, were likely to take precedence over official directives when the two conflicted. Trying to lead such a staff was like trying to play croquet in Wonderland; subordinates, like the mallets, balls, and wickets of the fairy tale, operated with a high degree of independence.

To the supporters of executive leadership, it was clear that the lateral pulls of political parties and individual legislators had to be reduced, and the incentives for public employees to exploit their offices for personal advantage eliminated. Only then could the other means of building up executive influence be made effective; only then could the President assert his authority over administration. So the executive leadership supporters joined the defenders of neutral competence in the drive toward a merit system of appointment, expecting that a bureaucracy chosen by objective standards would be at least as responsive to Presidential direction as to party and legislative pressures. A merit system of appointment controlled by a Civil Service Commission thus served the ends of two schools of thought; for different reasons, and in pursuit of different goals, they united behind it.

Similar factors apparently operated to promote the adoption of objective standards of practice for other activities corrupted by the spoils system. Political discrimination in public contracting, public works, government purchasing, granting of charters and franchises, distribution of benefits and subsidies, and the enforcement of the law, provided a harvest mainly reaped by state and local party and government leaders. These practices, too, gave a bit of leverage to executives in their legislative and political roles, but they did nothing for executive control of the executive branch. So the executive leadership school approved and worked for the adoption of rigorous statutory limitations, cutting party and individual legislators out of these processes as far as possible just as the civil service system freed the appointing process from their depredations. Here, too, though apparently striving for different objectives, the neutral competence and executive leadership groups joined hands.

Consequently, the flood of literature on public administration after World War I unanimously applauded many of the measures designed to take government out of politics. By the 'thirties, however, as the emphasis on executive leadership increased, evidences of discord grew more persistent.

III. THE EMERGING CONFLICT

In thirty years the number of federal civilian employees has more than quadrupled. If power were measurable, the federal bureaucracy's power would probably turn out to have increased by an even greater factor: Governmental policy is now formulated in administrative regulations and orders, as the growth of the Federal Register vividly attests; judicial proceedings before administrative agencies probably exceed in quantity those before the courts; licensing and administrative decisions regarding benefits and subsidies are the order of the day; and all of this is handled by administrative officials under the very broadest of mandates from Congress and the President. Much of our legislation originates in administrative agencies, and most proposed legislation is submitted to such agencies to determine what the President's position on it ought to be. A corresponding growth of administrative influence has taken place in all large-scale organizations, both governmental and private, but few have a record as dramatic in this respect as the federal government.

The growth of governmental bureaucracy in size and importance was subjected to vehement attacks in this country and abroad. For the most part, however, the attacks were disregarded, especially by political scientists, because it was clear that they were not aimed at the bureaucracy per se, but at the governmental programs administered by the civil servants. The programs themselves were too popular for their critics to assail directly with any real hope of success; the assault therefore took an oblique approach, hitting at what appeared to be a more vulnerable target. The criticism was therefore not taken very seriously in the study of public administration. Students of this subject became ardent and sometimes uncritical defenders of bureaucrats. Now that the controversy over the New Deal has subsided, however, the bureaucracy itself is more or less taken for granted, and attacks upon it are less frequent, less vehement, and less publicized than they once were. This has helped students of public administration to take a somewhat more dispassionate view of the bureaucracy, and some second thoughts may be at hand.

For though the mechanisms of neutral competence were remarkably successful in reducing the influence of the political parties on the administrative hierarchy, they did not necessarily increase the President's control over administration. Rather, they encouraged the development of "self-directing" groups within the bureaucracy, and these groups in turn cultivated their own sources of support among professional groups concerned with the subject matter over which the services have jurisdiction, among their clienteles, and among appropriate Congressional committees and subcommittees. The components of the "neutral" bureaucracy, by virtue of their expertness and information and alliances, have become independent sources of decision-making power, and Presidents will probably find them no easier to direct—indeed, perhaps even more intractable, than their partisan predecessors.

As a consequence, some of the standard devices for promoting neutral competence have been openly questioned in the literature of public administration. As noted earlier, the independence of regulatory commissions and government corporations has been vigorously criticized. The Brownlow Committee also sought to make personnel management an arm of the White House and to confine the Civil Service Commission to quasi-judicial functions and a role as "watchdog" of the merit system. This principle was endorsed recently by the staff of the Temporary (New York) State Commission on Coordination of State Activities, by a minority (comprising 11 members) of the Mayor's Committee on Management Survey of the City of New York, by the Sixth American Assembly, and, implicitly, by the present administration in Washington, under which the chairman of the Civil Service Commission serves as administrative head of that agency and is located in the executive mansion. A rising chorus of voices has also begun to call for decentralization of authority for personnel management to line departments, a position stated with particular clarity and force by Commissioner James K. Pollock of the first Hoover Commission in a minority report on personnel. The establishment of Schedule C in the federal government service in 1953, rolling back merit system protections from a number of positions of a policy-making and confidential character, despite the partisan components of the impetus behind this move, was in large measure an effort to preserve the power of the President over policy. More recently, the arguments of the second Hoover Commission for extension of civil service protections to the very highest administrative officials (in the form of a "senior civil service") have been sharply questioned. Recommendations for an institutionalized corps of political executives have been assailed as likely to weaken the President. The premises of the city-manager plan have been described as inapplicable to large cities, and some spirited defenses of elected mayors have appeared. All of these views have been reflected in the kinds of administrative improvements adopted in many jurisdictions in recent years. Other similar defections from the coalition between the neutrality and the leadership camps can be found in current literature and practice, but it is not necessary to belabor the point; patently, these straws in the wind are examples of the growing divergence between the two philosophies that makes it increasingly doubtful that their adherents will continue to support the same governmental theories or reforms.

Moreover, the philosophical divisions over structural values among the scholars have been intensified by differing political—i.e., program—views. Many of the champions of increased governmental activities, in the realms both of services (welfare, financial, industrial) and economic regulation, tend to rally behind chief executives and especially behind the President. The reason is fairly obvious: Demands for expansion of government service and regulation originate frequently (though not exclusively) in urban areas, and urban areas have their greatest political effect on the election of chief executives and their smallest impact on the state legislatures and Congress, where they are substantially under-represented. Thus executives generally tend to be more sympathetic to those demands than do the legislators, and those who favor an expanding role for government look to elected executives, as a rule, when they want to impress their preferences on governmental policy. Quite apart, then, from the concern about the organizational problems created by fragmentation of government, there are considerations of political preference and strategy that generate support for executive leadership.

By the same token, there are issues of political attitudes and tactics that engender enthusiasm for legislative bodies regardless of questions of representativeness. Legislatures, because of the composition and the sources of their political strength, offer the greatest leverage to those who resist the growth of governmental activities—or, more accurately, who oppose those governmental activities sought by urban populations. Not because legislatures are more representative, but because this is where the backers of a particular political attitude can exert their greatest political strength, many individuals recommend in their proposals for governmental reform that these bodies be strengthened both relatively and absolutely.

Finally, it might be inferred that some reformers distrust all politicians and electorates and pin their hopes on the expertise and efficiency of a professionalized bureaucracy. They seem to be moved not merely by a concern for governmental structure but by political values that include an implicit contempt for what we ordinarily understand to be the democratic process and an explicit respect for an aristocracy of talent that borders on a latter-day faith in technocracy.[10]

So the tendencies toward division reinforce each other, and there are no visible factors thrusting toward alliances like that fortuitous one developed by a peculiar conjunction of circumstances during the infancy of public administration as an academic and occupational specialty. As a result, the language of public administration is likely to become increasingly strategic and

---

[10]   There would seem to be an emergent split within this group. Some backers of professionalized public service are apparently thinking in terms of a corps of administrative generalists to occupy the top levels of administrative agencies regardless of agency subject matter. Others seem to conceive of an administrative elite of occupational specialists—engineers, lawyers, doctors, social workers, foresters, etc.

tactical in tone rather than "scientific." Just as the naked power issues of the legislatively oriented groups came to the surface in the recent efforts to weaken the Presidency—viz., the Twenty-Second Amendment, which reduces the leadership potential of a President in his second term; the efforts to strip away Presidential reorganization authority in 1953; the fight over the proposed Bricker Amendment; the continuing efforts to revamp the Electoral College in such a way as to reduce the political effectiveness of the urban-labor-liberal entente that has been partly responsible for the aggressive and expansive use of Presidential power—so too, many of the reorganization issues will be discussed in power terms in the future as the public administration groups aligned with the executive and with the bureaucracy, respectively, pull apart. The question that will be asked about suggested reorganizations is not, "What, according to the canons of management science, is the best organization?" but, "What will be the effect of this measure on the institution we support?" The differences in the answers will sharpen the theoretical distinctions between the wings of the public administration group and hasten estrangement of the factions.[11]

To many students of public administration trained in the 'twenties, 'thirties, and 'forties, the new atmosphere will be a strange and perhaps a bewildering one, fraught with hostilities. To students trained in the 'sixties, the literature of the earlier period, with its emphasis on "principles," may seem quaint and even naive. Political scientists of the remoter future, looking back, may well conclude that it is not easy to bridge the gap between a generation seeking to encourage the growth of a professional bureaucracy and a generation in turmoil over how to control it.

COPING WITH THE CIVIL SERVICE

Robert Dince

[From *Fortune,* June 5, 1978. Reprinted by permission of the publisher.]

We were all taught in high-school civics courses that Civil Service represented a major reform of American political life. Created in the 1880's, it was designed to end the "spoils system," under which victorious candidates for public office staffed government agencies with their cronies and supporters. In place of cronyism, Civil Service was supposed to enthrone the merit principle.

Among the many interesting lessons in civics that I learned during a recent three-year tour of duty in Washington was the extent to which the original conception has been stood on its head. Civil service today is designed to insulate federal personnel practices from the claims of merit. You learn very rapidly in government that if you want to get, or hold onto, good people and avoid being stuck with the lemons, you must learn how to thwart the Civil Service Commission and its regulations. Coming off the experience, I find myself an enthusiastic supporter of President Carter's proposals for reform-

---

[11] One may even hazard the guess that the American Society for Public Administration will remain firmly in the hands of the neutral competence group while the executive leadership school in public administration looks more and more to the American Political Science Association as its forum.

ing the system.

Viewed at ground level, the Civil Service Commission is an awesome antagonist. It is large, sluggish, slow to respond even to rather urgent requests for action, seemingly staffed by large numbers of unmotivated people. At the same time, it is almost passionately committed to the defense of its own procedures. The procedures are spelled out in the Civil Service code, and the newcomer to the government immediately perceives a message in the physical appearance of the code: it comes in binders that take up two feet of shelf space and is accompanied by additional binders, replete with exegetical material, that take up another five feet. The message is that you can forget about common sense when you make a personnel decision in the government.

One of my first encounters with the Civil Service involved our efforts to hire a research assistant to do certain kinds of statistical analysis. It happened that a young woman who seemed ideal walked in off the street and applied. At twenty-three, she had a graduate degree in public administration and also held enough undergraduate work in mathematics to enable her to cope with the kind of analysis required for the job. Best of all, she was obviously intelligent and highly motivated—and she very much wanted to work for the Comptroller of the Currency. Several different people in our department interviewed her, and all thought she would be ideal. If the Comptroller's office had been a private company, she would have been hired on the spot.

In the government, however, you can never act so decisively. Every individual who is hired must be formally certified by Civil Service as qualified for a particular job and at a particular government-service level. (The levels range from GS-1, which might be a clerk, to GS-18, which could be a highly skilled professional.) Furthermore, every job must have been previously described in detail to Civil Service, and the qualifications for the job—the skills, experience, academic degrees, etc—must also have been described. The writing of job descriptions is itself an immensely specialized and time-consuming task. Typically, an agency administrator, working with a specialist from his own personnel department, and following detailed guidelines from the Civil Service, could not get a new job description approved, or an old one changed, in less than two months, and four months would not be considered extreme. Inevitably, administrators tend to stick with job descriptions that were approved in the past, even if the actual job requirements have changed over the years. Furthermore, the qualifications listed in the job description may have been somewhat phony all along. At the professional level, the job description often calls for certain academic degrees that are not needed by someone actually doing the job. These degrees would have been made part of the description because (a) the Civil Service format requires great specificity in listing professional qualifications and (b) the administrator who originally listed the degrees was thinking of a particular person who had them—presumably someone he wanted to hire for the job.

In the case of the research assistant, the job we wanted to offer the young woman carried a GS-9 rating (then paying about $14,000). Unfortunately, the job description said that the qualifications for this particular job included graduate work in economics and/or a Master of Business Administration degree. We tried to argue that her own credentials were the equivalent of those demanded but we were turned down. Two months after she first applied, Civil Service ruled that she did not have the "pertinent educational experience" to be hired as a GS-9 research assistant.

We then talked the young woman into re-applying for the same job at a GS-7 level, where the pay would be lower (around $11,500 in her case) but where the specifications for research assistants were somewhat looser. But Civil Service continued to balk at her lack of any academic work in economics; after *six months* of negotiating, the best we could extract from the commission was an agreement that the young woman could be hired at a GS-5 level (earning around $9,300). When we reported this dismal outcome to our applicant, she gave up on government service and went to work for a bank.

Two footnotes might be dropped to this story. One is that even if the Civil Service had agreed to our original proposition, it would have taken six or eight or possibly even ten weeks to get the young woman cleared for hiring. For job applicants who don't already have jobs of their own—e.g., for recent college graduates—the molasses-like pace at which the government makes job decisions is a severe discouragement. Bright young people who are eager to get to work soon learn to steer clear of Washington.

Second, it is worth noting that we never did fill that research-assistant job in any satisfactory way. It proved impossible to find anyone we wanted who had the requisite credentials (and we shrank from the time-consuming task of rewriting the job description and getting it approved by Civil Service). The job is now being performed by a GS-5 clerk-typist enrolled in one of the agency's "upward-mobility" programs. She is a high-school graduate with far less technical ability than the woman we failed to hire, and the work she is doing is not nearly as good as the work our candidate could have done. However, there was no difficulty at all about getting the clerk-typist into the job. The government is very supportive of upward-mobility programs.

A story with a somewhat happier ending involved our efforts to hire a senior economist at a GS-15 level. Here again, we knew precisely whom we wanted to hire. He was a Ph.D. who had written a number of distinguished books on banking and had later worked in several regional offices of the Comptroller. The Civil Service confirmed him as qualified for the job we wanted to fill, and there seemed to be no reason why we couldn't immediately transfer him to Washington and install him as chief economist in the research division.

Just as we were about to do this, Civil Service told us it had another man whose credentials made him "the leading candidate." The form sent along by the commission indicated that he too had a Ph.D. and had been a full professor at a large university. Unlike our man, he was a veteran—which gave him the points to make him the leading candidate. Initially, of course, I had no way of knowing how well this man would suit us as a senior economist. But I did know that our own candidate was ideal; I also knew that it was absurd, in dealing with highly qualified professionals, to let the issue be decided by the fact that someone had served in the armed forces decades earlier.

In looking over the resume of the commission's candidate, I noticed an odd gap in his career; there appeared to be a period of around a year when he hadn't worked at all. Some discreet inquiries among friends in the academic world elicited the information that the man had been an alcoholic, unable to function for weeks at a time. The gap, it appeared, represented a long drying-out period.

However, alcoholism is not an argument that can be used against job candidates in the federal government these days. The official view is that alcoholism (like drug abuse) is an illness that is susceptible to treatment, not a disqualifying handicap. Even if the man was *still* an acholic, and still repeatedly turned up drunk at his place of work, the fact could not have been used against him provided only that he agreed to register in an accredited rehabilitation program. Obviously, therefore, further inquiries were in order.

We were lucky. The inquiries turned up the fact that he was not a Ph.D. after all—indeed, that he had dropped out of the graduate program he was enrolled in—and furthermore had never really been a full professor at that university. (He had taught briefly in some of its extension programs.) The Civil Service agreed to withdraw his candidacy, and we waited anxiously to see whether the commission would try to stick us with another alternative to our own man. Apparently, it couldn't find any one plausible, because we were allowed to hire him.

Administrators eager to hire their own people have various dodges that help them get around Civil Service requirements. One relatively innocent dodge is to post the required notice of a job opening during Christmas week—when a lot of the competitors for the job will be on vacation or at least thinking more about their shopping than their careers. A dodge that is less innocent, and that is now a bit of a sore point at the Comptroller's office, is to get your own candidate into a job by classifying him as "excepted." Civil Service regulations do not apply when certain kinds of openings, including those for lawyers and bank examiners, are being filled. In past years, our agency had a habit of hiring people whose jobs were definitely not excepted and classifying them as bank examiners. As a matter of fact, I was brought into the agency in the guise of a bank examiner. So were miscellaneous other professionals, including people in our personnel department, in computer services, and in consumer affairs. Unfortunately, the agency overdid it. There was an investigation and our chief personnel officer retired.

To a considerable extent, the Civil Service functions today as a kind of union. The intent, and effect, of most of those rigid procedures is to give government workers the kind of protection that is afforded in some union contracts. The procedures make it extremely difficult to fire government workers, or even to deny the periodic "merit" raises, or, indeed, rate their work unfavorably in the annual evaluations that are required. Any of these "adverse actions' may be contested by the worker, and one who is determined to assert his rights can force a series of fact-finding sessions and appeals. These are immensely time-consuming, their outcome is dubious, and most administrators conclude early on that they are to be avoided at all costs.

People new to the ways of Washington have trouble understanding how a raise can be virtually mandatory and yet solemnly proclaimed to be "for merit." But there is no doubt about the rules: every government-service level has ten salary grades, and every employee is entitled to periodic moves up in grade. When he gets to the top of his level-e.g., to GS-12/10-he is frequently able to move into the next level after a further interval. No matter how poor his performance has been, his superior cannot withhold the raise unless he is prepared for a major battle. At one point, I recall, the Comptroller's office was investigating the feasibility of taking action against a manager whose accounts showed some suspicious irregularities. In the middle of the investigation, we were notified by the personnel department that it was time for the manager's raise. I suggested to personnel that a merit raise would surely compromise any case we later tried to make against the manager in a fact-finding session. I was told the rules were inflexible: unless we were prepared to start the adverse action immediately, we had to put through the raise—which we did.

It's not entirely impossible to get rid of people. One technique is to give the undesirable worker a promotion accompanied by a transfer to a remote office. Workers may turn down lateral transfers, but when a promotion is involved, a turndown relieves the boss of any obligation to come up with further raises. In effect, the worker's career is over. If you happen to know that someone's family situation makes it impossible for him to leave the Washington area, a promotion and transfer to the Minneapolis regional office is one way to get rid of him.

In addition, it is often possible for an agency head to make a deal with senior people he wants to get rid of. Take the case of a GS-14 who is in his fifties and has become, over the years, a rather listless time server—a not unusual case in the government. The agency head can call him and suggest a deal along the following lines. The man will get a promotion and substantial raise—from, say, $40,000 to $47,500. He will also get the right to hang around for another couple of years, possibly in a branch office out of the boss's sight. In return, he will submit a letter of resignation, dated ahead. By working the additional years at the higher salary, the official being pushed out gets a major increase in the value of his pension and is therefore much less disposed to contest what is in effect a firing. (Government workers with thirty years of service may retire on full pension at age fifty-five. The pension benefit, which is ordinarily based on average pay during the three highest-paid years, is indexed; workers retiring from the U.S. government are almost alone among retired Americans in having no reason to fear inflation.)

Even when it is theoretically possible to fire someone outright, a prudent administrator will proceed cautiously. A determined adversary who knows his way around Washington can often turn a routine firing for incompetence into a kind of civil-liberties case.

Early last year, the Comptroller's research department hired a young man to be a research assistant at the GS-9 level. Soon after he was hired, his superiors turned very sour on him. He took forever to get his work done, was inclined to be quarrelsome, and generally seemed ineffective. For a period of several months, I listened to his superior lamenting about the trouble he'd had with the man. Finally, I suggested that a dismissal might be in order. "You mean I can do that?" his boss asked, his expression tightening visibly. I told him that the rules actually made it easy to fire people for cause during their first year on the job; until the first anniversary of their employment, they are "provisional employees" and lacked the protection afforded other workers. Before the day was over, the young man's boss had fired him.

It turned out, however, that getting rid of him was not as easy as I had assumed it would be. The young man got himself a lawyer and went to the Civil Service Commission, arguing, in effect, that sinister forces were behind the firing. Casting himself as a "whistle-blower", he contended that the Comptroller's office was hushing up a study on which he had been working. He claimed that the study showed banks were guilty of massive discrimination in mortgage lending—i.e., of redlining. He wasn't a very good researcher, but he had certainly found the kind of issue that will get you a lot of supporters in Washington these days.

Ultimately, the Civil Service ruled that his firing was in order, but it took six months of correspondence and fact-finding to get the ruling. And the ruling was by no means the end of the matter. Belief in the rectitude of whistle blowers is very prevalent in Washington, and the young man was soon receiving a respectful hearing in the press (the *Star* ran a sympathetic article about him) and on Capitol Hill. We received demands for information about the case from Senator Proxmire's office and from several Congressmen concerned with bank regulation.

We kept insisting (a) that the data we had collected did not show massive discrimination, (b) that in any case the data had been made public, and (c) that the young man was fired only because he was a poor worker. But any demand for information from the Hill tends to make bureaucrats jumpy, and there is no doubt in my mind that the young man would never have been forced out—he'd have simply been shunted aside somewhere—if we had suspected how much work it would take to get rid of him.

Because shunting people aside is so much easier than firing them, most sizable government agencies have a fair number of employees who do little or nothing, or at least are working at levels far below those for which they're being paid. My own guess is that the Washington Office of the Comptroller of the Currency had at least twenty-five such individuals, perhaps fifty—versus a total head count of about 500. In other words, 5 or 10 percent of those on the payroll might be thought of as deadwood.

I do not know whether, or in what form, Congress will ultimately pass the President's Civil Service reform legislation, but it is clear that only Congress can make a major dent in the system that now exists. A reform as thorough-going as the one that ended the spoils system is plainly called for. The system now in place has become a kind of spoils system for non-workers.

THE UNIVERSALITY OF ADMINISTRATION

H.A. Simon, D.W. Smithburg, and V.A. Thompson

[From Herbert A. Simon, Donald W. Smithburg, and Victor A. Thompson, *Public Administration*, (New York: Alfred Knopf, Inc., 1950), pp. 6-12. Reprinted by permission of the authors.]

Since administration is concerned with all patterns of cooperative behavior, it is obvious that any person engaged in an activity in cooperation with other persons is engaged in administration. Further, since everyone has cooperated with others throughout his life, he has some basic familiarity with administration and some of its problems. The boys' club, the fraternity, the church, the political party, the school, and even the family require administration to achieve their goals.

Much of this administration is unconscious—that is, not deliberately or formally planned—but it is administration nevertheless. The father is often considered the head of the household, but he is not consciously selected as such by a formal vote. Unless he is completely henpecked, he certainly performs administrative functions, making decisions for the family and assigning tasks to its members.

Most persons, while they are engaged in administration every day of their lives, seldom think formally about the process. That is, they seldom deliberately set out to consider the ways in which the cooperative activities of groups are actually arranged; how the cooperation could be made more effective or satisfying; what the requirements are for the continuance of the cooperative activity. In most of the simpler organizational situations in life—the family, for example—there are traditional and accepted ways of behaving that are gradually acquired during childhood and that are seldom the objects of conscious attention or planning. Like Moliere's hero who had talked prose all his life without knowing it, most persons administer all their lives without knowing it.

The governmental organizations whose administration is the subject of this book are more complex than these everyday administrative situations we are all familiar with. The difficulties of securing effective cooperative action in performing large and intricate tasks become so great that they force themselves upon the attention. Traditional, customary ways of behaving no longer suffice, and cooperation becomes conscious and requires planning. The "rules of the road" that govern family life and the relations among family members are informal, carried around in the heads of parents and children. The rules of the road that govern the relations among the employees of a government agency may fill ten volumes of a looseleaf "Administrative Manual."

If large-scale organizations are to accomplish their purposes; if the extremely complex interrelationships of an industrial era are not to break down, organizational life—its anatomy and its pathology—needs to be understood. Those who participate in and operate the formal organizations through which so much of our society's activity is channeled must know what makes cooperation effective and what hampers it. Either through experience or through formal education, or both, they must study administration. Our concern is with the formal study of public administration.

For purposes of study, administration can be divided into certain problem areas. The problem area to be studied in this book is that of public administration. By public administration is meant, in common usage, the activities of the executive branches of national, state, and local governments; independent boards and commissions set up by Congress and state legislatures; government corporations; and certain other agencies of a specialized character. Specifically excluded are special and legislative agencies within the government and nongovernmental administration.

The selection of the problem area is an arbitrary one, made partly because of a traditional academic breakdown of specialties; partly because of the necessity of limiting our attention to an area that can be mastered within a relatively limited period of time; and partly because there are certain problems and practices in government agencies that differ from those in other organizations.

Legislative and judicial agencies are excluded from books on public administration, but not because they do not have administrative problems. They do. Handling a bill in Congress often requires administration of a very delicate character; the proper presentation and consideration of a case in court requires administration of a high order. But because legislative and judicial bodies have problems peculiar to their structures, and because those problems require extensive treatment, legislative and judicial administration are not included in this book.

Legislatures and courts are, however, a part of the environment within which public administration must be carried on. The activities, attitudes, and methods of these agencies will often powerfully influence the process of administration in the organizations with which we are concerned. And so, while the operations of legislatures and courts will not be examined here directly or systematically, their effect upon public administration will have to be considered as the discussion progresses.

It has been customary in this country to make a sharp distinction between governmental and nongovernmental administration. In the popular imagination, governmental administration is "bureaucratic"; private administration is "business-like"; governmental administration is political; private administration is nonpolitical; governmental administration is characterized by "red tape"; private administration is not. Actually, the distinction is much too sharp to fit the facts. As we shall see in the course of this book, large scale public and private organizations have many more similarities than they have differences. It is possible, therefore, in examining the activities of public administration to use the results of research carried on in private business. In actual administration there is often a greater difference between small and large organizations than there is between public and private ones. For example, the differences in organization and in administrative problems between a hospital with 1,000 beds and one with 50 beds will be far greater than the differences that result from the fact that one hospital is privately owned and the other publicly owned.

SIMILARITIES BETWEEN PUBLIC AND PRIVATE ADMINISTRATION

The similarities between the problems of administration in public and private organizations can be readily observed when a private organization is taken over by the government. Not long ago the elevated railways and the surface lines in Chicago were transferred to public ownership. To the observer, the difference is imperceptible. The same tracks are there; the same cars are used; the same fare is charged (or was, until inflation caused an increase); the same time schedule is followed; the same employees do the same tasks and work for the same immediate bosses. Only in the financial organization of the company and in the replacement of a few top-level persons is there a change. The change in the financial organization changed the identity of the persons to whom interest on bonds is paid. It also allowed the company to raise capital for the installation of new equipment. The influence of the changes in top personnel is not yet observable. Both changes, however, could have been accomplished without a change in ownership. If the city of Chicago had sufficiently desired that the lines be left in the hands of private owners, provision could have been made for a subsidy to make new equipment possible. The private owners might have made the identical changes in personnel. Owned by LaSalle Street or City Hall, the transit system's major administrative problems remain the same.

Many of the same skills are required in public and private administration. A statistician might transfer from a large insurance company to the Bureau of Labor Statistics in Washington and find his tasks almost identical. He possesses skills that can be used by a great many organizations, public or private. Similarly, a doctor performing an appendectomy will use the same technique whether he is employed in an Army hospital or in private practice. General Dwight Eisenhower left the Army to become President of Columbia University. Two more different organizations would be hard to imagine. Yet it is likely that the administrative problems of the two organizations are sufficiently similar so that he had little difficulty in making an adjustment to this new position.

DIFFERENCES BETWEEN PUBLIC AND PRIVATE ADMINISTRATION

While the similarities between governmental and nongovernmental organizations are greater than is generally supposed, some differences nevertheless exist. Most often these are differences in degree rather than in kind.

For example, both governmental and nongovernmental organizations are usually based on law. Activities of a government agency are usually authorized by statute or executive order based on statutory or constitutional authority. All corporations and a good many other nongovernmental organizations operate under a legal charter. The officers of both types of organizations are legally required to carry out their activities within the law. However, the duties and responsibilities of the public administrator will usually be described by law in much greater detail than those of his private counterpart, and there will usually be greater possibilities for holding him accountable in the courts for the discharge of these duties in a lawful manner. For example, a corporation can ordinarily authorize its officers and employees to make purchases for it under any procedure the board of directors sees fit to approve. A public purchase, however, must usually satisfy numerous legal requirements with respect to advertising for bids, letting the contract to the lowest responsible bidder, authorizing the expenditure, and so forth. A contract to purchase equipment for a government agency may be invalidated by the courts for failure to follow these statutory procedures.

The public administrator may be the subject of Congressional criticism or investigation. For political and other reasons, legislative bodies frequently determine "who killed Cock Robin?" The extensive Congressional hearings to establish responsibility for the Pearl Harbor disaster are a good example. The private administrator may also be the subject of investigation, but he is much less likely to be, and then usually only in cases where he has business transactions with a government agency or in areas where his business is subject to public regulation. With the increasing scope of governmental regulation of business, however, his chances of being the object of public investigation are growing rapidly.

The private administrator is often given much more latitude in interpreting the relationship between his organization and the general welfare than is the public administrator. It is accepted that the former is in business primarily to further his private ends; the latter is expected to serve the public interest, and it is considered unethical for him to use the advantages of his position for personal gain. In 1947, governmental employees who speculated in the grain market were objects of public censure, even in cases where they possessed no "inside" information that gave them special advantage. Of course, the price and production policies of business may also be scrutinized when it is felt that they impinge upon the public welfare.

DIFFERENCES IN PUBLIC ATTITUDES TOWARD PUBLIC AND PRIVATE ADMINISTRATION

During World War II, the government found it necessary to "seize" the coal mines to insure continued production in the face of strikes by the miners. Such seizures consisted in hoisting an American flag over the mines, appointing an Army officer to run the mines—and nothing else. Yet the miners returned to work for the same bosses, doing the same work, under the same conditions. The only factors that had been added were the presence of a uniformed officer and a flag. The miners, however, apparently held a different attitude when the government was "running" the mines. They felt that it was somehow wrong or dangerous to strike against the government. This psychological factor led to a change in worker attitudes that, in turn, changed the administrative problem.

On the other hand, there is a widespread conviction that what governments do is inefficient and often corrupt. A common stereotype of the bureaucrat is an overbearing, lazy tax-eater. Stemming from the laissez-faire doctrine and the frontier tradition, this attitude is one that must constantly be taken into account by public administrators working with public problems. It poses problems not generally shared by private administrators.

There are certain, but largely undefined, limits in the extent to which the public administrator is allowed to influence (or to attempt to influence) public attitudes toward his agency's product. It is accepted that the businessman will advertise his particular brand of breakfast cereal in almost any way he finds profitable. Congress, on the other hand, has exhibited strong hostility toward "public relations" expenditures by government agencies that could be interpreted as attempts to obtain public approval for agency programs. Appropriations for such purposes are almost always among the first casualties of an economy drive.

The foregoing examples are merely illustrative, not an exhaustive listing or analysis of the possible differences between public and private administration. Apart from these differences, however, whether one is studying the administration of a church, a labor union, a corporation, or a government agency, many of the basic problems will be the same. To the extent that this is so, it is possible to work out a general theory of administration that will encompass all kinds of organizations.

A NECESSARY EVIL

Donald C. Rowat

[From *The Public Service of Canada*, No. 5 in Citizenship Series for the Canadian Forces, 1953, pp. 23-31. Reprinted by permission of the Queen's Printer, Ottawa]

In our casual, everyday conversation it is popular to associate very closely the words "government" and "red tape." The phrase is meant to imply excessive routine and paper work and consequent inefficiency, delay, reluctance to make a decision, and the rigid application of rules to individual cases. One of our favorite pictures of the public service is that of a dense jungle of red tape which public officials only half-heartedly try to hack their way through.

Those of us who have had close contacts with government departments know that this popular picture is greatly overdrawn, that it is just a caricature of the real public service. The most important reason for this distortion I think, is that almost every governmental program adversely affects some group. Such groups then try to justify their opposition to the government doing something they dislike by saying that it can't do anything well. They exaggerate every fault they can find with the government service and try to persuade others to their way of thinking.

SIZE AND COMPLEXITY

An obvious reason for red tape in the public service—yet one that its critics often fail to appreciate—is the sheer size and complexity of the job that the Government is trying to do. The resulting problems of coordination and control are such as those that face any large-scale organization, whether public or private. Yet since the Government of Canada is by far and away the biggest single enterprise in the country, these problems are that much more difficult to solve.

Those who argue that the public service should be more "business-like" forget that giant private corporations suffer from much the same problems of red tape. Any large organization is noted for the impersonal nature of its dealings with its customers or its public. Those at the top cannot deal personally with the thousands of persons with whom the organization comes into contact. They must instead lay down general rules and handle only unusual cases. As a result, they tend to deal mostly with paper, far removed from the actualities of real life. And those at the bottom, who do not have the power to change the rules, must either apply them rigidly or refer cases higher up for decision. They may not even know the rules or understand their meaning, and tend to lose touch with the objectives of the organization. Passing the buck is by no means a disease peculiar to public administration.

There are some causes of red tape, however, which are peculiar to public administration. These, it should be stressed, are not just characteristic of the public service of Canada, but of the administrative side of democratic government generally.

ACCOUNTABILITY AND EFFICIENCY

The most important of these causes is the control exerted over the public service in a democracy. This requires all manner of unavoidably cumbersome financial and other procedures designed to hold public servants accountable for what they do. Public servants are acutely aware of the fact that they are expected to make just and impartial decisions and that if they don't they may be criticized. Sometimes they are criticized even when they do. They must therefore keep copious records in order to explain and justify their actions. Since they are living in a "fish bowl" where every act is apt to be seen and noted, some, instead of making bold decisions, are tempted to hide behind a precedent or the exact letter of the law....

Another cause of red tape in the public service arises from the fact that it is a monopoly. It has no business rivals to stimulate it into efficiency in the fight for economic survival. And its employees often do not have as an incentive to surpass their fellows the prospect of a better job elsewhere. Some of them have such highly specialized jobs that opportunities for similar employment do not arise outside the service.

Closely related to this is the lack of a clear-cut basis for measuring efficiency. While the profit of a competitive business provides an automatic measure of efficiency, government departments exist primarily to render a public service. A credit balance at the end of the year is irrelevant and the problem is to measure the amount of service rendered for a given amount of money. The results of many broad governmental programs cannot be measured in this way. How can the Government tell, for example, whether preparedness is more efficiently served by adding an extra aircraft to the air force instead of spending the same amount of money for more guns? It is possible, however, to measure efficiency at the lower levels of administration where the objectives are more specific, and especially when physical units are involved. When, for example, the question is not how to defend Canada at the least cost, but rather how to turn out aircraft or equip soldiers at the least cost, it is quite possible to work out measures of efficiency that are based on cost accounting.

Although the lack of drive for efficiency and the difficulty of measuring efficiency are said to be characteristics of public administration, it is perhaps worth pointing out that they apply equally well to monopolies in private business. It should also be noted that a governmental substitute for the profit motive found in competitive business is the vigorous competition of individual departments for a slice of the taxpayer's dollar in their submissions to the Treasury Board. And an important part of the Treasury Board's job is to show a department how it can render greater service with the same amount of money—in other words, how it can become more efficient. The Treasury Board and its staff are becoming increasingly conscious of this important function.

The Civil Service Commission, too, is doing much to remove unnecessary red tape and to improve efficiency. It has the positive job of selecting the ablest candidates for public office, encouraging and promoting the best, and improving the performance and morale of all civil servants through a widespread training program. It has also created a comprehensive organization and methods service designed to study, develop and advise the departments on more efficient methods, procedures and organization. Already this service has paid for itself many times over through the savings brought about by its recommendations. As a result of the efforts of these and other efficiency experts one finds that in many respects the government is now more "business-like" than a good many businesses, and that on some things it can actually show the way to private industry.

No matter how much is done to eliminate red tape, however, like death and taxes it will always be with us, simply because much of it is a necessary evil of large-scale organizations and of democratic government. If we want things done in an organized way and in a democratic society, then we must be prepared to wrestle with a certain amount of red tape.

BUREAUCRATIC?

... The critics of government in democratic countries, for much the same reasons as they have given us the exaggerated picture of red tape, have adopted the word "bureaucratic"…to describe our…public service…. They are annoyed about it and do not realize that it is a necessary part of democratic control. But to call the system bureaucratic is most unfair and indicates that they do not understand the difference between unavoidable red tape and irresponsible bureaucracy.

Yet "bureaucratic" has been used so frequently in association with "red tape" that now the word bureaucracy is often used to mean simply the administrative side of any government. It has become what you might call a "weasel word"—one so slippery that, as Alice in Wonderland said, it can mean anything you want it to. Since the critics always use the word in its uncomplimentary sense, it is worth pointing out that the public service is not really bureaucratic in this sense.

It is true that, internally, those at the bottom of the departmental pyramids are controlled by a few officials at the top. But this is merely a necessary, though unfortunate, consequence of large-scale organization. It is quite wrong to infer from this that the system of government as a whole or that the citizens are controlled by a few at the top. In fact it is just the reverse. It is through having the public servants controlled by a few at the top that the citizens, through their representatives in Parliament, are able to control the vast administrative machine known as the public service of Canada. How else could a few hundred representatives in Parliament hold to account the hundreds of thousands of servants which the public employs?

And there is all the difference in the world between a system like ours, where elected representatives of the people direct the activities of public officials, and a totalitarian system in which bureaucrats direct the lives and thoughts of the people and arbitrarily maintain themselves in power.

The real key to this difference is the fact that under our system the topmost directors of the departments and agencies, the Ministers of the Crown, are themselves elected and keep their jobs only so long as they are supported by a majority of the citizens' representatives in Parliament. Provided there are free elections and an Opposition Party free to criticize the Ministers and to replace them if they lose the people's confidence, we need never fear that the top level of our public service will become bureaucratic. Indeed, one eminent student of our institutions summed up his conclusions on this question as follows: "The Canadian service can hardly be censured as an arrogant bureaucracy, lusting for power; it has been too fearful of political intervention and too uncertain of itself to exhibit the desire to dominate. In the past it might more often have been charged with timidity."

THE NATURE OF ADMINISTRATIVE RESPONSIBILITY

Carl J. Friedrich

[From "Public Policy and the Nature of Administrative Responsibility," in C. J. Friedrich and Edward S. Mason, eds., *Public Policy: A Yearbook of the Graduate School of Public Administration*, Harvard University, 1940, pp. S5, 8-10, 12-14, 19-20, 22-24 selected. Reprinted by permission of Harvard University Press and the President and Fellows of Harvard College.]

RESPONSIBILITY AND POLICY FORMATION

The starting point of any study of responsibility must be that even under the best arrangements a considerable margin of irresponsible conduct of administrative activities is inevitable. For if a responsible person is one who is answerable for his acts to some other person or body, who has to give an account of his doings (*Oxford English Dictionary*), it should be clear without further argument that there must be some agreement between such a responsible agent and his principal concerning the action in hand or at least the end to be achieved. When one considers the complexity of modern governmental activities, it is at once evident that such agreement can only be partial and incomplete, no matter who is involved. Once the electorate and legislative assemblies are seen, not through the smokescreen of traditional prejudice, but as they are, it is evident that such principles cannot effectively bring about the responsible conduct of public affairs, unless elaborate techniques make explicit what purposes and activities are involved in all the many different phases of public policy. It is at this point that the decisive importance of policy determination becomes apparent. Too often it is taken for granted that as long as we can keep the government from doing wrong we have made it responsible. What is more important is to insure effective action—of any sort. To stimulate initiative, even at the risk of mistakes, must nowadays never be lost sight of as a task in making the government's services responsible. An official should be as responsible for inaction as for wrong action; certainly the average voter will criticize the government as severely for one as for the other.....

In the light of the large amount of legislative work performed by administrative agencies, the task of clear and consistent policy formation has passed likewise into the hands of administrators, and is bound to continue to do so. Hence, administrative responsibility can no longer be looked upon as merely a responsibility for executing policies already formulated. We have to face the fact that this responsibility is much more comprehensive in scope.

THE NEW IMPERATIVE: FUNCTIONAL RESPONSIBILITY

It is interesting that the administrators themselves attach so little weight to the influence of parliamentary or legislative bodies. Leading Swiss officials—and Switzerland has as responsible a government service as any country in the world—told the author that "responsibility of the public service in Switzerland results from a sense of duty, a desire to be approved by his fellow officials, and a tendency to subordinate one's own judgment as a matter of course. Still, in a case like the arrival of Social Democrats into the Federal Council, it might happen that official conduct would be slow to respond to the new situation." They also felt that officials are not unwilling to allow a measure to lapse, although actually provided for in legislation, if considerable opposition is felt which the public might be expected to share. Thus a wine tax was quietly allowed to drop out of sight, just as the potato control act remained a dead letter in the United States. There are, of course, ways by which the legislature secures a measure of control that enables it to enforce responsibility, usually of the negative kind which prevents abuses. Legislative committees act as watchdogs over all expenditure.

What is true of Switzerland and the United States without "parliamentary responsibility" seems to be equally true of England and France. In both countries complaints against the increasing independence of officials are constantly being voiced. In a very important discourse, Sir Josiah Stamp called attention to the creative role the civil servant is called upon to play in Great Britain. "I am quite clear that the official must be the mainspring of the new society, suggesting, promoting, advising at every stage." Sir Josiah insisted that this trend was inevitable, irresistible, and therefore called for a new type of administrator. An editorial writer of *The Times*, though critical of this development, agreed "that the practice, as opposed to the theory, of administration has long been moving in this direction." He added, "In practice, they (the officials) possess that influence which cannot be denied to exhaustive knowledge; and this influence, owing to the congestion of parliamentary business and other causes, manifests itself more and more effectively as an initiative in public affairs." Testimony of this sort could be indefinitely multiplied; and as we are interested in practice, not in ideology, we must consider the question of responsibility in terms of the actualities. Such cases throw a disquieting light upon the idea that the mere dependence of a cabinet upon the "confidence" of an elected assembly insures responsible conduct on the part of the officials in charge of the initiation and execution of public policy, when those officials hold permanent positions....

It is objectionable to consider administrative responsibility secure by this simple device, not merely because of interstitial violations but because there is a fundamental flaw in the view of politics and policy here assumed. The range of public policy is nowadays so far-flung that the largely inoperative "right" of the parliamentary majority to oust a Cabinet from power belongs in that rather numerous group of rights for which there is no remedy. The majority supporting the Cabinet may violently disagree with this, that, and the other policy advocated and adopted by the Cabinet, but considerations of party politics, in the broadest sense, will throttle their objections because the particular issue is "not worth a general election" and the chance of the M.P.'s losing his seat. As contrasted with the detailed and continuous criticism and control of administrative activity afforded by Congressional committees, this parliamentary responsibility is largely inoperative and certainly ineffectual. When one considers the extent of public disapproval directed against Franklin D. Roosevelt's Congressional supporters who were commonly dubbed "rubber stamps," it is astonishing that anyone extolling the virtues of British parliamentarism should get a hearing at all. For what has the parliamentary majority in Britain been in the last few years but a rubber stamp of an automatic docility undreamt of in the United States?...

A DUAL STANDARD OF ADMINISTRATIVE RESPONSIBILITY

But are there any possible arrangements under which the exercise of... discretionary power can be made more responsible? The difficulties are evidently very great. Before we go any further in suggesting institutional safeguards, it becomes necessary to elucidate a bit more the actual psychic conditions which might predispose any agent toward responsible conduct. Palpably, a modern administrator is in many cases dealing with problems so novel and complex that they call for the highest creative ability. This need for creative solutions effectively focuses attention upon the need for action. The pious formulas about the will of the people are all very well, but when it comes to these issues of social maladjustment the popular will has little content, except the desire to see such maladjustments removed. A solution which fails in this regard, or which causes new and perhaps greater maladjustments, is bad; we have a right to call such a policy irresponsible if it can be shown that it was adopted without proper regard to the existing sum of human knowledge concerning the technical issues involved; we also have a right to call it irresponsible if it can be shown that it was adopted without proper regard for existing preferences in the community, and more particularly its prevailing majority. Consequently, the responsible administrator is one who is responsive to these two dominant factors: technical knowledge and popular sentiment. Any policy which violates either standard, or which fails to crystallize in spite of their urgent imperatives, renders the official responsible for it liable to the charge of irresponsible conduct.

In writing of the first of these factors, technical knowledge, I said some years ago: Administrative officials seeking to apply scientific "standards" have to account for their action in terms of a somewhat rationalized and previously established set of hypotheses. Any deviation from these hypotheses will be subjected to thorough scrutiny by their colleagues in what is known as the "fellowship of science." . . . If a specific designation were desirable, it might be well to call this type of responsibility "functional" and "objective," as contrasted with the general and "subjective" types, such as religious, moral, and political responsibility. For in the former case, action is tested in terms of relatively objective problems which, if their presence is not evident, can be demonstrated to exist, since they refer to specific functions. Subjective elements appear wherever the possibility of relatively voluntary choice enters in, and here political responsibility is the only method which will insure action in accordance with popular preference.

Similarly, John M. Gaus writes:

The responsibility of the civil servant to the standards of his profession, in so far as those standards make for the public interest, may be given official recognition.... Certainly, in the system of government which is now emerging, one important kind of responsibility will be that which the individual civil servant recognizes as due to the standards and ideals of his profession. This is "his inner check."

Yet this view has been objected to as inconceivable by one who claimed that he could not see how the term "responsibility" could be applied except where the governed have the power to dismiss or at least seriously damage the officeholder. Thus, with one stroke of the pen, all the permanent officials of the British government, as well as our own and other supposedly popular governments, are once and for all rendered irresponsible. According to this commentator, political responsibility alone is "objective," because it involves a control by a body external to the one who is responsible. He also claims that its standards may be stated with finality and exactitude and its rewards and punishments made peremptory. For all of which British foreign policy leading up to Munich no doubt provides a particularly illuminating illustration.

It seems like an argument over words. The words, as a matter of fact, do not matter particularly. If you happen to feel that the word "objective" spells praise, and the word "subjective" blame, it may be better to speak of "technical" as contrasted with "political" responsibility, or perhaps "functional" and "political" will appeal. Whether we call it "objective" or "functional" or "technical," the fact remains that throughout the length and breadth of our technical civilization there is arising a type of responsibility on the part of the permanent administrator, the man who is called upon to seek and find the creative solutions for our crying technical needs, which cannot be effectively enforced except by fellow-technicians who are capable of judging his policy in terms of the scientific knowledge bearing upon it. "Nature's laws are always enforced," and a public policy which neglects them is bound to come to grief, no matter how eloquently it may be advocated by popular orators, eager partisans, or smart careerists.

POLITICAL RESPONSIBILITY

The foregoing reflections must not deceive us, however, into believing that a public policy may be pursued just because the technicians are agreed on its desirability. Responsible public policy has to follow a double standard, as we stated before. We are entirely agreed that technical responsibility is not sufficient to keep a civil service wholesome and zealous, and that political responsibility is needed to produce truly responsible policy in a popular government. Discarding the wishful thinking of those who would tell us that Great Britain has solved this difficult problem, it is first necessary to repeat that such truly responsible policy is a noble goal rather than an actual achievement at the present time, and may forever remain so. All institutional safeguards designed to make public policy thus truly responsible represent approximations, and not very near approximations at that. One reason is the intrusion of party politics, already discussed; another is the tremendous difficulty which the public encounters in trying to grasp the broader implications of policy issues, such as foreign affairs, agriculture, and labor today. Concerning unemployment, all the general public really is sure about is that it should disappear. Many people, in defending Hitler, declare that, after all, he did away with unemployment. If you try to object by explaining what tremendous cost in national welfare this "accomplishment" has entailed, the average citizen is apt to be bewildered. "After all . . . ," he reiterates. . . .

SHALL WE ENFORCE OR ELICIT RESPONSIBLE CONDUCT?

...Responsible conduct of administrative functions is not so much enforced as it is elicited. But it has been the contention all along that responsible conduct is never strictly enforceable, that even under the most tyrannical despot administrative officials will escape effective control—in short, that the problem of how to bring about responsible conduct of the administrative staff of a large organization is, particularly in a democratic society, very largely a question of sound work rules and effective morale.... The whole range of activities involving constant direct contact of the administrator with the public and its problems shows that our conception of administrative responsibility is undergoing profound change. The emphasis is shifting; instead of subserviency to arbitrary will we require responsiveness to commonly felt needs and wants. The trend of the creative evolution of American democracy from a negative conception to a positive ideal of social service posits such a transformation. As the range of government services expands, we are all becoming each other's servants in the common endeavor of operating our complex industrial society. . . .

Another important problem which is closely related to the foregoing, and equally controversial, is the right of officials to talk and write about issues of general public policy, more particularly those on which they themselves possess exceptional information and understanding because of their official position. There was a time when officials were supposed never to speak their mind in public. But the American and other democratic governments have gradually relaxed these restrictions. It must seriously be doubted whether technical responsibility, which, as we have shown, is coming to play an ever more important role in our time, can be effectively secured without granting responsible officials considerable leeway and making it possible for them to submit their views to outside criticism. The issue is a very complex one. Opinions vary widely. People try to escape facing these difficulties by drawing facile distinctions, such as that officials might discuss facts but not policy. It might cogently be objected that facts and policies cannot be separated. Any presentation of facts requires a selection, and this selection is affected by views, opinions, and hence bears upon policy. What is worse, in many of the most important matters intelligent and well-informed students disagree frequently on what are the facts.

The simplest solution, and one to which the authority-loving politician has recourse without much hesitancy, is to forbid such public utterances altogether. It is undeniable that great inconveniences might and often do result from technical authorities' bringing out "facts which make the official policy appear in a questionable light." Hence instances of "gag rules" are quite frequent. At one time a federal department head ruled that no official in his organization was to give any more interviews, because one of them had annoyed him. Thereupon six reporters proceeded to that department and got six different stories, all of which were printed and sent to the administrative head to show him that his rule had been foolish and could not really be enforced. In this case the power of the press forced the abandonment of an unsound policy which would seriously interfere with making the administration responsible in the formulation and execution of policy. While many cautious administrators will aver that an official should not discuss policy, it seems wiser, in a democracy, to avoid such a gag rule. Many officials will hesitate to express themselves, anyway, for obvious reasons. A great deal depends upon the nature of the case. In matters of vital importance the general public is entitled to the views of its permanent servants. Such views may often provide a salutary check on partisan extravagances. Such views should be available not only to the executive but to the legislature and the public as well. Gag rules seek to insulate the specialist so that he is no longer heard. A large benefit is thus lost. Irrespective of what one thinks of the particular policies involved, a presidential order not to talk against administration bills to Congress is particularly doubtful, for Congress certainly is entitled to the advice and expert opinion of permanent officials of the government, who may be presumed to have a less partisan viewpoint on particular policy proposals. In fact, the rule can easily be circumvented by an official determined to make his views known: he can prime Congressional questioners to ask the right questions, and, as the officials must answer, their views become available to whole committees. This is true, but while it is alleged that no president would dare punish a man for what he says in answer to a Congressional query, it may often seem to the official undesirable to incur the presidential wrath. Hence no such rule should be allowed at all.

What applies to enlightening Congress really applies likewise to a wider field. It seems inexcusable that highly trained professional economists, for example, should be handicapped in addressing themselves to their colleagues in a frank and scientifically candid manner. Even when they are permitted to do so, they will be only too prone to be overcautious. The only sound standard in a vast and technically complex government such as ours is to insist that the public statements of officials be in keeping with the highest requirements of scientific work. If a man's superiors disagree with him, let them mount the same rostrum and prove that he is wrong; before the goddess of science all men are equal. Without this conviction the present volume could not have been conceived. In its pages men of science inside and outside the government service match their views and findings in a common effort to reach the right conclusions.

CONCLUSION

The ways, then, by which a measure of genuine responsibility can be secured under modern conditions appear to be manifold, and they must all be utilized for achieving the best effect. No mere reliance upon some one traditional device, like the dependence of the Cabinet upon majority support in Parliament, or popular election of the chief executive (neither of which exists in Switzerland), can be accepted as satisfactory evidence. At best, responsibility in a democracy will remain fragmentary because of the indistinct voice of the principal whose agents the officials are supposed to be—the vast heterogeneous masses composing the people. Even the greatest faith in the common man (and I am prepared to carry this very far) cannot any longer justify a simple acceptance of the mythology of "the will of the people." Still, if all the different devices are kept operative and new ones developed as opportunity offers, democratic government by pooling many different interests and points of view continues to provide the nearest approximation to a policy-making process which will give the "right" results. Right policies are policies which seem right to the community at large and at the same time do not violate "objective" scientific standards. Only thus can public policy contribute to what the people consider their happiness.

THE CASE FOR SUBSERVIENCE

Herman Finer

[From "Administrative Responsibility in Democratic Government," *Public Administration Review,* Summer, 1941, pp. 336-41, 350 selected. Reprinted by permission of the American Society for Public Administration.]

Are the servants of the public to decide their own course, or is their course of action to be decided by a body outside themselves? My answer is that the servants of the public are not to decide their own course; they are to be responsible to the elected representatives of the public, and these are to determine the course of action of the public servants to the most minute degree that is technically feasible. Both of these propositions are important: the main proposition of responsibility, as well as the limitation and auxiliary institutions implied in the phrase, "that is technically feasible." This kind of responsibility is what democracy means; and though there may be other devices which provide "good" government, I cannot yield on the cardinal issue of democratic government. In the ensuing discussion I have in mind that there is the dual problem of securing the responsibility of officials (a) through the courts and disciplinary controls within the hierarchy of the administrative departments, and also (b) through the authority exercised over officials by responsible ministers based on sanctions exercised by the representative assembly. In one way or another this dual control obtains in all the democratic countries, though naturally its purposes and procedures vary from country to country.

What are we to mean by responsibility? There are two definitions. First, responsibility may mean that X is accountable for Y to Z. Second, responsibility may mean an inward personal sense of moral obligation. In the first definition the essence is the externality of the agency or persons to whom an account is to be rendered, and it can mean very little without that agency having authority over X, determining the lines of X's obligation and the terms of its continuance or revocation. The second definition puts the emphasis on the conscience of the agent, and it follows from the definition that if he commits an error it is an error only when recognized by his own conscience, and that the punishment of the agent will be merely the twinges thereof. The one implies public execution; the other hari-kiri. While reliance on an official's conscience may be reliance on an official's accomplice, in democratic administration all parties, official, public, and Parliament, will breathe more freely if a censor is in the offing....

In the democratic system, however, there is either a direct declaration in the constitution of the primacy of the people over officeholders, whether politicians or employees, or else in authoritative documents or popular proverbs the constitutional omission is made good. Thus, in the Weimar Constitution, Article I declared the issuance of sovereignty from the people.

Thus, the Committee on Indian Reforms of 1934 said, "so there arise two familiar British conceptions; that good government is not an acceptable substitute for self-government, and that the only form of self-government worthy of the name is government through ministers responsible to an elective legislature." And thus, we are all familiar with the essential meaning of the American dictum, "Where annual election ends tyranny begins."

Democratic governments, in attempting to secure the responsibility of politicians and officeholders to the people, have founded themselves broadly upon the recognition of three doctrines. First, the mastership of the public, in the sense that politicians and employees are working not for the good of the public in the sense of what the public needs, but of the wants of the public as expressed by the public. Second, recognition that this mastership needs institutions, and particularly the centrality of an elected organ, for its expression and the exertion of its authority. More important than these two is the third notion, namely, that the function of the public and of its elected institutions is not merely the exhibition of its mastership by informing governments and officials of what it wants, but the authority and power to exercise an effect upon the course which the latter are to pursue, the power to exact obedience to orders. The Soviet government claimed (in the years when the claim seemed profitable to it internationally) that it was a democratic government; but its claim was supported by two arguments only, that the government worked for the good of the people, their economic well-being, and that the people were allowed to inform the government of their will through a multitude of institutions. The Soviet government never sought to employ with any cogency the third and really vital argument that it could be made to conform to the people's will by the people and against its own will. This last alone is responsibility in democratic government.

Democratic government proceeded upon the lines mentioned because the political and administrative history of all ages, the benevolent as well as the tyrannical, the theological as well as the secular, has demonstrated without the shadow of a doubt that sooner or later there is an abuse of power when external punitive controls are lacking. This abuse of power has shown itself roughly in three ways. Governments and officials have been guilty of nonfeasance,[12] that is to say, they have not done what law or custom required them to do owing to laziness, ignorance, or want of care for their charges, or corrupt influence. Again there may be malfeasance, where a duty is carried out, but is carried out with waste and damage because of ignorance, negligence, and technical incompetence. Third, there is what may be called overfeasance, where a duty is undertaken beyond what law and custom oblige or empower; overfeasance may result from dictatorial temper, the vanity and ambition of the jack in office, or genuine, sincere, public-spirited zeal. As a matter of fact, the doctrine of the separation of powers as developed by Montesquieu was as much concerned with the aberrations of public-spirited zeal on the part of the executive as with the other classes of the abuse of power. Indeed, his phrase deserves to be put into the center of every modern discussion of administrative responsibility, virtue itself hath need of limits. We in public administration must beware of the too good man as well as the too bad; each in his own way may give the public what it doesn't want. If we wish the public to want things that are better in our estimation, there is a stronger case for teaching the public than for the imposition of our zealotry. A system which gives the "good" man freedom of action, in the expectation of benefiting from all the "good" he has in him, must sooner or later (since no man is without faults) cause his faults to be loaded on to the public also.

As a consequence of bitter experience and sad reflection, democratic governments have gradually devised the responsible executive and an elected assembly which enacts the responsibility. Within the system, there has been a particular concentration on the subservience of the officials to the legislature, ultimately through ministers and cabinet in a cabinet system, and through the chief executive where the separation of powers is the essential form of the organization of authority. Where officials have been or are spoilsmen, the need for holding them to subservience is particularly acute, since the spoilsman has not even a professional preparation to act as a support and guide and guarantee of capacity. With career men, the capacity may be present. What is needed, however,

---

[12] I use the terms nonfeasance and malfeasance in a common sense, not a legal sense— they are convenient.

is not technical capacity per se, but technical capacity in the service of the public welfare as defined by the public and its authorized representatives.

Legislatures and public have realized that officials are monopolist no less than the grand men of business who have arrogated to themselves the exclusive control of the manufacture or sale of a commodity and therewith the domination, without appeal by the victim, of an entire sector of national life. The philosophy and experience of the Sherman Anti-Trust Act have significant applications to administrative procedures in public administration. The official participates in the monopoly of a service to society so outstanding that it has been taken over from a potential private monopolist by the government. This monopoly is exercisable through a sovereign agency armed with all the force of society and subject to no appeal outside the institutions which the government itself creates. This is to be subject to a potentially grievous servitude. . . .

To overcome the potential evils flowing from public monopoly, democratic governments have set up various controls. It is these controls, and especially their modern deficiencies, which seem to have worried Professor Friedrich into a position where he practically throws the baby out with the bath. He feels that there is need of some elasticity in the power of the official, some discretion, some space for the "inner check," and he sees also that existent controls (either intentionally or by the accident of their own institutional deficiencies) do actually leave some latitude to the official. He argues therefore that heavy and, indeed, primary reliance in the making of public policy and its execution should be placed on moral responsibility, and he pooh-poohs the efficacy of and need for political responsibility. He gives the impression of stepping over the dead body of political responsibility to grasp the promissory incandescence of the moral variety. . . .

But the remedy is not, as Professor Friedrich suggests, the institution of specific legislative policies which may please the heart of the technical expert or the technocrat. I again insist upon subservience, for I still am of the belief with Rousseau that the people can be unwise but cannot be wrong. . . .

In short, these various drawbacks of political control can be remedied. They can be highly improved, and it is therefore unnecessary to proceed along the line definitely approved by Professor Friedrich of more administrative policy-making. As a democrat, I should incline to the belief that the remedying of these drawbacks is precisely our task for the future. The legitimate conclusion from the analysis of the relationship between Parliament and administration is not that the administration should be given its head, but on the contrary that legislative bodies should be improved. Conceding the growing power of officials we may discover the remedy in the improvement of the quality of political parties and elections, if our minds are ready to explore. . . .

There is no need to over-stress the auxiliaries to political control. Such auxiliaries as approved by Professor Friedrich are: referenda by government departments, public relations offices, consultation of academic colleagues in order to temper "partisan extravagance," "education and promotional functions," the administrative scrutiny of a Congressman's mail. These are harmless enough.

But when Professor Friedrich advocates the official's responsibility to "the fellowship of science," the discard of official anonymity, the entry of the official into the political arena as an advocate of policy and teacher of fact versus "partisan extravagance," the result to be feared is the enhancement of official conceit and what has come to be known as "the new despotism."...

All these devices have their value, but let it be remembered that they do not and cannot commit and compel the official to change his course. Officials may, in spite of them, still think that what they are doing is for the good of the public, although the public is too ignorant to recognize what is for its good. However, the more the official knows of public reactions the better. My qualm is that the official is very likely to give himself the benefit of the doubt where the information he elicits admits of doubt, whereas when the legislative assembly asserts an opinion it also asserts a command.....

As for education—which should be part of the official's training before entry and then should be continued in various ways after entry—besides the purpose of technical excellence, it should be shaped to make the official aware of the basic importance of his responsibility to the parliamentary assembly, and the errors into which he will be liable to fall unless he makes this his criterion. He should realize the dangers in the belief that he has a mission to act for the good of the public outside the declared or clearly deducible intention of the representative assembly. . . .

The analysis reveals the following propositions as cogent and justifiable, in contradiction to Professor Friedrich's contentions.

Never was the political responsibility of officials so momentous a necessity as in our own era. Moral responsibility is likely to operate in direct proportion to the strictness and efficiency of political responsibility, and to fall away into all sorts of perversions when the latter is weakly enforced. While professional standards, duty to the public, and pursuit of technological efficiency are factors in sound administrative operation, they are but ingredients, and not continuously motivating factors, of sound policy, and they require public and political control and direction.

The public and the political assemblies are adequately sagacious to direct policy—they know not only where the shoe pinches, but have a shrewd idea as to the last and leather of their footwear: and where they lack technical knowledge their officials are appointed to offer it to them for their guidance, and not to secure official domination; and within these limits the practice of giving administrative latitude to officials is sound.

Contemporary devices to secure closer cooperation of officials with public and legislatures are properly auxiliaries to and not substitutes for political control of public officials through exertion of the sovereign authority of the public. Thus, political responsibility is the major concern of those who work for healthy relationships between the officials and the public, and moral responsibility, although a valuable conception and institutional form, is minor and subsidiary.

THE CRUCIAL LINK: PUBLIC ADMINISTRATION, RESPONSIBILITY, AND THE PUBLIC INTEREST

Herbert J. Storing

[From *Public Administration Review*, vol. 24, March 1964. Reprinted by permission of the American Society for Public Administration. This is a review of three books: Carl J. Friedrich, ed., *Nomos III: Responsibility* (Yearbook of the American Society of Political and Legal Philosophy) (The Liberal Arts Press. 1960); Carl J. Friedrich, ed. *Nomos V: The Public Interest* (Yearbook of the American Society of Political and Legal Philosophy) Atherton Press, 1962; and Harlan Cleveland and Harold D. Lasswell, eds., *Ethics and Bigness: Scientific, Academic, Religious, Political, and Military,* Conference on Science, Philosophy and Religion in Their Relation to the Democratic Way of Live, Inc., Harper & Brothers, 1962.]

Where men once said "the common good," we now say "the public interest"; where men once said "duty," we now say "responsibility." In these shifts of terminology lie much of the meaning and the problem of modern political thought, and therefore of thought about public administration.

The three volumes under consideration, containing together more than fifty essays clustered around some very general (and important) themes, provide a rich sample of contemporary opinion on what is widely regarded as the "soft" side of political science and public administration. The two volumes edited by Carl Friedrich, *Responsibility (Nomos III)* and *The Public Interest (Nomos V)*, are yearbooks of the American Society of Political and Legal Philosophy, of which Friedrich is founder and elder statesman, and are based on the papers and discussions at the society's 1958 and 1960 annual meetings. The papers in the Harlan Cleveland-Harold Lasswell collection were prepared for a 1960 Conference on Science, Philosophy, and Religion in Their Relation to the Democratic Way of Life. The breath-taking range of this volume—*Ethics and Bigness: Scientific, Academic, Religion, Political, and Military*—requires a preface and three introductions to get it properly launched; but the subject becomes somewhat less formidable as the student of public administration discovers that most of the essays are concerned with familiar problems of bureaucracy and responsibility. Obviously it is almost impossible to give an overall view of such volumes; moreover, the *Review's* policy leaves the commentator with a wide discretion in the exercise of his duty and encourages him to state and reflect a bit upon what seem to him to be the major issues. The result inevitably is that some essays—including some good ones—are not treated adequately or at all.

Perhaps the best place to begin is with the public interest and particularly with Glendon Schubert's and Frank Sorauf's attacks on it. These essays merit special consideration both because earlier articles by these authors helped foster the current round of discussion of the public interest and because of the vigor and, one gathers, the influence of their remarks.[13] There is, Schubert asserts, "no public-interest theory worthy of the name."[14] "Perhaps," concludes Sorauf, "the academicians ought to take the lead in drawing up a list of am-

---

[13]   See Frank Sorauf, "The Public Interest Reconsidered," *Journal of Politics,* vol. 19, pp. 616-39 (November 1957) and Glendon Schubert, "'The Public Interest' in Administrative Decision-Making," *American Political Science Review,* vol. 51, pp. 346-68 (June 1957). These two articles were taken as starting points by Charner M. Perry and Wayne A. R. Leys in a 1958-59 survey of the literature on the public interest done under the auspices of the American Philosophical Association. The conclusions were reported in *Philosophy and the Public Interest* (Committee to Advance Original Work in Philosophy, 1959) and are summarized in *Nomos V* in an essay by Leys. Schubert published his full study as *The Public Interest: A Critique of the Theory of a Political Concept* (Glencoe, Illinois: Free Press, 1960), from whihch his artacle inthe Nomos volume is drawn.

[14]   Friedrich, *The Public Interest,* p. 175.

biguous words and phrases 'which never would be missed.' For such a list I would have several candidates, but it should suffice here to nominate the 'public interest.'"[15]

CONCEPTUAL CRITICISMS OF "PUBLIC INTEREST"

Generally speaking, there are three major parts of the criticism of the meaningfulness and usefulness of "public interest": that the idea is undemocratic, that it is vague, and that it is unscientific. The belief that the idea of the public interest is undemocratic helps to agitate Schubert to impassioned scorn against what he calls the "idealists."[16] The argument is not very sophisticated. "According to idealist thought, congressmen are responsible neither to political parties nor to their own constituencies; they have a higher obligation to God and to their own consciences."[17] The argument at this level is sufficiently met by C. W. Cassinelli, who points out that 'the immediate and normally overriding responsibility of every official is to exercise his authority [allocated by the Constitution] to the best of his ability; but the public interest is still the final justification for this authority and for the constitution that confers it." The official "cannot avoid exercising discretion, and in doing so he often must act according to his own interpretation of the public interest."[18] Obviously this does not dispose of the problem; there *is* a question whether "public interest" is reconcilable with "democracy"—a question that a genuine exploration of "public interest" would have to take up. The absence from this volume of anything but oblique or superficial discussion of this central question, by either critics or defenders, testifies to the character and quality of much contemporary discussion of the public interest.[19] The fact is that its allegedly undemocratic character is the least important argument made by the critics of "public interest"—thus perhaps the willingness to stop at caricature. This is still a political question (and as such it comes into prominence when the theme shifts to responsibility); and academic discussions of "public interest" these days have a strikingly unpolitical character.

The second allegation against "public interest" is that it is hopelessly vague. "[W]e are widely reassured," says Sorauf, "that politics (and its study) is an art rather than a science, and that a certain genteel fuzziness—often masquerading as literary elegance—would not be out of place"[20] There are

---

[15] Ibid., p. 190.

[16] To enter into the questionable character of Schubert's approach and of his categories would require a detailed examination of his book, which would leave no space for anything else. Illustrative, perhaps, is the fact that although Schubert sets out in his book to deal with writing about the public interset during the last three decades, he finds it necessary to cast his net back some eighteen decades for his first "idealist"—a group known in one of his earlier formulations as "Platonists"—and that his catch turns out to be James Madison.

[17] Ibid., p. 166.

[18] Ibid., pp. 52-53.

[19] William S. Minor argues, for example: "The shared responsibility necessary to the development and maintenance of democratic relations within and among publics depends basically upon man's sincere search for evidence, because it is evidence rather than mere opinion which is useful in resolving conflicts of interest." Compare with *Federalist* 10.

[20] Friedrich, *The Public Interest,* p. 183.

grounds, in this volume and the others here considered, for such impatience, although it should be said that literary inelegance does not necessarily result in clarity and precision. To dissipate the vagueness of "public interest," its fundamental grounds and implications would have to be explored, which Schubert and Sorauf scarcely begin to do. One might begin by observing that the most interesting and revealing quality of the term is precisely the quality that the critics wish to throw out: its implication of a good. As a man's interest is what is good for him, so the public interest is what is good for the public; and we distinguish, therefore, as Hamilton does in *Federalist* 71, between the interests and the inclinations of the people.[21] However, the analogy between individual interest and public interest is problematical. While interest implies a good, it implies a relatively low or narrow good; it implies, moreover, an individual good. The first definition of interest in the Oxford Dictionary is "objectively concerned by having a *right* or title," and rights are primarily the possession of individuals. The foundation of the public interest, it appears, is individual rights. The beginning and the end of political life is the individual with his interest in and right to physical security and comfort; and the public interest is the maintenance of the conditions necessary for the enjoyment of those individual rights. One might at this point recall Madison's reference to "the permanent and aggregate interests of the community" and raise the question whether the public interest is a mere aggregate of individual interests or whether something else has to be added, and if the latter, what that something else can be and where it comes from.[22] These are serious difficulties and any fundamental discussion of "public interest" must face them; but (and this is the immediate point here) they are not difficulties arising out of *vagueness*.

Regarding more recent writers, it must be confessed that the charge of vagueness has more plausibility. To the rights enumerated in the Declaration of Independence we find writers here adding those of the Charter of Human Rights. Added to physical security and comfort, we find a right to individual development. Edgar Bodenheimer, expressing a general view, states the goal as "a well-ordered and productive community in which everybody has an opportunity to develop his capabilities to the fullest."[23] "Individual development" no doubt makes a better starting point than quibbling, as George Nakhnikian does, about whether Lasswell's assumption of the desirability of preserving human dignity is any good, since it would not be useful to those who are not in favor of human dignity.

Yet is there not some reason to doubt what Bodenheimer thinks no reasonable man will censure, namely, the aim of providing "the widest possible

---

[21] Compare with Ludwig Freund in Friedrich, *Responsibility* (The Liberal Arts Press, 1960), p. 35: "The problem of responsible leadership in a democracy begins here with the seemingly subtle, in reality rather definite distinctions between wants, desires, and the needs as synonyms of interest."

[22] See Edgar Bodenheimer's exploration of this question in Friedrich, *The Public Interest.* Here also Gerhard Colm suggests the interesting analogy of a play, in which producers, actors, and audience, all motivated by self-interest, "find a common ground under the spell of the play as a work of art" (p. 127); but he does not raise the question whether "common ground" might be found—for example, in commercial television—under a spell that no one would think of calling a work of art and what the consequences of different grounds might be for the quality and level of self-interest as well as the public interest.

[23] Ibid., p. 212.

opportunities for the activation of all human energies and talents. . ."?[24] Admirable as this aim may be in most cases, Bodenheimer himself recognizes that there are human energies and talents that ought not to be activated for the sake of the further development of the individual himself as well as the community at large. Yet in the end there does not seem to be any basis in this widespread view, which Bodenheimer represents well, for saying what "development" consists in; there is therefore no basis for saying what kinds of activities and talents ought to be encouraged and what discouraged.

Accompanying this emphasis on individual development is a concern in these essays with procedures, the rules of the game by means of which the open society prevents itself from falling apart.[25] There is a good deal of sensible discussion along these well-worn lines, with little disposition to inquire whether it is possible to give any meaningful and lasting procedural definition of the public interest when there is disagreement about the most important things. So far as the question is raised at all, the reply tends to be a formal one, as illustrated by Charner Perry's observation in *Ethics and Bigness*: ". . . the utilization of sources of agreement depends in large part on there being appropriate institutions for maximizing the results of limited agreement and for minimizing the disruptive effects of disagreement."[26]

Another way of attempting to dissipate the vagueness of "public interest" is to explore its meaning, not in the abstract, but in the context of a set of concrete circumstances and problems. This is the aim, for example, of Stephen K. Bailey's essay in *The Public Interest* and of his, James MacGregor Burns', and Paul N. Ylvisaker's essays in *Ethics and Bigness*. Yet although Ylvisaker's sharp, tight description of two cases of metropolitan decision making eschews any "genteel fuzziness" and all the essays are obviously motivated by a genuine perplexity about the public interest, in general and particular, a kind of tired cynicism is never far from the surface. What are we to make, for example, of Bailey's defense of the public interest as a "myth," which must, nevertheless, be given "rational content," and the value of which, it seems lies in its very moralistic vagueness?[27] Bailey seems to echo Pendleton Herring, who defined the public interest as a "verbal symbol" whose "value is psychological and does not extend beyond the significance that each responsible civil servant must find in the phrase for himself," and who yet saw the public interest as a *standard* for judging between one contending group and another: "Without this standard for judgment between contenders, the scales would simple be weighted in favor of victory for the strongest."[28] So on the one hand, there must be a standard if the law of the jungle is to be avoided; on the other

---

24 Ibid., p. 213.
25 See for example the essays by Gerhard Colm and Schubert in Friedrich, *The Public Interest*, Herbert J. Spiro in Friedrich, *Responsibility*, and Charner Perry and Richard McKeon in Cleveland and Lasswell, *Ethics and Bigness*.
26 Ibid., p. lx. Perry continues, "I think I have stated the main requirement regarding institutions in a pluralistic society: the requirement, namely, that they should be such as to extend cooperation beyond the limits of achieved doctrinal agreement and that they should be capable of utilizing for limited agreement the points of coincidence among the multiple strands of diverse myths and ideologies, and that they should be such as to minimize the bad effects of disagreement."
27 Friedrich, *The Public Interest*, p. 97.
28 E. Pendleton Herring, *Public Administration and the Public Interest* (McGraw-Hill Co., 1936), pp. 23-24, 377.

hand, there is no standard but rather an indefinite number of psychological, subjective feelings. The fruit of this tree is cynicism. The art of government or prudence, which these men seek to practice and to describe, is on their own principles groundless. Prudence cannot defend itself, as it once could, as being rooted in an understanding of the ends served because it is conceded that those ends are beyond or beneath rational understanding. Prudence cannot, therefore, defend itself against the attack that, far from being the legitimate pride of the practical man, it is but a poor substitute for the theory or science of instrumental decision making.[29]

These criticisms of its alleged undemocratic character and vagueness are, however, only a preface to the case against "public interest." At the heart of the case lies the third criticism; that it is unscientific. Schubert's root assumption is that if the concept of the public interest is to have any value, either as a guide to behavior or as a description of it, it must be capable of being made "operational," which, according to Schubert, "public interest" is not. This basic test is made more explicit by Sorauf. "Public interest," he explains, is one of the chief offenders in mixing together the "ought" and the "is," in confusing "the normative and the real." What is needed is, if not a completely "value-free" study of politics (because that is impracticable), "a maximum degree of separation of the two."[30] The purpose of this separation is to enable political scientists to get on with their scientific study of the "facts."

It is not clear what Schubert and Sorauf would have political scientists or politicians or citizens do with the "value" questions, if anything. There are some attempts in *The Public Interest*, the most interesting being that of William Minor, to show the beneficial effects of such a separation for politics as well as science; but the benefits remain shadowy—at least as vague, indeed, as anything that can be laid at the door of traditional talk about the public interest. There is a good deal of truth in Cassinelli's remark that "the critics often say, in effect, that since we have difficulty in deciding what is most desirable in politics, we should stop discussing the issue."[31] The happy situation of the economist, in this respect, has long attracted political scientists, but the economist can defend the partiality of his science by pointing out that there are others to deal with the whole—such as political scientists. As R. A. Musgrave says in *The Public Interest*,

> economic analysis has traditionally stopped short of certain non-economic implications of economic processes. Thus it might be argued that a continuous increase in the standard of living may be demoralizing, that pursuit of the profit motive harms the trader's soul, and so forth. Economists will not deny that the concept of the public interest must be broadened at some point to include such matters, but they would hold this to be outside their province.[32]

In view of their strong commitment to a "value-free" social science, it is interesting to observe that Sorauf uses the phrase "legitimate differences of interests" in the very essay in which he attacks the vague, nonoperational,

---

[29] See the exchange between Edward Banfield and Herbert A. Simon in *Public Administration Review*, Autumn 1957, and Winter 1958.
[30] Friedrich, *The Public Interest*, p. 186.
[31] Ibid., p. 47.
[32] Ibid., pp. 113-14.

value-laden term, "public interest,"[33] and that Schubert uses a similar term, "legitimate interests," in his book.[34] Even without the evaluating adjective, the term "interest" is full of difficulties from this scientific point of view. As Charner Perry points out, "'interest' does not denote an observable fact and is not operationally definable."[35] Any argument directed against the meaningfulness of "public interest" is equally applicable to "group interest," and most of the arguments in common use throw doubt on the concept of "interest" itself. A whole family of favorite babies will be thrown out with this bath.

Even more significant than Schubert's and Sorauf's unself-conscious use of "interest" and "legitimate interest" is the former's use of "responsibility." The first chapter of Schubert's book, *The Public Interest*, is entitled, "The Quest for Responsibility," and it begins with the observation that "the search for forms of government conducive to *responsible decision making* is as old as political philosophy" (italics added). To have said "conducive to decision making in the public interest" would have carried roughly the same meaning; it would surely have been no more vague, no more incapable of operationalization, no more unscientific. "Responsibility" is used throughout by Schubert in the same old general unscientific way that we used "public interest" in the past, until Schubert and other stern scientific patriarchs told us to stop. Schubert concludes his essay in the *Nomos* volume, as he concludes his book, with the argument that "if the public interest concept makes no operational sense . . . then political scientists might better spend their time nurturing concepts that offer greater promise of becoming useful tools in the *scientific study of political responsibility*" (italics added). One could again reverse the terms, talk about the lack of operational sense in political responsibility, and urge the development of better tools for the scientific study of the public interest. If it were not for the common knowledge that our most vocal scientific students of politics rarely subject themselves to a strict practice of what they preach, one might suspect the operation of a fairly simple shell game.

RESPONSIBILITY AS THE LINK

"Responsibility" is in even more frequent use today than "public interest." It is, moreover, more generally accepted as a respectable term, as Schubert's usage illustrates, perhaps because its "value" implications are a bit further from the surface. In any case, there is less emphasis here on attacking and defending the term and more concern with understanding it. One of the reasons for its popularity is that responsibility is, or appears to be, essentially a procedural criterion. Harlan Cleveland, for example, in his introduction to *Ethics and Bigness*, contends that ethical standards are "ultimately subjective, personal, individual" and that "each of us has both the freedom and the obligation to fashion his own ethical standards...."[36] Cleveland says that he cannot suggest an affirmative code of ethics for the government official (although in fact he does so), but he suggests a guiding question: "If I am publicly criticized, will I still feel that this is what I should have done, and the way I should have decided to do it?"[37] This is not a bad first step in the quest for responsi-

[33]　Ibid., p. 189.
[34]　Schubert, *The Public Interest*, p. 184.
[35]　Friedrich, *The Public Interest*, p. 245.
[36]　Cleveland and Lasswell, *Ethics and Bigness*, p. xlv.
[37]　Ibid.

bility, but it is surely no more than that. Cleveland takes for granted the desirability of the official making his public face the same as his private face, a simple view of the relation between the public and private that is understandably questioned in several of these essays. He fails to consider that Friedrich for example does take some notice of, the different audiences by whom the official's action might be criticized and to whom he might have to make explanation. He relies finally on the "feelings" of the official whose behavior may be questioned.

That is by no means unimportant; it is even sufficient for many practical purposes, but it is not fundamentally sufficient. Decent feelings require training and support. They require at least the support of a general opinion that there *are* standards of better and worse behavior. Yet, as Senator Eugene McCarthy points out in this same volume, that support tends to be lacking in contemporary American society: "When a leading scholar declares that 'the seat of ethics is in the heart'; when it is acceptable to assert that the only absolute is that there are no absolutes; when religious and philosophical leaders lend their names to a declaration of their faith in man's ability 'to make his way by his own means to the truth which is true to him'; we should not be surprised to find some government officials making up rules which may be convenient to their own purposes."[38]

Roland Pennock's provocative opening essay in *Responsibility* explores more fully the meaning of responsibility.

It is easy to get into muddles in connection with this term ["responsible government"], simply because we use it, often at the same time, in varying applications. We mean that the government is responsible to the electorate. . . it is accountable, in some not completely arbitrary fashion, for the exercise of its trust. But we also mean that it is morally responsible; that is, that it acts in a fashion that would be morally approved by disinterested observers (or by ourselves). It holds itself to account to high standards of duty, justice, and public welfare.[39]

Responsibility has, according to Pennock, two primary meanings: "(a) accountability and (b) the rational and moral exercise of discretionary power (or the capacity or disposition for such exercise), and . . . each of these notions tend to flavor the other."[40] Responsibility is a procedural liability to answer, to give an account, to give reasons; the last is not identical to the first but implicit in it. Thus, responsibility is a procedural liability, but, as Pennock's discussion suggests, an obligation to give reasons implies the distinction between good and bad reasons; the truly responsible man is one who can give good reasons for his behavior.

Regarding the popularity that the term "responsibility" enjoys today, Pennock makes this interesting suggestion:

"Rugged" individualism stressed rights; the [totalitarian] reaction against this philosophy emphasized duties; we may today, I believe, be seeing the emergence of a new individualism in which re-

---

[38] Ibid., p. 46.
[39] Friedrich, *Responsibility,* p. 10.
[40] Ibid., p. 13.

sponsibility is the central theme…. Responsibility," then, is a term for use in a complicated, dynamic, quasi-organic society. In criminal law and in morals, increased attention to this notion reflects a growing belief that relations between "individual" and "society" are too complicated and involve too much dynamic reciprocity or "feedback" to be dealt with adequately by the concept of "rights" and "duties," "guilt" and "innocence." In politics, too, the term "responsibility" is useful for a period when simple concepts like "will of the people" are recognized as inadequate, and when "responsible" government is distinguished from "responsive" government and even from public accountability, although it includes the latter.[41]

Whether the old concepts, such as "rights" and "duties," "guilt" and "innocence," are so inadequate as Pennock argues may be questioned. In particular, it may be doubted whether "duty" is necessarily so narrow and rigid and so devoid of the exercise of judgment and discretion as he suggests. It may be that Pennock is misled in this crucial respect by his narrow view of the history of ideas. The totalitarian notion of duty, which, according to Pennock, came as a reaction against rugged individualism, was a *false* notion of duty, as is now universally agreed and juridically settled, in the Western world at least; and totalitarianism may not be the best place to look for the meaning of duty. Nevertheless, the increased concern with responsibility to which Pennock points is significant as emphasizing—if in a broad and general way—a dissatisfaction with what he calls rugged individualism, a concern for the development of a "sense of responsibility" for broader interests than those of one's self or immediate groups, and a belief that man's "full development" requires, after all, some participation in a common good beyond a general interest in being left alone.

Perhaps nothing is more widely agreed upon by the writers of the essays in *Responsibility* and *Ethics and Bigness* than the vital need for an increased and more widespread "sense of responsibility" in the United States. But how is this to be achieved? How, indeed, even to begin? The faith in the efficacy for good of increased popular participation in government, so much a part of the discipline of public administration in its early days, is now shaken—and for good reason. We are not less democrats but less simple-minded democrats. "There was a time," Roland Egger says in *Ethics and Bigness,*

> when the enhancement of popular sovereignty—the maximization of public participation in decision making—was an effective counterweight to almost any excess in the concentration of political power, but none would today suppose that public participation could significantly improve the quality of the decision- making\process or relieve the President of the consequences of decisions. The extension of the franchise… is always a good thing, but it has nothing to contribute to the amelioration of the unbearable responsibility.[42]

The notion of the "will of the people" seems inadequate to us, as Pennock remarks, because we begin to see what the best theorists and practitioners of democracy have always known, that the problem is the *quality* of the will of the people, its "sense of responsibility." And we are on the way to under-

---

[41]   Ibid., pp. 18, 19.
[42]   Cleveland and Lasswell, *Ethics and Bigness*, pp. 285-86.

standing what our ablest democrats have also always known, that with the full emancipation of the many it is especially important to look to the place of the few—not the hereditary few or the privileged few or the wealthy few, but the few of capacity and devotion to the common good, on whom the growth of civic responsibility largely depends.

LEADERSHIP IN A DEMOCRACY

Norton Long, always provocative and often wise, is perhaps less successful in his essay in *Responsibility* in bringing into focus his hopeful picture of the responsible metropolitan citizen of the future than in sketching the too-familiar city dweller of today— "Like a Goth in the Roman Empire with his vote for a weapon, he may conceive himself as plundering an alien edifice."[43] But Long draws out the essential point:

> Democracy, as Irving Babbitt pointed out, even more than other regimes depends on the quality of its leadership. It depends on the self devotion of a natural aristocracy to the precarious leadership roles of a mass society. In fact the eliciting of the efforts of this natural aristocracy, its education for the responsible conduct of affairs and the provision of a significant and accessible *cursus honorum* are major requisites for institutionalizing responsible citizenship.[44]

American students of politics, whose nation's leaders include Washington, Hamilton, Lincoln, and the Roosevelts, have strikingly little to say about leadership in a democracy. Students of public administration have scarcely been willing even to consider the issue except when it can be confined within some technical prison. Philip Selznick has, it is true, pushed vigorously beyond the technical limits and made a preliminary foray into the land of genuine leadership. But Selznick, who is not represented in these volumes, is still far less influential or reflective of general opinion among students of government and public administration than, for example, Carl Friedrich. It is of course impossible here to do justice to the learning and wisdom which Friedrich has brought to this subject in his numerous writings, to which there are copious references in his essay in *Responsibility*. But when Friedrich suggests that "the responsible administrator is responsive to these two dominant factors, technical knowledge as well as popular sentiment,"[45] he differs in detail and sophistication but not in principle from the administrative writings of Woodrow Wilson and Frank Goodnow.

It is significant that Roland Egger and Don K. Price, in their valuable essays in *Ethics and Bigness*, turn to American political history—as did Leonard D. White—for the deeper instruction that the doctrines of management have failed to provide. It is significant too that, while they ably discuss administrative organization and management, both are led to pursue the question of political leadership. "[W]e have not quite accepted," Price argues, "in some of the important segments of our society, the primary assumption which is the foundation of responsibility for policy—that the most respected citizens of the nation will themselves consider political leadership their most important

---

43 Friedrich, *Responsibility*, p. 234.
44 Ibid., pp. 230-31.
45 Friedrich, *Responsibility,* p. 199.

calling."[46] Unquestionably we require, as Price points out, "the dedication of a higher order of ability to both the political and the administrative responsibilities of government",[47] and we will get no more than we are willing to pay for. But there is a further consideration, which is the theme of the one-page comment by David Truman that ends *Ethics and Bigness*. Short as it is, this comment contains perhaps the wisest observations in this very long and often very good volume. While acknowledging the force and quality of the Egger and Price essays, Truman makes a qualification or reservation which has, and is no doubt intended to have, deep implications.

> How [the ethical dilemmas of government] are faced, however, is not primarily dependent on whether "the most respected citizens of the nation will themselves consider political leadership their most important calling," as Price argues. Whether they assume leadership in this way or not may be of less consequence, given the apparent limits on the utility of the amateur in such affairs, than that the most respected citizens regard those who do accept the burden of political leadership as being engaged in *the society's* most important calling. This, it seems to me, is "the foundation of responsibility for policy," to use Price's phrase, the indispensable obligation of the chief beneficiaries of the system if it, and they, are to survive.[48]

The high turnover of our political executives, for example, is harmful not merely because it interferes with the business of government, but because of its effect on general opinion about what the business of government is and where it stands in comparison with other businesses. The lesson is all too evident. Having obeyed the call to public duty, the political executive scarcely learns to find his way to his office without asking directions before he is planning to leave it. It may be that not much can be done about the transient character of the political executive; certainly suggeststions for reform seem typically to be loose and superficial. It may be, indeed, that a large part of their work cannot be done well by amateurs. In any case, the difficulties at the level of the political executive make it all the more important to look to the quality, the education, and the self understanding of the permanent civil service.

The education of the civil servant is most deficient in its most important respect, and this includes not only his formal education but all of the instruction and advice aimed at him by the various representatives of the discipline of administration. The question of his responsibility—his duty, he may still say, especially if he is in military service—is that question about which the civil servant receives least instruction from his teachers and which is typically shrugged off with smug toleration or superficial relativism. He is in fact taught irresponsibility in the most important cases. He is taught to look to two standards: technical competence and popular will; beyond these he has no business to venture—and there are no higher standards anyway.

Yet it is where these standards are unavailable, or contradictory, or insufficient that he meets his most difficult and highest tests. How does he respond? If he can, he may try to avoid confronting such problems by securing himself in a narrow, comfortable haven of technical specialization and refus-

---

[46]   Cleveland and Lasswell, *Ethics and Bigness*, p. 447.

[47]   Ibid., p. 466.

[48]   Ibid., p. 468.

ing to leave it. Or, he may emulate the world of private affairs, where questions of responsibility are less complex. He may conclude that the fundamental implication of his training in "management" is that the civil service, like all other forms of social life, is organized on the principle of dog-eat-dog and that his problem is to divert as much as he can of the available resources—material, honorific, psychological—to the satisfaction of his own private desires. Better-hearted, or less touched by his administrative training, he may conscientiously try to do his duty. What is significant is that in this last case he will stand very much alone. Of course there are many other individuals trying to do the same thing; but their institutional backing is, to say the least, slim.

The conventions of American public life, general opinions about what is respectable and permissible, tend to draw the civil servant back from his highest public duties rather than to guide him toward them. Obviously there is no question here of solving the problem by legislating a code of ethics and brainwashing civil servants with it. Nor can it be ignored that the character of an educational system is profoundly affected by the character of the society; but the relation is a mutual one. Those who teach and write about administration and those who practice it help to form the character of the civil service and, through the civil service, of the community at large. It is due to his constraining education, as well as the powerful pull in American life of the private and the technical, that the civil servant has least understanding of his own doings when he is exercising his highest responsibility.

The question of responsibility is the link between the civil servant's particular business in government and that government's business. It is the link between his particular problem of whether, for example, at his own risk to fight hard for a project he believes to be in the public interest and the basic ambiguity in the notion of "the public interest": the tension between public wants and the public good. The understanding and practice of public administration begin in a willingness to confront that ambiguity. If, as Truman suggests, our society requires, "especially in its more privileged segments, a respect for and an understanding of the art of governing"[49] as society's most important calling, that respect and that understanding will have to grow first among men who practice and study those arts. Perhaps then, even in the United States, the executive of the private corporation might come to emulate the man who serves the common good, rather than the other way around.

RECOMMENDATION FOR A CIVIL SERVICE ADMINISTRATOR

President's Committee on Administrative Management

[From *Report of the Committee With Studies of Administrative Management in The Federal Government*, 1937, pp. 10, 11. Published by the United States Government Printing Office, Washington, D. C.]

The board form of organization is unsuited to the work of a central personnel agency. This form of organization, as stated elsewhere in this report, has everywhere been found slow, cumbersome, wasteful, and ineffective in the conduct of administrative duties. Board members are customarily laymen

---

[49] Ibid.

not professionally trained or experienced in the activities for which they are responsible. They remain in office for relatively short periods and rarely acquire the degree of expertness necessary to executive direction. The board form of organization also has a serious internal weakness. Conflicts and jealousies frequently develop within a board and extend downward throughout the organization causing cliques and internal dissensions disrupting to morale and to work. Board administration tends to diffuse responsibility, to produce delays, and to make effective cooperation or vigorous leadership impossible. The history of the Civil Service Commission has been no exception to this general rule.

Federal personnel management, therefore, needs fundamental revision. The Civil Service Commission should be reorganized into a Civil Service Administration, with a single executive officer, to be known as the Civil Service Administrator, and a nonsalaried Civil Service Board of seven members appointed by the President. This Board would be charged not with administrative duties but with the protection and development of the merit system in the Government. . . .

The adoption of the plan of a single-headed executive for the central personnel agency would give it a degree of unity, energy, and responsibility impossible to obtain in an administrative agency headed by a full-time board of several members. The Administrator should be selected on a competitive, nonpartisan basis by a special examining board designated by the Civil Service Board and should be appointed by the President, with the advice and consent of the Senate, from the three highest candidates passing the examination conducted to fill the post. In this manner careful attention would be given to the professional and technical qualifications required by the office and the merit principle would be extended to the very top of the Civil Service Administration. The President should be able to remove the head of this managerial agency at any time but would be required to appoint his successor in the manner stated above.

The Civil Service Administrator would take over the functions and activities of the present Civil Service Commission. In addition, he would act as the direct adviser to the President upon all personnel matters and would be responsible to the President for the development of improved personnel policies and practices throughout the service. From time to time he would propose to the President needed amendments to the civil-service rules and regulations. He would suggest to the President recommendations for civil-service legislation and would assume initiative and leadership in personnel management. . . .

Personnel management is an essential element of executive management. To set it apart or to organize it in a manner unsuited to serve the needs of the Chief Executive and the executive establishments is to render it impotent and ineffective. It may be said that a central personnel managerial agency directly under the President, with the primary duty of serving rather than of policing the departments, would be subject to political manipulation and would afford less protection against political spoils than a Civil Service Commission somewhat detached from the Administration. This criticism does not take into account the fact that the Civil Service Commission today is directly responsible to the President; its members are appointed by him and serve at his pleasure; they are not independent of the President and could not be made so under the Constitution. The reorganization of the Civil Service Commission as a central personnel managerial agency of the President would greatly advance the merit principle in the Government and would lead to the extension of civil service.

The valuable services that can be performed and the contributions that can be made by a lay board representing the public interest in the merit system should not be sacrificed, even though responsibility for actual administration is vested in a single Administrator. The placing of large powers of administration in the official makes it essential to preserve the value of vigilance and criticism that, in large measure, have been afforded by the rotation in office of lay-civil service commissioners who have hitherto supervised the staff work.

A fundamental flaw in the present organization of the Commission would be removed by the establishment of an Administrator and a Board. The Commission is now obliged to administer and to appraise and criticize its own administration. These functions are basically incompatible. An effective appraisal, critical and constructive, must be entirely detached from execution....

THE INADEQUACY OF A CIVIL SERVICE COMMISSION

James K. Pollock

[From "Additional Views of Commissioner Pollock," in Commission on Organization of the Executive Branch of the Government, *Personnel Management*, 1949, pp. 48-55 selected. Published by the United States Government Printing Office, Washington, D. C.]

1.   THE PROBLEM OF DECENTRALIZATION

There seems to be no disagreement over the general idea of decentralizing personnel administration in the Federal Government. Past experience has amply demonstrated the utter inability of a single central agency to cope with the multitude of problems involved in the personnel management of 2,000,000 employees.

The issue, however, is raised by the question: How much decentralization will actually take place and under what conditions?

The report recommends that personnel administration be decentralized under "standards approved by The Civil Service Commission." While the definition of "standards" is not clear, there is good reason to believe that it means "procedural standards." Judged not only by current practices of the Civil Service Commission, but also by their very nature, such standards invariably tend to be artificial, inflexible, centralizing, and in total effect, produce a dead hand in personnel administration.

I cannot join with my colleagues in recommending a program of decentralization wrapped in the red tape of detailed, centralized, procedural controls. The report is not clear in specifying what functions now discharged by the central agency should in the future be taken over by the operating departments. It fails to indicate that any reduction will be made in the size of the central or field staffs of the Civil Service Commission, what its future role will be, or what kind of an organization structure it will have. Indeed, from the language of the report one cannot even conclude that decentralization will be extended beyond the limits currently permitted.

I, therefore, wish to make my position clear as to what I mean by decentralization of personnel operations.

I recommend to the Congress that a complete decentralization of personnel management be made to the responsible heads of the Federal agencies.

They should be free to develop personnel programs suitable for their varying needs. This decentralization should apply to all phases of personnel management, including employee relations, training, recruitment, selection, classification, compensation, reductions in force, and dismissals.

The decentralization which is needed must be full-bodied and vigorous, under standards that will not force agencies to conform to uniform procedural ritual, but which will measure results in terms of the success of management to recruit and retain a superior staff, and which will permit originality, innovation, and experimentation in developing the art of personnel administration.

2. A MODERN CONCEPT OF PERSONNEL MANAGEMENT

While a complete decentralization of personnel management to the executive agencies is the first step that must be taken to make possible real improvements in personnel administration, this step cannot be considered an end in itself. If the majority of the departments and agencies themselves continue to be absorbed in the same legalistic, procedural, paper-processing techniques which characterize so much of present personnel practices in the Federal Government, no real gains can be expected.

The whole approach to personnel administration must be changed. There must be a "triumph of purpose over technique." Each agency must face anew the questions: What are the purposes of personnel management? What should it strive to do?

Certainly the objectives of intelligent personnel management are to obtain competent employees, and having them, to provide the climate which will be most conducive to superior performance, proper attitudes and harmonious adjustments. This is a problem of human relations, requiring an understanding of human motivation. It is a problem of satisfying the needs of individuals within the context of agency needs.

Personnel management must do this by directing its attention to problems of orientation, placement working conditions, on-the-job training, and counseling. The employee must be made to feel that he belongs in the organization, that he is creatively, not passively participating, and that he is contributing to its total effort. All these are factors now too much neglected, but nevertheless vital to high morale in working-group situations.

This does not necessarily mean that a certain amount of administrative routine and paper work is not essential in personnel administration. or that attempts to develop scientific measures should not be encouraged. It means that much of the ritual which now passes for science must he abandoned. It means that paper processes and the encumbrances of petty restrictive devices, largely mechanical and legalistic—once necessary perhaps to thwart the spoilsman—must give way to a greater need, the need for developing within each agency a competence, an esprit de corps, and a mission of service far beyond that attained even in our best operated agencies at the present time.

In terms of modern management, this means that we must develop a personnel program which has more concern with people than with procedures; which gives more attention to motivation, incentives, and morale than to the refinements of written examinations, pay plans, and service ratings. In short the modern approach implies less preoccupation with the apparatus of personnel transactions and more concern with results measured in terms of the quality, morale, and performance of the personnel.

3. THE ROLE OF THE CENTRAL AGENCY

If a real decentralization of personnel administration is to be accomplished along the lines indicated, there will of course, be no need for a central agency of either the size or the structure of the present Civil Service Commission. Its large divisions of examining and placement, investigations, classification, and service records can be eliminated as well as most of its field offices. The retirement operation could be transferred to the Office of General Services. The latter agency could also undertake the recruitment for common classes of positions, largely clerical and custodial, as a central service to the operating departments. Employee records would be maintained only in the operating agency files.

The role of the central agency would be radically changed so that it would become a real staff arm to the President. It would serve him both as advisor on personnel policy and in cultivating a modern approach to personnel management within the departments and agencies of the executive branch. Its staff would be small, but should constitute a corps of highly competent individuals with an understanding of and sympathy for the newer approach to personnel management.

The staff would act principally as consultants to the departments, assisting them in revamping present programs so that the human relations aspects of personnel management will be emphasized. This staff would encourage innovation and experimentation in agency personnel programs, and would act as a medium of exchange of information on successfully operating programs throughout the Government. They would stimulate in-service training, help departments solve troublesome personnel problems; and measure the results of agency personnel management by standards which evaluate the success of the agency (a) in recruiting, leading, and retaining competent personnel, and (b) in getting the Government's work accomplished at a high level of quality, and public satisfaction.

Only in instances where an agency fails to develop such a progressive program or defaults in carrying it out would the authority of the President be invoked to effect such changes in staff or in program as may be required.

4. THE CASE FOR A SINGLE PERSONNEL ADMINISTRATOR

Our Commission has unanimously rejected the Civil Service Commission form of organization because it has served only to perpetuate the evils of inaction, delay, and administrative meddling which have characterized its operations for so many years. The majority has accepted, however, what is essentially a compromise—a continuance of the commission, but a division of responsibility within it—thus making the chairman alone responsible for administration.

While this compromise might prove to be workable in administrations when both strong leadership is displayed by the chairman and a considerable degree of restraint and cooperation is exercised by the other commissioners, in my opinion, this form of organization has little to recommend it as a permanent institutional arrangement. It attempts to preserve a commission form of organization and, at the same time, to provide for a division of function and responsibility among its members which in practice will be difficult to achieve.

In effect, it elevates the chairmanship to a much higher position than the other commissionerships in terms of authority, prestige, and accessibility to the President. This situation can hardly be expected to produce harmonious relationships within the commission. Furthermore, it thrusts the burden for successful execution of the program upon a chairman who is expected to pursue policies in the formulation of which he has only one vote out of three.

While there is unanimity of opinion among the members of the Commission as to the superiority of a single administrator for prompt and efficient administration, the form of organization recommended by the majority is advanced only in the interest of "protecting the merit system." The question thus remains as to whether the protective functions would in fact be weakened if the central agency were headed by a single administrator.

It is my conviction that a statute outlawing political favoritism in the appointment of Federal employees, coupled with enlightened agency management, is sufficient to provide adequate protection. This combination has proved to be effective in the case of the Tennessee Valley Authority. In the opinion of many, including former members of the Civil Service Commission, the usefulness of the commission form of organization to preserve the merit principle is grossly exaggerated. If, however, Congress should feel that an organization device is necessary for protective purposes, that interest could best be served, in my opinion, by a part-time advisory board of distinguished citizens.

INDEPENDENT CIVIL SERVICE COMMISSIONS AND EXECUTIVE POWER

William W. Shaw

[From *Public Personnel Review*, 14 July 1953, selected. Reprinted by permission of the Public Personnel Association.]

In recent days many individuals, both in and out of the public service, have put forward the thesis that public personnel administration should exist only as a part of the executive power—not be independent of it. They state that an executive must carry out the laws through the bureaucracy if he is to fulfill his oath of office. They maintain that only through the processes of delegation can the executive carry out the commands of the law as declared by constitutions, legislatures, and courts. They say that if the executive cannot control the human beings in the executive branch of government, he cannot faithfully execute the laws. Therefore, it is maintained, a public personnel agency must be under executive power, not independent of it.

HISTORY OF CONTROL OF EXECUTIVE POWER

The ideal long held in man's history of a necessary balance being maintained between governmental power and individual freedom can never be achieved, but this ideal we strive for without letup. In this struggle the relation of public personnel administration to executive power is also of concern. Many persons have held that public bureaucracy as a tool of executive power too often negates man's liberties.

No one can read the ideological struggles of ancient, medieval, and modern man reflecting the events of the day, championing one side of the struggle or the other, without seeing example after example of the necessity of limiting executive power. Running throughout the history of Western man is the basic tenet that executive power should be under law, not above it. Natural law, Divine law, immemorial custom, the doctrine of tyrannicide, constitutionalism, and pluralism have always been utilized to control excessive executive power. It has been of major concern in the United States.

Our founding fathers established controls over executive power in the Constitution. As in other respects, however, these controls were not expressed so minutely as to be unadaptable to the times or reflect the vigor of individuals elected to executive office. Much was left free to be controlled by electoral will, judicial review, legislative control, and the play of pressure groups. Nonetheless, executive power contains, and continues to contain many indefinable, undelineated, and reserve powers ready to be exercised by the necessities of the day—as seen by a vigorous, forceful executive.

In the states, the supremacy of the legislature still exists, and executive power remains far weaker than in the federal government. In recent years, however, the strengthening of the powers of the governor, the rise of the council-manager plan, and the strong-mayor form of city have rapidly been building up executive power in state and local governments.

GROWTH OF EXECUTIVE RESPONSIBILITY—AND POWER

The growth of executive power reflects the situation of the times. The myriad of services rendered to the people, their complexity, and the demand for quick action all lend ammunition to the argument that executive power be concentrated and that it be given powers equivalent with its responsibilities .

The attitudes and thoughts as well as the methodology of many government administrators have been influenced by the reputed efficiency and speed of large—scale enterprise. The rise of the corporation brought with it a delineation between policy and administration-the establishment of a hierarchy to obtain results. Military and church administration has also been cited as added evidence of the desirability of building up executive power to get things executed efficiently, economically, and in a "business-like manner." As part of executive power, bureaucracy, carrying out that power, has been thought of by some to be the instrument of executive power.

THE EXECUTIVE VERSUS THE CIVIL SERVICE COMMISSION

The idea of the rule of law and not men has sometimes been lost sight of in present-day efforts to increase executive power and thereby make government more efficient. In the long struggle to provide for proper balance in order to protect liberties, there arises in each era the necessity to reassess the way in which we are proceeding. In recent years the idea of an independent Civil Service Commission, distinct and separate from the chief executive, has been frowned upon. There has been an increasing outcry to do away with a civil service commission and substitute the single personnel officer. Since this officer would be responsible to the chief executive, power over personnel administration would be transferred to the executive.

Frequently, however, in practice, in the day-by-day operations of government, career officers and employees have experienced the excesses of executive power much as they have experienced the excesses of legislative and judicial power. To many, in the course of the routine of the day's work, the command of executive power has been to ignore the law, delay the law, wink at the law, or in many other ways seek to use the expertness of bureaucracy to forestall, misinterpret, or abuse the requirements of law.

The situations in which this frequently occurs are not situations of magnitude but of minuteness. The attack is one of chipping away rather than slicing great chunks. In this manner slow deterioration of the services results; hopeless despair descends upon the bureaucracy. The liberties, along with the efficiency and economy of administration, are lost to the people.

THE DANGER OF PROFESSIONALISM

The early important reason for the establishment of civil service commissions and the fight to maintain their independence resulted from what used to be called "the excesses of the spoils politicians." Does there not also exist a danger in "the excesses of professionalism"? Today we see professionals holding executive power and under the guise of professionalism often times resorting to excesses. Whether the excesses of executive power stem from the rottenness of spoils excess or whether it is garbed in the desire to provide efficiency, expertness, or economy, the end result might be the same. Too great an assumption of power by any one arm of government is dangerous.

THE ROLE OF THE BUREAUCRACY

The personnel agency has responsibility for a very important segment of government. No one can read the literature in the field of public administration without seeing a sizable segment of that literature being devoted to the problems of public personnel administration. Those in responsible authority for this important area of public administration need to be aware of the responsibility of protecting the rule of law against excesses of power, executive or any other. There must be a retention of the independence of the bureaucracy if, under the modern state, the liberties of our people are to be maintained. All too frequently, the course of history has shown the danger of concentrating power in an unbalanced state in any government. If the bureaucracy can preserve its allegiance to the law, to the heritage of our constitutionalism, it is one more pathway by which the liberties of our people can be maintained in this modern world of governmental complexity, vastness, and speed.

He today who controls bureaucracy controls the power of the state. The slowness of judicial review and legislative investigation and the inability of public inquiry to be present at the time events take place give great fountainheads of power to the executive. A bureaucracy, however, by law being able to maintain independence from the absolutism of executive power, and dedicated to the responsibility of preserving the heritage of man under the concept of the rule of law, can do much to preserve the liberties which Western man down through the ages has so preciously won. The countervailing power of an independent civil service commission can do much to provide a bureaucracy with the climate in which it can apply the rule of law when excesses of executive power may be contemplated.

THE ROLE OF THE CIVIL SERVICE COMMISSION

Mere establishment, however, of an independent civil service commission cannot guarantee the results its proponents desire. There have been too many so-called "independent commissions" that turn out to be subservient rather than independent. It, therefore, is clear that the method of appointing an independent civil service commission is the determining factor in whether it is possible for it to remain independent. The methods of appointing civil service commissions in Cincinnati, New Orleans, Philadelphia, and the State of Louisiana are being watched to see how effective are these methods in the light of experience. So far, there is every indication that these commissions are doing a successful piece of work and maintaining their independence.

It is much more difficult, however, to devise methods by which independence can be integrated with cooperation. A modern civil service agency must help the executive provide the services essential to a modern personnel program, for example, in-service training, employee communication programs, suggestion systems, grievance procedures. Since a close relation between management and employee groups is necessary if these programs are successful, independence may be a deterrent.

It is true, however, that if a civil service commission is composed of members who understand the problem of hierarchy and if directors of personnel serving the commissions are well-trained and experienced in modern personnel administration, there need exist no roadblock to management-employee cooperation. Independence might also help convince the public at large as well as employee and management groups of the objectivity and impartiality of the commission and its staff in the development of modern personnel practices and procedures. On the other hand, if the personnel function, by law, was made a part of the chief executive, public opinion might well consider it to be political rather than professional.

THE CITY MANAGER AND THE CIVIL SERVICE COMMISSION

Such statements, however, may be questioned when we consider the forms of government springing up which accept the executive as professional. For example, the City Manager form of government clearly provides for professional management. The rapid growth of this form of government at municipal and county levels is a striking feature of recent times. It is not so easy, therefore, for the proponents of an independent civil service commission to refuse to be integrated when professional competency is at the helm. The proponents, however, of an independent civil service commission allege that this movement is too recent to give up the gains of the past. Some of them see the possibility that city managers, as they increasingly emphasize the necessity of sound public relations, give indication that they may become enmeshed with political realities. In other words, public relations may soon become political and it is therefore too early to determine whether the independent civil service commission should go. The mere existence of a city manager does not necessarily mean that professionalism is here to stay. And, even if it is, there is still need for a countervailing power to act as a brake upon the excesses of a stronger executive....

THE CASE FOR THE SENIOR CIVIL SERVICE

Leonard D. White

[From *Personnel Administration,* 19 Jan.-Feb., 1956, pp. 4-9. Reprinted by permission of the Society for Personnel Administration.]

On December 2, 1882, Senator Henry L. Dawes of Massachusetts, arguing for the passage of the Pendleton Act, declared, "The method of appointment to office in this country has got to be changed. It can be administered but little longer in the methods of the past. It has outgrown those methods adapted for an old system of things never sufficient for them; but it was never dreamt by those who created it . . . that 200,000 office-holders can be appointed in the methods that were fit and proper for the appointment of 1,000."

This argument points up the present position of the top executive career service of the Federal Government. It can hardly go on without change if it is to fulfill contemporary and future demands. The methods of constituting and maintaining it have not changed substantially since the 1930's they were inadequate then for the much less difficult burden of that day. A substantial alteration of some sort is overdue.

This indeed has been the opinion of every official or unofficial body that has considered the matter for nearly a quarter century. The Commission of Inquiry on Public Service Personnel reached this conclusion in 1935. Floyd W. Reeves and Paul David confirmed it in their report to the President's Committee on Administrative Management in 1937. The President's Committee on Civil Service Improvement (the Reed Committee) said the same thing. Agency reports after World War II came to the same conclusion. This long-repeated recommendation for more systematic means of building and maintaining a stronger career service in the highest levels has now been reduced by the Task Force on Personnel and Civil Service of the second Hoover Commission to a concrete plan. The plan has been endorsed by the Hoover Commission.

WHAT IS THE SENIOR CIVIL SERVICE?

Before stating the advantages of the proposal, it may be useful to summarize its provisions. The proposed Senior Civil Service is envisaged as a corps of from 1,500 to 3,000 men and women drawn typically from employees holding classified competitive positions in Grade GS-15 and rising into the super-grades (GS-16, 17 and 18). They are to be selected by a Senior Civil Service Board comprising three qualified citizens, the Director of the Bureau of the Budget, and the Chairman of the U.S. Civil Service Commission or their alternates. Candidates are to be nominated by their agencies, with their consent, after at least five years in the career service, on the basis of demonstrated administrative ability and promise of the highest order. In principle (and eventually in fact), it is expected that they will have had experience in line and staff, in headquarters and field, and preferably in more than one agency.

The Senior Civil Service will be concerned with professional management at levels immediately below that of top political command. The task force included in this range of positions includes the assistant secretary for administration, some deputy assistant secretaries, bureau chiefs and division chiefs, the heads of such services as budgeting and personnel in large agencies, and the deputy heads of staff agencies dealing with substantive problems. They are expected to occupy a politically neutral position, and must avoid emotional attachments to controversial policy issues that would make them unacceptable to either political party.

The task force proposed to take these positions out of their present job classification status and give to the members of the Senior Civil Service a personal rank or status equivalent to that of a general or flag officer in the armed services. This recommendation is designed to ensure both stability and flexibility of assignment. Corresponding to rank status is the obligation, within reason, to serve where the needs of the service require. Rank status does not confer a claim to any particular assignment or indeed to service in any given agency. It does confer the right to continued employment—the right to be used in the public service and not to be dispossessed from the service for partisan or personal reasons. Removal for cause would of course not be affected, and there is additional provision for "selecting out" any members whose competence proves inadequate.

Two observations are necessary preliminaries to stating the case for the Senior Civil Service. (1) Neither the task force nor the Hoover Commission are committed to all the details of the proposal. They may require modification in the light of further discussion by those who have to make the decision. They are proposed as a consistent and rational plan to meet an acknowledged need. If the present plan is not wholly appropriate, then it is the duty of critics to propose alternatives, which in turn may be subjected to constructive criticism. It is not enough merely to object. (2) In asserting the need for better means of sustaining a high quality professional corps of administrators, it is in no way intended to cast imputations upon the able men and women who now occupy top level career positions. Their intelligence, skill, and devotion are recognized on all sides. What we need is more men and women of equal quality, more assurance that they will be forth-coming when needed, and greater certainty of stable tenure.

WHAT THE SENIOR CIVIL SERVICE WOULD DO

The advantages of some such plan as the Senior Civil Service are these:

it conserves more certainly than at present the best career service talent at the highest professional levels; it increases the flexibility of assignment and reassignment; it provides the political top command with a tested supply of experienced executives; it induces much better training and development facilities; and it is a new incentive to able and promising younger men and women to make the Federal service their life work.

1. *The higher a Federal employee rises in the career ladder the more he is exposed to the cross-fire of policy or political controversy and in consequence the greater his danger of being squeezed out of the Federal service.* Schedule C[50] presumably has the effect of reducing this hazard to a certain degree by frankly putting policy-determining and confidential positions in an unprotected category. The Task Force on Personnel and Civil Service did not accept Schedule C as other than a temporary expedient. It believed also that the line between the policy top command and the permanent career service had not been properly drawn, since some division chiefs and many bureau chiefs were withdrawn from the career service. The task force drew the line just above the bureau chief level, reserving most department-wide positions for the political branch of the public service but including bureau and subordinate levels for the career service. The task force recognized, however, that bureau chiefs would not escape from the hazards of political or other forms of warfare and reprisal if in fact they took any share in the defense of policy. Hence the need of a senior civil service politically neutral, protected from the necessity of making public policy decisions, and foregoing any overt position with regard either to partisan politics or controversial measures.

To strengthen the foundations for permanence of employment at the highest career levels the task force consequently recommended:

(1) That a senior civil servant should make no public or private statements to the press, other than of a purely factual nature.

(2) He should make no public speeches of a political character.

(3) He should not contribute to campaign funds.

(4) He should avoid testimony before congressional committees on political questions, while remaining at the service of the committee for background information, relevant data, and technical advice.

(5) He should avoid public identification with any political party.

One of the marks of viability of the proposed Senior Civil Service will be its capacity to deserve the confidence of both political parties. That such a state of affairs had not been fully achieved in 1958 is borne out by the record. On the other hand, it is progressively in course of achievement, and needs only an established policy to become effective.

To conserve the administrative know-how of present and future members of Grades GS 1S17-18 for the use of both political parties would be a substantial step forward.

2. *Another handicap which has bogged down many efforts to meet both emergency and normal problems is the difficulty of reassignment of men holding high responsible career posts.* The difficulty is partly personal; men do not welcome

---

[50] Positions excluded from the career service because of being political-policy-determining, or of a confidential character.

change from an office with which they are thoroughly familiar and in which they are doing good work. The problem is made more bothersome by the difficulty of foreseeing future career possibilities and of adjusting to new personalities and working conditions. Moreover, there is a natural and in many respects a desirable attachment of career employees to "their" organizations. There is, nevertheless, a great need for a relatively small number of career men with a service-wide, rather than a departmental, point of view. The members of the Senior Civil Service are to be granted a type of tenure-personal rank independent of the particular position held and substantial security against discrimination—that is designed to lessen this handicap. As a counterpoise, senior civil servants are expected to serve where needed most.

This rule does not mean that they would be universally interchangeable. It does mean that they are not to be hemmed in by departmental or agency boundaries. It assumes that there are broad areas of government activity reaching into and across a cluster of departments and agencies within any part of which a senior civil servant would feel at home. Finance, transportation, conservation, the social services are examples. The higher ranges of the auxiliary services such as budgeting, personnel, accounting, and purchasing provide another class of services within which a top level career man could move with relative ease from agency to agency.

There is another aspect of this matter: an incoming administration would be under no obligation to keep a senior civil service man in his present position. It has an obligation, which is normally in its own interest and already recognized as such, to find him an appropriate employment in some appropriate agency and function.

3. *The senior civil service would provide a tested corps of career executives fully prepared to work with each incoming administration.* Many years ago Daniel Webster declared, "The army is the army of the country; the navy is the navy of the country; neither of them is either the mere instrument of the administration for the time being, or of him who is the head of it." This doctrine is generally accepted also for the civil service of the country, and needs only slight extension to cover what is now the most exposed section of the career service.

It is common knowledge that the first months of a new administration mark little progress and often seem confused and uncertain. Some of this confusion is inevitable, but some could be avoided by the availability of a top administrative service that would both ensure an orderly transition and bring competent help in such readjustments as seemed desirable. The complement of this aspect of the Senior Civil Service is more effective and speedy recruitment of a more experienced political top command: the under secretaries, assistant secretaries, assistants to these and corresponding officials, and principal substantive staff agency heads.

4. *A Senior Civil Service cannot be extemporized overnight.* The decision to create such a corps will necessarily involve corollary decisions, themselves of much importance. Among these the necessity of more and better executive training programs stands high on any list. The Senior Civil Service is to be recruited from within, and it will require new types of experience and indoctrination to prevent the dangers of inbreeding. The desirable range of early experience in staff and line, headquarters and field operations can be readily achieved. More difficult will be the psychological preparation of potential

candidates: their quick perception of the proper function of the political command; the niceties of their adjustment to changing policy; the absence of emotional attachments on their part either to policies or individuals that are under replacement; the code of professional behavior that will be needed both to protect themselves and to guide them under exposure to powerful forces in society; the forms of intercourse not only with secretaries and assistant secretaries but with business leaders, generals, admirals, and international authorities—all these and much more will be a necessary part of their equipment. Such men can now be found in the Federal service and to them will fall a large share of the practical task of forming such a corps as that proposed.

5. *The Senior Civil Service, once a fact, would be a strong inducement to well-qualified young men and women to enter the public service and remain in it.* The drop in the number of applicants for the Junior Management Assistant examination is serious, although it would go too far to assert that college and university graduates are engaged in a boycott of government employment. The hard fact is that the Federal Government competes in the open market for the services of these men and women. Business, banking, transportation, productive enterprise everywhere eagerly seeks the best of each college generation. Government has never been on equal competitive terms. One basic reason is that the height of a successful public service career has never been clear; the challenge of government work has never been made plain; the ultimate opportunities have always been obscure. The Senior Civil Service would provide a challenge and an opportunity that has never been available, and that could not fail to meet with a needed response from highly qualified young men and women.

BOLD CONSTRUCTIVE ADVANCE NEEDED

The necessity for some improvement in the institutional foundations of the Federal civil service can no longer be doubted. The only real issue is how to proceed. This question will have to be decided in the first instance by the President of the United States, and eventually by Congress, since legislation will be required at some points of the Hoover Commission proposals. The present top level career service will doubtless be consulted and their views are entitled to consideration. They should advise without reference to their own personal participation in the Senior Civil Service. The question is whether such an institutional arrangement, or some improvement thereof, would be in the public interest. Individual participation is another matter, to be determined later, person by person.

It was the view of the Task Force on Personnel and Civil Service that two decades of drift and patchwork amidst foreign and domestic crises have left the American personnel system for top career posts not far advanced beyond its position in the 1930's. It is generally agreed that this position is unsatisfactory and inadequate. The task force was satisfied that a bold constructive advance is now needed both to maintain our present supply of administrative talent and to provide more certainly for its future plenishment.

THE CASE AGAINST THE SENIOR CIVIL SERVICE

Everett Reimer

[From *Personnel Administration*, 19 March-April, 1956, pp. 31-38 selected. Reprinted by permission of the Society for Personnel Administration.]

That our Federal service needs more able, devoted senior civil servants no one can deny, nor the fact that those we have are underpaid, under-privileged, and sometimes under-utilized. All right-thinking men might therefore be expected to support a program designed to raise the pay, increase the prerogatives, and foster the wider use of these indispensable men and women. And so they would if they could still their doubts that these would be the principal and reasonably certain results of the program.

The proposed Senior Civil Service is a speculator's dream—promising great returns on a very modest investment. Traditionally a competent, devoted, senior government service, be it civilian or military, has been the fruit of a career system. The proposal of the Commission on Organization of the Executive Branch of the Government would produce the fruit without first planting and nurturing the tree. This, of course, is not impossible, as the horticultural grafters have demonstrated.

There are excellent reasons why a graft was preferred by the Personnel Task Force of the Commission to the arduous process of starting from scratch, and these reasons are more fundamental than merely the desire to save time. To develop an integrated service-wide career system in the Federal civil service would indeed be a formidable task. It would require, first of all, a measure of governmental planning which has never characterized the Federal civil service: an estimation of the number and type of skilled administrators needed in the future far enough in advance to allow for their recruitment and training.

It would require, furthermore, that the entrance jobs of these future administrators be earmarked, and also the jobs in the career ladders they would ascend and the jobs to which they would eventually graduate.

Finally, it would require that we recruit a group of persons able to absorb the skills and attitudes required in the senior administrative positions and reserve for them the best opportunities for training and development. By any criterion the members of this group would constitute an "elite," not only after arriving at senior status but from the time of their selection.

It is easy to see what fundamental problems and resistance such a career system would encounter in our Federal Government-problems which the Commission's proposal carefully avoids. The Senior Civil Service, as proposed, includes no forward planning process. It earmarks no specific classes of jobs for senior civil servants. It makes no provisions for recruitment or training and creates no elite, except post facto. But it remains to be seen whether a by-pass of these points of major resistance may not also by-pass the expected rewards—whether the fruits heretofore developed on a career tree can be grafted onto the native wood of our Federal service.

This is not the time and place to argue the merits of a unified governmental career service. Where the virtues or vices of such a system are touched upon in this discussion the comment is upon the proposal for a Senior Civil

Service and not upon a nonexistent proposal to establish an inclusive career system in the Federal Government. It would not, after all, be fair to argue on the one hand that the Senior Civil Service will not give us the fruits of a career system and on the other that even if it did we wouldn't like them.

CAN THE SENIOR CIVIL SERVICE BE COMPETENTLY STAFFED?

One of the great virtues of a career system is that it provides security and incentive, throughout their job careers, for individuals initially chosen to adorn eventually the top ranks of the service. What reason have we to believe that a service which fails—as our civil service does—to provide this continuing security and incentive to people of the highest caliber will produce enough qualified candidates for a Senior Civil Service?

If the odds that the best men and women would remain in the service were even, the answer might be given in terms of pure probability. But most experienced persons would agree that the odds are against the best people remaining. Private industry offers a better combination of economic security and incentive for the most able, universities offer more security and a freer choice of work, political posts and issues beckon those who can afford to follow their lure.

Against similar lures the military services are able to retain a high proportion of their West Point and Annapolis men: first because these men commit themselves to their career early in life and second because *it is a career.* Even when circumstances are unfavorable these men know that their advancement is merely delayed. The odds are that the best men will remain in the Service for they know that they will be the future generals and admirals and also what responsibilities and prerogatives this entails.

Even the existence of a Senior Civil Service will not square the odds for civil servants. For who can know whether he will be selected for the Senior Service even if he negotiates the uncertain way to the top ranks? And if he is selected there is still no guarantee of the kind of responsibility and authority he will have. Status as a Senior Civil Servant will provide him with a superior license to hunt for a job, plus a little longer shrift in the service if his hunting luck turns sour.

The proposal for a Senior Civil Service makes no provision for the training of the men who are to graduate into its ranks, except to suggest that in the future the selection criteria for entrance into the Service shall include breadth and variety of previous experience. The probable effectiveness of this requirement in changing the present practices of government agencies and civil servants will be assessed later. It is enough here to point out that these present practices tend to produce specialists and to raise the question whether a competent corps of administrative generalists can be recruited from among agencies whose personnel systems are geared to the production of specialists.

What we clearly need is a method of attracting men and women of the first rank to the Federal civil service, keeping them there, developing their executive capacities, and then of seeing that these capacities are used in the most responsible administrative posts. The present civil service system is ill adapted to this task and the proposed Senior Civil Service offers little correction of its major structural deficiencies. How then is the Senior Civil Service to be staffed, under the proposed rules, with more than a handful of men deserving of rank and title?

WILL THE SENIOR CIVIL SERVICE BE USED?

Since there is no provision for the mandatory use of senior civil servants in any class of job, their use will presumably depend upon their individual prestige and upon the prestige of the Service. But if the preceding analysis is sound, if the civil service tends to lose its best men to private enterprise, to the universities, and to politics, including political posts in the Federal service; if, furthermore, it tends to produce specialists rather than flexible executives, then there will not be enough men and women available who could give the Senior Service the prestige it will need.

The prestige of the Senior Civil Service could, of course, be assured by keeping it initially small. Instead of building up rapidly to a size of fifteen hundred members, as the Commission proposes, the new service could be limited to those who would clearly give it prestige. But this would scarcely solve the problem of the use of the Service, for the few clearly well-qualified senior civil servants are now in positions from which it would be difficult to detach them and in which they are probably already making their maximum contribution.

The voluntary use of the Senior Civil Service thus poses a dilemma—the demand for its members can be stimulated only by so restricting the supply as to make it impossible to meet the demand. Nor should this conclusion appear arbitrary or mere juggling with words when we remember that the proposed creation of the new service is itself, essentially, a sleight-of-hand performance. Our present undersupply of senior bureaucrats is to emerge from the magician's hat sparkling new, ready to function in new jobs with new competence and prestige. But the employing officers, those who will have to utilize the new creation, are themselves insiders. Will the hat trick convince them?

If nothing happens after the new service is created, if job changes do not increase because the accolade of rank is confined to the demonstrably deserving few who have already found their niche, the granting of rank and title will scarcely appear justified. If, on the other hand, rank is conferred upon those whose qualifications are not broadly recognized—granting even that they may deserve the recognition—what will be the result? It seems probable that for every appointing officer who accepts evaluation of the Senior Civil Service Board, and employs a member he would not otherwise have employed, there will be many who will regard the Board's action as simply conferring privilege upon the favored few. And the skeptics will be justified, if not by the facts, then by the appearance of seeming to create by edict what was not seen before.

The grafting operation tends to defeat its own purpose insofar as gaining recognition and use of the Senior Civil Service is concerned. Even if we assume that the formal requirements of career systems are fictions it is still apparent that they are persuasive fictions. Most people believe that a special system of selection, training, and advancement, geared to the basic function of an organization, will actually produce a leadership elite. They are less likely to believe that naming a man a Senior Civil Servant and conferring a rank upon him will make him anything he was not before—except more enviable.

Failure to use the new Service would of course compound the mischief. If not used it would lose its attraction to any except the self-seekers. Among those on the outside, the belief would be strengthened that this was a club designed for the advantage of its members. This belief in turn would further limit the use of the Service and its attraction for potential members who could add to its prestige and usefulness.

But let us not assume that the impossibility of recruiting enough well-qualified senior civil servants or the proposition that the new Service will not be used has been demonstrated. All that has been shown is that the task force proposal provides no assurance on these points, and furthermore that the odds may not be favorable. The possibility remains that the Task Force has created in the Senior Civil Service a potent piece of magic which, given a favorable start, will create the conditions for its own success. Let us examine this proposed dynamism in a little more detail to get a better notion of how its own characteristics will affect the odds for and against its success.

POLITICAL NEUTRALITY

One of the most striking features of the proposal, especially in its more detailed description by the Task Force, is the insistence on the political neutrality of the senior civil servants. The principal quid-pro-quo for the new rank and title seems to be, in fact, a new pledge of political neutrality. Off-hand, the bargain appears too reminiscent of Esau's selling his birthright. Is this really the way to attract men who will lend prestige to the Senior Civil Service?

Every administration has to use men who have opposed either its party or its programs, simply because the affairs of the nation are of too great moment to be entrusted to the competence inherent in only half its citizens. Can competence which has to be employed in spite of policy and party differences be excluded from the inner ranks without at the same time denying to these ranks many of the most important positions? Or take it the other way. Should men whose devotion to a program has coincided with their support of a party now responsible for administering the program be denied the rank and title of Senior Civil Servant? If so, there goes another batch of competent men—and good jobs.

What kind of men are going to be attracted to a service in which they may not give a Congressional committee their opinion on program policy but are forced to hide behind the neutrality of their service? What kind of men are going to subject even their membership on a school board to the possible intervention of their guile? Granted that civil servants have to give up some kinds of political participation; many people feel that the Hatch Act—as interpreted—already goes too far in proscribing activities which have nothing to do with spoils, and that activities—in nonpartisan municipal affairs, for example—are prohibited if it appears only that an influential politician might object to them. If the senior civil servant is to be still further politically emasculated, prevented, for example, from participating in the defense of a proper political scope for civil servants, then the attractions of the Service will be confined to a peculiar breed indeed, scarcely to men who would recommend themselves for responsibility in high positions.

The notion that administration can be divorced from policy and even from politics has been badly damaged in recent years. Even those who continue to believe in the separation, in terms of the theory and practice of public administration, must admit the reluctance of competent men to leave value judgments in the hands of others. If the Senior Civil Service is to attract the men who will give it the prestige it needs to be successful, it appears that the part of wisdom would be to loosen, not tighten, the shackles of the Hatch Act.

THE CONCEPT OF PERSONAL RANK

This is the key concept of the proposed Senior Civil Service. Rank is to inhere in the individual member and to determine his salary and perquisites regardless of the job he occupies. To question the value of this concept as an element of the Service may appear at first like questioning the value of the lens to the eye. It is the only formal element of a career system included in the proposal. If the Senior Civil Service is to be an entering wedge for a career system, how can we eliminate personal rank and have anything left?

The difficulty is precisely that in the absence of other elements of a career system the granting of personal rank to members of the Senior Civil Service cannot be justified. In a career system the range of responsibilities and authority which go with a given rank are specified and so are the steps which have to be mounted to achieve the rank. Both rank and the right to it are therefore respected. In the proposed Senior Civil Service, however, rank is to be a privilege conveyed by the fiat of a board, and this rank is depended upon to lend its dignity to any job its holder may occupy. This is getting the cart before the horse, placing a burden upon the concept of rank which it was not designed to carry.

The ranks of General, Admiral, or Foreign Service Officer, Class I, are justified by the assignments reserved for their holders. Occasionally, of course, the obverse is true. One of the virtues of rank is that it can be used to define the importance of an assignment, but when this is done the capital which has been invested in the rank, by virtue of the assignments normally reserved to it, is being expended.

Personal rank could be introduced into a Senior Civil Service after such a Service had been established long enough to be defined by the jobs reserved for its members. But if rank is introduced earlier it is not likely to be respected but to be regarded as a mark of undeserved privilege.

Actually rank is not essential to the proposed workings of the Service. It is a convenience for which less convenient substitutes could be found. The temporary assignment of senior civil servants to jobs below their grade level could be arranged as such assignments are now arranged; through interagency loan or through the temporary reclassification of jobs. The obstacles and delays which make these methods undesirable could be minimized in the case of members of the Senior Civil Service through appropriate general agreements.

Undoubtedly the Senior Civil Service would lose some of its glamour if personal rank were initially left out of its formula. It would probably get off to a slower start, but it might well be a sounder one.

NATURAL RIVALS AND SURVIVAL POWER

The case against the Senior Civil Service consists thus far in showing that no provision is made to insure an adequate supply of qualified members or to insure that the members of the Service will be used as it is proposed they should be. A look at two of the principal features of the proposed service has not been reassuring, but has suggested that these features will hinder rather than help in the recruitment of a qualified membership and in gaining appropriate use and acceptance of the Service. Nevertheless, the preceding arguments could be characterized as somewhat general and as depending upon assumptions which are hard to prove one way or the other. Let us look therefore at some of the more specific environmental obstacles which a Senior Civil Service will encounter. The proposition to be supported is that the Federal Government does not provide a favorable environment for a Senior Civil Service.

EXISTING FEDERAL CAREER SYSTEMS

It is almost a commonplace that the Federal service is not a career system but contains many. In addition to the Post Office, the Foreign Service, the T.V.A., and the military services, there are scores of bureaus which maintain specialized selection, training, and promotion systems designed to meet their own future leadership requirements. It will not be difficult to get the senior personnel of these departments and bureaus to accept rank and title in the Senior Civil Service for they will have nothing to lose thereby and something to gain. To get them to function as senior civil servants, however, will be a horse of another color. By accepting temporary assignment outside their own bureau they would jeopardize their position on the ladder they have spent a lifetime climbing. By accepting an outsider into their ranks at top levels, they would simply be inviting competition for themselves.

If the Senior Civil Service could itself command a Government-wide group of jobs these risks might be justified. If in their earlier careers these men had had an opportunity to move from bureau to bureau, the odds against moving at the peak of their careers would be less. As it stands, however, the career systems which are established, which do command a definite set of jobs, in which men have been trained and into which they were originally recruited, will have all the advantage over a new system with little to recommend it except the prospect of adventure. The advantage of a bureau in keeping its men against the lure of broader experience will hold, moreover, at all grade levels until the Senior Civil Service becomes a serious competitor to the bureau in offering dependable long-term career prospects.

THE CONGRESS AND THE SENIOR CIVIL SERVICE

The parliamentary system is undoubtedly one of the great allies of an integrated governmental career system, and almost as surely the United States Congress is one of the principal obstacles to such an institution. It is no longer spoils but influence over the bureaucracy which is at issue, and in a struggle between the executive and the legislature which under our system of government is inevitable and legitimate, the Congressional strategy is clearly to divide and conquer. This is the principal reason why so much autonomy and separatism exist among the bureaus of the executive branch. It is also the reason why the Congress will not be neutral with respect to the Senior Civil Service. We must assume that the Congress will permit the establishment of such a service; otherwise we are debating an academic issue. It cannot be assumed, however, that the Congress will meekly accept the ground rules which have been spelled out by the Personnel Task Force or even the more general versions of these rules contained in the Commission recommendation.

The hardest thing to imagine is that the Congress will permit a civil servant to avoid testifying on policy issues on the ground that he is a civil servant. Our Congressional committee chairmen are old Washington hands, of older vintage frequently than our senior bureaucrats. But both are veterans in comparison with the political leadership of the executive departments; moreover, they are veterans who know each other and who understand, among themselves, where policy is made and carried out and where the money comes from. No Senior Civil Service which undertakes to block their free communication is going to last for five minutes.

Another thing the Congress will find hard to swallow is that a civil servant should be granted permanent title to a salary, regardless of what he does— this is what the concept of rank as envisioned in the Senior Civil Service will be boiled down to by Congressional critics. A Congressman is of course paid for what he is rather than for what he does, but then a Congressman has to get this privilege renewed periodically and on a competitive basis. A military officer is also paid on this basis, but he also has to face a periodic, competitive re-evaluation. Furthermore, both the Congressman and the officer had originally to surmount a specific set of hurdles. It will be hard to convince Congressmen that the past and future obligations laid upon the senior civil servant are equivalent in character to [their] own and those of the military officer and that they are equally deserving of rank.

SUMMARY OF THE CASE AGAINST

The proposal for a Senior Civil Service has now been weighed and found wanting on three separate scales. First, it was found to make no sufficient provision either for an adequate supply of qualified members or for an appropriate use of this membership. Second, two of the principal characteristics of the Service, as proposed, were evaluated as weaknesses rather than strengths: (a) an excessive insistence on political neutrality was held to inhibit the recruitment of the ablest men and to be unacceptable to the Congress; and (b) the granting of rank, without a concomitant provision for assignments justifying the rank, was held to make the Service vulnerable to its critics. Finally, the proposed Service was adjudged too weak to counter the resistance which must be expected from the entrenched career systems of the government and from the Congress. . . .

HAVE PUBLIC EMPLOYEES THE RIGHT TO STRIKE?—NO

H. Eliot Kaplan

[This and the following selection are from the *National Municipal Review,* 30 September, 1941, pp. 518-28, 551 (Kaplan's slightly abridged). Reprinted by permission of the National Municipal League.]

Expansion of government in fields viewed heretofore as within the exclusive province of private enterprise prompts the suggestion that the relationship between government and civil employees needs to be considered anew. Where employees in private industry are brought into the civil service it is not surprising that they carry over earlier precedents and customs, and with them ideas which may prove to be inimical to government administration and impractical of application in the public service. Two major factors have tended to persuade some people toward new concepts of the relationship between government and its employees: (1) the National Labor Relations Act, which significantly excepts government service from its application, and (2) extension of governmental activities—the transition from a policing and regulatory government to a servicing government.

At the outset it should be made clear that the right of public employees to organize for their mutual welfare as they see fit must not be denied. The only issues that need concern us are, first, to what degree should public employees be permitted to affiliate with outside labor unions or organizations, and second, to what extent should the rights and privileges accorded to private employee unions and organizations be extended to similar associations of public employees.

Many civil service employee organizations have long been affiliated with public employee organizations of other jurisdictions. Many of them have been affiliated with labor unions—local, state, and national. Both the A.F. of L. and the C.I.O. have been vying with each other in persuading civil employees to join their ranks.

The people are generally aware of their responsibility for the economic welfare of their own employees. They are also aware that public employees owe a certain responsibility to the people.

The issue is not solely whether the public employee should be devoted exclusively to the people's interest but rather whether he should be responsible only to the people and not to a political boss, a demagogue, or a labor leader. Fundamentally, that is the crux of the problem. If we miss this concept of public employee responsibility to the people alone, under our democratic system, we are bound to misunderstand the proper relationships in public employment.

Just how far public employees should be permitted to join with outside labor unions must depend on what the purposes of such affiliation may be and the obligations assumed by public employees under such outside affiliation. Political machines and arrogant administrators have, of course, thrown many a monkey wrench into attempts of civil service employees to organize. They have sought to control employee organizations for their own political or administrative purposes—a practice which closely resembles a "company union" idea. In attempting to meet this occasional difficulty we must be careful not to permit other abuses or practices equally detrimental to the people's interests to take its place.

PURPOSES OF AFFILIATION

The public may view with suspicion any affiliation between public employee organizations and outside labor unions unless there is some patently direct interest which they both share. One can well understand a community of interest between carpenters in civil service positions and carpenters in private employment, for instance, or between machinists or motormen in their respective fields. But what desirable purpose can there be in an affiliation of a union of municipally employed clerks, patrolmen, gas inspectors, or engineers with a C.I.O. or A.F. of L. union of hodcarriers, instrument-makers, or garment workers, other than the selfish purpose of overawing a city or state administration or a department head, by a show of solidarity, into making unwarranted concessions which cannot be justified on their merits and which may be against the public interest? One would have to be naive indeed to assume that administrative officials can exercise their judgment untrammeled by a combined, highly organized pressure group, particularly if the labor or employee leadership falls into unscrupulous hands.

It is one thing for civil employees in a local jurisdiction to affiliate with other civil employees in a state or national organization for their mutual welfare in educating public opinion as to their common needs and seeking to persuade the people toward certain policies affecting them. It is another thing, however, for civil employees to affiliate with outside labor unions primarily for the purpose of using their combined strength to coerce action that may be utterly inimical to the people's interests and to employ methods which run counter to orderly governmental and democratic procedure. The people must not tolerate the use of the civil service by irresponsible labor leaders for purposes that could place the people at the mercy of their very own employees, such as a sympathetic strike, wherein civil employees are dragged into a situation in which they themselves have no direct interest. It is conceivable that they can be used in some cases actually to overcome the will of the majority in a community, particularly when the tactics employed to coerce action in private industry are injected to coerce administrative action.

If this seems fantastic, let us weigh the implications of the civil employees' strike recently called in Racine, Wisconsin. There the employees of the city, aided by affiliated labor unions, brought pressure on the mayor and city council to meet their demands for salary increases. The city officials felt that the demands were unwarranted and resisted them. The city employees went out on strike. Other labor unions, it is alleged, threatened to join them in a sympathy strike. A hurried meeting of the city officials was called and, to prevent tie-up of the city's business and [to] safeguard the people, officials yielded to the demands of the city employees.

THE PEOPLE PARAMOUNT

We must appreciate that it is for the people alone to decide what rights or privileges may or may not be granted to public employees by the people's representatives. Public officials act for the people, not for themselves—even if administrators seem to forget that elementary principle occasionally. The right to strike against themselves—the people—can be granted to public employees in given cases and under such circumstances as the people may choose. It is analogous to the privilege granted individuals by the people to sue the state. Regardless of private injury or loss, an individual may sue the state—the people—only to the extent granted by the people. In other words, not until the people recognize by law the right of public employees to refuse to obey their superior officers under specified circumstances and strike against the actions of public officials, is there any "right" of public employees to strike. No employee has the right to interfere with the orderly conduct of public affairs or to interrupt public services for the people without the people's consent. That is the difference between private and public employment.

It would be foolish to suppose that existing relationships between administrative officials and public employees are ideal even under the best administered merit system of today. Public employees should be granted the privilege to negotiate with public officials on matters of concern both to employees and the people whom they serve, such as the fixing of wages, hours, and conditions of employment, sick leave privileges, etc., or to adjust and remedy grievances. Unfortunately, this privilege is too often denied them. Arrogant administrative "bosses" can be as tyrannical as the worst despot in private enterprise. But even so, the civil employees may not take it [into] their own hands to interfere with the orderly functioning of government by striking against such a public tyrant. Do they strike against him or against the people? True, the majority of the people directly or indirectly are responsible for that arrogant administrator. But we cannot sanction the right of public employees to resort to a strike to force the people to oust the recalcitrant administrator who may have been elected or appointed for a fixed term. That is a right which the people reserve to themselves.

Who is to determine whether the particular administrator (representing the people) is right or wrong, the civil service employees? Suppose the administrator is trying to protect the public from concerted selfish action on the part of the people's employees, as in the case of an unreasonable wage demand far beyond the ability of the taxpayers to meet. Ought we permit employees to quit work and so attempt to coerce the administrator into granting their demand? Suppose an employee organization or a labor union affiliate disapproves of the dismissal of one of its number and all the employees walk out on the people in protest? This has actually occurred in more than one jurisdiction. Where does one draw the line as to just how far employees may go in attempting to coerce administrative action against the public interest? These are questions that need be given thought in any appraisal of the relationships in public employment.

MORALE IMPORTANT

It is, of course, decidedly in the public interest that those serving the people be a satisfied and contented group. Morale of their employees is a matter of vital importance to the people. The kind of service the people will get from their public servants will depend in large measure upon the treatment the public employees get from the people.

It is essential to the people's interest, however, that conditions of employment in the civil service be remedied in more or less the same general manner and orderly means as is to be expected of any other change of public policy. Civil employees have as great, and in many respects greater, opportunities to educate public opinion toward their view of problems as has any other class of citizens. If the people do not yet see it their way, it is up to the employees to crystallize public sentiment in their direction. If the method at their disposal is too slow for them, then they may properly agitate for a change in methods and machinery for more effectively and speedily meeting their problems.

Of course, public employees have the right to strike—if by that we mean that any individual has the right to quit his job. There is no general statutory prohibition outlawing strikes of public employees.[51] Whether or not they have the right, however, is beside the point. Unwillingness of public employees by concerted action to serve the public can hardly be condoned. There is no inherent right of public employees collectively to refuse to serve the people and still retain the privilege of continuing in the service of the people. We would not recognize the right of motorists to refuse to pay their automobile license fees but still insist upon the privilege of running their autos on the public highways merely because they did not like the gasoline tax. It is no less offensive to the public interest for an employee because of a strike to decline to run the elevators in a public office building than for a hospital nurse to leave a dying patient and join a strike parade. A motor bus operator of a city-owned transit line may no more abandon his bus full of passengers to join in a "sympathy strike," than may a fireman leave a burning building to answer a strike call.

Many mental gymnastics have been indulged in by those who should know better in attempting to distinguish between the rights and privileges of public employees in one and another type of government service. It is easy for them to postulate that a policeman or fireman or health officer should not have the right to strike because that would rob society of an imperative protection. They would distinguish the "usual" governmental function from services they consider proprietary. They seize upon the classic case of a public utility taken over by a municipality and see no reason why the employee relationship should change merely because the city operates the utility in place of the private company.

Those who argue thus forget that the people have not chosen to take over a public utility until public necessity required it.[52] A utility or function assumed by a city becomes a service for the people. Simultaneously, the relationship of employees to the people must perforce change. Many municipal functions and services of a proprietary nature have heretofore been accepted in the same light of "usual" government service as have the police, fire, and health agencies. Water supply services, collection of garbage, and similar services have been long performed by municipalities. What was not a public need yesterday may become one tomorrow. The rights and privileges of individual employees under private ownership must yield to the public interest. The people become the new "boss" and the employees the people's public servants. Attempts to distinguish between one kind of public function wherein employees may continue to have the rights accorded them as private employees, and another kind wherein such rights are denied, just begs the question....

NO "SUPER-AGENCY"

In private enterprise the relationship between employers and employees can always be subjected to government regulation, supervision, or even

---

[51] This is no longer true. Legislation passed in 1946 and in 1947 prohibits strikes by public employees in the federal government and in eleven states. [original Ed.]

[52] For an excellent inquiry into this assumption and into the realities of the internal life of organized interests, see Grant McConnell, *Private Power and American Democracy* (New York: Knopf, 1966); S.M. Lipset et al., *Union Democracy* (New York: Anchor, 1962); and Raymond Bauer et al., *American Business and Public Policy* (New York: Atherton, 1963).

control. There is no "super-agency" that can step in to control, regulate, or supervise disputes between public employees and the people except the people themselves, through their representatives. Public employees, like any other class of citizens, have an equal right through orderly processes under our democratic form of government to petition the legislature and public officials for redress of grievances, adjustment of claims, and acceptance of their views. To encourage any class of citizens to ignore, or abandon in defiance of authority, such orderly procedure to gain its ends, no matter how justified its action may appear to be, would defeat our democratic process.

The public must guard against a potential danger that may be as formidable and uncontrollable as our dubious political organization machines—a self-perpetuating labor dictatorship, which could conceivably overcome the will of the people through control of governmental machinery manned by public employees. This is not a possibility to be dismissed as too fantastic. Situations have already arisen in some jurisdictions which should warn us to apply the brakes immediately. . . . The concepts of labor relations common to private enterprise and the practices indulged in by capital and labor are not practicable or desirable in the civil service.

HAVE PUBLIC EMPLOYEES THE RIGHT TO STRIKE?—MAYBE
Sterling D. Spero

The right to strike is regarded as so important a factor in the maintenance of human freedom that the state guarantees its exercise despite the public inconvenience and the social dislocations which strikes frequently cause. Time and again American legislators have rejected proposals to abrogate that right. Anti-strike proposals got nowhere during the threatened railway tie-up of 1916 which led to the passage of the Adamson eight-hour law. Many anti-strike bills died in committee during World War I when this country was an actual participant. President Harding's suggestions to prevent railway strikes at the time of the shopmen's walkout in 1922 received no serious consideration. The present Congress, despite the articulateness of anti-labor members and their strong outside support, has not enacted anti-strike legislation affecting national defense industries.

When it comes to its own employees, however, the state takes a different attitude. "The right to strike against the government is not and cannot be recognized," declared Mayor LaGuardia during the recent transit controversy. "No government employee can strike against his government and thus against the whole people, " said President Hoover in the 1928 campaign. That government employees cannot strike, President Roosevelt told a press conference a few years ago, was "a matter of common sense." These are representative statements. It is significant that on this issue the conservative Herbert Hoover is in complete agreement with Mayor LaGuardia and President Roosevelt, whose political strength is in no small measure based on organized labor's support.

What is there about government employment which makes the denial of a right regarded as so essential elsewhere so apparently simple and obvious a proposition? Can the proposition be founded on the functions which government workers perform? These, on examination, appear little different from those of other workers.

The functions of government workers fall roughly into four broad catagories—administrative, industrial, service, and law enforcement. The administrative functions are similar to those which any business or institution must carry on in order to operate. They include filing, auditing, correspondence, clerical, and so-called office work of various kinds. These functions are incidental to the conduct of any establishment. Their wider importance is measured by the importance of the functions to which they are incidental.

The industrial functions of government are directly comparable with private industry. Battleships are built in navy yards and battleships are built in private plants. What logic is there in the government denying the right to strike in the former case and permitting the right in the latter? Ordnance is made at the Rock Island Arsenal, which is run by the army, and at the Midvale Steel and Ordnance Company's plant, which belongs to a private corporation. Why is it "common sense" to deny the right to strike at the arsenal and allow it at the company?

The service functions of the government—the conduct of utilities, educational institutions, hospitals, welfare agencies—likewise parallel or compete with the work of private organizations. Until last year New York had private and public subway lines. Strikes actually took place on the former lines some years ago. Yet when the city took over these same lines it was solemnly declared: "The right to strike against the government is not and cannot be recognized."

Those engaged in the administrative, service, and industrial functions of government account for the overwhelming majority of government employees. The comparatively small number which remain are engaged in the work of law enforcement, the only governmental activities not directly comparable with work outside. These are traditionally and peculiarly functions of public authority. Yet law enforcement is dependent upon far more than the work of policemen or public inspectors. Like all social processes in complex modern society it is dependent upon the running of the whole social machine. New York or Chicago could not be policed at night if employees of private lighting companies did not keep the lights on. Law could hardly be enforced and public order could hardly be maintained if privately owned transportation and communication systems ceased to operate.

The fact is that the continuity of governmental functions depends upon cooperation of society as a whole quite as much as the rest of society depends upon the functioning of government. In many instances the work of privately employed workers is actually of greater immediate social concern than the work of civil servants. Compare, for example, the immediate effects of a strike in the Department of the Interior or even a strike of public school teachers with a strike of privately employed milk drivers.

A CHALLENGE TO AUTHORITY

It thus becomes increasingly clear that government's denial of the right of its employees to strike cannot be based upon the ground of the harm which the cessation of their work might cause. It is based rather upon the ground that government as custodian of final authority in the land cannot permit those whom it hires to carry on its work to challenge its authority. The preservation of this concept of public authority is regarded as far more important than the immediate interests served by the functioning of particular agencies.

The famous Boston police strike in 1919 was caused because the responsible officials refused to accept a reasonable settlement which they regarded as compromising their authority. In the same year the city of Cincinnati forced a strike of its firemen in much the same way. In Colorado Springs, in the midst of a controversy over wages, the mayor dismissed the entire fire department without making any provision for the protection of the city. In all these cases, and in many similar ones, the wrath of the community was turned against the virtually locked-out employees, while the authorities who were responsible for the protection of the community were praised for defending law, order, and public authority.

The denial of the right of government workers to strike largely takes the form of statements by executive authorities. The only legislation on the subject, aside from two statutes enacted in the wake of the Boston police strike making it a misdemeanor for policemen or firemen of the District of Columbia to strike, is indirect. Federal employees are not forbidden to strike. The law merely states that "membership in any . . . labor organization of postal employees not affiliated with any outside organization imposing an obligation or duty upon them to engage in any strike, or proposing to assist them in any strike, against the United States" shall not constitute cause for reduction in rank or removal. This applies only to postal workers. No other class of federal employees is mentioned.

There are a number of other statutory provisions, both federal and state, which might be invoked to bar public service strikes although they were not enacted for such purpose. These deal principally with conspiracy against the government. The courts have never passed directly on the public service strike issue. . . . However, the courts have in a number of cognate cases involving undertakings affected with the public interest made their disapproval of such strikes so clear and defined the power of government to prevent or break them so broadly that there is little question as to how they would act if government workers should walk out.

NO STRIKE POLICY

One of the most significant aspects of the strike question in the government services is the attitude of the employees themselves. There is not a single organization in the United States composed entirely of government employees which has a strike policy. Those affiliated with either the A.F. of L. or the C.I.O. as well as some independent unions have no-strike provisions in their constitutions. Despite such provisions there have been some municipal strikes within the jurisdiction of these unions, particularly among fire fighters. As in private industry such strikes have been for better working conditions or for union recognition. Practically all such strikes occurred in the early stages of unionization when unsatisfactory working conditions which brought the union into being were still uncorrected or when the authorities attempted to break up the movement.

Most of the membership of organizations composed wholly of public employees is in the traditional services which are non-industrial in character. These organizations have sought their objectives through legislative means.

Some of these groups have lobbies of strength and influence. This is particularly true of the postal organizations, whose objective has been to carry the legislative method of fixing conditions as far as possible and to limit and narrow the discretion and authority of the supervisory officials. The postal workers feel that the influence of their lobby is substantial while their power in the department is slight. One reason for this, and this is true in some other government services also, is that the postal employee works for a government monopoly. There is no other business to which the special skills and training of a postal clerk would be of value. If he loses his government job he must seek an entirely different type of employment. This weakens him in his relations with the department.

WORKERS IN SERVICE

Quite the opposite, however, is true of the government's industrial workers. These are organized in the regular unions of their crafts, trades, or industries. a machinist or a pattern-maker can work in a navy yard or for a private firm. Washington printers or pressmen are not dependent upon even the huge Government Printing Office for employment. These workers view their governmental employer with none of the awe and respect that departmental clerks and administrators bestow upon him. They are members of their trade or industry first and government employees only incidentally. They can and do go from government jobs to private jobs and back again depending upon which employer has the better offer to make. These employees concede no special rights to the governmental employer. They insist upon their right to strike and have on occasion exercised it.

In most of these services, both federal and local, wages are fixed upon the basis of prevailing rates for comparable work through formal or informal collective bargaining or negotiation. The expansion of the public service into the field of economic activity, one of the marked characteristics of the day, will bring a larger and larger number of industrial workers into the service. Experience has already shown that they will not easily be cut to the pattern of the conventional civil servant and that they will not readily surrender methods of dealing with their employer which have proved successful. During the days of federal operation of the railroads during World War I railway workers resisted attempts to apply to them the federal rules on political activity in the civil service. They struck even during war time against the United States Railroad Administration.

The attitude of the transit workers in New York City is another case in point. Here, despite all the protestations of the press and the local administration that the city could not bargain with its workers and that it would not yield to strike threats, the city yielded when the strike date approached and entered into negotiations with its organized employees.

It is, of course, impossible to guess whether the union would have struck if the city had not yielded on all essential points. It is significant that the union twice in a little over a year went to the extent of authorizing a strike in the face of most explicit denials of the right by the municipal authorities.

THE RIGHT TO STRIKE

It is clear that no mere denial of the right to strike will of itself prevent strikes if workers regard their grievances sufficiently great to assume the risks. Strikes under such circumstances damage the authority of the sovereign, the very thing the denial of the right to strike seeks to preserve. The governmental employer, in order to maintain his authority in the face of illegal strikes, must demonstrate his power by punishing the offending workers and calling upon his military forces to break the strike and restore operations. The generally undesirable consequences of such procedure hardly require elaborate description.

The state, of course, has the right, where the necessity of maintaining its existence and preserving public peace, order, and safety require it, to use its military arm, but such circumstances are as likely to result through interruptions in private industry as in the public service. At any rate the use of military power is an extreme and extraordinary measure to be resorted to only under exceptional circumstances.

When the state denies its workers the right to strike merely because they are government employees, it defines common labor disputes as attacks upon public authority and makes the use of drastic disciplines and armed force a method of handling otherwise simple industrial relations.

The use of the state's ultimate force for the protection of the public interest is different from the subordination of a large and growing section of the labor movement to governmental power. Such subordination is a dominant characteristic of totalitarian society. If the government services were small and inconsequential the issue would still be of importance. But with the public services in all their branches employing one tenth of all the wage earners in the land, and expanding at an ever-increasing rate, the issue becomes one of major moment. A free labor movement among these millions of workers is their only effective check upon the greatly enhanced power which expanding governmental activity gives to public authorities.

The power motive, recent history teaches, is as important an exploiting force as ever was the profit motive. Labor is thus faced with a serious dilemma if the government insists upon denying it that right which is the ultimate guarantee of its freedom. An expanding public service will mean a creeping totalitarian trend as a larger and larger section of the working population is obliged to surrender its ultimate right to strike as a consequence of its public employment. This is one great danger.

There is also another danger. The labor movement may, in order to preserve its freedom, resist the expansion of government activity, thus creating a disintegrating social trend by rendering government ineffective to meet the problems of the times. Both of these possibilities present infinitely greater threats to our society than the remote possibility of a labor dispute which might result in the temporary interruption of some government service.

PART 4

Independent Civil Servants and the Rule of Law

The material presented in the previous section can all be understood as bearing on the general issue of responsibility and control of public administration. This general issue will continue indefinitely to draw the attention of serious people because it cannot be resolved in a simple way, nor can either of the two relevant considerations be sacrificed to the other. That is, the effective administration of the public will does require in practice something like the rule of politically neutral merit. The experience of this country prior to the Pendleton Act proves that proposition beyond reasonable doubt. However, every step we take in the direction of shielding civil servants from the wrong sort of political control, from corrupt politics, must also in practice operate as a barrier against legitimate and proper instruments of political control. The attempt to discover in just what way civil servants are to be held politically responsible, and at just what level of responsibility, will always have to depend on the lessons of partially relevant experience adapted to changing circumstances.

There is, however, an additional consideration regarding the effect of neutral public administration and *politics* that carries beyond the scope of responsibility and control, although it involves these things. This consideration arises most obviously in connection with the independent regulatory commissions, although it is present in every instance of wide, discretionary authority being exercised by public administrators under broad grants from the legislature. Here the concern is only indirectly for democratic, political control. Primarily it is the rule of law that is thought to be threatened. The classic argument was made by Friedrich von Hayek, for example in his *Road to Serfdom*. Hayek observes a distinction between two alternative modes of exercising authority. On one hand, the authority may be given an end and charged to find and implement the means that its practical reasoning tells it are appropriate. This, of course, is in the nature of administration. On the other hand, authority may simply proscribe certain behavior, irrespective of whatever defense might be offered for it as serving a good end. This sort of authority is in the nature of law. Thus an example of a law would be "Thou shalt not kill." The law flatly proscribes what otherwise might be done, presumably for some useful purpose.

Hayek has shown, rather convincingly, that the rule of law is practically incompatable with comprehensive social and economic planning of the type engaged by British socialists. The United States has encountered the issue for itself at various times, especially in its attempts at wage and/or price controls. Hayek proposed, therefore, that the rule of law should be strengthened and defended as a way of preserving the vitality of the free market economy. Moreover, Hayek showed that democracy also hangs in the balance, because it is practically inconceivable that democratic self-government could operate except according to the modality of law. That is because we can imagine a people directly forbidding themselves certain behavior; but if instead they only authorize an administrator to figure out the best means to bring about an end, they are in fact more subject to the rule of "experts" than to themselves. Still, ultimately Hayek's defense of the rule of law is rooted in neither the requirements of economic prosperity nor democracy; and he warns against over-valuing either of these things. *The* importance of the rule of law is personal freedom, a term which Hayek defines in the manner of a classic Liberal as freedom from *arbitrary* authority.

Hayek is today almost a patron saint of the conservative disposition. It is therefore interesting that his argument has been adopted and given a somewhat progressive spin by Theodore Lowi, in his *The End of Liberalism*. Lowi avers no disagreement with Hayek, and in fact cites him approvingly. Still, what especially bothers Lowi about what he too senses as the near abandonment of the rule of law is that it allows public policy to be made through a brokering of the special interests most directly concerned, to the exclusion of the general public or the public's interest. Independent regulatory commissions and administrative agencies exercising wide discretion are in practice always going to be captives of the specific interests that they ought to govern. The solutions Lowi offers are a return to and vigorous enforcement of the rule in *A.L.A. Schecter Poultry Corp. v. United States* (1935) wherein the Supreme Court tried to articulate a Constitutional limit on Congress' power to delegate authority to administrative agenies. Where it is simply impossible for Congress to recover the authority it has allowed to be farmed out, Lowi recommends that bureaus and agencies themselves behave in a more lawful mode, i.e. to dictate and develop administrative law. In the context of this abbreviated suggestion Lowi asserts his admiration for Kenneth Culp Davis' *Administrative Law Treatise*, which is probably the most authoritative work in the field.

While not as influential as Hayek, Lowi's work has certainly struck a responsive chord with a wide audience. For these two writers to have been so well regarded by such different, even opposing, camps suggests either that at least one of them is inconsistent or that the position from which they both start may be question-begging. In fact, their position *is* question-begging. The fundamental advantages that both Hayek and Lowi see as belonging to the rule of law, its simplicity and generality, are really just the positive consequences of its crudeness, and sometimes that makes it insufficient. Sometimes discretion in its administration is a practical necessity. Does the United States suffer from too much administrative discretion? Is this even a meaningful question? Does the *Schecter* case really offer a rule that can distinguish legitimate from illegitimate discretion? Could there be such a rule?

The selections offered here include two statements, by the Brownlow

Commission and the First Hoover Commission, expressing concern over the independence of the independent regulatory commissions. Following is a selection from Lowi's *End of Liberalism* wherein he identifies "interest-group liberalism" as the consequence of the gradual weakening of the rule of law. Shortly after its publication, Harvey Mansfield Jr. subjected Lowi's book to a searching and far-reaching criticism in which he argued that Lowi's antipathy towards the special interests and his defense of law is in fact an unwitting sophistry. The sophistry is that whereas Lowi calls for a government that is willing and able to face the issue of social justice directly and enact policies that are unabashedly moral, he does not actually make an argument in behalf of any substantive moral conclusions or show that any particular distribution of good and bad is just. Mansfield also argued that the sophistical character of Lowi's argument is a consequence of Lowi's not being able to think beyond the limits of Liberalism, and its abstraction from the issue of justice. This judgment leads Mansfield to criticize Lowi's rhetoric as damaging to the decent *modus vivendi* that is the best one can hope for among members of a Liberal society.

If in the performance of their day-to-day duties public administrators must sometimes operate with reference to the notion of the public's interest, or common good, it would be well for them to have considered carefully Lowi's argument, together with Mansfield's critique—to have digested them slowly and with repeated rumination. The debate helps us think through the meaning of Liberal government's abstraction from the question of the common good, and hence to gain a perspective on that question that is more sophisticated than either moralistic naivete or jaded cynicism. We can be grateful for its existence.

THE HEADLESS "FOURTH BRANCH"

The President's Committee on Administrative Management

[From *Report of the Committee with Studies of Administrative Management in the Federal Government*, 1937, pp. 39–42. Published by the United States Government Printing Office, Washington, D. C.]

Beginning with the Interstate Commerce Commission in 1887, the Congress has set up more than a dozen independent regulatory commissions to exercise the control over commerce and business necessary to the orderly conduct of the Nation's economic life. These commissions have been the result of legislative groping rather than the pursuit of a consistent policy. This is shown by the wide variety in their structure and functions and also by the fact that just as frequently the Congress has given regulatory functions of the same kind to the regular executive departments.

These independent commissions have been given broad powers to explore, formulate, and administer policies of regulation; they have been given the task of investigating and prosecuting business misconduct; they have been given powers, similar to those exercised by courts of law, to pass in concrete cases upon the rights and liabilities of individuals under the statutes. They are in reality miniature independent governments set up to deal with the railroad problem, the banking problem, or the radio problem. They constitute a

headless "fourth branch" of the Government, a haphazard deposit of irresponsible agencies and uncoordinated powers. They do violence to the basic
theory of the American Constitution that there should be three major branches
of the Government and only three. The Congress has found no effective way
of supervising them, they cannot be controlled by the President, and they are
answerable to the courts only in respect to the legality of their activities.

MIXTURE OF EXECUTIVE AND JUDICIAL FUNCTIONS

The independent regulatory commissions create a confusing and difficult situation in the field of national administration. There is a conflict of principle involved in their make-up and functions. They suffer from an internal
inconsistency, an unsoundness of basic theory. This is because they are vested
with duties of administration and policy determination with respect to which
they ought to be clearly and effectively responsible to the President, and at the
same time they are given important judicial work in the doing of which they
ought to be wholly independent of Executive control. In fact, the bulk of regulatory commission work involves the application of legislative "standards" of
conduct to concrete cases, a function at once discretionary and judicial, and
demanding, therefore, both responsibility and independence.

The evils resulting from this confusion of principles are insidious and
far-reaching. In the first place, governmental powers of great importance are
being exercised under conditions of virtual irresponsibility. We speak of the
"independent" regulatory commissions. It would be more accurate to call them
the "irresponsible" regulatory commissions, for they are areas of unaccount-
ability. It is not enough to point out that these irresponsible commissions have
of their own volition been honest and competent. Power without responsibility has no place in a government based on the theory of democratic control,
for responsibility is the people's only weapon, their only insurance against
abuse of power.

But though the commissions enjoy power without responsibility, they also
leave the President with responsibility without power. Placed by the Constitution at the head of a unified and centralized Executive Branch, and charged
with the duty to see that the laws are faithfully executed, he must detour around
powerful administrative agencies which are in no way subject to his authority
and which are, therefore, both actual and potential obstructions to his effective
over-all management of national administration. The commissions produce
confusion, conflict, and incoherence in the formulation and in the execution of
the President's policies. Not only by constitutional theory, but by the steady and
mounting insistence of public opinion, the President is held responsible for the
wise and efficient management of the Executive Branch of the Government.
The people look to him for leadership. And yet we whittle away the effective
control essential to that leadership by parceling out to a dozen or more irresponsible agencies important powers of policy and administration.

At the same time the independent commission is obliged to carry on
judicial functions under conditions which threaten the impartial performance
of that judicial work. The discretionary work of the administrator is merged
with that of the judge. Pressures and influences properly enough directed toward officers responsible for formulating and administering policy constitute
an unwholesome atmosphere in which to adjudicate private rights. But the

mixed duties of the commissions render escape from these subversive influences impossible.

Furthermore, the same men are obliged to serve both as prosecutors and as judges. This not only undermines judicial fairness; it weakens public confidence in that fairness. Commission decisions affecting private rights and conduct lie under the suspicion of being rationalizations of the preliminary findings which the commission, in the role of prosecutor, presented to itself.

The independent commission, in short, provides the proper working conditions neither for administration nor for adjudication. It fails to provide responsibility for the first; it does not provide complete independence for the second.

THE ADMINISTRATIVE PROBLEM

The independent commissions present a serious immediate problem. No administrative reorganization worthy of the name can leave hanging in the air more than a dozen powerful, irresponsible agencies free to determine policy and administer law. Any program to restore our constitutional ideal of a fully coordinated Executive Branch responsible to the President must bring within the reach of that responsible control all work done by these independent commissions which is not judicial in nature. That challenge cannot be ignored.

At the same time, the commissions present a long-range problem of equal or even greater seriousness. This is because we keep on creating them. Congress is always tempted to turn each new regulatory function over to a new independent commission. This is not only following the line of least resistance; it is also following a fifty-year-old tradition. The multiplication of these agencies cannot fail to obstruct the effective over-all management of the Executive Branch of the Government almost in geometric ratio to their number. At the present rate we shall have forty to fifty of them within a decade. Every bit of executive and administrative authority which they enjoy means a relative weakening of the President, in whom, according to the Constitution, "the executive power shall be vested." As they grow in number his stature is bound to diminish. He will no longer be in reality the Executive, but only one of many executives, threading his way around obstacles which he has no power to overcome.

We have watched the growth of boards and commissions transform the executive branches of our State governments into grotesque agglomerations of independent and irresponsible units, bogged by the weight and confusion of the whole crazy structure. The same tendency in national administration will bring the same disastrous results. That tendency should be stopped.

It is imperative that we discover some technique or principle by which the work done by our present regulatory commissions, together with such new regulatory tasks as arise in the future, may be handled without the loss of responsibility for policy and administration and without the undermining of judicial neutrality. Is there not some way to retain the major advantages that the commissions aim to secure and, at the same time, to get rid of their basic unsoundness?

REDISTRIBUTION OF FUNCTIONS

The following proposal is put forward as a possible solution of the independent commission problem, present and future. Under this proposed plan

the regulatory agency would be set up, not in a governmental vacuum outside the executive departments, but within a department. There it would be
divided into an administrative section and a judicial section. The administrative section would be a regular bureau or division in the department, headed
by a chief with career tenure and staffed under civil-service regulations. It
would be directly responsible to the Secretary and through him to the President. The judicial section, on the other hand, would be "in" the department
only for purposes of "administrative housekeeping," such as the budget, general personnel administration, and material. It would be wholly independent
of the department and the President with respect to its work and its decisions.
Its members would be appointed by the President with the approval of the
Senate for long, staggered terms and would be removable only for causes
stated in the statute.

The division of work between the two sections would be relatively simple.
The first procedural steps in the regulatory process as now carried on by the
independent commissions would go to the administrative section. It would
formulate rules, initiate action, investigate complaints, hold preliminary hearings, and by a process of sifting and selection prepare the formal record of
cases which is now prepared in practice by the staffs of the commissions. It
would, of course, do all the purely administrative or sub-legislative work now
done by the commissions--in short, all the work which is not essentially judicial in nature. The judicial section would sit as an impartial, independent body
to make decisions affecting the public interest and private rights upon the
basis of the records and findings presented to it by the administrative section.
In certain types of cases where the volume of business is large and quick and
routine action is necessary, the administrative section itself should in the first
instance decide the cases and issue orders, and the judicial section should sit
as an appellate body to which such decisions could be appealed on questions
of law.

This proposed plan meets squarely the problems presented by the independent commissions. It creates effective responsibility for the administrative
and policy-determining aspects of the regulatory job and, at the same time,
guarantees the complete independence and neutrality for that part of the work
which must be performed after the manner of a court. It facilitates and strength-
ens administrative management without lessening judicial independence.

The plan has, furthermore, the great advantage of adaptability to varying conditions. With the administrative and judicial sections under the roof of
the same department, the details of their organization could be worked out
experimentally by Executive order. The precise division of labor between them
could also be readily modified in the light of experience, and the shifting of a
function from one section to the other would not raise the major jurisdictional
controversies that sometimes result from proposals to alter the status or duties of an independent commission.

Furthermore, the principle of the plan does not have to be applied with
exact uniformity to every commission. The requirement and present practices
of each commission may be taken into consideration in carrying out this principle.

There is nothing essentially novel or startling about the proposed plan.
There are numerous precedents and analogies which refute the suggestion
that it is revolutionary or dangerous.

In the first place, we should remember that for thirty years important regulatory functions have been carried on by the executive departments. The powers of the Secretary of Agriculture under the Packers and Stockyards Act are essentially the same in nature and importance as those of the regulatory commissions. And there are over twenty regulatory laws similarly administered. By common consent the departments have done this work well. And yet, under this arrangement the judicial phases of the regulatory process, involving important rights of property, are handled by politically responsible, policy-determining officials, a system far more open to attack than the proposed plan which carefully places the adjudication of private rights in an independent judicial section.

In the second place, the idea of giving those phases of the administrative process which involve policy and discretion to a different agency from that which issues orders or makes decisions after the manner of a court is a very old one. We find this principle working comfortably in our legislative courts, such as the Customs Court and the Court of Claims, or in that pseudo-court, the Board of Tax Appeals. These bodies decide cases originating in the process of administration and presented to them by administrative officers. It is true that they are not handling cases which are precisely the same as those coming before our regulatory commissions, but they are established as they are in order that the functions of administration need not be imposed upon the officials who are charged with the adjudication of private rights and the public interest. This same segregation of function lies at the heart of the proposed plan.

A groping after the same principle is found, in the third place, in those departments and agencies in which have been set up appellate bodies, judicialized in varying degrees, which sift and review the preliminary decisions and orders of administrative officers. This device has long been in operation in the Patent Office, the Immigration and Naturalization Service, the Veterans' Administration, the Treasury, and elsewhere. Here again we recognize the desirability of separating the task of ultimate decisions upon private rights from the preliminary steps in which there is a larger element of administrative discretion.

Finally, a close scrutiny of the way in which the more important regulatory commissions handle their work indicates that the division of functions between the proposed administrative and judicial sections is merely a formalizing by statutory enactment of the division of labor that has already been set up within the commissions themselves. In nearly every case the commissioners devote the major part of their time and energy to the deciding of cases and the issuance of orders on the basis of the records and findings prepared by the examiners, attorneys, and other officers making up the commission's staff. The division of labor is, of course, very rough and tentative, and there is no corresponding division of responsibility between the commissioners and their subordinates. But the fact that that division of labor has emerged, not under any legal compulsion, but because it has proved a normal and convenient method of getting the commission's work done, is significant for our present purposes.

The process of setting the proposed plan in motion would in a sense be merely the following of a path already roughly picked out. The present commissioners as a body would assume the status of a judicial section. The present staff of the commission under a responsible administrative chief could, with a minimum of disruption, be molded into an administrative section. It is difficult to see how the transition could be very disturbing or why the plans should not work smoothly and efficiently.

USE OF THE INDEPENDENT REGULATORY COMMISSION

First Hoover Commission's Task Force on Regulatory Commissions

[From *Commission on Organization of the Executive Branch of the Government, Task Force Report on Regulatory Commissions,* 1949, pp. 18-28 (abridged). Published by the United States Government Printing Office, Washington, D. C.]

In view of the strong criticisms made in the 1937 Report of the President's Committee on Administrative Management, we have considered the needs for independent regulatory commissions and their advantages, and have investigated whether their disadvantages outweigh any benefits they may offer. In particular, as outlined below, we sought to find whether the independence of these agencies has caused serious failures in coordination between them and the executive branch.

Finding. On the basis of the actual experience revealed in the staff reports, we have concluded that the independent commission is a useful type of agency for regulation under certain conditions and should be continued for such specialized tasks.

This chapter sets forth our reasons for these conclusions.

A. NATURE OF THE REGULATORY TASKS

The most basic fact about the independent regulatory commissions is the similarity of the situations with which they were designed to deal. The differences among the fields assigned to each agency are obvious, but the underlying likeness in the character of their problems is even more striking.

In each case, Congress was convinced that the industry or activity required Federal regulation to correct existing or threatened abuses. Congress could specify generally the kinds of regulation to be imposed, but its ability to legislate detailed rules was limited. For example, with respect to carriers or utilities it could direct the regulation of rates, service, entry into the field, financial structures, and the relations between competing carriers. In varying degrees it has so directed with respect to railroads, motor carriers, air carriers, water carriers, pipe lines, telephone and telegraph service, gas pipe lines, and electrical utilities.

Or, in another field, Congress could determine to prohibit methods of competition which are not socially desirable or activities of employers or employees which impede collective bargaining.

Or Congress could decide that securities issues should be regulated to insure full disclosure of information for investors, or that securities exchanges should be supervised to insure a fair market free from improper practices. Again, Congress can decide that credit and money should be controlled in the public interest.

Congress can prescribe broad standards to carry out these purposes. Thus it can direct that rates be fair and just; that service be reasonable; that carriers or utilities should be allowed to enter the business only when it will serve public convenience and necessity; and that the entrant must be fit, willing, and able to perform the service. It can forbid unfair methods or practices and may be able to specify some of the activities forbidden.

But in these fields Congress can seldom prescribe detailed rules which are self-enforcing. What is a fair rate depends on many circumstances; and these circumstances may change as time passes and economic conditions or the technology of the industry change. The same is true of reasonable service. Similarly, whether a carrier or utility should be allowed to serve a particular route or area depends on many factors which will vary as the industry evolves, the need for such service grows or declines, and so forth.

Thus effective regulation does not permit a rigid and detailed statute.

In the first place, Congress cannot possibly devote the time and effort which would be required to develop an intelligent scheme of detailed rules at the time the statute is adopted. To do so would require expertness which members of legislature could hardly achieve along with the discharge of their other duties.

In the second place, even if time and skill were available, the solution of many of these problems of regulation can be worked out only by trial and error, and thus could not be embodied in a definitive statute unless Congress were prepared to devote continuous attention to adapting and applying the statute in the light of experience.

In the third place, the conditions of the industry and the economic context in which it operates are constantly changing in some degree. In some fields, such as air carriers or communications, the rate of development is so rapid as to be staggering. In others, such as railroads, conditions change more slowly but still change as new and competing services develop.

The upshot is that Congress must delegate wide latitude to some agency in order to keep regulation in such areas sufficiently flexible and adapted to the varying conditions and methods.

B. ADVANTAGES OF INDEPENDENT COMMISSIONS

The delegation of discretionary power to regulate private business activities creates certain basic problems in ensuring that regulation is administered fairly and so as not to impede operations unduly. The independent commission finds its justification in meeting these problems.

Impartiality of Regulation

The wide latitude in effective regulation opens the door to favoritism and unfairness in administration. The regulated interests are powerful and often influential. The privileges which the regulatory agencies can grant or withhold are often of great value, and regulation will obviously have a tremendous impact on the profits, service, and finances of the industry involved.

This combination of wide discretion on the part of officials, and strong motives for influencing the officials on the part of the regulated industry, involve serious risks of corruption and unfairness. If the agency is subject to partisan or political influence or control, this will not only defeat the public purposes of regulation and unfairly benefit the influential, but will also tend to impair the public confidence in the democratic process and the effectiveness of government acting generally. Thus, in the interest of fairness to the individuals concerned, of attainment of the public objectives, and of the maintenance of the integrity of government, there is a vital necessity for assuring that such regulatory agencies are insulated from partisan influence or control to the maximum extent feasible.

The independent commission was designed to meet this need. The number of members and their security of tenure are intended to assure freedom from partisan control or favoritism. The group is able to resist outside influence more effectively than an individual and each member is free from a threat of removal as a source of pressure. Moreover, since the activities of the commission may be more subject to public scrutiny than would be a single bureau in a large department, there is a greater opportunity for exposure of pressures or improper actions. Finally, while provisions for hearings and similar safeguards against arbitrary actions are not peculiar to commissions, they may be more effective when combined with group action.

So far as our staff reports and the comments of others have revealed, the independent commissions have largely achieved freedom from direct partisan influence in the administration of their statutes. With few exceptions, the actions of the commission appear to be above suspicion of favoritism or partiality. Our examination does not indicate any significant effort on the part of the President to interfere with the specific decisions of any of these agencies. In some instances, the President appears to have interested himself in the general policies of some of the agencies and to have had some influence on them. The propriety of such influence will be discussed in the next chapter of the report.

Many members of Congress, however, appear to feel free to concern themselves, on behalf of their constituents, with the handling of specific cases. The staff reports indicate that all these agencies receive such inquires regarding matters ending before them. Many of these take the form of requests for expediting decisions or obtaining prompt action by the commissions. As far as appears, such requests do not seem to have improperly influenced the action of most of the commissions. Doubtless, many of these inquiries are casual or routine without any threat of pressure, but others imply or suggest more active interest. In any event, such activity creates an unhealthy atmosphere for the commissions to carry on their work in, and tends to impair their reputation for nonpartisan and impartial administration.

Group Policy Making and Decisions

A distinctive attribute of commission action is that it requires concurrence by a majority of members of equal standing after full discussion and deliberation. At its best, each decision reflects the combined judgment of the group after critical analysis of the relevant facts and divergent views. This provides both a barrier to arbitrary or capricious action and a source of decisions based on different points of view and experience.

This process had definite advantages where the problems are complex, where the relative weight of various factors affecting policy is not clear, and where the range of choice is wide. A single official can consult his staff but does not have to convince others to make his views or conclusions prevail.

The member of the commission must expose his reasons and judgments to the critical scrutiny of his fellow members and must persuade them to his point of view. He must analyze and understand the views of his colleagues if only to refute them.

Experience indicates that these advantages have been in large measure achieved by the commissions. The several members often bring to light aspects missed by the staff or their colleagues. Each brings to bear a different background and experience, and sometimes a specialized knowledge. Deliberation has certainly reduced the likelihood of capricious decision, and promoted objectivity.

But group action has its disadvantages as well. Undoubtedly, decisions are more time-consuming, especially as the number of members increases. The necessity for considering various approaches and points of view and attempting to resolve them into a group decision inevitably takes substantial time.

One consequence may be slowness by the commission in reaching individual decisions or difficulty in disposing of a large volume of cases. The Labor Board presents such a situation largely because the heavy work load is larger than can be handled by such methods. The Interstate Commerce Commission has also been criticized for the length of time it takes after cases are submitted for decision. But in most agencies this is not a pressing problem.

The cost of group action appears more clearly in the areas of neglect or omission. As will be discussed later, the commissions tend to concentrate too exclusively on decision of the day-to-day cases without fitting them into a framework of more basic issues of program, standards, and planning.

Because the deliberative process is time-consuming, it seems clear that it should be used only where its special advantages are necessary.

Yet, as will appear from later discussion, the commissions have gene rally failed to restrict its use to such areas, and have tended to handle as a group many matters which can be dealt with more expeditiously and efficiently by an individual. This is especially true of administrative matters and routine actions. As a result, too little time has frequently been available for thorough discussion and deliberation of the more fundamental issues for which group judgment is uniquely useful. Our recommendations later in this report attempt to deal with this problem.

Finding. Despite the cost of the method of consultation and deliberation, we are convinced that it is a valuable process for arriving at wise policies and decisions in areas allowing so wide a choice. It is one of the major contributions of the commission form to sound regulation

Familiarity or Expertness

The purpose of regulation should be to correct or prevent abuses without impeding the effective operation of the industry or imposing unnecessary expense or waste. This can be done only if regulation is framed with knowledge of the conditions of the industry. Otherwise, the rules will either fail to achieve their purposes or needlessly interfere with private management.

As has been said, the regulated industry is frequently complex or highly technical. Its problems can be understood only on the basis of constant study and analysis of the developments in the industry. Thus the regulating agency must be able to give continuous attention to the area of regulation in order to achieve this essential familiarity or expertness.

The commission form is designed to assure expertness or at least familiarity with the problems of the regulated field both through the members of the commission and through the staff. Devoting their full time to the particular industry or activity, the staff and members become fully familiar with the technical aspects of the industry and its basic problems through their day-to-day contacts. . . .

Continuity of Policy

So long as the regulated industry remains in private hands, one other objective is essential. Despite public regulations, the private managers remain responsible for operation of the industry. They must take the initiative in introducing new and improved methods and in expanding the operations of their companies to meet the future demands for service. In order to enable private industry to plan ahead, the regulatory agency must seek to achieve as much stability in policy and methods as is consistent with continuously adapting regulations to meet changing conditions. So far as feasible, managers should be able to rely on uniformity and continuity of underlying policy.

In the independent commission, this objective is sought largely through the number and tenure of the members of the commission. The long terms expiring at staggered intervals, and the restraints on removal of members are designed to assure that the composition of the commission changes slowly despite changes in administration. Thus, as has been said, the older members and the staff are available to educate the new appointees in the problems of the industry and the policies of the commission. Moreover there is less likelihood of sudden change in policy since decisions are made by group consultive action. . . .

C. COORDINATION WITH ACTIVITIES OF OTHER AGENCIES

Nature of the Problem

One of the objections most frequently asserted against the independent commission is that its freedom from direct responsibility to the President prevents effective discharge of his duties and impairs coordination of the activities and policies of these agencies with those of other parts of the executive branch. Frequently, this criticism appears to be based mainly on theoretical or doctrinal grounds and not on actual failures of coordination or conflicts among agencies.

The brief review in the preceding chapter of the limitations on the independence of these commissions indicates that the notion that they operate in complete isolation from the remainder of the Government is unreal; in fact the extent of independence is a matter of degree. The members of the commissions are clearly not under the direction of the President as members of his Cabinet are considered to be, but they are subject to the powers of the President and Congress over appointments and other matters already discussed, and to the influence of public opinion.

One of the major purposes of our staff studies was to discover, so far as possible, whether lack of coordination is a serious problem in the practical operation of the Government. Each of the staff reports reveals how the varied pressures or influences on the independent commissions have tended to keep them operating within the framework of general policy and objectives prevailing at the particular time, and to prevent most of the theoretical difficulties implicit in independence aside from these practical constraints. . . .

Finding. The point to be emphasized here is that the study of the separate agencies forces the conclusions that lack of coordination is not an insuperable obstacle with respect to the independent commission. As has already been stated, some problems do exist and should be dealt with. But on the whole, coordination is needed in more limited areas than might be supposed a priori, and has been achieved in most of the major fields through interdepartmental committees or more informal techniques.

D. SUMMARY CONCLUSION ON THE USE OF INDEPENDENT COMMISSIONS

The preceding discussion sets forth our reasons for concluding that the independent commission has an essential place for certain types of governmental regulation. On the basis of experience, it appears to have definite advantages. Where regulation requires constant adaptation to changing economic and industry conditions, and wide discretion must be delegated to the administrative agency, the independent commission provides a means for insulating administration from partisan influence or favoritism and obtaining the benefits of continuity of attention and consultative judgments.

In reaching this conclusion we do not suggest that the advantages of this type of agency have been fully realized under all conditions or in all cases. Like other institutions, this one has had its ups and downs. The performance of some of the commissions is far better than that of the others. And, as discussed later, the administration of a number of the commissions has left much to be desired. But to a large degree these agencies do seem to have achieved many of the advantages which led to their creation.

We have also concluded that the independence of these commissions does not create insoluble problems of coordination with the rest of the Government which should prevent their use for tasks calling for their special advantages. On this question, the actual experience is far more convincing than theory.

INTEREST-GROUP LIBERALISM

Theodore Lowi

[From Theodore Lowi, *The End of Liberalism* 2nd ed. (New York: W.W. Norton & Company, 1979) pp. 50-63. Reprinted by permission of the author and publisher.]

The frenzy of governmental activity in the 1960s and 1970s proved that once the constitutional barriers were down the American national government was capable of prompt response to organized political demands. However, that is only the beginning of the story, because the almost total democratization of the Constitution and the contemporary expansion of the public sector has been accompanied by expansion, not contradiction, of a sense of distrust toward public objects. Here is a spectacular paradox. It is as though each new program or program expansion had been an admission of prior governmental inadequacy or failure without itself being able to make any

significant contribution to order to well-being. It is as though prosperity had
gone up at an arithmetic rate while expectations, and therefore frustrations,
had been going up at a geometric rate—in a modern expression of Malthusian
Law. Public authority was left to grapple with this alienating gap between
expectations and reality.

Why did the expansion of government that helped produce and sustain
prosperity also help produce a crisis of public authority? The explanation pursued throughout this volume is that the old justifications for expansion had too
little to say beyond the need for the expansion itself. An appropriate public
philosophy would have addressed itself to the purposes to which the expanded
governmental authority should be dedicated. It would also have addressed itself to the forms and procedures by which that power could be utilized. These
questions are so alien to public discourse in the United States that merely to
raise them is to be considered reactionary, apolitical, or totally naive.

Out of the emerging crisis of public authority developed an ersatz political formula that bears no more relation to those questions than the preceding political formula. The guidance the new formula offers to policy formulations is a set of sentiments that elevated a particular view of the political process above everything else. The ends of government and the justification of
one policy or procedure over another are not to be discussed. The process of
formulation is justified in itself. As observed earlier it takes the pluralist notion that government is an epiphenomenon of politics and makes out of that a
new ethics of government.

There are several possible names for the new public philosophy. A strong
candidate would be *corporatism*, but its history as a concept gives it several
unwanted connotations, such as conservative Catholicism or Italian fascism.
Another candidate is *syndicalism*, but among many objections is the connotations of anarchy too far removed from American experience. From time to
time other possible labels will be experimented with, but, since the new American public philosophy is something of an amalgam of all of the candidates,
some new terminology seems to be called for.

The most clinically accurate term to capture the American variant of all
these tendencies is *interest-group liberalism*. It is liberalism because it is optimistic about government, expects to use government in a positive and expansive role, is motivated by the highest sentiments, and possesses a strong faith
that what is good for government is good for the society. It is interest-group
liberalism because it sees as both necessary and good a policy agenda that is
accessible to all organized interest and makes no independent judgement of
their claims. It is interest-group liberalism because it defines the public interest as a result of the amalgamation of various claims. A brief sketch of the
working model of interest-group liberalism turns out to be a vulgarized version of the pluralist model of modern political science: (1) Organized interests
are homogenous and easy to define. Any duly elected representative of any
interest is taken as an accurate representative of each and every member.[1] (2)
Organized interests emerge in every sector of our lives and adequately repre-

---

[1] For an excellent inquiry into this assumption and into the realities of the internal life
of organized interests, see Grant McConnell, *Private Power and American Democracy* (New York: Knopf, 1966); S.M. Lipset et al., *Union Democracy* (New York:
Anchor, 1962); and Raymond Bauer et al., *American Business and Public Policy* (New
York: Atherton, 1963).

sent most of those sectors, so that one organized group can be found effectively answering and checking some other organized group as it seeks to prosecute its claims against society.[2] And (3) the role of government is one of insuring access to the most effectively organized, and of ratifying the agreements and adjustments worked out among the competing leaders.

This last assumption is supposed to be a statement of how a democracy works and how it ought to work. Taken together, these assumptions amount to little more than the appropriation of the Adam Smith "hidden hand" model for politics, where the group is the entrepreneur and the equilibrium is not lowest price but the public interest.

These assumptions are the basis of the new public philosophy. The policy behavior of old liberals and old conservatives, of Republicans and Democrats, so inconsistent with the old dialogue, is fully consistent with the criteria drawn from interest-group liberalism: *The most important difference between liberals and conservatives, Republicans and Democrats, is to be found in the interest group they identify with. Congressmen are guided in their votes, presidents in their programs, and administrators in their discretion by whatever organized interest they have taken for themselves as the most legitimate; and that is the measure of the legitimacy of demands and the only necessary guidelines for the framing of the laws.*

It is one thing to recognize that these assumptions resemble the working methodology of modern political science. But is quite another to explain how this model was elevated from a hypothesis about political behavior to an ideology about how our democratic polity ought to work.

THE APPEALS OF INTEREST-GROUP LIBERALISM

The important inventors of modern techniques of government were less than inventive about the justifications for particular policies at particular times. For example, Keynes was neither a dedicated social reformer nor a political thinker with an articulated vision of the new social order.[3] Keynes helped discover the modern economic system and how to help maintain it, but his ideas and techniques could be used to support a whole variety of approaches and points of view:

> Collective bargaining, trade unionism, minimum-wage laws, hours legislation, social security, a progressive tax system, slum clearance and housing, urban redevelopment and planning, education reform, all these he accepted but they were not among his preoccupations. In no sense could he be called the father of the welfare state.[4]

These innovators may have been silent on the deeper justification for expanding government because of the difficulty of drawing justification from the doctrines of popular government and majority rule. Justification of posi-

---

2   It is assumed that countervailing power usually crops up somehow, but when it does not, government ought to help create it. See John Kenneth Galbraith, *American Capitalism* (Boston: Houghton Mifflin, 1952). Among a number of excellent critiques of the so-called pluralist model, see especially William E. Connolly, ed., *The Bias of Pluralism* (New York: Atherton 1969).

3   Alvin H. Hansen, *The American Economy* (New York: McGraw-Hill, 1957), p.152.

4   Ibid., pp. 158-59. Keynes himself said, "The Class War will find me on the side of the educated bourgeoisie" (Ibid., p. 158).

tive government programs on the basis of popular rule required, above all, a belief in and support of the supremacy of Congress. The Abdication of Congress in the 1930s and thereafter could never have been justified in the name of popular government; and, all due respect to members of Congress, they made no effort to claim such justification. Abdication to the Executive branch on economic matters and activism in the infringement of civil liberties produced further reluctance to fall back upon Congress and majority rule as the font of public policy justification. Many who wished nevertheless to have majority rule on their side sought support in the plebiscitary character of the presidency. However, presidential liberals have had to blind themselves to many complications in the true basis of presidential authority, and their faith in the presidency as a representative majority rule came almost completely unstuck during the late 1960s and thereafter.[5]

This is precisely what made interest-group liberalism so attractive. It had the approval of political scientists because it could deal with so many of the realities of power. It was further appealing because large interest groups and large memberships could be taken virtually as popular rule in modern dress. And it fit the needs of corporate leaders, union leaders, and government officials desperately searching for support as they were losing communal attachments to their constituencies. Herbert Hoover had spoken out eloquently against crass individualism and in favor of voluntary collectivism. His belief in this kind of collectivism is what led him to choose, among all his offers, to be Secretary of Commerce in 1921.[6] And the experts on government who were to become the intellectual core of the New Deal and later Democratic administrations were already supporting such views even before the election of Franklin D. Roosevelt. For example,

> [The national associations] represent a healthy democratic development. They rose in answer to certain needs.... They are part of our representative system.... These groups must be welcomed for what they are, and certain precautionary regulations worked out. The groups must be understood and their proper place in government allotted, if not by actual legislation, then by general public realization of their significance.[7]

After World War II, the academic and popular justifications for interest-group liberalism were still stronger. A prominent American government textbook of the period argued that the "basic concept for understanding the dynamics of government is the multi-group nature of modern society or the modern state."[8] By the time we left the 1960s, with the Democrats back in

---

[5] For a critique of the majoritarian basis of presidential authority see Willmoore Kendall, "The Two Majorities," *Midwest Journal of Political Science* 4 (1960): 317-45. The abdication by Congress to the Executive Branch will come up again and again throughout this volume.

[6] For an account of Herbert Hoover's political views and his close relationship to the New Deal, see Grant McConnell, *Private Power,* pp. 62 ff; and Peri Arnold, "Herbert Hoover and the Continuity of American Public Policy," *Public Policy* (Autumn 1972).

[7] E. Pendleton Herring, *Group Representation before Congress* (Baltimore; Johns Hopkins Press, 1929), p. 268. See his reflections of 1936 in Chapter 2 of that book.

[8] Wildfred Binkley and Malcom Moos, *A Grammar of American Politics* (New York: Knopf, 1950), p. 7. Malcolm Moos became an important idea man in the Eisenhower Administration.

power, the justifications for interest-group liberalism were more eloquent and authoritative than ever. Take two examples from among the most important intellectuals of the Democratic Party, writing around the time of the return of the Democrats to power in 1960. To John Kenneth Galbraith, "Private economic power is held in check by countervailing power of those who are subjected to it. The first begets the second."[9] Concentrated economic power stimulates power in opposition to it, resulting in a natural tendency toward equilibrium. This is not merely theoretical for Galbraith, although he could not possibly have missed its similarity to Adam Smith; Galbraith was writing a program of positive government action. He admitted that effective countervailing power was limited in the real world and proposed that where it was absent or too weak to do the job, government policy should seek out and support it and, where necessary, create the organizations capable of countervailing. It should be government policy to validate the pluralist theory.

Arthur Schlesinger summarized his views for us in a campaign tract written in 1960. To Schlesinger, the essential difference between the Democratic and Republican Parties is that the democratic Party is the truly multi-interest party:

> What is the essence of multi-interest administration? It is surely that the leading interests in society are all represented in the interior processes of policy formation—which can be done only if members or advocates of these interests are included in key positions of government.[10]

Schlesinger repeated the same theme in a more sober and reflective book written after John Kennedy's assassination. Following his account of the 1962 confrontation of President Kennedy with the steel industry and the later decision to cut taxes and cast off in favor of expansionary rather than stabilizing fiscal policy, Schlesinger concludes,

> The ideological debates of the past began to give way to a new agreement on the practicalities of managing a modern economy. There thus developed in the Kennedy years a national accord on economic policy—a new consensus which gave hope of harnessing government, business, and labor in rational partnership for a steadily expanding American economy.[11]

A significant point in the entire argument is that the Republicans would disagree with Schlesinger on the *facts* but not on the *basis* of his distinction. The typical Republican rejoinder would be simply that the Democratic administrations are not more multi-interest than Republican. In my opinion this would be almost the whole truth.

The appeal of interest-group liberalism is not simply that it is more realistic than earlier ideologies. There are several strongly positive reasons for its appeal. The first is that it helped flank the constitutional problems of federalism that confronted the expanding national state before the Constitution was completely democratized. A program like the Extension Service of the De-

---

[9] Galbraith, *American Capitalism*, p. 118.

[10] Arthur Schlesinger, Jr., *Kennedy or Nixon—Does It Make Any Difference?* (New York: Macmillan, 1960), p. 43.

[11] Arthur Schlesinger, *A Thousand Days*, as featured in the *Chicago Sun-Times*, January 23, 1966, section 2, p. 3.

partment of Agriculture got around the restrictions of the Interstate Commerce clause by providing for self-administration by a combination of land-grant colleges, local farmer and commerce associations, and organized commodity groups (see Chapter 4). These appeared to be so decentralized and permissive as to be hardly federal at all. With such programs we begin to see the ethical and conceptual mingling of the notion of organized private groups with the notions of local government and self-government. Ultimate, direct interest-group participation in government became synonymous with self-government; but at first it was probably a strategy to get around the inclination of the Supreme Court to block federal interventions in the economy.

A second positive appeal of interest-group liberalism, strongly related to the first, is that it helped solve a problem for the democratic politician in the modern state where the stakes are so high. This is the problem of enhanced conflict and how to avoid it. The contribution of politicians to society is their skill in resolving conflict. However, direct confrontations are sought only by so-called ideologues and outsiders. Typical American politicians displace and defer and delegate conflict where possible; they face conflict squarely only when they must. Interest-group liberalism offered justification for keeping major combatants apart and for delegating their conflict as far down the line as possible. It provided a theoretical basis for giving to each according to his claim, the price for which is a reduction of concern for what others are claiming. In other words, it *transformed access and logrolling from necessary evil to greater good.*

A third and increasingly important positive appeal of interest-group liberalism is that it helps create the sense that power need not be power at all, control need not be control, and government need not be coercive. If sovereignty is parceled out among groups, then who is out anything? As a major *Fortune* editor enthusiastically put it, government power, group power, and individual power may go up simultaneously. If the groups to be controlled control the controls, then "to administer does not always mean to rule."[12] The inequality of power and the awesome coerciveness of government are always gnawing problems in a democratic culture. Rousseau's General Will stopped at the boundary of the Swiss canton. The myth of the group and the group will is becoming the answer to Rousseau and the big democracy. Note, for example, the contrast between the traditional and the modern definition of the group; Madison in *Federalist 10* defined the group ("faction") as "a number of citizens, whether amounting to a majority or minority of the whole who are united and actuated by some common impulse of passion, or of interest, *adverse to the right of other citizens, or to the permanent and aggregate interests of the community*" (emphasis added). Modern political science usage took that definition and cut the quotation just before the emphasized part.[13] In such a manner pluralist theory became the handmaiden of interest-group liberalism, and interest-group liberalism became the handmaiden of modern American positive national statehood, and the First Republic became the Second Republic. (This is the first of many references to the passage of the United States into a new republic. The detailed analysis of this transformation is in Chapter 10.)

---

[12] Max Ways, "Creative Federalism and the Great Society," *Fortune,* January 1996, p. 122.
[13] David Truman, *The Governmental Process* (New York: Knopf, 19510. P. 4.

Evidence of the fundamental influence of interest-group liberalism can be found in the policies and practices of every Congress and every administration since 1961. The very purpose of this book is to identify, document, and assess the consequences of the preferences that are drawn from the new public philosophy. President Kennedy is an especially good starting point because his positions were clear and because justification was especially important to him. His actions were all the more significant because he followed the lines of interest-group liberalism during a period of governmental strength, when there was no need to borrow support from interest groups. But whatever he did in the name of participation, cooperation, or multi-interest administration, and whatever President Johnson did in the name of "maximum feasible participation" and "creative federalism," so did President Eisenhower and President Nixon and Ford do in the name of "partnership." This posture was very much above partisanship, and that is precisely what makes it the basis of what we can now call the Second Republic. *Fortune* could rave its approval of the theory of "creative federalism," despite its coinage by Lyndon Johnson, as "a relation, cooperative and competitive, between a limited central power and other powers that are essentially independent of it . . . a new way of organizing Federal programs . . . [in which simultaneously] the power of states and local governments will increase; the power of private organizations, including businesses, will increase; the power of individuals will increase."[14] Similarly, one of the most articulate officials during the Kennedy-Johnson years could speak glowingly of the Republican notion of partnership: "To speak of 'federal aid' simply confuses the issue. It is more appropriate to speak of federal support to special purposes . . . [as] an investment made by a partner who has clearly in mind the investments of other partners—local, state, and private."[15]

In sum, leaders in modern, consensual democracies are ambivalent about government. Government is obviously the most efficacious way of achieving good purposes, but alas, it is efficacious because it is coercive. To live with that ambivalence, modern policy-makers have fallen prey to the belief that public policy involves merely the identification of the problems towards which government ought to be aimed. It pretends that though "pluralism," "countervailing power," "creative federalism," "partnership," and "participatory democracy" the unsentimental business of coercion need not be involved and that unsentimental decisions about how to employ coercion need not really be made at all. Stated in the extreme, the policies of interest-group liberalism are end-oriented but ultimately self-defeating. Few standards of implemental law have been replaced by the requirement of contingency. As a result, the ends of interest-group liberalism are nothing more than sentiments and therefore not really ends at all.

THE FLAWED FOUNDATION OF INTEREST-GROUP LIBERALISM: PLURALISM

Everyone operates according to some theory or frame of reference, or paradigm—some generalized map that directs logic and conclusions, given certain facts. The influence of a paradigm over decisions is incalculably large.

---

14   Ibid., p. 122. See also *Wall Street Journal*, March 16, 1966 for another positive treatment of creative federalism.

15   Francis Keppel, while assistant secretary for education, quoted in *Congressional Quarterly, Weekly Report*, April 22, 1966, p. 833.

It helps define what is important among the multitudes of events. It literally programs the decision-maker toward certain kinds of conclusions. People are unpredictable if they do not share some elements of a common theory. Pragmatism is merely an appeal to let theory remain implicit, but there is all too much truth in Lord Keynes's epigram, which was for this reason chosen as the opening quotation to Part I. Interest-group liberals have the pluralist paradigm in common and its influence on the policies of the modern state has been very large and very consistent. Practices of government are likely to change only if there is a serious re-examination of the theoretical components of the public philosophy and if that reexamination reveals basic flaws in the theory. Because they guide so much of the analysis of succeeding chapters, contentions about the fundamental flaws in the theory underlying interest-group liberalism ought to be made explicit here at the outset. Among the many charges to be made against pluralism, the following three probably best anticipate the analysis to come.

1. The pluralist component has badly served liberalism by propagating the faith that a system built primarily upon groups and bargaining is self-corrective. Some parts of this faith are false, some have never been tested one way or the other, and others can be confirmed only under very special conditions. For example, there is the faulty assumption that groups have other groups to confront in some kind of competition. Another very weak assumption is that people have more than one salient group, that their multiple or overlapping memberships will insure competitions, and at the same time will keep competition from becoming too intense. This concept of overlapping membership is also supposed to prove the voluntary character of groups, since it reassures us that even though one group may be highly undemocratic, people can vote with their feet by moving over to some other group to represent their interests. Another assumption that has become an important liberal myth is that when competition between or among groups takes place the results yield a public interest or some other ideal result. As has already been observed, this assumption was borrowed from laissez-faire economists and has even less probability of being borne out in the political system. One of the major Keynesian criticisms of market theory is that even if pure competition among factors of supply and demand did yield an equilibrium, the equilibrium could be at something far less than the ideal of full employment at reasonable prices. Pure pluralist competition, similarly, might produce political equilibrium, but the experience of recent years shows that it occurs at something far below an acceptable level of legitimacy, or access, or equality, or innovation, or any other valued political commodity.

2. Pluralist theory is also comparable to laissez-faire economics in the extent to which it is unable to come to terms with the problem of imperfect competition. When a program is set up in a specialized agency, the number of organized interest groups surrounding it tends to be reduced, reduced precisely to those groups and factions to whom the specialization is most salient. That almost immediately transforms the situation from one of potential competition to one of potential oligopoly. As in the economic marketplace, political groups surrounding an agency ultimately learn that direct confrontation leads to net loss for all the competitors. Rather than countervailing power there is more likely to be accommodating power. Most observers and practitioners continue to hold on to the notion of group competition despite their

own recognition that it is far from a natural state. Galbraith was early to recognize this but is by no means alone in his position that "the support of countervailing power has become in modern times perhaps the major peacetime function of the Federal government."[16] Group competition in Congress and around agencies is not much of a theory if it requires constant central government support.

3. The pluralist paradigm depends upon an idealized conception of the group. Laissez-faire economics may have idealized the enterprise and the entrepreneur but never more than the degree to which the pluralist sentimentalizes the group, the group member, and the interests. We have already noted the contrasts between the traditional American or Madisonian definition of the group as adverse to the aggregate interests of the community with the modern view that groups are basically good things unless they break the law or the rules of the game. To the Madisonian, groups were a necessary evil much in need of regulation. To the modern pluralist, groups are good, requiring only accommodation. Madison went beyond this definition of the group to a position that "the regulation of these various interfering interests forms the principal task of modern legislation." This is a far cry from the sentimentality behind such notions as "supportive countervailing power," "group representation in the interior processes of... ,"and "maximum feasible participation."

THE COSTS OF INTEREST-GROUP LIBERALISM

The problems of pluralist theory are of more than academic interest. They are directly and indirectly responsible for some of the most costly attributes of modern government: (1) the atrophy of institutions of popular control; (2) the maintenance of old and the creation of new structures of privilege: and (3) conservatism in several senses of the word. These three hypotheses do not exhaust the possibilities but are best suited to introduce the analysis of policies and programs.

1. In *The Public Philosophy*, Walter Lippmann was rightfully concerned over the "derangement of power" whereby modern democracies tend first toward unchecked elective leadership and then toward drainage of public authority from elective leaders down into the constituencies. However, Lippmann erred if he thought of constituents as only voting constituencies. Drainage has tended toward "support-group constituencies," and with special consequences. Parceling out policy-making power to the most interested parties tends strongly to destroy political responsibility. A program split off with a special imperium to govern itself is not merely an administrative unit. It is a structure of power with impressive capacities to resist central political control.

When conflict of interest is made a principle of government rather than a criminal act, programs based upon such a principle cut out all of that part of the mass of people who are not specifically organized around values salient to the goals of that program. The people are shut out at the most creative phase of policy-making—where the problems are first defined. The public is shut out also at the phase of accountability because in theory there is enough accountability to the immediate surrounding interests. In fact, presidents and congressional committees are most likely to investigate an agency when a

---

[16]   *American Capitalism*, p. 136.

complaint is brought to them by one of the most interested organizations. As a further consequence, the accountability we do get is functional rather than substantive; and this involves questions of equity, balance, and equilibrium, to the exclusion of questions of the overall social policy and whether or not the program should be maintained at all. It also means accountability to experts first and amateurs last; and an expert is a person trained and skilled in the mysteries and technologies of that particular program.[17]

Finally, in addition to the natural tendencies, there tends also to be a self-conscious conspiracy to shut out the public. One meaningful illustration, precisely because it is such an absurd extreme, is found in the French system of interest representation in the Fourth Republic. As the Communist-controlled union, the Confederation Generale du Travail (CGT), intensified its participation in postwar French government, it was able to influence representatives of interests other than employees. In a desperate effort to insure that the interests represented on the various board were separated and competitive, the government issued a decree that "each member of the board must be *independent of the interests he is not representing.*"[18]

2. Programs following the principles of interest-group liberalism tend to create and maintain privilege; and it is a type of privilege particularly hard to bear or combat because it is touched with a symbolism of the state. Interest-group liberalism is not merely pluralism but is *sponsored* pluralism. Pluralists ease our consciences about the privileges of organized groups by characterizing them as representative and by responding to their "iron law of oligarchy" by arguing that oligarchy is simply a negative name for organization. Our consciences were already supposed to be partly reassured by the notion of "overlapping memberships." But however true it may be that overlapping memberships exist and that oligarchy is simply a way of leading people efficiently toward their interests, the value of these characteristics changes entirely when they are taken from the context of politics and put into the context of pluralistic government. The American Farm Bureau Federation is no "voluntary association" if it is a legitimate functionary within the extension system. Such tightly knit corporate groups as the National Association of Home Builders (NAHB), the National Association of Real Estate Boards (NAREB), the National Association for the Advancement of Colored People (NAACP), or the National Association of Manufacturers (NAM) or American Federation of Labor-Congress of Industrial Organizations (AFL-CIO) are no ordinary lobbies after they become part of the "interior processes" of policy formation. Even in the War on Poverty, one can only appreciate the effort to organize the poor by going back and pondering the story and characters in *The Three Penny Opera*. The "Peachum factor" in public affairs may be best personified in Sargent Shriver and his strenuous efforts to get the poor housed in some kind of group before their representation was to begin (see especially Chapter 8).

The more clear and legitimized the representation of a group or its leaders in policy formation, the less voluntary its membership in that group and the more necessary is loyalty to its leadership for people who share the interests in question. And, the more widespread the policies of recognizing and

---

[17] These propositions are best illustrated by the ten or more separate, self-governing systems in agriculture, in Chapter 4.

[18] Mario Einaudi et al., *Nationalization in France and Italy* (Ithaca: Cornell University Press, 19550, pp. 100-101. (Emphasis added.)

sponsoring organized interest, the more hierarchy is introduced into our society. It is a well-recognized and widely appreciated function of formal groups in modern society to provide much of the necessary everyday social control. However, when the very thought processes behind public policy are geared toward these groups they are bound to take on the involuntary character of *public* control.

3. The conservative tendencies of interest-group liberalism can already be seen in the two foregoing objections: weakening of popular control and support of privilege. A third dimension of conservatism, stressed here separately, is the simple conservatism of resistance to change. David Truman, who has certainly not been a strong critic of self-government by interest groups, has, all the same, provided about the best statement of the general tendency of established agency-group relationships to be "highly resistant to disturbance": New and expanded functions are easily accommodated, provided they develop and operate through existing channels of influence and do not tend to alter the relative importance of those influences. Disturbing changes are those that modify either the content or the relative strength of the component forces operating through an administrative agency. In the face of such changes, or the threat of them, the "old line" agency is highly inflexible.[19]

If this already is a tendency in a pluralistic system, then agency-group relationships must be all the more inflexible to the extent that the relationship is official and legitimate.

Innumerable illustrations will crop up throughout the book. They will be found in new areas of so-called social policy, such as the practice early in the war on Poverty to co-opt neighborhood leaders, thereby creating more privilege than alleviating poverty (see Chapter 8). Even clearer illustrations will be found in the economic realm, so many, indeed, that the practice is synthesized in Chapter 10 as "a state of permanent receivership." Old and established groups doing good works naturally look fearfully upon the emergence of competing, perhaps hostile, new groups. That is an acceptable and healthy part of the political game—until the competition between them is a question of "who shall be the government?" At that point conservatism becomes a matter of survival for each group, and a direct threat to the public interest. Ultimately this threat will be recognized.

THE NEW REPRESENTATION: A SECOND REPUBLIC?

If ambivalence toward government power is a trait common to all democracies, American leaders possess it to an uncommon degree. Their lives are dedicated to achieving it, and their spirits are tied up with justifying it. They were late to insist upon the expansion of national government, and when the expansion finally did begin to take place, it only intensified the ambivalence. *With each significant expansion of government during the past century, there has been a crisis of public authority. And each crisis of public authority has been accompanied by demands for expansion of representation.*

The clearest case in point is probably the first, the commitment by the federal government, beginning with the Interstate Commerce Act of 1887, to intervene regularly in the economic life of the country. The political results of

---

[19]   *The Governmental Process,* pp. 467-68.

the expansion were more immediate and effective than the economic consequences of the statutes themselves. The call went out for congressional reform of its rules, for direct election of senators, for reform in nominating processes, for reform in the ballot, for decentralization of House leadership, and so on. The results were dramatic, including "Reed's Rules" in the House, direct election of senators, the direct primary movement, the Australian ballot, and the "Speaker Revolt." This is also the period during which some of the most important national interest groups were organized.

Expansion of government during the Wilson period was altogether intertwined with demands by progressives for reform and revision in the mechanisms of representation: female suffrage (Nineteenth Amendment), the short ballot, initiative, referendum and recall, great extensions of direct primaries, the commission form of city government, and the first and early demands for formal interest representation—leading to such things as the formal sponsorship of the formation of Chambers of Commerce by the Commerce Department, government sponsorship of the formation of the Farm Bureau movement, the establishment of the separate clientele-oriented Departments of Labor and Commerce, and the first experiments with "self-regulation" during the World War I industrial mobilization.

The Roosevelt revolution brought on more of the same but made its own special contribution as well. Perhaps the most fundamental change in representation to accompany expanded government was the development and articulation of the theory and practice of the administrative process (see Chapter 5). Obviously the more traditional demands for reform in actual practices of representation continued. Reapportionment became extremely important; demands for reform produced the Administrative Procedure Act and the congressional reforms embodied in the 1946 LaFollette-Monroney Act. But probably of more lasting importance during and since that time has been the emergence of interest-group liberalism as the answer to the problems of government power. The new jurisprudence of administrative law is a key factor, to me the most important single factor. The new halo words alone indicate the extent to which new ideas of representation now dominate: *interest representation, cooperation, partnership, self-regulation, delegation of power, local option, creative federalism, community action, maximum feasible participation,* Nixon's *new federalism,* and even that odd contribution from the 1960s New Left—*participatory democracy.*

In whatever form and by whatever label, the purpose of representation and of reform in representation is the same: to deal with the problem of power—to bring the democratic spirit into some kind of psychological balance with the harsh reality of government coerciveness. The problem is that the new representation embodied in the broad notion of interest-group liberalism is a pathological adjustment to the problem. Interest-group liberal solutions to the problem of power provide the system with stability by spreading a *sense* of representation at the expense of genuine flexibility, at the expense of democratic forms, and ultimately at the expense of legitimacy. Prior solutions offered by progressives and other reformers built greater instabilities into the system by attempting to reduce the lag between social change and government policy. But that was supposed to be the purpose of representation. Flexibility and legitimacy could only have been reduced by building representation upon the oligopolistic character of interest groups, reducing the number of competitors, favoring the best organized competitors, specializing politics around agencies, ultimately limiting participation to channels provided by pre-existing groups.

Among all these, the weakest element of interest-group liberalism, and the element around which all the rest is most likely to crumble, is the antagonism of (the) interest-group liberal solution to formalism. The least obvious, yet perhaps the most important, aspect of this is the antagonism of interest-group liberalism to law. Traditional expansions of representation were predicated upon an assumption that expanded participation would produce changes in government policies expressed in laws that would very quickly make a difference to the problems around which the representation process had been activated. Since the "new representation" extends the principle of representation into administration, it must either oppose the making of law in legislatures or favor vague laws and broad delegations that make it possible for administrative agencies to engage in representation. This tends to derange almost all established relationships and expectations in a republic. By rendering formalism impotent, it impairs legitimacy by converting government from a moralistic to a mechanistic institution. It impairs the potential of positive law to correct itself by allowing the law to become anything that eventually bargains itself out as acceptable to the bargainers. It impairs the very process of administration itself by delegating to administration alien material—policies that are not laws and authorizations that must be made into policies. Interest-group liberalism seeks pluralistic government, in which there is no formal specification of means or of ends. In a pluralistic government there is, therefore, no substance. Neither is there procedure. There is only process.

DISGUISED LIBERALISM

Harvey Mansfield Jr..

[From *Public Policy* volume XVIII, Fall 1970, number 5. Reprinted with permission of the author and the publisher, the President and Fellows of Harvard College. The page and chapter references in parentheses within the body of this chapter are Professor Mansfield's, and they refer to Professor Lowi's book *The End of Liberalism* (New York: W.W. Norton & Company, 1969.)]

Theodore Lowi has written a book, *The End of Liberalism*,[20] which deserves to be read carefully, and because it is timely, will probably be read widely. It is timely as another radical critique of liberalism, summing up and adding to the troubles of that doctrine in politics and political science with a sprightly style that shows every good humor but offers no mercy. Its merit, however, is to approach a radical critique of liberalism in the sense of a clear understanding. Lowi sees contemporary liberalism as the use of disguised power for forgotten moral purposes, and "the end of liberalism" in a new, overtly moral "juridical democracy." This "juridical democracy" proves to be less interesting than the critique of liberalism that is supposed to validate it; indeed, the critique works as well on the author's proposed "public philosophy" as on his intended target. We shall consider first Lowi's critique, next his own proposal, and last, liberal-

---

[20] Theodore Lowi, *The End of Liberalism: Ideology, Policy, and the Crisis of Public Authority* (New York: Norton, 1969), xiv 322 pp.

ism in the longer perspective of political philosophy, from which we see in the present more danger to liberty than to liberalism.

I

Lowi devotes nine of the ten chapters in his book to his critical analysis of contemporary liberalism in America. In them he argues comprehensively that liberalism has lost sight of the need to coerce and the duty to be moral. Its blindness is not just a blink or a wink but a general and settled incompetence. Lowi considers areas of policy outside the latest concerns—agriculture, commerce, and labor—and an instrument of policy not recently in public discussion, administration, as well as the more sensitive hurts or bellyaches of today in the cities—housing, welfare, and education; and to complete the picture, he also takes up foreign policy. Everywhere the defect is the same, except in foreign policy, which nicely complements the defect of domestic policy. Liberals, the men who run the country and hold "the new public philosophy," fail to take "unsentimental decisions about how to employ coercion" (p. 85) and thus give out their problems, which are the country's problems, to be solved by those groups who are held or claim to be most vitally affected by the problem.

Liberals have developed the use of power disguised by delegation to such groups so far that it can no longer be considered merely their favorite tactic. In the indiscriminate use of delegation, in the permission given by governing liberals to "interest groups" not only to administer the laws that apply to them but also to make the rules and even to formulate the problems, it is clear that the liberal tactic has become the soul of liberalism, or rather that liberalism has lost its soul, its sense of direction. It has surrendered its reforming purpose to the interests of society as presently constituted. It has become profoundly conservative, though unconsciously so; for liberals today are so far from constituting a power elite that they are fearful of exercising power and (one may add to Lowi's analysis) ashamed of being an elite, in sum, incapable of conspiracy. Liberalism has become "interest-group liberalism," the practice and doctrine of self-government by a "self" that has forgotten the need for government and believes in the reality only of its parts.

As for the practice, Lowi speaks especially of "the new feudalism" in agriculture, by which he means the self-regulation that began with the Federal Extension Service and that flourished under the New Deal. Instead of working to a plan of what ought to be done in agriculture as a whole, the Extension Service offers the services that interest groups (in this case the American Farm Bureau Federation particularly) say farmers want and that committees of Congress, organized mostly by interests, agree they should have. Lowi has found ten such separate and autonomous triangles of central agency, local interests, and congressional committees in agriculture today. Where oligopoly does not exist, as in agriculture, it must be created; where it does exist, it need only be endorsed. Such is the practice of two other "clientele agencies," the Departments of Commerce and Labor. Lowi admits that the two agencies have had this special character from their birth before the New Deal, but he argues that their special character has been made the ruling tendency of government by the New Deal and even more by Presidents Kennedy and Johnson.

His example of this tendency is the War on Poverty (chapter 8), in which the poor have been organized to fight poverty by being organized. The intent of this operation, one might say in elaboration of Lowi, was apparently to treat the poor as another interest group, to be urged into existence by the sponsorship of its loudest and least acquiescent spokesmen. Thus has interest-group liberalism moved unconsciously from endorsing interests based on some qualification that contributes to the common good to establishing groups whose "interest" is merely a need. A farm program to make farmers rich makes sense, if not wisdom; but a poverty program to establish and then abolish the poor makes sense only to those few spokesmen who become very rich in money or prestige by their poverty. Presidents Kennedy and Johnson treated the poor like an estate of the realm, rather than as they were in the 'thirties, "the human exhaust of capitalism" (p. 243) or as they are today, according to Lowi, the victims of injustice. Their confusion of intent between abolishing and organizing the poor has in practice merely reinforced the status quo, for example fragmentation in New York and machine dominance in Chicago.

In liberal doctrine liberal practice finds its justification or "apology" (p. 313). This "doctrine" is not a philosophic teaching but "the public philosophy," i.e., the dominant opinions of our day as shown in the policies of government and the political science of what might be called, agreeably to all concerned, the unphilosophical side of the profession. Lowi's objection to the apologetic political science of interest-group liberalism is moral rather than philosophic; and so his theme is the errant axioms of liberal practice rather than the theoretical roots. He wishes to recover "an independent and critical political science," and thinks that this can be done by moral objection alone. The moral man confronts a choice more than or rather than the chosen, and so the moral as such is at a distance from present practice or the Establishment. Lowi's political science is free to *choose* differently from the present "public philosophy" and consequently free to *think* differently. Its freedom comes from choosing differently, not from thinking differently. Thus political science that feels obliged to apologize cannot be independent and critical, just as a government that cannot plan for reform must surrender to its interest groups. This conclusion would seem to overlook the possibility of apologizing because something better is unattainable and finding one's independence in thinking or understanding. Speaking from within the unphilosophical side of the profession, Lowi reproaches that side for its neglect of morality; and to make the reproach sting, he calls such neglect conservatism (pp. 90, 244). He does not consider whether neglect of morality might be studious, unlike the unthinking policies of liberals in government—a deliberate, willful resistance to moral judgment justified by an opinion about facts and values which he ought to confront and refute (p. 313). He signals "a need to break the thirty-year moratorium on consideration of first premises that has characterized modern political science" (pp. ix, 47, 55), but it must be said that he has only lifted, and not violated, the ban.

Lowi contrasts the new public philosophy of liberalism with the old public philosophy of capitalism, for he believes the crucial change in recent American politics was accomplished thirty years ago (in 1937; see above), in the Roosevelt revolution that decided "that in a democracy there can be no effective limit to the scope of governmental power." This first premise, then established against the fear of the state that capitalist ideology had made dominant, does not need to be reconsidered now. Perhaps he makes this remark more with intent against revived anarchism on the Left than against surviving *laissez-faire* purists on the Right. At any rate he wants to work from this principle as established, because it makes obsolete the usual distinction between liberals and conservatives that has confused public discussion since the time of the New Deal. *This* battle of the New Deal has been won. We are all liberals in *this* sense. It is time now to see how conservative the New Deal was in the *use* of unlimited power, in its delegation of power to interest groups. Lowi is so concerned to make this point that he passes up the opportunity to compare interest-group liberalism with precapitalist or preindustrial liberalism, especially the eighteenth-century liberalism (and radicalism) that was responsible for the American constitution. He knows of course that interest-group liberalism has a source in Madison's political science, and he prefers Madison's definition of "faction" to the contemporary understanding of "interest group" because it has a moral element (a faction is "adverse to the right of other citizens, or to the permanent and aggregate interests of the community," quoted, p. 296). But he does not make an analysis, and so he does not make clear to what extent his "juridical democracy" returns to or departs from the principles of the framers of the Constitution. This analysis would be important for judging the practical as well as the moral and theoretical soundness of his proposal. With such an analysis, he would have risked only imputation of deference to an earlier revolution which might have been called forth from the bullhorns of the advocates of revolution in our day.

When Americans adopted the new public philosophy, they accepted positive government, but they did not understand the necessity and the requirements of planning. Planning is necessary because society does not operate automatically to desired ends as if by an invisible hand, in the way that capitalist ideology supposed the free market could order itself. In rediscovering the importance of the many groups in a free society, liberal political science avoided the inevitability of Marxist class conflict and the automaticity of capitalist individual competition, and thus seemed to open the way for rational planning by government in administration. "Rationality applied to social control is administration" (p. 27), for only by administration can men be brought to live together when the complexity of modern technology divides them and forces them apart. Because of its pluralism, liberal political science seemed capable of understanding the necessity of administration, as opposed to capitalism and Marxism, and indeed it called attention to the importance of private administration by groups. But in regard to public administration it succumbed to the myth of the automatic society and concluded that government is merely a process, an epiphenomenon of the reality of groups. Thus New Deal delegation was enshrined in the political science of Robert Dahl and David Truman, two living, smiling political scientists who for their prominence have recently suffered through many tests of their good humor.

Lowi's account of administration is unclear. He criticizes the liberal political science for believing in an automatic society, and yet gives it credit for seeing that administration is more than responsive to changes in society. According to liberal political science as Lowi sees it, administration is bargaining, a kind of imperfect competition where the bargainers have "market power," yet apparently self-regulative because the political scientists do not see the role of "separate government" (p. 48) nor do they appreciate the need for it. Lowi understands government as planning and hence as separate: regulative, reforming, and coercive. Government is above society and the politics of society. Yet he also assumes that modern, democratic government is representative, which means that it comes out of society (pp. 95, 290). What lifts government above society is "democratic formalisms" (p. 291), that is, laws with clear standards of administration and coercive sanctions as opposed to informal bargaining that accomodates injustice and leads to disrespect for the law (p. 149). But the "formalisms" must somehow be made representative by consent if government is to remain representative; and so they seem to rest on the whim or prejudice of an electorate, surely on the informal reality of an appeal to the people. At times Lowi seems to reach out tentatively for the Aristotelian notion of the regime (politeia) that forms society, but because of his unexplained acceptance of representative government, he never grasps it. He attacks Dahl for supposing that government is mostly peaceful adjustment; Dahl fails to notice the vast category of administration, where men adjust peacefully because coercion in the form of law remains discreetly but immediately in the background (p. 52). Yet in Lowi's view consent or at least unprotesting assent seems to be behind coercion, so that government would seem after all to be mostly a peaceful adjustment by which people bargain with their liberty for security. I shall return to this issue.

This system of interest-group liberalism and its public philosophy have brought us now to a crisis in public authority, "the spectacular paradox" of a constitution almost totally democratized and its government increasingly felt to be illegitimate (p. 68). Our rulers, the liberals, have parceled out parts of problems that belong together to competing groups to solve as those groups think fit or according to their bargaining power. The liberals do not consult the interest of society as a whole. They see problems in parts, which is to say that they refuse to see problems. From this mistake comes a failure of realism—and a failure of idealism. Liberals are unrealistic because they pretend it is unnecessary to coerce in the interest of the whole, and unidealistic because they cannot coerce for a moral end. Our government must find the nerve to coerce by restoring its "formalisms" so that it can consider problems as a whole, i.e., morally. Coercion, formalism, morality are the central incapacities of interest-group liberalism. Of these, the key is formalism, for the formalism of democracy somehow assures that the interest of the whole is consulted, therefore that moral questions are raised and answered, and finally that coercion is undertaken overtly and unsentimentally. By "formalisms" Lowi means, as we have seen, laws with clear standards for administrators and judges. Together he could have called them "legality" if he had wished to emphasize the strong "law and order" component of his thinking. But like President Nixon, Lowi is a "law and order with justice" man, and he adopts the name "juridical democracy" to describe his proposed public philosophy.

II

Juridical democracy does not hide either its power or its intention. It is overtly moral and it is unafraid of weeping, wailing, and teeth-gnashing among its "terror-stricken" (p. 281) opponents. But what is the morality of juridical democracy? Lowi, in a book attacking liberals for not raising moral questions, raises none himself and offers no moral arguments. He only makes moral assertions, from which it appears that moral means equality or democracy. It is as if morality were a thing whose significance would be known once its absence were appreciated, like beer forgotten on a picnic.

Lowi does give the principal moral conclusion of juridical democracy in America now, a verdict against residents of suburbs. His book culminates or concludes in an attack on residents of suburbs, and of suburbs, on Chicago suburbs (p. 277), and of Chicago suburbs, on Kenilworth, the home as he says of Senator Charles Percy (pp. 197, 277, 278, 281). Whatever this means, the suburb in general is "an instrument by which the periphery can exploit the center." It is "a parasite," Lowi specifies, "whose residents can enjoy the benefits of scale and specialization without sharing in the attendant costs" (p. 197). These parasites, he believes, are responsible for the outstanding ill in America today, the inferior adjustment of the Negro to life in the city, as compared to previous classes of immigrants. One might explain this inferiority of adjustment by the racial inferiority of the Negro, but this possibility "we must reject—at least until every other possible explanation is exhausted" (p. 195)— apparently for reasons of humanity or patriotism. A second possibility is that the urban Negro likes his life of "disorder, destruction, protest, burning, pillaging, narcotics, numbers, gang warfare and rule by extortion"; to think otherwise is middle-class parochialism, and to act otherwise is middle-class tyranny. Lowi prudently rejects this possibility for reasons of common sense, and moves to the third explanation, which he prefers. In the 1930s, he says, suburban city fathers acquired and used legal powers to erect political barriers to the development of the central city. As the suburbs gained political independence of the city, they became havens for escapers, rather than merely well-to-do neighborhoods, and the residents of suburbs were enabled to avoid making a contribution to the city's old function of educating immigrants and other "flotsam and jetsam of industrial society."

To rediscover the whole, or the public, we must recapture the suburbs for the city. In the United States there are national citizenship and state citizenship, one's public character as created by the Constitution and its grant of power to each state; but there is no city citizenship (p. 273). To remake city citizenship and to recover its vital function of education, we must use federal power to put pressure on the states through grants-in-aid and tax rebates, and then the states must destroy the corporate cities within them who are their legal creatures. Metropolitan regional organization will not suffice, for the legal fiction of home rule would survive and continue to foster selfish unconcern for the problems of the city. Today the states can best destroy the corporate city and remake the city through public education, by busing Negro schoolchildren. It would be massive busing, for each school district in the entire metropolitan area, perhaps even each school, would have the same percentage of blacks. This measure would remove an important incentive to escape the city and a valuable attraction in the hideout, says Lowi more delicately than I (p. 280). This, then, is what juridical democracy means for us today. It would be unfair to say that Lowi has written a three-hundred page statement to demand busing, and called it *The End of Liberalism.*

Lowi does not seem to have any idea of what kind of democrat his democracy should encourage or create. More specifically, what kind of man should an American Negro and an American suburbanite be, besides not being a dope fiend or a parasite? If the city teaches citizenship, what does and what should it teach? Lowi proposes a great enlargement of modest busing experiments now or recently in effect. He wants to send very many black children to the suburbs as an indirect method of improving their status from freed men to free men. But why not do it directly? Why is this method of putting the education of black children into the hands of suburbanites, or if there will be entirely new school districts, into the hands of an interest group of professional educators or agitators—and this without any guidelines or principles to serve as the source of guidelines, not to mention clear standards— why is this any different from delegating farmers' problems to the American Farm Bureau? The effect of this proposal, should it succeed against the wishes of the terror-stricken parasites, would not be hard to predict: The present competition of trends would continue. I mean the competition between the propensity of the Negro to become middle class when he gets the chance and the propensity of the white middle class suburbanites, especially the young ones, to adopt some of those ways of the Negro which derive from his former status as slave—a slouchy posture, a shuffling gait, shiftless habits, gaudy attire, throbbing music, and the various addictions.[21] At present, the latter propensity is ahead, and I believe Lowi's proposal, by destroying what remains of the isolation and virtue of middle class youth, would greatly accelerate its progress and increase its lead. For this reason, and also because the punishment would fit the crime, it might be better to send white children into the ghettoes. In sum, after it is decided who teaches whom, the result would be a subtle endorsement of the status quo, with bargaining advantage given by law to one propensity or the other. It would be another solution by disguised government delegated to private parties, in which no one raises the moral question of what ought to be done.

If it is moral to restrict the privileges of suburbanites, why is it moral to retain them at all? Why stop with busing? Why not make people live in the suburb or central city by lot and then change periodically? This idea is not new either in theory or in practice, and we ought to know whether to adopt it or advocate it or hope for it. What we need is a moral argument, if not a numerical measure, that will say which equal persons will receive equal treatment and that will balance contribution and need. Equipped with this argument and informed by a closer look at circumstances, we could judge whether suburbs should exist as well as whether they should have legal autonomy.

Lowi uses Henry George's idea of unearned increment against the sanctity of suburban real estate values, and he says in italics: "The private profit from public facilities must be calculated in social terms" (p. 281). But to be complete, this kind of calculation must also consider the social profit in private terms. For example, what does society owe to Henry George? Does not Theodore Lowi at least owe him a rent for his idea of unearned increment? More generally, what does the American people owe for the contribution to society made by the managerial, professional, and creative talent of those who live in the suburbs? We would be justified in despising this talent altogether for its money-grubbing, its power-seeking, or its aesthetic vanities only if we were willing to dispense with its products. As things are, and in the absence of a general accounting between society and Henry George or Theodore Lowi or the University of Chicago, it cannot be assumed that society is underpaid.

Early liberalism, the liberalism of Hobbes and Locke, assumed that a

---

[21]   There are other, better ways of a slave, his patience, endurance, and capacity for enjoyment; but these do not appeal to our modern, liberal youth.

free society could not survive and prosper without a liberal aristocracy of talented men. This aristocracy would be acceptable to a society based on the natural equality of men if it were rewarded according to its social contribution. This could be done in a way all would understand if the aristocracy were based on the principle of equality of opportunity, rather than noble family, even though the ordinary man is as effectually excluded from the suburbs or whatever by lack of talent as by inferior birth. The fact of aristocracy is less evident, and its ascendancy less odious, when individuals from all classes can rise and when all classes profit from their rise. In this disguise of aristocracy it is important that the talented (in effect, the successful) be paid in money, a universal coin, rather than in privileges that obviously set men off from each other. As regards suburbs, it could be said that differences between rich and poor would still be irritating if they lived cheek by jowl, with slums in the back yards of the mansions. Suburbs at a distance from slums keep the rich and the poor from living in fear and envy, while the poor take the comfort they clearly do take from the possibility that some part of this luxury may one day belong to them or to their children or to one of their children.

This reasoning is not a noble defense, but the society to be defended is not noble but large and free, with freedom for artists and intellectuals as well as for bankers and corporation executives. When freedom means freedom of choice, it must be expected that most people will choose to have products that require and support an "aristocracy," often including some unsavory characters, always including some whose talents do not redeem their mediocre qualities. Lowi seems to want this kind of free society, but he is unwilling to swallow the unsentimental analysis that must serve as an "apology" for it. He does not face the necessity of social aristocracy in our liberal society and hence does not appreciate the necessity of disguising it in our liberal democracy. Instead he argues for a free society of equals making their own morality by making their own laws and holding their administrators to account. The latter are an elite with great powers, Lowi observes, but they seem to be confined to the higher echelons of government, where they can be "peacefully cashiered" (pp. 187, 304). It is a picture that reminds one of Rousseau in his political mood and that requires a small and homogeneous society which does not resemble contemporary America in the least.

The connection between law and morality is the most refreshing of Lowi's themes. For him, the law is the great sustainer rather than the enemy of morality, which itself is principally a matter of public character rather than the private conscience. Lowi is not for doing your own thing either individually or in your interest group. While strong for the civil rights of the Negro, Lowi is dead against black separatism. Legal support for it would be as evil as was legal prohibition of integration (p. 279). But still, despite his speaking of "public character," in this opinion he sees morality as the elimination of privilege, not as the promotion of character. For he does not say what the character of an American should be, into which the Negro is to be integrated. If law is an instrument of morality, there should be some nonlegal moral ends or virtues that the law wishes to promote. What are they? From this standpoint it is not enough for the law, or its proponents, to say that its end is the achievement of a society in which integration is totally illegal and the law is absolutely obeyed. This would reduce the law to fiat, although (or still worse) to a universal fiat, since the "public character" of society would be merely the result of universalizing its private character. This private character, the individual citizen, would have no other specification than that he was capable of being universalized, or that he could be adjusted to integration with other individual citizens having the same noble qualification. Seeing this point, Lowi criticizes liberalism for having "the mentality of a world of universalized ticket-fixing: Destroy privilege by universalizing it" (p. 292). But if it is as wrong to fix tickets for everybody as for a few, a priori formality cannot be the rule of justice (p. 290) and formalism cannot be its only, unfailing instrument. Since Lowi has decided that suburban living is an unjust privilege, he would have to show how busing black children to the suburbs differs from universalized ticket-fixing.

When law is used as an instrument of morality in the way Lowi uses it, the use is not fundamentally illiberal; it is fundamentally liberal. It is the reassertion of absolute sovereignty for its original liberal purpose. Early liberalism considered men to be natural equals or created equal; and so all government had to be by consent. At the same time, government was seen to be very necessary because some men, claiming natural superiority or divine election, will try to lord it over their equals. A society of natural equals, then, needs government of unlimited scope, that is, an enormous inequality of political power, in order to protect its equality. This equality, of course, is natural, not social: The very equality which keeps me from governing you enables you to use your freedom to become a better author or businessman than I if your talents are better, unless by doing so you interfere too much with my freedom. Modern or liberal equality leads primarily to freedom and consequently to government, but government is no less absolute for being consequential or instrumental to freedom. Liberal government must first gather all power to itself so as to be sure that all citizens understand the meaning of natural equality, and then, after this assertion, relax, in a mood often called conservative, and license individuals in their groups to pursue happiness as they see it, consistently with such pursuit by others. Hobbes was the author of the doctrines of absolute sovereignty and of pluralism both, and of the former in order to be author of the latter.

What Lowi presents as the inconsistency of interest-group liberalism—first gathering power, then releasing it by delegation—is not an inconsistency but the planned strategy of modern liberalism. Before liberalism can tolerate a plural society of groups, it must first be rid of illiberal groups. The original illiberal group was the Church, a group that claimed divine appointment to govern or to interfere in government; and that group had to be opposed and tamed by an assertion of absolute sovereignty that could reach into its sanctuaries, which had previously enjoyed legal exemptions and protections. Just as Lowi's juridical democracy seems to be the liberalism he criticizes, so his attack on the suburbs resembles nothing so much as the anticlericalism that has always been the soul or animus of liberalism. But whether suburbanites are truly the priests of our day, condemning the vanities of the age while living off the fat of the land, may be left to the judgment of those who are willing to compare them with radicals in the streets, middlemen in the media, and professors in universities. Lowi's contribution is to remind interest-group liberalism of the danger of illiberal groups, which for reasons of humanitarian optimism and misguided scientific positivism it had taken lightly.

In thinking this time to assert sovereignty, Lowi advances the idea of administration rather than representation. Representation in the formulation of policy, and the increasing democracy of representation, he takes for granted; he wants to stress that laws enacted democratically need to be "implemented absolutely" or "carried to absolute finality" (p. 271). It is interest-group liberalism that tries to administer "by spreading a sense of representation" (p. 95). Yet administration, a modern invention as Lowi says, is so far from being essentially opposed to representation as to require it and further it. Lowi says that "the function of representation" is "to bring the democratic spirit into some kind of psychological balance with the harsh reality of the coerciveness of government" (p. 95). It is characteristic of the modern "democratic spirit," one should add, not to wish to govern (as the poor might wish to govern the rich) but to wish not to be governed. This must be added because for most men government is not such a harsh reality when they are governing someone else; why could not the poor make government a harsh reality for the rich? This "democratic spirit" is really a representative spirit arising from the natural equality of men. Since in modern democracy all are included in the *demos*, the democrats govern themselves, not the rich. Lacking the satisfaction of governing others, they need some "psychological balance with the harsh reality of the coerciveness of government." In plainer language, they need a disguise for the harsh reality.

"Administration" in the modern sense is part of the disguise which as a whole we call representation. Lowi indicates as much when, in speaking of administration, he refers to internalized coercion that "can be called legitimate" because it is "well enough accepted to go unnoticed" (p. 52). "Administration" is distinct from "legislation" in a way that makes it possible for policy to seem nonpartisan. Government seems harsh not so much because it is coercive as when the coercion seems partisan and from a party not your own. Coercion can be "internalized" and go unnoticed or be accepted if it begins with an act of consent, necessarily partisan, and concludes in the particular command of a nonpartisan rule of law. When you are coerced by the law, it is very consoling to be told that you made the law by participating in an election; and it is more convincing to hear, on the contrary but in addition, that the law is being applied without reference to yourself. By the system of representation the law says to the citizen: You are coercing yourself and besides, if that is not enough, nobody is coercing you in particular and therefore nobody in particular is coercing you. In modern representative government we notice both party government and nonpartisan administration. It required an unprecedented frankness to admit that government is partisan and a complementary pretence to deny that it is so in administration.

This nonpartisan administration requires, according to Lowi, an administrative class which in the United States is weak and fragmented, and needs to be strengthened, as well as a Supreme Court above partisan politics, which operates to Lowi's satisfaction. Juridical democracy, in order to be representative, needs undemocratic institutions, suburbs of the central city so to speak. Even democracy is government, the government of whoever the majority may be, and government must be hidden by means of such institutions. The effect and, I suppose, the intention of Lowi's "juridical" is to qualify his "democracy." It would be a courtesy and an enlightenment to his fellow intellectuals not to hide this fact from them.

This comprehensive book has a single chapter on foreign policy entitled

"Making Democracy Safe for the World: On Fighting the Next War." The implication that liberalism has made democracy too aggressive is reduced to the charge that American foreign policy since World War II has been consistently oversold, exaggerating the Communist threat and promising too much in remedy. Lowi believes the cause is an inflated presidency created by a series of liberal presidents. They have tried to compensate for the lack of formal authority in American government by blowing up international crises so that they can take crisis actions that will bring them the authority they cannot get formally. The charge is unproven and the explanation fanciful. Lowi might have developed the subtitle of this chapter, which suggests a doubt of the liberal propensity to hope for a society without coercion and peace with a capital P or perpetual peace. He excuses the peace marchers who seem more guilty of this fault than the presidents. He asks that we read all of Locke's *Second Treatise* so that we appreciate "the separation of the 'federative power,' by which Locke means, 'what is to be done in reference to foreigners'" (p. 187). This quotation points rather to Locke's refusal to adopt liberal internationalism than to formal limitations on the presidency. In paragraph 148 of the *Second Treatise* one finds Locke's declaration that though the federative power is conceptually distinct from the executive, they belong together in practice.

In sum, Lowi has not presented a political science that is "independent and critical" of the reigning liberalism of our day. Nor does he attempt to be independent and critical of "the revolution of our time" (p. 272), though he takes no party position. If we wish to think independently and critically about both, we should look in the history of liberal political philosophy for the reason of Lowi's most interesting point: to see why liberalism is compelled to disguise its use of power. In this compulsion can be found the two permanent, contrary tendencies of liberalism, the realism characteristic of contemporary "interest-group liberalism" and the idealism of the reaction against it.

III

The political philosophy of liberalism began with Machiavelli, though Machiavelli was not the founder of liberalism. He was the first to teach that man was born a needy being, not merely in having needs but in being unprovided in his most essential needs, having no advantages and receiving no inheritances except what he receives or gets from other men. Man has received no gifts from God or from nature—only the need or perhaps the promise of gifts. Being needy and naked, and living in an unwelcome environment, man must acquire the goods to supply his needs, and he must keep on acquiring. God and nature have not even done him the favor of indicating how much is enough, or if they have, it is not clear that this indication is in the interest of man. Man must "acquire the world"; he must take it away from God or nature. In this acquisition other men are both an aid and a hindrance. A man cannot acquire successfully without the cooperation of other men, but he also cannot acquire unless he does it single-mindedly, that is, unless he loses —or rather, perfects—his capacity of self-promotion. When men cooperate for acquisition, they cooperate as long as it is useful for each; their common object has no chance of becoming a mutual goal.

So men do cooperate with one another, but since they cooperate for acquisition, they cooperate for advancement, which means self-advancement. All advancement is ultimately if not immediately at someone else's expense, and so acquisition means acquisition from other men. For Machiavelli, acquisition is chiefly political, with the understanding that the goal of politics is mastery and mastery in the simple sense by "one alone." It is not chiefly economic, with the hope that the energies of mastery can be diverted to the never-ending diminution of scarcity. Government is the necessary instrument and the highest goal of acquisition; and if government means mastery, it could also be called, as we do, with an eye more to the receiving end, oppression. Government is oppression, open or disguised. But will it not of necessity be primarily disguised? Since no power is secure unless it is expanding, and no expansion can occur without taking from someone else, government is under the necessity of disguising its intentions. It must use fraud. It must use the winning smile or the bland disclaimer because, behind them, the intention must always be hostile. If the intention did not have to be hostile, then it could be shown openly. It might be thought that an established power, having risen with fraud, could then afford to forget its past, stand on principle, and avow its intention. But no power can afford to do so, though many former powers thought they could, for power is not secure or "established" unless it is expanding. The strong must excel the weak in fraud, or else they will not be strong for long. To be strong means to be strong in fraud. Machiavelli, to repeat, was not opposed to cooperation and trust. He once said: Never ask for a man's weapon, saying "I want to kill you with it." Just ask for the weapon, and when you have it you can do your will. In cruder words: Never break your trust until it has been built up to the point where it is profitable to do so.

Now this argument, which has been very much compressed from the graceful presentation and deep penetration of Machiavelli's writings, was taken up and transformed by Thomas Hobbes, who was, I think, the founder of liberalism. He began as did Machiavelli with man in a state of neediness, and he called this condition the state of nature. In the state of nature all men are equal or roughly equal if judged by the standard to which any man, at his discretion, can appeal—their ability to kill each other. All men being equal in the ability to kill, none has power over another by nature or by virtue of his superior natural endowments; and so all have an equal right to life, a natural right of self-preservation. But since all have an equal right to life and a pressing need to secure their lives, the state of nature is the war of all against all. No government is possible there because you cannot trust the other fellow to lay down his weapon if you lay down yours. Trust, and thence government, become possible by the authorization of a common power over us all. Hobbes calls him our representative, the artificial person who acts for us and ensures that everyone keeps his promises. The sovereign representative is created by a promise of all to obey, which enables him to secure, while limiting, the liberty of all. Justice, the central virtue for Hobbes, is keeping promises, and this justice replaces Machiavelli's understanding of fraud as the basis of government.

To make a very realistic beginning has always been the great supposed advantage of liberalism. No one can say that Hobbes's state of nature is a Garden of Eden, and yet when correctly understood it shows how men can trust one another on a purely human basis without reference to something above or beyond man. It seems to show how we can control ourselves. We do it by *consent*. Government is by consent, each man transferring the power to secure his absolute natural right to life to the sovereign representative, and receiving in return a qualified civil right to live in freedom and security. The principle of legitimacy (to use a contemporary term) is one's own. The question of legitimacy is not, Is this government good? It is: Did you authorize it? If it is your government, if the government represents you, then you have no right of complaint about what it does. To authorize the government and then refuse to obey it would be going back on your word, a kind of self-contradiction, which is the essence of injustice.

Thus the typical issue in liberal politics is over the legitimacy or the representativeness of the government, not over its goodness. Questions of goodness are likely to be restated as questions of legitimacy. If the government does something wrong or suffers a misfortune, the typical solution proposed is to make it more representative or (as is also said today) to restructure it. The proposal may be to change the size of the legislature of the method of electing the President, or in foreign affairs to adopt a policy of self-determination, or (for Lowi) to restructure the school districts of the central city and the suburbs. Argument over such proposals, after the principle of consent has been established, has contributed to the success of liberal politics, for if government ever became perfectly representative to everyone's satisfaction, we might see just how necessary oppression is for us. We might see ourselves as the beasts Hobbes says we are in the state of nature. Government seems not to be coercive because it is government by consent, and especially when we can argue about the meaning or the application of consent. Imagine a perfect blend of black, white, and every other kind of power; then we might have to face the reality of power and of ourselves. We might become aware of that to which we must consent and begin to wonder about the very principle of consent.

This is not an immediate danger. It might seem reasonable that liberal political philosophy, having established the principle of government by consent, would go on to consider what good policies the people should consent to. But in practice (as I believe was intended), the principle of consent has shown a remarkable capacity to become preoccupied with itself. Liberal politics seem to have been chiefly the politics of consent, in which the issue has been the meaning of consent or the method of representation. Conservatives, reactionaries, and radicals become involved in the same issue and thus testify unwillingly or unconsciously to its power. The reason why this issue is paramount in liberal politics can be seen in the right of consent. Consent is not merely expedient for governments, but it is the right of the governed. To assert this right it is necessary to abstract from the policies of government, in which governments show what they think to be expedient. In consequence, the people's attention is diverted from the worth of policy to its formulation, from the uses of power to its legitimation by consent. Liberal politics consists in the assertion and the reassertion of this right, because the purpose of liberal politics, as of any politics for its supporters, is to enable liberals to show that they are liberals, even while claiming to have discovered the end of liberalism. The liberal diversion from the uses of power is related to the following fragment of Machiavellian fraud, taken from the original: "Wounds and other injuries that a man voluntarily inflicts on himself, by choice, are much less painful than those inflicted by others." This is the liberal principle of consent without its characteristic system, universality and morality.

Modern youth reacts in disgust against this realism, against justice based on self-interest that looks to an accomodation of the power struggle by the methods of consent or bargaining. There must be no more merely mechanical solutions, they say. We must ask what is right ideally and proceed to it without fear, favor, or compromise. We must be idealistic as opposed to realistic. It would be sophisticated and wrong to deny that such idealism derives from the moral philosophy of Kant. Kant carefully meant something splendid and difficult when he referred to his position as "idealism" (or "critical idealism"), in shocking contrast to the shoddy, loose idealism of our day. Yet the latter is derived from the former.

Kant invented what he called a priori morality in reaction against the realism of early liberalism. A priori morality is prior to experience, which means, not based on consideration of any facts that might seem morally relevant. It is not based on the facts of human behavior in the state of nature, as was Hobbes's (now dubbed) "empirical" morality. Not considering the facts, a priori morality does not surrender to them; it does not excuse immorality even if it seems to be required by our environment or prompted by our nature. Therefore it is both pure and powerful to a degree unmatched by any previous morality: pure, because uncontaminated by expediency, and powerful, because unhindered by the doubts that arise from considering expediency. To achieve a priori morality you must not look at any facts about yourself or your situation. Above all, you must not consider yourself as a human being but as a rational being. More precisely, you must consider yourself as a rational being who is not necessarily human, who does not necessarily have a human body; for it is the belief that the rational being needs the human body which is the source of all the concessions to selfishness that characterize empirical, so-called morality. When you separate rational being from human being, you become capable of the "categorical imperative" of acting as if the maxim of your action could be a universal rule applicable everywhere to all rational beings.

Kant did not break with the liberal principle of consent. By means of a priori morality he put man beyond the reach of God or nature, except for what man could posit for himself. He kept the principle of consent because his formula made it the duty of all, rather than the privilege of the few gentlemen, to be moral. But a priori morality has the political implication that government by consent of human beings becomes government of rational beings. This apparently remote theoretical distinction makes a crucial difference in practice. Whereas a government must actually get the consent of a human being, who has actually to pull a lever in a voting machine, it can assume the consent of a rational being. Rational beings are all alike, and one or a few can serve for all. This difference was used by certain thinkers and nonthinkers after Kant who did not believe in rational beings, but who wished to be able to assume, rather than get, the consent of the people.

This is the idealist theory; what is the program for action? How can the idealist proceed against the "political moralists," those who conform morality to political necessities? The answer is confrontation politics, the idea of which is stated in Kant's essay on perpetual peace. Kant says there: Let us force the political moralists, the power-brokers, to confess that they rest on might, not right. Let us make them use force to defend themselves, and their attachment to power and vested interests will be manifest. At the same time, the very presence of those who have no secrets because they have no attachments and who publicize their aim of perpetual peace because it is a universal aim will confound the political moralists, for it will show that moral men can ignore their supposed necessities and sacrifice their interests. In this confrontation (Kant does not use the word, but his essay has the effect) the legitimacy of government collapses because it loses its disguise. It is revealed to be the government of an immoral few (Kant expects it will be few) who merely want to defend their lives and their property by an immoral use of prudence. Prudence is immoral for the idealist because the rational being has nothing to defend. He does not live in a human body, much less in a suburb.

In confrontation politics Kant's rational being has been replaced today by Nietzsche's willing being, but the hostility to prudence and self-preservation remains. While consent was designed to legitimize the greatest use of force, the least use is now taken to cause the loss of legitimacy. The reason is that the idealist, a universal being whether rational or willing, carries all idealism in himself. Instead of gathering consent by counting noses, the idealist speaks for all idealism; and therefore he speaks out. Any consideration for the sensibilities of live, empirical human beings would constitute an immoral and irrational concession to expediency.

In judging Kant's idealism and the idealism of the will or activism that is prevalent today, we note that the confrontation remains a diversion like the liberal diversion. It is a diversion from the sense of the proposal or "demands" to the bad conscience of the power-holders, which, being liberals, they are bound to have. They may be impressed by the implicit argument on the character of morality. Forgetting that it is easy for the young to be idealistic, they may praise them for their spirit of sacrifice. Or more typically, the liberal power-holders will see the challenge of morality as a problem of consent, and bewail the emergence of a communication gap. But one can wonder about these rational or willing beings, the idealists. It is easy for the young to be idealistic since they have no vested interests, no wives, no children, no property. They do have incomes, however. Nothing is more impressive about American youth than the fact that they have incomes. And where there is income, there is property. Among the young property used to give rise, with little prompting by their elders, to what were known as "expectations," which with some instruction were supposed to encourage sobriety and prudence. Today society guarantees expectations for most, and the young can spend themselves in forcing it to extend the guarantee to all so that all can be as free as they. Still there is property, however disguised as belonging to "society." Behind every income stands one's own; that was Machiavelli's point. If the income is not economic, it is psychic: the joy of righteousness, of condemnation and—the open secret of idealism—of mastery.

The fraud or diversion of idealism is its formalism, which could be defined in politics as the promotion of form without regard to matter. For human beings, matter is the human body that is ineluctably one's own. Idealism pretends to ignore one's own and in fact universalizes it, as in Lowi's example of universal ticket-fixing. The result is a regime in which idealists somehow, unintentionally and reluctantly, would receive the biggest prize of all; they would rule. And, in order to rule, they would have to descend to realism. This hardly surprising result would be very appropriate to conclude any political reasoning but an idealist's. It seems, then, that despite the weaknesses of liberalism, despite the present discomfiture of the "white liberal," we are not at the end of it and have not seen the last of him. True to its nature, liberalism engenders itself in the disguise of opposition to itself; the idealist is a disguised realist. Liberalism in one or several of its forms or perversions will last as long as the opposition to it does not question the Machiavellian premise that all government is essentially oppression. The premise has been questioned, not by idealists but by the ancient writers who constitute the true alternative to liberalism. Failing a revival of their thought, which would require a radical questioning of all modernity, one who wishes to understand liberalism from without can use its two tendencies, moralistic and mundane, according to the times.

In present circumstances the moralistic tendency of liberalism would seem to be the greater danger. If liberalism does not seem on the point of expiring, liberty in the mundane sense of consent is in jeopardy. To understand this danger, one would have to take up the development within idealism from Kant to Nietzsche and existentialism, or from rational to activist idealism. A review of Lowi's book is not the place for this inquiry because Lowi, to his honor, favors a somewhat archaic pre-New Deal, Middle-American "progressivism" over the more fashionable West Coast university and New York literary activism. Yet it is remarkable that he does not consider the problem of gaining consent for his program of juridical democracy. How will he build and keep the majority behind it? Since he wishes to take advantage of the law-abidingness (pp. 247, 269), how will he protect the rights of the "terror-stricken" minority opposed to it? Lowi might reply that he wants to give effect to consent in democratic majorities by isolating administration from consent. His book is devoted to the advocacy of formalism in administration, as opposed to the mechanical solutions of interest-group liberalism that mix execution with gaining consent. He could be reminded that nothing is more mechanical than a moralistic formalism, which could be compared to majority tyranny without the majority. Lowi's particular proposals for abolishing the legal autonomy of suburbs, busing Negro children, promoting an administrative class, and requiring the regulatory agencies to adopt more formal practices are more liberal, or more conservative, or more reasonable than his advocacy of "a legitimate revolution" (p. 270) would let appear. But they can become revolutionary in the illegitimate sense if they are put forward in revolutionary rhetoric with a spirit of moral intransigency. Disguised liberalism is no substitute for moderation, and reasonable proposals, to be reasonable, must be reasonably proposed.

Part 5

Decision-Making Theory and Performance Budgeting

To many of the early civil service reformers, the problem of responsibility and control of the politically neutral bureaucracy appeared to be an external one. That is, they thought that the requirements of efficient and effective administration were what they were; and they could be discovered by a sustained study of administration itself. Such a study would lead ultimately to a genuine, practical science. To be sure, the recommendations of such a science might have to be compromised or qualified by the additional considerations that public administration be subject to political control; but that did not embarrass the attempt to develop an administrative science. The whole idea from the beginning, in Wilson and Goodnow, was that research and study would reveal that administration had principles of its own, subordinate to but not derivative from political considerations. Common sense seemed to support the notion that just as manufacturing a hatchet is something different from chopping down a cherry tree, so too is the organizing of human beings into an administrative agency something different from the agency's performing its task. Organizing the agency requires addressing a host of issues in "organizational communication," personnel recruitment, promotion, reward and punishment, and so on. Surely there must be *some* answer to the question of how these things are to be done in the best way. The job of those who were educating public administrators was to find them. If this were not done, government would be moribund. The whole effect of the civil service reform movement would be nil, or perhaps even negative.

But is there, can there be, a science of administration? That is, can there exist *principles* of administration *per se*? The early attempts to discover and articulate such principles foundered on the fact that administration is a process; but the principle that defines and governs any particular process is the end in which the process is completed. Therefore, knowing how to do something or how to organize an agency to do something *would* depend on knowing what it is that is to be done. Since an attempt at developing a science of administration had to abstract from the end, the actual consequence was to produce propositions that were true only in certain circumstances that were presumed to hold, and/or to be vapidly general. To be sure, the work of such early students of administration as Luther Gulick and Lyndon Urwick, F. W.

Willoughby, or Leonard White do deserve a measure of deference for the seriousness of their pursuit of principles. When Urwick, for example, explained that the task of an executive is to perform those duties suggested by the acronym "PODSCORB", (The letters stand for planning, organizing, staffing, directing, co-ordinating, reporting, and budgeting.) he said something that probably was useful towards overcoming the numbing and intimidating quality of the term "executive leadership" by breaking it down into subordinate parts. It is not obvious that students of administration and public administration today are gaining anything more useful than PODSCORB if their approach to executive leadership begins with the kind of psychological issues involved in, say, Theory Z or Total Quality Management techniques. Indeed, many of the same criticisms apply.

As most of the early students of public administration were able to admit, however, their field had not discovered genuine principles that would make it a science. For a time this may have seemed excusable due to the infancy of the field. However, Herbert Simon was able to show that infancy was not the problem. Rather the problem was precisely that the attempt to articulate a science of administration had concentrated on recommendations as to means in abstraction from ends, and as long as that was true, it could never produce anything more compelling than proverb-like admonitions. The problem with proverbs is that they are "iffy"; in some situations they work, but in others one would be better advised to follow a precisely opposite course, for which one might appeal to a different proverb. "Look before you leap," is bad advice where it would be better to remember that "He who hesitates is lost." There is simply no answer to Simon's argument. Therefore if progress towards a science of administration is to be made, a fundamentally different orientation would be needed.

Simon dubbed his new orientation "decision-making theory." He argued that the aims of efficient and effective administration could be achieved only where there was clarity, i.e. non-arbitrariness regarding the end to be served. All issues of administrative process and structure, then, depend on such clarity. But how is that to be attained? The answer was, by way of the *decision*. A decision is to be distinguished sharply from the sort of reasoning or deliberation about which means are to be chosen to achieve one's end. The whole point is that since reasoning about means presumes an end, the identification of the end cannot be the fruit of such reasoning. Indeed, the identification of an end is not, strictly speaking, a rational activity at all. It has to be arbitrary, and self-consciously so, precisely to put an end to further questioning as to its defensibility according to some still more inclusive end. Only if the starting point of practical reasoning is a flat "so be it" can it be a foundation for unambiguous recommendations or commands. The intentionally positive part of Simon's work was to articulate the conditions whereby such decision-making might actually occur.

The work of Herbert Simon inaugurated a genuine revolution in the fields of administration and public administration. Afterwards, things would never look as they did in the texts of White or Willoughby. This is not to say that the revolution was altogether successful on Simon's terms. Simon had asserted what might be understood as a positivism applied to practical reasoning. As such it generated a wave of responses from people whose arguments bear the stamp of a philosophical sophistication that Simon's lack. The most outstanding example by far of such critical responses was Herbert J. Storing's chapter on Simon in *Essays in the Scientific Study of Politics*, a series of essays which he edited. This chapter, too long to be included in the present collection, was in fact so careful and thorough in its discussion of the implicit consequences of Simon's approach that it may even have seemed to some readers as unrelenting overkill. Professor Edward Banfield's critique of Simon turns on the same fundamental point as Storing's and is presented more briefly. To state the matter as shortly as possible, Banfield and Storing observe that perfect arbitrariness in decision-making would require canvassing an actual infinity of alternative ends; but one simply cannot pass through an actual infinity—not even with the mind's eye. Some restriction of the field is necessary, therefore some notion of salience or relevance must be relied on. But while Simon is forced to admit this, he says in response only that one should do one's best to be as clear as possible. He therefore fails to consider whether such clarity, and arbitrariness, may not undermine the ability of an organization of human beings to have recourse to the necessarily unarticulated restrictions with which limited rationality must operate.

The debate that Simon generated has largely been about his premises rather than about how to employ his recommendations. That is, it has been somewhat theoretical and as such it might not seem to requite direct engagement by students who are studying public administration with hopes for a career in the civil service. On the contrary, insofar as public administration includes techniques of budgeting, today's students do confront the implications of decision-making theory quite directly. The whole issue of "P.P.B.S." (Planning, Programming, and Budgeting Systems), which was first tried out at the federal level in Robert McNamara's defense department, can be viewed as an effort to apply administrative rationality as Simon understood it to the way government bureaus and agencies think about what is to be done. This is because P.P.B.S. shares with Simon's decision-making theory the same hostility to ambiguity and inexplicitness regarding the premises of practical reasoning, believing these to be the main source of confusion and inefficiency. This section, therefore, concludes with a presentation of Samuel Greenhouse's description and defense of P.P.B.S., followed by one of Professor Aaron Wildavsky's many salvos criticizing the whole idea as politically naive and even damaging to what he calls "political rationality". Doubtless, this argument for a time so dominated discussion in the field, especially notably in the *Public Administration Review,* that it bred annoyance among professionals; and the effectual collapse of the technique in the federal bureaucracy following the Johnson Administration has made the whole issue seem, mercifully, passe. Here as elsewhere, the abandonment of an issue does not indicate its resolution or its unimportance. In revisiting the whole debate over P.P.B.S. one notices that its partisans do in fact exhibit a certain political naivete in comparison with their opponents, who shrewdly remind them of the limits of practical reasoning. Still, our situation today forces us to ask what we are left with once that point has been made. The fundamental question is how can the *limitedness* of rationality require or even tolerate an *argument* in its defense? Despite the cleverness of such defenses as are implied by the title of Charles Lindblom's famous article, "The Science of Muddling Through," in truth respecting the *status quo,* or "muddling," is rendered more difficult, not less so, when it is recognized as merely that.

THE PROVERBS OF ADMINISTRATION

Herbert A. Simon

[This selection and the continuation of Simon's paper under the following topic are from *Public Administration Review*, 6 ,Winter, 1946, pp. 53-57 and 58-61 selected. Reprinted by permission of the American Society for Public Administration.]

A fact about proverbs that greatly enhances their quotability is that they almost always occur in mutually contradictory pairs. "Look before you leap!"—but "He who hesitates is lost."

This is both a great convenience and a serious defect—depending on the use to which one wishes to put the proverbs in question. If it is a matter of rationalizing behavior that has already taken place or justifying action that has already been decided upon, proverbs are ideal. Since one is never at a loss to find one that will prove his point—or the precisely contradictory point, for that matter—they are a great help in persuasion, political debate, and all forms of rhetoric.

But when one seeks to use proverbs as the basis of a scientific theory, the situation is less happy. It is not that the propositions expressed by the proverbs are insufficient; it is rather that they prove too much. A scientific theory should tell what is true but also what is false. If Newton had announced to the world that particles of matter exert either an attraction or a repulsion on each other, he would not have added much to scientific knowledge. His contribution consisted in showing that an attraction was exercised and in announcing the precise law governing its operation.

Most of the propositions that make up the body of administrative theory today share, unfortunately, this defect of proverbs. For almost every principle one can find an equally plausible and acceptable contradictory principle. Although the two principles of the pair will lead to exactly opposite organizational recommendations, there is nothing in the theory to indicate which is the proper one to apply.[1]

It is the purpose of this paper to substantiate this sweeping criticism of administrative theory, and to present some suggestions—perhaps less concrete than they should be—as to how the existing dilemma can be solved.

SOME ACCEPTED ADMINISTRATIVE PRINCIPLES

Among the more common "principles" that occur in the literature of administration are these:

1. Administrative efficiency is increased by a specialization of the task among the group.

2. Administrative efficiency is increased by arranging the members of the group in a determinate hierarchy of authority.

3. Administrative efficiency is increased by limiting the span of control at any point in the hierarchy to a small number.

---

[1]   Lest it be thought that this difficulty is peculiar to the science—or "art"—of administration, it should be pointed out that the same trouble is shared by most Freudian psychological theories, as well as by some sociological theories.

4. Administrative efficiency is increased by grouping the workers, for purposes of control, according to (a) purpose, (b) process, (c) clientele, or (d) place. (This is really an elaboration of the first principle but deserves separate discussion.)

Since these principles appear relatively simple and clear, it would seem that their application to concrete problems of administrative organization would be unambiguous and that their validity would be easily submitted to empirical test. Such, however, seems not to be the case. To show why it is not, each of the four principles just listed will be considered in turn.

SPECIALIZATION

Administrative efficiency is supposed to increase with an increase in specialization. But is this intended to mean that any increase in specialization will increase efficiency? If so, which of the following alternatives is the correct application of the principle in a particular case?

1. A plan of nursing should be put into effect by which nurses will be assigned to districts and do all nursing within that district, including school examinations, visits to homes or school children, and tuberculosis nursing.

2. A functional plan of nursing should be put into effect by which different nurses will be assigned to school examinations, visits to homes of school children, and tuberculosis nursing. The present method of generalized nursing by districts impedes the development of specialized skills in the three very diverse programs.

Both of these administrative arrangements satisfy the requirement of specialization—the first provides specialization by place; the second, specialization by function. The principle of specialization is of no help at all in choosing between the two alternatives.

It appears that the simplicity of the principle of specialization is a deceptive simplicity—a simplicity which conceals fundamental ambiguities. For "specialization" is not a condition of efficient administration; it is an inevitable characteristic of all group effort, however efficient or inefficient that effort may be. Specialization merely means that different persons are doing different things—and since it is physically impossible for two persons to be doing the same thing in the same place at the same time, two persons are always doing different things.

The real problem of administration, then, is not to "specialize," but to specialize in that particular manner and along those particular lines which will lead to administrative efficiency. But in thus rephrasing this "principle" of administration, there has been brought clearly into the open its fundamental ambiguity: "Administrative efficiency is increased by a specialization of the task among the group in the direction which will lead to greater efficiency."

Further discussion of the choice between competing bases of specialization will be undertaken after two other principles of administration have been examined.

UNITY OF COMMAND

Administrative efficiency is supposed to be enhanced by arranging the members of the organization in a determinate hierarchy of authority in order to preserve "unity of command."

Analysis of this "principle" requires a clear understanding of what is meant by the term "authority." A subordinate may be said to accept authority whenever he permits his behavior to be guided by a decision reached by another, irrespective of his own judgment as to the merits of that decision.

In one sense the principle of unity of command, like the principle of specialization, cannot be violated; for it is physically impossible for a man to obey two contradictory commands—that is what is meant by "contradictory commands." Presumably, if unity of command is a principle of administration, it must assert something more than this physical impossibility. Perhaps it asserts this: that it is undesirable to place a member of an organization in a position where he receives orders from more than one superior. This is evidently the meaning that Gulick attaches to the principle when he says:

> The significance of this principle in the process of coordination and organization must not be lost sight of. In building a structure of coordination, it is often tempting to set up more than one boss for a man who is doing work which has more than one relationship. Even as great a philosopher of management as Taylor fell into this error in setting up separate foremen to deal with machinery, with materials, with speed, etc., each with the power of giving orders directly to the individual workman. The rigid adherence to the principle of unity of command may have its absurdities; these are, however, unimportant in comparison with the certainty of confusion, inefficiency, and irresponsibility which arise from the violation of the principle.

Certainly the principle of unity of command, thus interpreted, cannot be criticized for any lack of clarity or any ambiguity. The definition of authority given above should provide a clear test whether, in any concrete situation, the principle is observed. The real fault that must be found with this principle is that it is incompatible with the principle of specialization. One of the most important uses to which authority is put in organization is to bring about specialization in the work of making decisions, so that each decision is made at a point in the organization where it can be made most expertly. As a result, the use of authority permits a greater degree of expertness to be achieved in decision-making than would be possible if each operative employee had himself to make all the decisions upon which his activity is predicated. The individual fireman does not decide whether to use a two-inch hose or a fire extinguisher; that is decided for him by his officers, and the decision is communicated to him in the form of a command. However, if unity of command, in Gulick's sense, is observed, the decisions of a person at any point in the administrative hierarchy are subject to influence through only one channel of authority; and if his decisions are of a kind that require expertise in more than one field of knowledge, then advisory and informational services must be relied upon to supply those premises which lie in a field not recognized by the mode of specialization in the organization. For example, if an accountant in a school department is subordinate to an educator, and if unity of command is observed, then the finance department cannot issue direct orders to him regarding the technical, accounting aspects of his work. Similarly the director of motor vehicles in the public works department will be unable to issue direct orders on care of motor equipment to the fire-truck driver.

Gulick, in the statement quoted above, clearly indicates the difficulties to be faced if unity of command is not observed. A certain amount of irresponsibility and confusion are almost certain to ensue. But perhaps this is not too great a price to pay for the increased expertise that can be applied to decisions. What is needed to decide the issue is a principle of administration that would enable one to weigh the relative advantages of the two courses of action. But neither the principle of unity of command nor the principle of specialization is helpful in adjudicating the controversy. They merely contradict each other without indicating any procedure for resolving the contradiction.

If this were merely an academic controversy—if it were generally agreed and had been generally demonstrated that unity of command must be preserved in all cases, even with a loss in expertise—one could assert that in case of conflict between the two principles, unity of command should prevail. But the issue is far from clear, and experts can be ranged on both sides of the controversy. On the side of unity of command there may be cited the dictums of Gulick and others. On the side of specialization there are Taylor's theory of functional supervision, Macmahon and Millett's idea of "dual supervision," and the practice of technical supervision in military organization.

It may be, as Gulick asserts, that the notion of Taylor and these others is an "error." If so, the evidence that it is an error has never been marshaled or published—apart from loose heuristic arguments like that quoted above. One is left with a choice between equally eminent theorists of administration and without any evidential basis for making that choice.

What evidence there is of actual administrative practice would seem to indicate that the need for specialization is to a very large degree given priority over the need for unity of command. As a matter of fact, it does not go too far to say that unity of command, in Gulick's sense, never has existed in any administrative organization. If a line officer accepts the regulations of an accounting department with regard to the procedure for making requisitions, can it be said that, in this sphere, he is not subject to the authority of the accounting department? In any actual administrative situation authority is zoned, and to maintain that this zoning does not contradict the principle of unity of command requires a very different definition of authority from that used here. This subjection of the line officer to the accounting department is no different, in principle, from Taylor's recommendation that in the matter of work programming a workman be subject to one foreman, in the matter of machine operation to another.

The principle of unity of command is perhaps more defensible if narrowed down to the following: In case two authoritative commands conflict, there should be a single determinate person whom the subordinate is expected to obey; and the sanctions of authority should be applied against the subordinate only to enforce his obedience to that one person.

If the principle of unity of command is more defensible when stated in this limited form, it also solves fewer problems. In the first place, it no longer requires, except for settling conflicts of authority, a single hierarchy of authority. Consequently, it leaves unsettled the very important question of how authority should be zoned in a particular organization (i.e., the modes of specialization) and through what channels it should be exercised. Finally, even this narrower concept of unity of command conflicts with the principle of specialization, for whenever disagreement does occur and the organization members revert to the formal lines of authority, then only those types of specialization which are represented in the hierarchy of authority can impress themselves on decision. If the training officer of a city exercises only functional supervision over the police training officer, then in case of disagreement with the police chief, specialized knowledge of police problems will determine the outcome while specialized knowledge of training problems will be subordinated or ignored. That this actually occurs is shown by the frustration so commonly expressed by functional supervisors at their lack of authority to apply sanctions.

SPAN OF CONTROL

Administrative efficiency is supposed to be enhanced by limiting the number of subordinates who report directly to any one administrator to a small number—say six. This notion that the "span of control' should be narrow is confidently asserted as a third incontrovertible principle of administration. The usual common-sense arguments for restricting the span of control are familiar and need not be repeated here. What is not so generally recognized is that a contradictory proverb of administration can be stated which, though it is not so familiar as the principle of span of control, can be supported by arguments of equal plausibility. The proverb in question is the following: Administrative efficiency is enhanced by keeping at a minimum the number of organizational levels through which a matter must pass before it is acted upon.

This latter proverb is one of the fundamental criteria that guide administrative analysts in procedures simplification work. Yet in many situations the results to which this principle leads are in direct contradiction to the requirements of the principle of span of control, the principle of unity of command, and the principle of specialization. The present discussion is concerned with the first of these conflicts. To illustrate the difficulty, two alternative proposals for the organization of a small health department will be presented— one based on the restriction of span of control, the other on the limitation of number of organization levels:

1. The present organization of the department places an administrative overload on the health officer by reason of the fact that all eleven employees of the department report directly to him and the further fact that some of the staff lack adequate technical training. Consequently, venereal disease clinic treatments and other details require an undue amount of the health officer's personal attention.

    It has previously been recommended that the proposed medical officer be placed in charge of the venereal disease and chest clinics and all child hygiene work. It is further recommended that one of the inspectors be designated chief inspector and placed in charge of all the department's inspectional activities and that one of the nurses be designated as head nurse. This will relieve the health commissioner of considerable detail and will leave him greater freedom to plan and supervise the health program as a whole, to conduct health education, and to coordinate the work of the department with that of other community agencies. If the department were thus organized, the effectiveness of all employees could be substantially increased.

2. The present organization of the department leads to inefficiency and excessive red tape by reason of the fact that an unnecessary supervisory level intervenes between the health officer and the operative employees, and that those four of the twelve employees who are best trained technically are engaged largely in "overhead" administrative duties. Consequently, unnecessary delays occur in securing the approval of the health officer on matters requiring his attention, and too many matters require review and re-review.

The medical officer should be left in charge of the venereal disease and chest clinics and child hygiene work. It is recommended, however, that the position of chief inspector and head nurse be abolished and that the employees now filling these positions perform regular inspectional and nursing duties. The details of work scheduling now handled by these two employees can be taken care of more economically by the secretary to the health officer, and, since broader matters of policy have, in any event, always required the personal attention of the health officer, the abolition of these two positions will eliminate a wholly unnecessary step in review, will allow an expansion of inspectional and nursing services, and will permit at least a beginning to be made in the recommended program of health education. The number of persons reporting directly to the health officer will be increased to nine, but since there are few matters requiring the coordination of these employees, other than the work schedules and policy questions referred to above, this change will not materially increase his work load.

The dilemma is this: in a large organization with complex interrelations between members, a restricted span of control inevitably produces excessive red tape, for each contact between organization members must be carried upward until a common superior is found. If the organization is at all large, this will involve carrying all such matters upward through several levels of officials for decision and then downward again in the form of orders and instructions—a cumbersome and time-consuming process.

The alternative is to increase the number of persons who are under the command of each officer, so that the pyramid will come more rapidly to a peak, with fewer intervening levels. But this, too, leads to difficulty, for if an officer is required to supervise too many employees, his control over them is weakened. If it is granted, then, that both the increase and the decrease in span of control has some undesirable consequences, what is the optimum point? Proponents of a restricted span of control have suggested three, five, even eleven as suitable numbers, but nowhere have they explained the reasoning which led them to the particular number they selected. The principle as stated casts no light on this very crucial question. One is reminded of current arguments about the proper size of the national debt.

A CRITICISM OF THE DECISION-MAKING SCHEMA

Edward C. Banfield

[From *Public Administration Review*, 17, Autumn, 1957, pp. 278-8.5. Reprinted by permission of the author and the American Society for Public Administration. Page and chapter references within the body of this chapter are Professor Banfield's and refer to Professor Simon's book, *Administrative Behavior*, 2nd ed. (New York: Macmillan, 1957.)]

In his Introduction to the second edition of *Administrative Behavior*, Herbert A. Simon observes that he might claim some sort of prophetic gift in having incorporated in the title and subtitle three of the currently most fashionable words in social science— "behavior," "decision-making," and "organization." It is because it deals with these fashionable themes in a fashionable way (if he were not so modest he might claim credit for making the fashion as well as for discerning it) that his book deserves re-examination after a decade. Except for the addition of the Introduction, the text is unchanged.

Simon's intention was to make a methodological contribution. There are, he said in the preface to the first edition, no "adequate linguistic and conceptual tools for realistically and significantly describing even a simple administrative organization—describing it, that is, in a way that will provide the basis for scientific analysis of the effectiveness of its structure and operation." It was to supply this lack that *Administrative Behavior* was written, and it is with this in mind, of course, that it should be criticized.

In this review, Simon's main methodological points will be considered one by one. They are three.

1. The "principles" of the "usual" administrative theory (he refers especially to the work of Gulick and Urwick) are really "proverbs,"— for almost every principle one can find an equally plausible and acceptable contradictory principle. A real science of administration will avoid this fatal defect.

2. A proper science of administration must be based upon "operational" concepts; the creation of a suitable set of concepts is the first task of theory.

3. Decision-making is the appropriate conceptual scheme.

"PRINCIPLES" ARE "PROVERBS"

Simon is easily able to show that there are fundamental ambiguities in the "principles" of the usual administrative theory. Span of control should be narrow. But the number of organizational levels should be kept to a minimum. "Although the two principles of the pair will lead to exactly opposite organizational recommendations, there is nothing in the theory to indicate which is the proper one to apply." (p. 20) The difficulty with the usual theory is, he says, that it treats as "principles of administration" what are really "criteria" for describing and diagnosing administrative situations.

To make them useful, some way must be found of wedding the advantages associated with one criterion with the incompatible advantages associated with the competing ones. To choose between the advantages of a narrow span of control on the one hand and those of a small number of levels of organization on the other, it is necessary to measure all advantages against the single criterion of efficiency. (p. 36)

This, Simon points out, is a matter for empirical research. The real shortcoming of the usual theorists, then, is that they have not gone on to do the empirical research which would reveal the concrete circumstances in which the various criteria appropriately apply.

Clearly any theorist will produce "proverbs" unless and until empirical research is done to provide a basis for knowing which propositions to invoke in particular circumstances. (Simon himself is in no danger of producing proverbs, however, for he limits himself to the construction of a vocabulary and does not engage in theorizing; "no principles of administration are laid down," he says in the preface, using the word which caused Gulick and Urwick so much trouble.)

There are two "indispensable conditions" to the empirical research which is necessary to turn proverbs into scientific analysis:

> First, it is necessary that the objectives of the administrative organization under study be in concrete terms so that results, expressed in terms of these objectives may be accurately measured. Second, it is necessary that sufficient experimental control be exercised to make possible the isolation of the particular effect under study from other disturbing factors that might be operating on the organization at the same time. (p. 42)

In the literature of administration, Simon observes, only a handful of research studies, most of them at the periphery of organization, satisfy these fundamental conditions. In the field of public administration, almost the sole example is the series of studies that were conducted in the public welfare field to determine the proper case loads for social workers. (p. 43)

Simon does not consider *why* there is this extraordinary lack. One reason, perhaps, is that organizations—especially public ones—do not generally have ends which are concrete enough in content to provide an unambiguous criterion by which to choose among the competing advantages associated with the various diagnostic criteria. Sometimes it is hard to say whether a particular organization has any objective at all other than survival. Often organizational objectives exist only as vague generalities. As Simon himself observes (p. 5), "Goals or final objectives of governmental organization and activity are usually formulated in very general and ambiguous terms—'justice,' 'the general welfare,' or 'liberty.'" Even in those rare instances where objectives are highly concrete, there is not likely to be an ordering such that the researcher can know how much of one advantage the organization would willingly forgo for the sake of gaining a certain amount of another advantage which is different in kind.

If the organization has no relevant objectives, or if its objectives conflict, obviously the researcher cannot weight his diagnostic criteria by them. He may, of course, ask the organization to accommodate him by clarifying its objectives or by thinking up new ones. He may even suggest to it some objectives which would help to produce a plausible research result without doing violence to such general ends as may already have been declared. This is not always possible, of course, for the researcher may not have the cooperation of the organization. And even when it is possible, it is not an altogether satisfactory solution to the problem, since it only shifts the burden of being arbitrary from the researcher to the organization itself.[2] Simon's other "indispensable condition" is hardly less unrealizable. Very rarely is it possible to isolate the particular effect under study from other, disturbing factors operating within the organization. One may approximate—but not achieve—"controlled" conditions in the study of case workers, a large number of whom are performing essentially the same task under essentially similar conditions.[3] But one can do little or nothing to eliminate disturbing elements when one studies an operation which is not routine; here the "disturbing elements"—a certain personality, that an election is in the offing, and so on—are inseparable from the phenomenon under study.

If one cannot study important matters under controlled conditions, one must either seek out unimportant ones which can be scientifically studied or

---

[2]   As an example of proper method, Simon cites a study by himself and others which sought to fix the optimum work load for professional staff in the California State Relief administration. the relief agency had two conflicitng aims: (a) to determine eligibility accurately, and (b) to keep down administrative expense. Somehow the relative importance of these objectives had to be fixed if Simon and his associates were to determine what case load was best. How was this weighting of objectives accomplished? "It was believed," the study says, "that an agency would not wish to carry the thoroughness of its investigations much beyond the point where prompter removal of ineligibles would be more than balanced by the increased operating expense." In other words, the researchers imputed an objective to the organization. The imputation seems plausible. But might not a relief agency be willing to spend rather large sums to avoid declaring ineligible someone who was really eligible? How large? Doubtless the Internal Revenue Service would gladly spend more than would be recovered in order to catch tax criminals. See Simon et al., *Determining Work Loads for Professional Staff in a Public Welfare Agency* (Bureau of Public Administration, University of California, Berkeley, 1941), p. 4.

[3]   In the study of work loads which he cites as a model Simon and his associates tried hard to control the disturbing factors (ibid., Chapter IV). It is obvious, however, that they did not succeed. The study was conducted "substantially in duplicate in two relatively dissimilar areas [of Los Angeles] in order to obtain some notion of the stability of results to be expected under different conditions of operation." (p. 3) But the situation in Northern California was certainly different from that in either of the Los Angeles districts; thus some disturbing factors were disregarded. Moreover, it was impossible to control the disturbing effect of events which were occurring while the study was in progress: the relief administration was in a political battle which resulted in personnel cuts. "These events," Simon wrote, "combined with a series of conflicts for control within the agency, created an atmosphere of uncertainty and apprehension that was noticeable throughout the experiment." (p. 65) The experiment itself was a disturbing factor, of course. "On February 13 a meeting of the Vernon intake workers revealed considerable dissatisfaction with the experiment. The workers were not able to adjust themselves to the different loads, and complained of the nervous reaction and strain from participation in the experiment." Workers in the other district, however, "appeared to enjoy the experiment, experienced no difficulty in adjustment, and felt under no nervous strain or tension." (pp. 65-66) By use of statistical techniques (described in a footnote on page 40) Simon and associates satisfied themselves that they had "eliminated or at least minimized" the effects of these and other disturbing factors. They did not, at any rate, indicate any reservations as to the applicability of their study to the state as a whole or to a subsequent time.

reconcile oneself to relying on common sense (meaning here judgment which does not rest entirely upon logical or nonarbitrary grounds).

The latter is, of course, what administrators do every day. The administrator who invokes the twin "proverbs" of span of control and level of organization, for example, considers as best he can how the various advantages associated with each appear in terms of the vague objectives of his organization. In doing this he tries to abstract as well as he can from what he thinks are the disturbing factors in the situation. Simon tells him that he does not perform these operations with exactitude. But Simon does not recognize that, even if there were plenty of time and money, exactitude would be impossible except with regard to the least interesting matters.

So far the analysis of Simon's position has proceeded upon the basis of what was said in the first edition. In the Introduction to the new edition he seems to acknowledge some of these difficulties. With reference to the two "indispensable conditions" of empirical research he says:

> I no longer believe that this passage [he refers to Chapter II, pp. 41-44] is a particularly good description of the kind of empirical research that is needed in administration. Organizations are complex structures, and the importance of any particular factor in the design of such a structure will depend on many circumstances. Hence we can hardly hope for a set of invariant "weights" to apply to the design problem. I expect that for a long time to come, research in administration will be more concerned with identifying and understanding the basic mechanisms that are present in systems of organizational behavior than with assigning numbers to designate the importance of these mechanisms. (p. xxxiv)

It is hard to judge how far this repudiation is intended to go. If it is that he no longer believes empirical research can yield a scientific basis for choice among competing diagnostic criteria ("proverbs"), one would expect him to acknowledge that much of his case against the usual theorists has disappeared. Apparently this is not the conclusion to be drawn, for the Introduction restates the case against the usual theorists ("Alas, the indictment stands" [p. xiv]) and even makes it stronger: the principles of the usual theorists, he now says, are "essentially useless."

THE BASIS OF A PROPER SCIENCE

Another fault Simon finds with the usual theory is that its terms are ambiguous. Before a science can develop principles, he says, it must possess concepts. The first task of administrative theory, accordingly, is to develop a set of concepts that will permit the description, in terms relevant to the theory, of administrative situations. To be scientifically useful, these must be operational; "that is, their meanings must correspond to empirically observable facts or situations." (p. 37)

This is, of course, a highly ambiguous explanation of the term "operational." But Simon illustrates his meaning with his concept of "authority." "Authority," he says, "may be defined as the power[4] to make decisions which guide the actions of another." (p. 125) The advantage of this definition is that

---

[4] On this and other pages he also defines it as a "relationship."

it is "in purely objective and behavioristic terms." As Simon says, "It involves behaviors on the part of both superior and subordinate. When, and only when, these behaviors occur does a relation of authority exist between the two persons involved. When the behaviors do not occur there is no authority, whatever may be the 'paper' theory of organization." (p. 125)

Two objections must be made to Simon's position. One is that narrowly behavioristic concepts are likely to obscure the making of the distinction which it is the purpose of a good conceptual scheme to facilitate. The other is that, strictly speaking, such concepts are usually impossible. Both points may be illustrated with Simon's example.

One could not, on the basis of his definition, distinguish the "authority" of a stick-up man from that of a boss. In both cases the "subordinate" accepts the premises of the "superior" as the basis of his action. A scientific vocabulary should facilitate the making of analytically significant distinctions in this case, distinctions referring to the circumstances which cause a subordinate to accept, or not accept, the premises of the other. Simon, however, unwilling to sacrifice his behavioristic view, defines the concept so as to dissolve the needed distinctions. One may, he says (p. xxxv), reconstitute them as needed under new terms. But although the purpose of his book is to construct a vocabulary for the description and analysis of administrative situations, Simon never does offer additional concepts by which to distinguish the authority of the stick-up man from that of the boss or the authority of one boss from that of another.

Despite the straining and the pretense, Simon's concept of authority is not really defined in "objective and behavioristic terms." It is not because it cannot be. If one merely observes the behavior, including the verbal behavior, of two persons, one cannot tell whether they are in what Simon calls a relationship of authority. One cannot find out if A is accepting the premises of B without getting knowledge of the subjective state of both A and B. Acting as if the other's premises are accepted is, of course, not what Simon defines as authority.

With the other key concepts in the "vocabulary" which it is the main purpose of his book to construct, Simon has less trouble. The reason is that he does not attempt to define them behavioristically and does not note the most glaring ambiguities in them.

Take the concept "decision," for example. Simon says that any selection among action possibilities, whether conscious or unconscious, is a decision. (P. 4) Sleepwalkers, madmen, and newborn babes are, presumably, decision-makers. But what is an "action"? (Is not acting action also?) Abolishing a bureau is an action, but so are picking up a telephone, pressing a buzzer, and signing a letter, and an action of the first type is constituted of numberless actions of the second type. Most decisions in organizations, Simon says, are not made by any single individual; a major decision is "almost always a composite process" involving the interaction of many decisions both of individuals and by committees and boards. (p. 222) "Who really makes the decisions?" he asks rhetorically. "Such a question is meaningless," he answers, "—a complex decision is like a great river, drawing from its many tributaries the innumerable component premises of which it is constituted." (p. xii)

How then does one identify the object to be studied? One cannot always tell by observing an administrator, or even by asking him, whether he has made a decision (either in the sense of having made a choice personally or in the sense of having given formal recognition to the outcome of a "composite" choice). He may not himself know whether he has made a decision, especially if the "decision" has been not to decide. The same sort of ambiguity exists with regard to other important concepts in Simon's scheme. What, precisely, is a "consequence?" (p. 66) Was the industrial revolution a consequence of the Protestant reformation? Is it possible to say that one decision is more nearly "rational" than another? Supposing, for example, that one decision is made after a careful consideration of alternative strategies but with little attention to the consequences which would follow from them? Is this decision more or less "rational" than one made with little consideration of alternatives but a careful review of probable consequences? And if it is meaningless to say that one decision is more rational than another, how is the concept to be used?

With regard to all of those concepts one may paraphrase what Simon says of Gulick, "What is to be considered as a function [phenomenon] depends entirely upon language and techniques. If the English language has a comprehensive term which covers both of two subpurposes [phenomena] it is natural to think of the two together as a single purpose [phenomenon]." The difference between them is that Gulick was trying to theorize about administration, not constructing "adequate linguistic and conceptual tools" for describing administrative organization "in a way that will provide the basis for scientific analysis. . . ." (p. xlv)

DECISION-MAKING: THE APPROPRIATE CONCEPT

Much administrative analysis, Simon says, proceeds by selecting a single criterion (or "proverb") and applying it to an administrative situation to reach a recommendation, while the fact that equally valid, but contradictory, criteria exist which could be applied with equal reason, but with a different result, is conveniently ignored. "A valid approach . . . ," he concludes, "requires that all the relevant diagnostic criteria be identified. . . ." (p. 36)

A good conceptual scheme, then, will tend to be logically complete or systematic, and will therefore direct attention to all relevant features of the situation. A scheme built around the concept "decision" meets these specifications, Simon thinks. In fact, he implies, it is the only one which will. He writes,

What is a scientifically relevant description of an organization? It is a description that, so far as possible, designates for each person in the organization what decisions that person makes, and the influences to which he is subject in making each of these decisions. (p. 37)

The qualifier "in so far as possible" is very important, for, as noted, Simon believes major organizational decisions are composites and it is meaningless to ask who really makes them. Nevertheless, in so far as an empirical referent can be found for the concept "decision," it is this which should be the object of study.

The idea of identifying all relevant diagnostic criteria implies, of course, knowledge of some comprehensive criterion by which to judge what is relevant and what is not. Simon provides such a criterion in the principle (strictly speaking, it is a definition) of "efficiency." "The theory of administration," he says in the first edition, "is concerned with how an organization should be constructed and operated in order to accomplish its work efficiently." (p. 38) Efficiency (which he elaborates in Chapter IX) is therefore the nuclear concept around which others are organized and which gives them their relevance and systematic character.

Decisions which are rational are more likely to lead to efficiency than ones which are not. Thus "rationality" (which he discusses in Chapters IV and V) becomes another organizing category with the help of which one can discover what diagnostic criteria are, or are not, relevant. It turns out, then, that what is needed is a full account of the influences which tend to make the decision-makers more or less rational; knowing these, the organization can manipulate itself by manipulating them—it can alter influences so as to make decisions more rational and outcomes more efficient. Thus the construction of an efficient organization is "a problem in social psychology" (p. 2)—a particularly interesting problem, Simon might have added, because the organization itself is both "psychologist" and "society."

Although it is certainly not the only useful conceptual scheme and for some purposes may even lead the investigator away from the things which are most interesting, and although its concepts are not as "operational" as one might wish, the decision-making scheme unquestionably has a great deal of the merit claimed for it. If it does not identify all of the relevant diagnostic criteria, it at least identifies many.

It has one serious defect, however. As was remarked above, organizations do not generally have concrete, consistently ordered objectives. To the extent that their ends are vague or inconsistent, the idea of efficiency is inapplicable. Efficiency refers to a relation between valued inputs and valued outputs. If there is no way of knowing what is valued or how much it is valued in relation to something else, one cannot speak of efficiency. And if it is not possible to say what is for the organization an efficient situation, it is not possible either to say what are for it rational decisions.

In his introduction to the new edition, Simon takes some account of these problems. He has come to the conclusion that it is utterly unreal to regard men in organizations as engaged in "maximizing"—what they really do is look for a situation which is satisfactory or "good enough." Whereas in the first edition "administrative man" was a "maximizer" (p. 39), in the introduction to the second (but not, of course; in the body of the book, that being unchanged) he is a "satisficer." (p. xxvi) Simon justifies this change on the grounds that the "satisficing" model is a "correct" description whereas the other was not. Here he seems to forget that the concepts of efficiency and rationality were not put forward simply as "sociological" descriptions of the behavior of men in organized groups; they were also intended, as he explained in an appendix (p. 253), as the basis of a "practical" (recommendative) science of administration—one that would describe "good" administration, i.e., how men would behave "if they wished their activity to result in the greatest attainment of administrative objectives with scarce means." He may now feel that the concepts of efficiency and rationality are too unrealistic to be useful even as guides to a "practical" science of administration. He does not, however, say this in so many words.

He cannot argue that the new "satisficing" model takes the place of the old "maximizing" one in a "practical" as distinguished from a "sociological science of administration." For the "satisficing" model, if he is correct, tells us how men actually do behave in organizations, not how they would behave "if [not an utterly unrealistic assumption, surely] they wished their activity to result in the greatest attainment of administrative objectives with scarce means." Presumably the model appropriate for a "practical" science of administration is somewhere between the merely descriptive "satisficing" one and the not-descriptive-enough "maximizing" one.

Of these important matters Simon in the *Introduction* to the new edition says nothing. Instead, he ceases to concern himself with what he called the "practical" science of administration, i.e., "good" administration. In the first edition, the theory of administration "is concerned with how an organization should be constructed and operated in order to accomplish its work efficiently" (p. 38) and the principle of efficiency "follows almost immediately from the rational character of 'good' administration." (p. 39) In the *Introduction*, however, "Administrative theory is peculiarly the theory of intended and bounded rationality—of the behavior of human beings who satisfice because they have not the wits to maximize." (p. xxiv)

He has destroyed the rationale of the old conceptual scheme without offering any new one and without, apparently, being aware of what he has done.[5] A valid approach, he said, requires that all relevant diagnostic criteria be identified. But now, so far as "good" administration is concerned, he has no basis for judging what criteria are relevant and what are not.

AN EVALUATION

It may be asked, in the words Simon used of the usual theory, "Can anything be salvaged which will be useful in the construction of an administrative theory?" The answer, too, may be given in his words: "As a matter of fact, almost everything can be salvaged."

Simon is right in asserting that the "principles" of administrative theory are really "diagnostic criteria" and that empirical research must be done before they can be applied in particular situations. He is wrong, however, in implying that the "usual" theory is peculiarly defective in this regard. The principles of any theory including Simon's own (if he were to get beyond the stage of vocabulary construction) are diagnostic criteria or, to use the attention-getting word, "proverbs." They are "essentially useless," however, only if no empirical basis is found for deciding which of them to invoke. Simon is right in asserting that as a matter of logic empirical research should accurately measure results in terms of organizational objectives defined in concrete terms and the particular effects under observation should be isolated from disturbing factors. But he is wrong in supposing that either of these conditions can be met to a significant extent in the ordinary, and especially the important, cases. It is useful to have the logic of the matter clarified. But unless this clarification is accompanied by a frank avowal that the logic may be irrelevant to the real situation and unless directions are

---

[5] He says in the Introduction that he has "few, if any, major changes to propose in the fundamental conceptual framework." But he appears reluctant to acknowledge changes when he sees them. He says, for example (p. xxxii), that he has always regarded the "premise" as the appropriate unit for analysis. He did make much use of the concept in the first edition, to be sure, but it was "decision," not "premise," which he presented as the basic building block of theory. The word "premise" did not even appear in the index.

given as to how to proceed when the logical way is closed, the researcher is left in a quandary. He may keep himself methodologically pure by studying only those matters to which the logic has some application. Unfortunately, these are not the important ones.

Simon is right in demanding that terms be unambiguously defined. But here, too, he is wrong in supposing that methodological refinement can be had without cost. Some concepts crucial to the discussion of behavior cannot be defined "behavioristically" without ceasing to refer to what it is crucial to discuss. "Authority" is a good example; if Simon had succeeded in defining it behavioristically, it would only have been by extracting from it all of the meaning that it is useful for it to have. Fortunately, he does not deal with the ambiguities in "decision" and related concepts. These are serious enough to impede the thoughtful researcher, but there is reason to fear that if he had applied himself to resolving them his conceptual scheme would have been cut loose from reality. Conceptual clarity, like other virtues, can be carried too far for this world.

Simon is right, also, in claiming relevance and completeness for the rational decision-making schema. It is not the only good schema and it is not a particularly new one. But it is a good one or, rather, it would be a good one if the concept "decision" were defined so as to exclude outcomes that are not in any sense the product of deliberation—a condition Simon would surely reject. It is too bad that Simon kicked the props out from under the decision-making schema by discovering that administrative man, instead of seeking a maximum, seeks only what is "good enough." If efficiency and rationality, or some approximation thereto, are not to be looked for, what model of "good" administration is to be put in their place?

"My present forecast—and a rather confident one," Simon says, in the *Introduction* to the new edition, "is that when a second decade has passed this book will sound a bit old-fashioned." (p. ix) Let us hope not, for the fashion seems to be moving in the wrong direction. *Administrative Behavior*, at any rate, was a better book ten years ago than it is now.

"THE DECISION-MAKING SCHEMA": A REPLY

Herbert A. Simon

[From *Public Administration Review*, 18, Winter, 1958, pp. 60-63. Reprinted by permission of the American Society for Public Administration.]

Professor Edward Banfield published in the Autumn, 1957, issue of the *Public Administration Review* (in the form of a review of *Administrative Behavior*) a defense of proverbs and "wisdom"—a defense against the austerities and pretensions of the scientific method. His lines had so much more the tone of advocate than of judge, that I should like the privilege of pleading the case of the opposing party. I will not dispute whether the three topics he discusses are my "main methodological points," as he asserts, but will simply consider each of them in turn.[6] The first has to do with the "proverbs of administra-

---

[6] I should not like anyone to interpret my silence on other points Mr. Banfield makes as agreement with them. In the interest of brevity, I have restricted my reply to a few central issues.

tion"; the second with the need for operationalizing the concepts of our science; the third with decision-making as a schema for analyzing administrative processes.

THE PROVERBS AGAIN

Mr. Banfield agrees that the usual "principles" are fundamentally ambiguous and mutually contradictory, but despairs of experimental science as a means for resolving the ambiguities and contradictions.

If one cannot study important matters under controlled conditions, one must either seek out unimportant ones which can be scientifically studied or reconcile oneself to relying on common sense (meaning here judgment which does not rest entirely upon logical or nonarbitrary [sic] grounds)

The latter is, of course, what administrators do every day. The administrator who invokes the twin "proverbs" of span of control and level of organization, for example, considers as best he can how the various advantages associated with each appear in terms of the vague objectives of his organization.

The trouble is, "of course," that administrators don't weigh the competing proverbs nearly as often as they should, with the result that we have periodic fads and fashions in organization. For a long while, reorganization studies could always be counted on to recommend a reduction in span of control—whatever the existing span was (the "levels" proverb was not even in the literature until it was put there by James Worthy and me). At the present time "flat" organizations are all the rage.

A second example: I have seen not one but a dozen large organizations plump for "decentralization" without even bothering to examine just how much centralization or decentralization they already had. It is an observed fact that large numbers of business organizations are advocating decentralization of their labor relations activities (and are believing that they are practicing it) at the very time that they are centralizing them further. Neither Mr. Banfield's common sense nor my science has been applied to questions of organization nearly as much as his remarks imply, and there is plenty of room for the improvement of administrative organization through the application of both.

If present knowledge is unsatisfactory, Mr. Banfield would still doubt whether scientific method (and experimentation, in particular) can help us. He introduces into evidence a study in which I participated, which I have no desire to defend in detail (since I could do better now with fifteen years of hindsight), but which I am prepared to defend in general.

In order to derive policy recommendations from the findings of the study, we had to weigh a number of administrative objectives—accuracy of eligibility determination versus service to clients, for example. Mr. Banfield observes, correctly, that the weighing is in itself a value judgment and not empirically testable. (This is the main point of Chapter 3 of *Administrative Behavior,* also clearly stated in the study he refers to.) Since the study had applied aims as well as methodological objectives, its authors took the empirically tested findings (about the consequences for various goals of changing work loads), combined these with the objectives the administrators of the agency said they wished to accomplish (these were not "imputed" by the researchers), and arrived at a policy recommendation. There is nothing unusual or "unscientific" about this procedure, since the authors made clear what value premises they were accepting, and where values left off and facts began.

In consuming food, I attach values both to good nutrition and to gustatory pleasure. I sometimes eat too many calories because I enjoy them; and I sometimes don't eat as many as I otherwise would for nutrition's sake. The numbers and kinds I eat are much influenced by what has been learned about human physiology and nutrition, even though this scientific knowledge is relevant to only one of my two goals in eating, and contributes nothing to the weighing of them. What distinguishes this knowledge from common-sense proverbs of the eat-well-but-not-too-much variety is that it tells me how much (i.e., about 2,500 calories per day) is enough and not too much. If we applied Mr. Banfield's argument literally to nutrition—as he does to administration— we would conclude that the science of nutrition has contributed nothing to the practical arts of eating. I can't accept the conclusion.

To answer Mr. Banfield's specific query, the "principles" are useless because, at best, they preach moderation without giving any measure of the consequences of departing from moderation in any direction. Even if we know how much weight we wish to give to various goals, the proverbs (unlike studies of the kind he objects to) provide us with no connections between actions and consequences. Mr. Banfield makes more technical criticisms of our empirical study, criticisms that were made first by the authors of the study. They, too, would have liked to reduce the unreliability of their data. The route to reliability, however, is more likely to lie through more, and more careful, experimental and observational studies than through a return to "common-sense" methods for examining complex situations and drawing conclusions from them.

In saying this, I am not taking the controlled experiment as the model for all science. Celestial mechanics is a good example of successful non-experimental (until Sputnik) science whose conclusions are based on a single case history. We badly need reliable general methods for observing and drawing inferences from the single case; but we need methods that are more objective, less subject to the "filtering" of the observer, than those [with which] the arts of history, biography, and journalism have provided us. Mr. Banfield can surely see the missing premise in his argument when he says, in effect: scientific method hasn't taken us very far in organization theory; *therefore,* let's go back to common sense.

The preceding paragraphs will answer Mr. Banfields question as to how far the repudiation of pages 41-44 of *Administrative Behavior* is intended to go. I hope it is clear that I do not accept the dilemma of either studying unimportant matters scientifically, or important ones by common sense. The third route—studying important matters scientifically—is a steep and rocky one, but the only one, I am convinced, that leads to our destination.

OPERATIONAL DEFINITIONS

Mr. Banfield uses the definition of "authority" to illustrate his argument that "narrowly behavioristic concepts are likely to obscure the making of the distinctions which it is the purpose of a good conceptual scheme to facilitate." He says that, from the definition in *Administrative Behavior,* he can't distinguish the authority of a stick-up man from that of a boss. This is true—it is equally true that from the definition of "mammal" in Webster, I can't distinguish a mule from a man. Authority is defined on page 125. The gentle reader who perseveres to pages 130-133, or who reads the chapter on authority in *Public Administration* (written with my former colleagues Smithburg and Thompson), will find the stick-up man distinguished from the boss. The point in having a common term covering the influence relation in both cases is that there is, in fact, an important generic similarity. In most organizations I have examined or lived in, negative sanctions (which I understand to be the peculiar earmark of the stick-up man's authority) are not absent as pillars of authority. In fact, their presence raises some of the same problems for the boss that the stick-up man faces, and that have been remarked on in discussions of pedagogical uses of punishment.

Mr. Banfield's second point on operationalism is that, while I have criticized Gulick for not defining the "unit function," I have lapsed in not defining the "unit decision." The point he misses is that if we have a structure made up of parts within parts within parts—and so on—we need to define "unit part" only if we intend to attribute some property to unit parts that is not shared by compound parts. Mr. Gulick makes use of the concept of an organization having a single unitary function, while I do not make use of the concept of a unitary decision. Hence, he needs such a distinction, while I do not. As a matter of fact, an attempt is made in *Public Administration* to provide Mr. Gulick's concept with operational content and hence to make it useful for organizational science (see the discussion in that volume of "unitary organizations" and "operational goals"). Likewise, since decisions can become, and usually do become, premises in other decisions, Mr. Banfield doesn't need to be concerned about the location of *the* decision. There isn't any "the decision."

THE DECISION-MAKING SCHEMA

Mr. Banfield imputes to me something less than complete candor for asserting in the introduction to the second edition that the "decision premise" rather than the "decision" was the building block of my theory. I didn't say that I never called "decision" a building block, since I can't find "building block" in the index; but I do remember that I called "decision" the "heart of administration." I often mix metaphors; seldom that badly.

The important point, and one that does not involve any change in framework from the first edition, is that throughout the book the principal technical means that is employed to analyze the decision process is to dissect decisions into their component premises and then to study where the premises come from. The actual outline of Chapters 7 through 10 is based on this idea, and the point is stated explicitly and *ad nauseam* in the text, e.g., on pages 96, 123, 220, 223. In a casual search, I found 42 occurrences of the term "premises" in the text, together with many synonyms, like "elements." I don't know what Mr. Banfield is trying to prove when he asserts that I appear "reluctant to acknowledge changes" when I see them, but he used a singularly poor example to prove it. What he should have concluded was that "the book does not have an adequate index."

Mr. Banfield is right in observing that in the introduction I place more emphasis on "satisficing" and less on "maximizing" than in the original text. Far from refusing to acknowledge this change, in the new introduction I describe the first edition as "schizophrenic" on this point, and refer to my change in view again on page xxxv.

Now has this change, as Mr. Banfield claims, "destroyed the rationale of the old conceptual scheme"? The change certainly does not interfere with the process of analyzing decisions in terms of the premises that enter into them—which is the conceptual scheme. What Mr. Banfield means is that the change, like his recognition that there may be multiple and incommensurable goals in organizations, adds one further link to the process of going from propositions in a "pure" or "sociological" science of administration—to policy recommendations in the "applied" science of administration.

Under favorable circumstances, a criterion of maximizing guarantees that there will be a single, uniquely determined "best" course of action; the criterion of satisficing provides no such guarantee. My argument is that men satisfice because they have not the wits to maximize. I think this is a verifiable empirical proposition. It can be turned around, if anyone prefers: If you have the wits to maximize, it is silly to satisfice. Since my views on this subject are spelled out in greater detail in the essays in Part 4 of *Models of Man*, I will say no more here.

IN CONCLUSION

Mr. Banfield has a lot to say about what he's against. He has little to say about what he's for. I have inferred that what he is for is "common sense" and "wisdom," and I think this is a fair reading of his lines and of his books. He would be more candid if he presented the case against "wisdom" with the same fervor with which he presents the case against "science." Since he has not done so, I will state briefly what it is:

1. We have applied "wisdom" to administration for 2,000 years. It has allowed us to carry out many administrative tasks reasonably well. However, I don't detect much progress from the "wisdom" literature in administrative theory during the past fifty years. Aristotle and the Hoover Commissions sound much alike, except that the former was a good deal more sophisticated than the latter about the relation of politics to administration.
2. Many other areas of human knowledge began to progress—in both their theoretical and applied aspects—when scientific method was applied to them. I refer not primarily to the physical sciences, but to the much closer parallel of biology and medicine. You can find the same kinds of impassioned pleas for "wisdom" in medicine a century ago as we find in administration today. Meanwhile, the sale of Lydia Pinkham's Vegetable Compound has fallen off; the sale of thyroid extract has increased.

As knowledge advances—and it will—administrative practice will come to rest largely on scientifically tested knowledge of fundamental underlying mechanisms. Moreover, the present generation will see very rapid progress in this direction.

PPBS: RATIONALE, LANGUAGE, AND IDEA RELATIONSHIPS

Samuel M. Greenhouse

[From *Public Administration Review*, Vol. 26, December, 1966, pp. 271-277. Samuel Greenhouse is a member of the Administrator's Advisory Council, Veterans Administration, Washington D.C. Reprinted with permission of the American Society of Public Administration.]

An understanding of what the Planning-Programming-Budgeting System (PPBS) purports to be and to do for the U.S. Government rests, I believe upon recognizing the primacy and interplay of two PPBS ingredients. These two "molecules"—as they stand individually, contribute proportionately, interact, and interdepend—compose the vital core of PPBS.

Let me begin by identifying the two ingredients, as a prelude to defining and discussing them.

A single concept, dealing with the accountability of the Federal agency apparatus, forms the philosophic base of the PPBS structure.

The main structural members of PPBS are eight terms with definitions so special that, in effect, PPBS has a "language all its own." True, one of the words and phrases in this language is really new. But each is used so very differently in the PPBS context that earlier-entrenched images (which our minds seem to conjure up whenever the terms are heard) may in some cases prevent comprehension. The eight terms are: objectives, programs, program alternatives, outputs, progress measurements, inputs, alternative ways to do a given job, and systems analysis. A true understanding of PPBS cannot derive from reliance upon the traditional definitions of these terms. Each has a particular meaning and significance in the rearrangement of established ideas which PPBS represents.

The fresh design which emerges from this rearrangement, rather than the individual ideas themselves, is what is new about PPBS.[7] But in rearranging, in linking and relating the ideas, a trimming and fitting had to take place. Through this tailoring process, the terms remained unchanged while the ideas (which the terms had so long and effectively stood for) took on subtle differences of flavor and shade. Given these new meanings, the terms have become coordinates with distinct functions, hierarchical placements, and highly significant relationships within the flow and overall framework of PPBS.

THE BASIC CONCEPT: ACCOUNTABILITY

PPBS is a multi-purpose system. If it is implemented and instrumented soundly, it should have a variety of uses. Only one of these—and perhaps not the most important one, although it is receiving predominant attention at this stage—is the improvement of individual Federal agency operations. Whether the regulation of Federal agency activities is a key purpose or not, the careful

---

[7]   In this regard, PPBS is not surprisingly like many conceptual "innovations." It is often said that there is "nothing new under the sun." That many discoveries consist in rearranging and regrouping ideas which are, individually, already known, does not diminish the usefulness of the results. The important question is whether and in what direction PPBS may prove useful.

installation of PPBS in the individual agencies is of surpassing importance, because the agencies are indispensable building blocks in the overall system. That is to say, PPBS could not exist disembodied from the individual agencies, even if the main purpose of PPBS were, say, to accelerate the economic growth of the United States rather than to introduce a new technique of agency management. This may help to explain why the bedrock concept of PPBS concerns the matter of Federal agency accountability.

Now, what is the PPBS concept, and how is it different?

The PPBS concept is that each Federal agency is accountable to the President[8] for the production of goods and services, and more particularly, for the distribution of these goods and services to the American people.

This is a considerable departure indeed, for, until PPBS, the Federal agency apparatus was considered to be held accountable by, and to, the President for providing the Presidency with "administrative support." Application of this vague concept has become more difficult as the Federal apparatus has grown and diversified. Our Presidents have become too busy to locate, identify in specifics, and hold direct reins of responsibility.

The PPBS accountability concept focuses the attention of each agency on the question: What is our business? The PPBS concept provides a basis for particularizing the answers to the question: Accountable for specifically what products (goods or services), delivered to whom?

The PPBS concept matches the reality of today's Federal agency operations, demonstrating once again that "theory interprets established fact." The agencies are producing goods and services, and distributing them to the American people.[9] What PPBS adds to this reality is the assumption that product delivery to the American public is the central purpose of agency operation rather than merely a happenstance or a by-product of other, more characteristic purposes.

Of course, all Federal agencies perform other functions besides distributing goods and services to the public. For example, each agency generates goods and services for purely internal uses; for the use of other agencies; or for the President and Congress. However, an understanding of PPBS depends upon recognizing that all "inside-the-government" efforts and interchanges are considered subordinate to the central purpose. Inside-government activities are not pertinent for PPBS accountability. Unless this is recognized, the ideas which underlie the terms "objective," "program," "output," and "input" cannot be clearly discerned nor can the interplay of these terms be comprehended. The discussions of output and input allude in greater detail to this crucial matter.

If the agencies are to be held accountable for discharging the central purpose of distributing agency-produced goods and services to the American public, the public becomes, conceptually speaking, the market for the agencies' products and services. Thus, the explicit business of each Federal agency is to satisfy the public's actual and potential market demands for the agency's particular product/service lines. Accountability discharge becomes subject to

---

8   And to the Congress.
9   In some cases, the agencies contract for goods and services, and perform the distribution function themselves. So long as the production is government financed, and performed under government auspices, it can be regarded the same way, for PPBS purposes, as in government production.

evaluation in terms of each agency's success in (1) gauging the nature and proportions of the market demands, and (2) fulfilling these demands.

OBJECTIVES

With this background, it becomes clear that the apex-term of the PPBS idea-structure is "objectives." As the preceding discussion indicates, a more precise way to visualize the idea here denoted is to expand the term to "market objectives." Each agency is supposed to generate explicit market objectives, to make possible a genuine agency-wide understanding and a common agency approach toward their achievement. Satisfactory market objectives would, one supposes, provide specific grounds upon which to base the answers to three questions[10] about *each* main class of items produced by a given agency:

What class of goods or services is contemplated for production? (Each agency has at least one main class of items, or product line; most agencies have more than one.)

What market group is each product line (good or service) intended to satisfy? (Some agencies have readily identifiable groups of customers, e.g., veterans; other agencies serve fluid and only temporarily associated groups, such as air travelers.)

What specific needs, of the market group served, is the product designed to satisfy? (For example, if the American Indian, say, were assumed to need help in achieving economic well-being comparable to the "national average," what indications of this need might be cited in support of programmatic intentions?)

If this theme correctly interprets PPBS, customer-oriented market objectives are destined to become key standards for agency self-appraisal and accountability. Such standards are quite common for private industry, except that total sales volume is a more readily obtainable index of market needs and satisfactions than will be available in government.

Allowing for the absence of various profit mechanisms in government, the effect of PPBS will be to bring governmental practice to a somewhat closer approximation of common industrial practice than has been possible before.

PROGRAMS

What idea underlies the term "program"? In PPBS language, a program is a package which encompasses each and every one of the agency's efforts to achieve a particular objective or set of allied objectives.[11] If the objective were to provide economic assistance to the American Indian, the program would be composed of all agency activities and expenditures put to that purpose.

Bear in mind that this idea of program is very different from the traditional governmental usage. Prior to PPBS, all agencies used the term to characterize functions and professional disciplines. Hence, "procurement," "data management," "engineering," and many other activities were called programs. The habit persists even now, because PPBS has not yet succeeded in making its point.

---

10   These questions appear useful to the author to illustrate the concept of market demand which PPBS implies. They are not found in the available PPBS literature.

11   Whenever the term "objectives" is used hereafter, it should be read as "customer-oriented market objectives."

Those agencies which did not understand the new meaning of the term in advance of generating their initial PPBS "program structures," will certainly need to redo program structures if PPBS is ever to gain solid ground. Individual activities, functions, and professional disciplines are the very antitheses of programs in the PPBS sense. The whole PPBS idea is to facilitate the drawing together, the summation of all agency efforts to meet particular objectives, so that the validity of each program may be assessed in terms of overall approach, dimension, and costs and may be compared with other competing programs, potential or existing. It should be recognized, then, that in the future, a program which mirrors (corresponds with) a given agency's established organization structure will be a rarity, unless the agency happens to have only one program. An agency with a functional-type organization must break down functional efforts and apportion them among programs, in order to successfully sum each program.[12]

As the foregoing discussion may have indicated, there is a strong conceptual relationship between objective(s) and program. In "PPBS language," there are no objectives recognized except those which suggest a program designed specifically to fulfill them; and there can be no recognized entity describable as a program unless it is designed to accomplish explicit objectives (customer oriented market objectives).

PROGRAM ALTERNATIVES

The term "program alternatives" is next in the PPBS hierarchy.[13] Within any one agency, this term means other possible programs besides those already decided upon. Consequently, it suggests a comparison of two or more programs (i.e., two or more possible approaches) toward fulfilling *the same market objective(s)*. For example, as in the hypothetical case mentioned earlier, suppose that an agency wanted to accomplish the objective of raising the economic well-being of the American Indian to some mythical level such as the national average. Presumably, any one of several programs, existing or new, might succeed in bringing this about. The agency would wish to choose the "best" program for the purpose, and to disregard other program alternatives. Or, it might simply wish to evaluate a number of program alternatives so that, having selected one, it could demonstrate the wisdom of the selection by revealing the inadequacies (in the discarded programs) which the comparative evaluation had uncovered.

OUTPUT

In PPBS language, an output must have, conceptually speaking, all of the following properties:

It is a product (either a good or a service).

It is produced by a Federal agency, or is produced under the agency's auspices.

---

[12] However, it is not required that there be change in the established organization structure; merely a change in the accounting will do.
[13] Of course, these PPBS terms may be considered in any order, but the author finds the order of presentation given here easiest to work with for definition purposes.

It is an outgrowth of a particular program (i.e., it is the result of a calculated program effort).

It is the sort of product which can be appropriately singled out as an indicator of program results. (Logically, therefore, it must be a program end-product, and an important one, at that.)

It is considered by the agency as satisfying an explicit market objective (or related set of objectives).

The foregoing list of properties should serve to illustrate the connective tissue which runs all the way through PPBS. That is, the idea of output is inseparably linked to the earlier discussed ideas of market objectives and program(s). And this idea-connection is highly significant for interpreting the PPBS notion of output. It means that many types of products which the agencies have been accustomed to regard as outputs can no longer be so regarded. PPBS has preempted the word, so to speak, for a much narrower, sharper-focused usage than the traditional one. In order to be considered an output in PPBS language, the good or service produced must satisfy an explicit market objective and must be an indicator of program results.

Let us appraise a few items traditionally considered outputs, in light of these definitional criteria. Suppose that an agency decides upon a program to build schools. The agency's procurement division places a series of contracts with construction firms. One month later, the agency's statistical division prepares and forwards to the agency director a "construction progress report." Are the contractual documents properly countable as outputs? No! Is the statistical report an output No! Why? Neither the documents nor the report satisfies a customer-oriented market objective, and neither represents an indicator of program achievement (although both of them do represent divisional, that is, internal, achievements).

They are intermediate, or contributory products, rather than outputs in the PPBS sense.

What would constitute *program* achievement, and thus be an output in the PPBS sense of the word, could in the example cited above be the number of schools built, number of new classrooms available, or number of new classroom seats set into place.

The distinction between intermediary or contributory products and output is a very critical matter, insofar as understanding PPBS is concerned. If we would follow the logic-structure of PPBS, we must reconstitute our thinking. We must consider many of the things we are accustomed to producing (and claiming output-credit for) as mere intermediates. This is not so illogical as it may first appear to be. Coal is the output of a miner, but is only a contributing factor for the completion of industrial processes, rather than an output of any of those processes. In turn, the processes' outputs are, or may be, salable commodities. One man's output is, to another man, merely a contribution to *his* output. The logic of how to classify an item, such as coal, depends entirely upon the intent and purpose of the classification, rather than upon some immutable principle. For purposes of PPBS output, the government's many agencies may be regarded as analogous to the separate divisions of any large corporation. The corporate outputs, in any such enterprise, are only those items produced to reach the public. Neither those items consumed by and for the production processes themselves, nor those exchanged between the corporate divisions, are regarded by the corporation as outputs.

Given the realization that this is the output focus of PPBS, we can now get a clearer fix on the PPBS idea of progress measurement.

PROGRESS MEASUREMENT

The notion that progress should be measured in some fashion is not likely to trouble many people. The question that may be vexing some students of PPBS is: What does PPBS want us to measure? Or, put in another way: What does PPBS regard as *progress* in a given program?

If output means only those programmatic end-products which satisfy explicit market objectives, then program *fulfillment* must imply that *both* of two conditions have occurred:

The output which had been planned has materialized, *and*;

The output distribution which had been intended has been completed.[14]

If that is fulfillment, then progress must imply one of two questions, depending upon what stage the program happens to be in at the time when progress is measured:

Either, how closely does the production progress match planned progress?

Or, how well is the output distribution proceeding, as compared with the distribution plan?

INPUT

Of all the words in the special language of PPBS, input is probably the easiest to grasp, because the PPBS definition is fairly close to the traditional usage of the term. If all of the inputs to a given program were expressed in dollars, the sum would comprise the total costs incurred by the program (during the time period that the program had been in effect). In other words, the total quantity of manpower, facilities, equipment, and materials applied to the program, expressed in either units or dollars. is the program input. Note, however, that the facilities, equipment, and materials applied may, in a given program, include some intermediate or contributory products.[15]

ALTERNATE WAYS TO DO A GIVEN JOB

The concept of "alternate ways to do a given job" is input related, insofar as PPBS is concerned. The "given job" notion means that the output to be

[14]   At this early stage in the evolution of PPBS, with the distribution aspect not yet generally recognized, few agencies' plans give distribution intentions any prominence. Where on-going programs are concerned, particularly, the agencies have tended to disregard distribution consideration altogether. If PPBS "makes it," this situation will change.

[15]   In which case, we may be classifying as *inputs*, for PPBS purposes, some items which would have been classified, in pre-PPBS days, as *outputs*. But remember: don't duplicate inputs—that is, whether summarizing input units or input dollar costs, don't count both the intermediate/contributory products *and* the manpower, facilities, equipment, or materials that were used *in their production*. Count either one or the other as input but not both.

produced and the distribution pattern for that output have already been decided upon. The question, at any phase of the program subsequent to the decision-point becomes: Can we alter the production or distribution *technique* and by so doing improve either:

> The timing of the production or delivery, or
>
> The quantity or quality of the item(s) being produced, or,
>
> The unit or total cost of the production or delivery?

Every one of the three questions above is input-oriented. That is why defining the term "program alternatives" separately (as was done earlier) is advantageous. True, the word "alternatives" appears in both "program alternatives" and "alternative ways to do a given job." The first is output-related; it suggests substituting an entirely different program (and therefore a different output or outputs) for a program already planned or in progress. On the other hand, "alternative ways to do a given job" takes the program as given, and raises possibilities for changing the mix of inputs, and thereby redirecting the program.

Viewed in another way, the first involves policy questions, while the second involves operational matters. It is quite useful to distinguish between these two, as an aid in placing responsibility. That is to say, any single group of executives need not, sometimes should not, and often cannot answer both types of questions. However, the agency head, able in a given case to distinguish the PPBS situation as either policy or operations, is well on the way toward getting appropriate action taken, because he will know which group of his executives to contact.

SYSTEMS ANALYSIS

Of the eight terms characterized as important for understanding PPBS, only systems analysis remains to be discussed.

In the foregoing, the attempt has been to establish a distinct identity for PPBS. If this has succeeded, the reader already knows that systems analysis isn't PPBS, and that PPBS isn't systems analysis. The number of people who appear to regard these two things as one and the same is astounding.

Purely for purposes of differentiating the two, PPBS may be captioned as a bag of promises, concepts and relationships; whereas systems analysis may be captioned as a bag of techniques attached to a way of approaching problems. No disparagement of the latter is intended. To the contrary. The cause of technique is not advanced by confounding it with the very content to which it can be most profitably applied.

If systems analysis isn't synonymous with PPBS, what is it? More particularly, what is it insofar as PPBS is concerned?

A capsule definition would be: systems analysis is the application of "benefit-cost" analytical techniques to several areas of the PPBS anatomy.[16]

From the standpoint of the individual Federal agencies, two PPBS areas are especially amenable to benefit-cost techniques. One is the posing and evaluation of program alternatives, i.e. ascertaining the benefit-cost advantage (if any) of shifting to different outputs and/or distribution patterns so as to sat-

---

[16]   In the broader context represented by economic theory, benefit-cost techniques have been described for a century as "marginal utility" analysis.

isfy market objective(s) better. The other is the measurement of progress in a given program, i.e. ascertaining the benefit-cost advantage (if any) of changing the input mix so as to produce and/or distribute the output more efficiently.[17] In either case, the function of the systems analyst is to diagnose the benefit-cost situation as it exists so that the agency head may have the opportunity to make his decision on a benefit-cost basis if the circumstances suggest to him that such is the appropriate basis. If other considerations suggest to the agency head that the decision should be predicated upon different or broader criteria than simply benefit and cost, that remains his prerogative. He should have the benefit-cost data in any case, so that he can know what sacrifice, if any, the exercise of the prerogative entails.

The preceding only skims the surface of systems analysis. A more complete treatment is beyond the scope of an essay on the nature of PPBS.

SUMMARY

What is PPBS? It is a structure with a base unusual for government, and with key structural members so interdependent that comprehension must extend to all, or true perception of the "building" is impeded. The base is accountability in the citizen market. Therefore, the objectives must be product supply and distribution. Accordingly, programs are conceived and executed as production/distribution entities. Consequently, program alternatives are different production/distribution entities which might offer better benefit-cost ratios than existing ones. End-products become the only items construed as outputs. And, progress is viewed and measured in terms of output/distribution timing and effectiveness vs. planned timing and effectiveness. Hence, the inputs are "whatever resources it takes to get the production-distribution job done." As a result, alternative input-mixes become important comparison bases within any given program. Finally, systems analysis contributes diagnosis and appraisal to the whole.

Those familiar with PPBS will have noted the omission of many details. The workaday requirements in planning, programming, and budgeting; the preparation and time-phasing of "program memoranda" and "program and financial plans"; the problems and reasoning associated with below-the-first-tier program structuring; the many different ways in which the cost-benefit approach and techniques (marginal utility theory) may be applied—all of these have been omitted or touched lightly, in large part because they have been treated thoroughly and in depth by many. Hopefully, the details will take on greater meaning within the framework of the "larger architecture" which this essay has sought to delineate.

---

[17] A special and very useful application of systems analysis, which overlaps both foregoing cases, is the benefit-cost evaluation of program expansion/contraction.

THE POLITICAL ECONOMY OF EFFICIENCY

Aaron Wildavsky

[From *Public Administration Review,* Vol. 26, December 1966, pp. 292-310 Reprinted with permission of the American Society of Public Administration.]

There was a day when the meaning of economic efficiency was reasonably clear.

An objective met up with a technician. Efficiency consisted in meeting the objective at the lowest cost or in obtaining the maximum amount of the objective for a specified amount of resources. Let us call this "pure efficiency". The desirability of trying to achieve certain objectives may depend on the cost of achieving them. In this case the analyst (he has graduated from being a mere technician) alters the objective to suit available resources. Let us call this "mixed efficiency." Both pure and mixed efficiency are limited in the sense that they take for granted the existing structure of the political system and work within its boundaries. Yet the economizer, he who values efficiency most dearly, may discover that the most efficient means for accomplishing his ends cannot be secured without altering the machinery for making decisions. He not only alters means and ends (resources and objectives) simultaneously but makes them dependent on changes in political relationships. While he claims no special interest in or expertise concerning the decision apparatus outside of the market place, the economizer pursues efficiency to the heart of the political system. Let us call this "total efficiency." In this vocabulary, then, concepts of efficiency may be pure or mixed, limited or total.

A major purpose of this paper is to take the newest and recently most popular modes of achieving efficiency-cost-benefit analysis, systems analysis, and program budgeting—and show how much more is involved than mere economizing. *Even at the most modest level of cost-benefit analysis, I will try to show that it becomes difficult to maintain pure notions of efficiency. At a higher level, systems analysis is based on a mixed notion of efficiency. And program budgeting at the highest levels leaves pure efficiency far behind its over-reaching grasp into the structure of the political system. Program budgeting, it turns out, is a form of systems analysis, that is, political systems analysis.*

These modes of analysis are neither good for nothing nor good for everything, and one cannot speak of them as wholly good or bad. It is much more useful to try to specify some conditions under which they would or would not be helpful for various purposes. While such a list could not be exhaustive at this stage, nor permanent at any stage (because of advances in the art), it provides a basis for thinking about what these techniques can and cannot do. Another major purpose of this paper, therefore, is to describe cost-benefit and systems analysis and program budgeting as techniques for decision-making. I shall place particular stress upon what seems to me the most characteristic feature of all three modes of analysis: the aids to calculation designed to get around the vast areas of uncertainty where quantitative analysis leaves off and judgment begins.

COST-BENEFIT ANALYSIS

One can view cost-benefit analysis as anything from an infallible means of reaching the new Utopia to a waste of resources in attempting to measure the unmeasurable.[18]

The purpose of cost-benefit analysis is to secure an efficient allocation of resources produced by the governmental system in its interaction with the private economy. The nature of efficiency depends on the objectives set up for government. In the field of water resources, where most of the work on cost-benefit analysis has been done, the governmental objective is usually postulated to be an increase in national income. In a crude sense, this means that the costs to whomever may incur them should be less than the benefits to whomever may receive them. The time streams of consumption gained and foregone by a project are its benefits and costs.

The aim of cost-benefit analysis is to maximize "the present value of all benefits less that of all costs, subject to specified restraints."[19] A long view is taken in that costs are estimated not only for the immediate future but also for the life of the project. A wide view is taken in that indirect consequences for others—variously called externalities, side-effects, spillovers, and repercussion effects—are considered. Ideally, all costs and benefits are evaluated. The usual procedure is to estimate the installation costs of the project and spread them over time, thus making them into something like annual costs. To these costs are added an estimate of annual operating costs. The next step involves estimating the average value of the output by considering the likely number of units produced each year and their probable value in the market place of the future. Intangible, "secondary," benefits may then be considered. These time streams of costs and benefits are discounted so as to obtain the present value of costs and benefits. Projects whose benefits are greater than costs may then be approved, or the cost-benefit ratios may, with allowance for relative size, be used to rank projects in order of desirability.

UNDERLYING ECONOMIC AND POLITICAL ASSUMPTIONS

A straightforward description of cost-benefit analysis cannot do justice to the powerful assumptions that underlie it or to the many conditions limiting its usefulness. The assumptions involve value judgments that are not always recognized and, when recognized, are not easily handled in practice. The limiting conditions arise partly out of the assumptions and partly out of severe computational difficulties in estimating costs, and especially benefits. Here I can only indicate some major problems.

---

[18]   A. R. Prest and R. Turvey, "Cost-Benefit Analysis: A Survey," *The Economic Journal,* Vol. LXXV, December, 1965, pp. 683-75. I am much indebted to this valuable and discerning survey. I have also relied upon: Otto Eckstein, "A Survey of the Theory of Public Expenditure Criteria," in *Public Finances: Needs, Sources, and Utilization,* National Bureau of Economic Research (New York, Princeton University Press, 1961), pp. 439-504. Irving K. Fox and Orris C. Herfindahl, "Attainment of Efficiency in Satisfying Demands for Water Resources," *American Economic Review,* May, 1964, pp. 198-206. Charles J. Hitch, *On the Choice of Objectives in Systems Studies* (Santa Monica, The RAND Corporation, 1960). John V. Krutilla, "Is Public Intervention in Water Resoources Development Conducive to Economic Efficiency," *Natural Resources Journal,* January, 1966, pp. 60-75. John v. Krutilla and Otto Eckstein, *Multiple Purpose River Development* (Baltimore, Johns Hopkins Press, 1958). Roland N. McKean, *Efficiency in Government Through Systems Analysis with Emphasis on Water Resources Development* (New York, 1958).

[19]   Prest and Turvey, *ibid.,* p. 686.

Cost-benefit analysis is based on superiority in the market place,[20] under competitive conditions and full employment, as the measure of value in society. Any imperfection in the market works against the validity of the results. Unless the same degree of monopoly were found throughout the economy, for example, a governmental body that enjoys monopolistic control of prices or outputs would not necessarily make the same investment decisions as under free competition. A similar difficulty occurs where the size of a project is large in comparison to the economy, as in some developing nations. The project itself then affects the constellation of relative prices and production against which its efficiency is measured. The assumption based on the classical full employment model is also important because it gives prices special significance. Where manpower is not being utilized, projects may be justified in part as putting this unused resource to work.

The economic model on which cost-benefit analysis depends for its validity is based on a political theory. The idea is that in a free society the economy is to serve the individual's consistent preferences revealed and rationally pursued in the market place. Governments are not supposed to dictate preferences nor make decisions.

This individualist theory assumes as valid the current distribution of income. Preferences are valued in the market place where votes are based on disposable income. Governmental action to achieve efficiency, therefore, inevitably carries with it consequences for the distribution of income. Projects of different size and location and composition will transfer income in different amounts to different people. While economists might estimate the redistributive consequences of various projects, they cannot, on efficiency grounds, specify one or another as preferable. How is this serious problem to be handled?

Benefit-cost analysis is a way of trying to promote economic welfare. But whose welfare? No one knows how to deal with inter-personal comparisons of utility. It cannot be assumed that the desirability of rent supplements versus a highway or dam can be measured on a single utility scale. There is no scientific way to compare losses and gains among different people or to say that the marginal loss of a dollar to one man is somehow equal to the gain of a dollar by another. The question of whose utility function is to prevail (the analyst versus the people involved, the upstream gainers versus the downstream losers, the direct beneficiaries versus the taxpayers, the entire nation or a particular region, and so on) is of prime importance in making public policy.

The literature on welfare economics is notably unable to specify an objective welfare function.[21] Ideally, actions would benefit everyone and harm

---

[20]   In many important areas of policy such as national defense it is not possible to value the product directly in the market place. Since benefits cannot be valued in the same way as costs, it is necessary to resort to a somewhat different type of analysis. Instead of cost-benefit analysis, therefore, the work is usually called cost-effectiveness or cost-utility analysis.

[21]   A. Bergson, "A Reformulation of Certain Aspects of Welfare Economics," *Quarterly Journal of Economics*, February, 1938; N. Kaldor, "Welfare Propositions and Interpersonal Comparisons of Utility," *Economic Journal*, 1939, pp. 549-52; J. R. Hicks, "The Valuation of Social Income," *Economica*, 1940, pp. 105-24; I. M. D. Little, *A Critique of Welfare Economics* (Oxford, 1950); W. J. Baumol, *Welfare Economics and the Theory of the State* (Cambridge, 1952); T. Scitovsky, "A Note on Welfare Propositions in Economics," *Review of Economic Studies*, 1942, pp. 98-110; J. E. Meade, *The Theory of International Economic Policy*, Vol. II: *Trade and Welfare* (New York, 1954).

no one. As an approximation, the welfare economist views as optimal an action that leaves some people better off and none worse off. If this criterion were applied in political life, it would result in a situation like that of the Polish Diet in which anyone who was damaged could veto legislation. To provide a way out of this impasse, Hicks and Kaldor proposed approval of decisions if the total gain in welfare is such that the winners could compensate the losers. But formal machinery for compensation does not ordinarily exist and most modern economists are highly critical of the major political mechanism for attempting to compensate, namely, log-rolling in Congress on public works projects.[22] It is a very imperfect mechanism for assuring that losers in one instance become winners in another.

Another way of dealing with income distribution is to accept a criterion laid down by a political body and maximize present benefits less costs subject to this constraint. Or the cost-benefit analyst can present a series of alternatives differing according to the individuals who pay and prices charged. The analyst must not only compute the new inputs and outputs, but also the costs and benefits for each group with whom the public authorities are especially concerned. No wonder this is not often done! Prest and Turvey are uncertain whether such a procedure is actually helpful in practice.[23]

Income redistribution in its most extreme form would result in a complete leveling or equality of incomes. Clearly, this is not what is meant. A more practical meaning might be distributing income to the point where specific groups achieve a certain minimum. It is also possible that the operational meaning of income redistribution may simply be the transfer of some income from some haves to some have nots. Even in the last and most minimal sense of the term it is by no means clear that projects that are inefficient by the usual economic criteria serve to redistribute income in the desired direction. It is possible that some inefficient projects may transfer income from poorer to richer people. Before the claim that certain projects are justified by the effect of distributing income in a specified way can be accepted, an analysis to show that this is what actually happens must be at hand.

Since the distribution of income is at stake, it is not surprising that beneficiaries tend to dominate investment decisions in the political arena and steadfastly refuse to pay for what they receive from government tax revenues. They uniformly resist user charges based on benefits received. Fox and Herfindahl estimate that of a total initial investment of three billion for the Corps of Engineers in 1962, taxpayers in general would pay close to two-thirds of the costs.[24] Here, greater use of the facilities by a larger number of beneficiaries getting something for nothing inflates the estimated benefits which justify the project in the first place. There may be a political rationale for these decisions, but it has not been developed.

In addition to redistributing income, public works projects have a mul-

[22] For a different view, see James M. Buchanan and Gordon Tullock, *The Calculus of Consent: Logical Foundations of Constitutional Democracy* (Ann Arbor, University of Michigan Press, 1962).

[23] Prest and Turvey, op. cit., p. 702. For a contrary view, see Arthur Maas, "Benefit-Cost Analysis: Its Relevance to Public Investment Decisions," Vol. LXXX, *The Quarterly Journal of Economics,* May, 1966, pp. 208-226.

[24] Irving K. Fox and Orris C. Herfindahl, "Attainment of Efficiency in Satisfying Demands for Water Resources," *American Economic Review,* May, 1964, p. 200.

titude of objectives and consequences. Projects may generate economic growth, alleviate poverty among some people, provide aesthetic enjoyment and opportunities for recreation, improve public health, reduce the risks of natural disaster, alter travel patterns, affect church attendance, change educational opportunities, and more. No single welfare criterion can encompass these diverse objectives. How many of them should be considered? Which are susceptible of quantification? The further one pursues this analysis, the more impassable the thicket.

LIMITATIONS IN THE UTILITY OF COST-BENEFIT ANALYSIS

One possible conclusion is that at present certain types of cost-benefit analysis are not meaningful. In reviewing the literature on the calculus of costs and benefits in research and development, for example, Prest and Turvey comment on "the uncertainty and unreliability of cost estimates...and...the extraordinarily complex nature of the benefits...."[25]

Another conclusion is that one should be cautious in distinguishing the degree to which projects are amenable to cost-benefit analysis.

...When there are many diverse types of benefits from a project and/or many different beneficiaries it is difficult to list them all and to avoid double counting. This is one reason why it is so much easier to apply cost-benefit analysis to a limited purpose development, say, than it is to the research and development aspects of some multi-purpose discovery, such as a new type of plastic material. . . . It is no good expecting those fields in which benefits are widely diffused, and in which there are manifest divergences between accounting and economic costs or benefits, to be as cultivable as others. Nor is it realistic to expect that comparisons between projects in entirely different branches of economic activity are likely to be as meaningful or fruitful as those between projects in the same branch. The technique is more useful in the public-utility area than in the social-services area of government.[26]

If the analysis is to be useful at all, calculations must be simplified.[27] The multiple ramifications of interesting activities can be taken into account only at the cost of introducing fantastic complexities. Prest and Turvey remark of one such attempt, that "This system . . . requires knowledge of all the demand and supply equations in the economy, so is scarcely capable of application by road engineers."[28] They suggest omitting consideration where (1) side effects are judged not terribly large or where (2) concern for these effects belongs to another governmental jurisdiction.[29]

If certain costs or benefits are deemed important but cannot be quantified, it is always possible to guess. The increasing use of recreation and aesthetic facilities to justify public works projects in the United States is disapproved by most economists because there can be a vast, but hidden, inflation of these benefits. For example, to attribute the same value to a recreation day on a reservoir located in a desert miles from any substitute source of water as to a day on an artificial lake in the heart of natural lake country is patently wrong. Economists

[25]   Prest and Turvey, *op. cit.*, p. 727.
[26]   *Ibid* ., pp. 729, 731.
[27]   David Braybrooke and Charles Lindblom, *A Strategy for Decision* (New York, 1963).
[28]   Prest and Turvey, *op. cit.*, p. 714.
[29]   *Ibid.* p. 705.

would prefer to see recreation facilities listed in an appendix so that they can be taken into account in some sense, or, alternatively, that the project be presented with and without the recreation facilities, so that a judgment can be made as to whether the additional services are worth the cost.[30]

Economists distinguish between risk, where the precise outcome cannot be predicted but a probability distribution can be specified, and uncertainty, where one does not even know the parameters of the outcomes. The cost-benefit analyst must learn to live with uncertainty, for he can never know whether all relevant objectives have been included and what changes may occur in policy and in technology.

It is easy enough to cut the life of the project below its expected economic life. The interest rate can be raised. Assumptions can be made that costs will be higher and benefits lower than expected. All these methods, essentially conservative, are also highly arbitrary. They can be made somewhat more systematic, however, by sensitivity analysis in which length of life, for instance, is varied over a series of runs so that its impact on the project can be appraised.

Lessening uncertainty by hiking the interest or discount rate leads to greater difficulties, for the dominance of "higher" criteria over economic analysis is apparent in the frustrating problem of choosing the correct interest rate at which to discount the time streams of costs and benefits essential to the enterprise. Only an interest rate can establish the relationship between values at different periods of time. Yet people differ in preferences for the present versus the intermediate or long-run value. Moreover, the interest rate should also measure the opportunity cost of private capital that could be used to produce wealth elsewhere in the economy if it had not been used up in the form of tax income spent on the project under consideration. Is the appropriate rate the very low cost the government charges, the cost of a government corporation like TVA that must pay a somewhat higher rate, the going rate of interest for private firms, or an even higher rate to hedge against an uncertain future? As Otto Eckstein has observed, "...the choice of interest rates must remain a value judgment."[31]

If the efficiency of a project is insensitive to interest costs, then these costs can vary widely without mattering much. But Fox and Herfindahl discovered that if Corps of Engineer projects raised their interest (or discount) rate from 2 5/8 to 4, 6, or 8 percent, then 9, 64, and 80 percent of their projects, respectively, would have had a benefit-cost ratio of less than unity.[32] This single value choice among many has such large consequences that it alone may be decisive.

[30] See Jack L. Knetch, "Economics of Including Recreation as a Purpose of Water Resource Projects," *Journal of Farm Economics,* December, 1964, p. 1155. No one living in Berkeley, where "a view" is part of the cost of housing, could believe that aesthetic values are forever going to remain beyond the ingenuity of the quantifier. There are also costs and benefits, such as the saving and losing of human life, that can be quantified but can only be valued in the market place in a most peculiar (or ghoulish) sense. See Burton Weisbrod, *The Economics of Public Health; Measuring the Economic Impact of Diseases* (Philadelphia, 1961), for creative attempt to place a market value on human life. Few of us would want to make decisions about public health by use of this criterion, not at least if we were the old person whose future social value contribution is less than his cost to the authorities.

[31] Otto Eckstein, *op. cit.*, p. 460.

[32] Fox and Herfindahl, *op. cit..* p. 202.

THE MIXED RESULTS OF COST-BENEFIT ANALYSIS

Although cost-benefit analysis presumably results in efficiency by adding the most to national income, it is shot through with political and social value choices and surrounded by uncertainties and difficulties of computation. Whether the many noneconomic assumptions and consequences actually result in basically changing the nature of a project remains moot. Clearly, we have come a long way from pure efficiency, to verge upon mixed efficiency.

Economic analysts usually agree that all relevant factors (especially nonmarket factors) cannot be squeezed into a single formula. They therefore suggest that the policy maker, in being given the market costs and benefits of alternatives, is, in effect, presented with the market value he is placing on nonmarket factors. The contribution of the analyst is only one input into the decision, but the analyst may find this limited conception of his role unacceptable to others. Policy makers may not want this kind of input; they may want the answer, or at least an answer that they can defend on the basis of the analyst's legitimized expertise.

The dependence of cost-benefit analysis on a prior political framework does not mean that it is a useless or trivial exercise. Decisions must be made. If quantifiable economic costs and benefits are not everything, neither would a decision-maker wish to ignore them entirely. The great advantage of cost-benefit analysis, when pursued with integrity, is that some implicit judgments are made explicit and subject to analysis. Yet, for many, the omission of explicit consideration of political factors is a serious deficiency.

The experience of the Soil Conservation Service in lowering certain political costs may prove illuminating. For many years the Service struggled along with eleven major watershed projects involving big dams, great headaches, and little progress. Because the watersheds were confined to a single region, it was exceedingly difficult to generate support in Congress, particularly at appropriations time. The upstream-downstream controversies generated by these projects resulted in less than universal local approval. The SCS found itself in the direct line of fire for determining priorities in use of insufficient funds.

Compare this situation with the breakthrough which occurred when SCS developed the small watershed program. Since each facility is relatively inexpensive, large numbers can be placed throughout the country, markedly increasing political support. Agreement on the local level is facilitated because much less land is flooded and side payments are easier to arrange. A judicious use of cost-benefit analysis, together with ingenious relationships with State governors, places the choice of priorities with the States and yet maintains a reasonable level of consistency by virtue of adherence to national criteria. Errors are easier to correct because the burden of calculation has been drastically reduced and experience may be more easily accumulated with a larger number of small projects.

Consider the situation in which an agency finds it desirable to achieve a geographical spread of projects in order to establish a wider base of support. Assume (with good reason) that cost-benefit criteria will not permit projects to be established in some states because the value of the land or water is too low. One can say that this is just too bad and observe the agency seeking ways around the restriction by playing up benefits, playing down costs, or attacking the whole benefit cost concept as inapplicable. Another approach would be to recognize that federalism—meaning, realistically, the distribution of indulgences to State units—represents a political value worth promoting to some extent and that gaining nation-wide support is important. From this perspective, a compromise solution would be to except one or two projects in each State or region from meeting the full requirement of the formula, though the projects with the highest benefit-cost ratio would have to be chosen. In return for sacrificing full adherence to the formula in a few instances, one would get enhanced support for it in many others.

Everyone knows, of course, that cost-benefit analysis is not the messiah come to save water resources projects from contamination by the rival forces of ignorance and political corruption. Whenever agencies and their associated interests discover that they cannot do what they want, they may twist prevailing criteria out of shape: Two projects may be joined so that both qualify when one, standing alone, would not. Costs and benefits may be manipulated, or the categories may be so extended that almost any project qualifies. On the other hand, cost-benefit analysis has some "good" political uses that might be stressed more than they have been. The technique gives the responsible official a good reason for turning down projects, with a public-interest explanation the Congressman can use with his constituents and the interest-group leader with his members.

This is not to say that cost-benefit analysis has little utility. Assuming that the method will continue to be improved, and that one accepts the market as the measure of economic value, it can certainly tell decision makers something about what they will be giving up if they follow alternative policies. The use of two analyses, one based on regional and the other on national factors, might result in an appraisal of the economic costs of federalism.

The burden of calculation may be reduced by following cost-benefit analysis for many projects and introducing other values only for a few. To expect, however, that the method itself (which distributes indulgences to some and deprivations to others) would not be subject to manipulation in the political process is to say that we shall be governed by formula and not by men.

Because the cost-benefit formula does not always jibe with political realities—that is, it omits political costs and benefits—we can expect it to be twisted out of shape from time to time. Yet cost-benefit analysis may still be important in getting rid of the worst projects. Avoiding the worst where one can't get the best is no small accomplishment.

SYSTEMS ANALYSIS

The good systems analyst is a "chochem," a Yiddish word meaning "wise man," with overtones of "wise guy." His forte is creativity. Although he sometimes relates means to ends and fits ends to match means, he ordinarily eschews such pat processes, preferring instead to relate elements imaginatively into new systems that create their own means and ends. He plays new objectives continuously against cost elements until a creative synthesis has been achieved. He looks down upon those who say that they take objectives as given, knowing full well that the apparent solidity of the objective will dissipate during analysis and that, in any case, most people do not know what they want because they do not know what they can get.

Since no one knows how to teach creativity, daring, and nerve, it is not surprising that no one can define what systems analysis is or how it should be practiced. E. S. Quade, who compiled the RAND Corporation lectures on systems analysis, says it "is still largely a form of art" in which it is not possible to lay down "fixed rules which need only be followed with exactness."[33] He examined systems studies to determine ideas and principles common to the good ones, but discovered that "no universally accepted set of ideas existed. It was even difficult to decide which studies should be called good."[34]

Systems analysis is derived from operations research, which came into use during World War II when some scientists discovered that they could use simple quantitative analysis to get the most out of existing military equipment. A reasonably clear objective was given, and ways to cut the cost of achieving it could be developed, using essentially statistical models. Operations research today is largely identified with specific techniques: linear programming; Monte Carlo (randomizing) methods; gaming and game theory. While there is no hard and fast division between operations research and systems analysis, a rough separation may perhaps be made. The less that is known about objectives, the more they conflict, the larger the number of elements to be considered, the more uncertain the environment, the more likely it is that the work will be called a systems analysis. In systems analysis there is more judgment and intuition and less reliance on quantitative methods than in operations research.

Systems analysis builds models that abstract from reality but represent the crucial relationships. The systems analyst first decides what questions are relevant to his inquiry, selects certain quantifiable factors, cuts down the list of factors to be dealt with by aggregation and by eliminating the (hopefully) less important ones, and then gives them quantitative relationships with one another within the system he has chosen for analysis. But crucial variables may not be quantifiable. If they can be reduced to numbers, there may be no mathematical function that can express the desired relationship. More important, there may be no single criterion for judging results among conflicting objectives. Most important, the original objectives, if any, may not make sense.

It cannot be emphasized too strongly that a (if not the) distinguishing characteristic of systems analysis is that the objectives are either not known or are subject to change. Systems analysis, Quade tells us, "is associated with that class of problems where the difficulties lie in deciding what ought to be done—not simply how to do it—and honors go to people who . . . find out what the problem is."[35] Charles Hitch, the former Comptroller of the Defense Department, insists that:

> … learning about objectives is one of the chief objects of this kind of analysis. We must learn to look at objectives as critically and as professionally as we look at our models and our other inputs. We may, of course, begin with tentative objectives, but we must expect to modify or replace them as we learn about the systems we are studying—and related systems. The feedback on objectives may in some cases be the most important result of our study. We have never undertaken a major system study at RAND in which we are able to define satisfactory objectives at the beginning of the study."[36]

---

[33]   E. S. Quade, *Analysis for Military Decisions* (Chicago, 1964), p. 153.
[34]   *Ibid.,* p. 149.
[35]   *Ibid.,* p. 7.
[36]   Charles J. Hitch, *op. cit.,* p. 1.

Systems analysts recognize many good reasons for their difficulties in defining problems or objectives. Quade reaches the core: "Objectives are not, in fact, agreed upon. The choice, while ostensibly between alternatives, is really between objectives or ends and non-analytic methods must be used for a final reconciliation of views."[37] It may be comforting to believe that objectives come to the analyst from on high and can be taken as given, but this easy assumption is all wrong. "For all sorts of good reasons that are not about to change," says Hitch, "official statements of national objectives (or company objectives) tend to be nonexistent or so vague and literary as to be non-operational."[38] Objectives are not only likely to be "thin and rarified," according to Wohlstetter, but the relevant authorities "are likely to conflict. Among others there will be national differences within an alliance and within the nation, interagency, interservice, and intraservice differences...[39]

Moreover, even shared objectives often conflict with one another. Deterrence of atomic attack might be best served by letting an enemy know that we would respond with an all-out, indiscriminate attack on his population. Defense of our population against death and destruction might not be well served by this strategy,[40] as the Secretary of Defense recognized when he recommended a city-avoidance strategy that might give an enemy some incentive to spare our cities as well. Not only are objectives large in number and in conflict with one another, they are likely to engender serious repercussion effects. Many objectives, like morale and the stability of alliances, are resistant to quantification. What is worth doing depends on whether it can be done at all, how well, and at what cost. Hence, objectives really cannot be taken as given; they must be made up by the analyst. "In fact," Wohlstetter declares, "we are always in the process of choosing and modifying both means and ends."[41]

Future systems analysts are explicitly warned not to let clients determine objectives. A suggestive analogy is drawn with the doctor who would not ignore a patient's "description of his symptoms, but . . . cannot allow the patient's self diagnosis to override his own professional judgment."[42] Quade argues that since systems analysis has often resulted in changing the original objectives of the policy-maker, it would be "self-defeating to accept without inquiry" his "view of what the problem is."[43]

I have stressed the point that the systems analyst is advised to insist on his own formulation of the problem because it shows so closely that we are dealing with a mixed concept of efficiency. Adjusting objectives to resources in the present or near future is difficult enough without considering future states of affairs which hold tremendous uncertainty. Constants become variables; little can be taken for granted. The rate of technological progress, an opponent's estimate of your reaction to his latest series of moves based on his reaction to yours, whether

[37] E. S. Quade, *op. cit.,* p. 176.

[38] Charles J. Hitch, *op. cit.*, pp. 4-5.

[39] Albert Wohlstetter, "Analysis and Design of Conflict Systems," in E. S. Quade, *op. cit.*, p. 121.

[40] See Glenn H. Snyder, *Deterrence and Defense* (Princeton, 1961) .

[41] Wohlstetter in Quade, *op. cit.*, p. 122.

[42] E. S. Quade, *op. cit.*, p. 157. Quade attempts to soften the blow by saying that businessmen and military officers know more about their business than anyone else. But the import of the analogy is clear enough.

[43] *Ibid.*, pp. 156-157.

or not atomic war will occur, what it will be like, whether we shall have warning, whether the system we are working on will cost anything close to current
estimates and whether it will be ready within five years of the due date—on
most of these matters, there are no objective probabilities to be calculated.

An effective dealing with uncertainty must be a major goal of systems
analysis. Systems analysis is characterized by the aids to calculation it uses,
not to conquer, but to circumvent and mitigate some of the pervasive effects
of uncertainty. Before a seemingly important factor may be omitted, for example, a sensitivity analysis may be run to determine whether its variation
significantly affects the outcome. If there is no good basis for calculating the
value of the factor, arbitrary values may be assigned to test for extreme possibilities. Contingency analysis is used to determine how the relative ranking of
alternatives holds up under major changes in the environment, say, a new
alliance between France and Russia, or alterations in the criteria for judging
the alternatives, such as a requirement that a system work well against attacks from space as well as earth. Contingency analysis places a premium on
versatility as the analyst seeks a system that will hold up well under various
eventualities even though it might be quite as good for any single contingency as an alternative system. Adversary procedures may be used to combat
uncertainty. Bending over backwards to provide advantages for low ranking
systems and handicaps for high ranking systems is called a fortiori analysis.
Changing crucial assumptions in order to make the leading alternatives even,
so that one can judge whether the assumptions are overly optimistic or pessi-
mistic, is called break-even analysis.[44] Since all these methods add greatly to
the burden of calculation, they must be used with some discretion.

A variety of insurance schemes may also be used to deal with uncertainty. In appraising what an opponent can do, for instance, one can assume
the worst, the best, and sheer inertia. In regard to the development of weapons, insurance requires not one flexible weapon but a variety of alternatives
pursued with vigor. As development goes on, uncertainty is reduced. Consequently, basic strategic choice involves determining how worthwhile paying
for the additional information is by developing rival weapons systems to the
next stage. The greater the uncertainty of the world, the greater the desirability of having the widest selection of alternative weapons to choose from to
meet unexpected threats and opportunities. Alchian and Kessel are so wed-
ded to the principle of diversified investment that they "strongly recommend
this theorem as a basic part of systems analysis."[45] As a form of calculation,
systems analysis represents a merger of quantitative methods and rules of
thumb. First, the analyst attempts to solve the problem before he knows a
great deal about it. Then he continuously alters his initial solution to get closer
to what he intuitively feels ought to be wanted. Means and ends are continuously played off against one another. New objectives are defined, new assumptions made, new models constructed, until a creative amalgam appears

---

[44]   Herman Kahn and Irwin Mann, *Techniques of Systems Analysis* (Santa Monica, The
       RAND Corporation, 1957), believe that "More than any single thing, the skilled use
       of *a fortiori* and break-even analyses separate the professionals from the amateurs."
       They think that convincing others that you have a good solution is as important as
       coming up with one.
[45]   Armen A. Alchian and Reuben A. Kessel, *A Proper Role of Systems Analysis* (Santa
       Monica. RAND Corporation 1954) p.9.

that hopefully defines a second best solution, one that is better than others even if not optimal in any sense. In the famous study of the location of military bases conducted by Albert Wohlstetter and his associates at the RAND Corporation, widely acknowledged as a classic example of systems analysis, Wohlstetter writes:

> The base study…proceeded by a method of successive approximations. It compared forces for their efficiency in carrying a payload between the bases and targets without opposition either by enemy interceptors or enemy bombers. Then, it introduced obstacles successively: first, enemy defenses; then enemy bombardment of our bombers and other elements needed to retaliate. In essence, then, the alternative systems were tested for their first-strike capability and then they were compared for their second-strike capacity. And the programmed system performed in a drastically different way, depending on the order in which the opposing side struck. In the course of analyzing counter-measures and counter-counter-measures, the enemy bombardment turned out to be a dominant problem. This was true even for a very much improved overseas operating base system. The refueling base system was very much less sensitive to strike order. It is only the fact that strike order made such a difference among systems contemplated that gave the first-strike, second-strike distinction an interest. And it was not known in advance of the analysis that few of the programmed bombers would have survived to encounter the problem of penetrating enemy defenses which had previously been taken as the main obstacle. The analysis, then, not only was affected by the objectives considered, it affected them.[46]

The advantage of a good systems study is that by running the analysis through in theory on paper certain disadvantages of learning from experience may be avoided.

If the complexity of the problems encountered proved difficult in cost-benefit analysis, the burdens of calculation are ordinarily much greater in systems analysis. Many aspects of a problem simply must be put aside. Only a few variables can be considered simultaneously. "Otherwise," Roland McKean tells us, "the models would become impossibly cumbersome, and… the number of calculations to consider would mount in the thousands."[47] Formulas that include everything may appear more satisfactory but those that cannot be reduced "to a single expression are likely to convey no meaning at all."[48] Summing up their experience, Hitch and McKean assert that:

> … analyses must be piecemeal, since it is impossible for a single analysis to cover all problems of choice simultaneously in a large organization. Thus comparisons of alternative courses of action always pertain to a part of the government's (or corporation's) problem. Other parts of the over-all problem are temporarily put aside, possible decisions about some matters being ignored, specific decisions about others being taken for granted. The resulting analyses are intended to provide assistance in finding optimal, or at least good, solutions to

[46]   Albert Wohlstetter in E. S. Quade, *op. cit.,* pp. 125-26.
[47]   R. N. McKean, "Criteria," in E. S. Quade, *op. cit.,* p. 83.
[48]   E. S. Quade, *op. cit.,* p. 310.

sub-problems: in the jargon of systems and operations research, they are sub-optimizations.[49]

Although admitting that much bad work is carried on and that inordinate love of numbers and machines often get in the way of creative work,[50] practitioners of systems analysis believe in their art. "All of them point out how the use of analysis can provide some of the knowledge needed, how it may sometime serve as a substitute for experience, and, most importantly, how it can work to sharpen intuition."[51] Systems analysis can increase explicitness about the assumptions made and about exclusions from the analysis. The claim is that systems analysis can be perfected; sheer intuition or unaided judgment can never be perfect.

Yet there is also wide agreement that systems analysts "do philosophy,"[52] that they are advocates of particular policy alternatives. What Schelling calls "the pure role of expert advisor" is not available for the analyst who "must usually formulate the questions themselves for his clients."[53] Beyond that, Wohlstetter argues that systems analysts can perform the function of integrating diverse values. New systems can sometimes be found that meet diverse objectives.[54] The politician who gains his objectives by inventing policies that also satisfy others, or the leader of a coalition who searches out areas of maximum agreement, performs a kind of informal system analysis.

All these men, however, work within the existing political structure. While cost-benefit analysis may contain within it implicit changes in existing governmental policies, it poses no direct challenge to the general decision-making machinery of the political system. Program budgeting is a form of systems analysis that attempts to break out of these confines.

PROGRAM BUDGETING

"It is always important, and perhaps especially so in economics, to avoid being swept off one's feet by the fashions of the moment."[55]

"So this new system will identify our national goals with precision..."[56]

On August 25, 1965, President Johnson announced that he was asking the heads of all Federal agencies to introduce "a very new and revolutionary system" of program budgeting. Staffs of experts set up in each agency would define goals using "modern methods of program analysis." Then the "most effective and the least costly" way to accomplish these goals would be found.[57]

Program budgeting has no standard definition. The general idea is that

[49] Charles J. Hitch and Roland N. McKean, *The Economics of Defense in the Nuclear Age* (Cambridge, Harvard University Press, 1961) p. 161.

[50] See Hitch on "Mechanitis—Putting ....machines to work as a substitute for hard thinking." Charles Hitch, "Economics and Operations Research, A Symposium. II," *Review of Economics and Statistics, August,* 1958, p. 209.

[51] E. S. Quade, *op. cit.,* p. 12.

[52] *Ibid.,* p. 5.

[53] T. C. Schelling, "Economics and Operations Research, A Symposium. V., Comment," *Review of Economics and Statistics,* August, 1958, p. 222.

[54] Albert Wohlstetter in E. S. Quade, *op. cit.,* p. 122.

[55] Prest and Turvey, *op. cit.,* p. 684.

[56] David Novick, Editor, *Program Budgeting* (Cambridge, Harvard University Press, 1965), p. vi.

[57] *Ibid .,* pp. v-vi.

budgetary decisions should be made by focusing on output categories like governmental goals, objectives, end products or programs instead of inputs like personnel, equipment, and maintenance. As in cost-benefit analysis, to which it owes a great deal, program budgeting lays stress on estimating the total financial cost of accomplishing objectives. What is variously called cost-effectiveness or cost-utility analysis is employed in order to select "alternative approaches to the achievement of a benefit already determined to be worth achieving."[58]

Not everyone would go along with the most far-reaching implications of program budgeting, but the RAND Corporation version, presumably exported from the Defense Department, definitely does include "institutional reorganization to bring relevant administrative functions under the jurisdiction of the authority making the final program decisions." In any event, there would be "information reporting systems and shifts in the power structure to the extent necessary to secure compliance with program decisions by the agencies responsible for their execution."[59] Sometimes it appears that comprehensiveness—simultaneous and complete examination of all programs and all alternatives to programs every year—is being advocated. Actually, comprehensiveness has been dropped (though not without regret) because "it may be too costly in time, effort, uncertainty, and confusion."[60] There exists considerable ambivalence as to whether decisions are implicit in the program categories or merely provide information to improve the judgment of governmental officials.

Programs are not made in heaven. There is nothing out there that is just waiting to be found. Programs are not natural to the world; they must be imposed on it by men. No one can give instructions for making up programs. There are as many ways to conceive of programs as there are of organizing activity,[61] as the comments of the following writers eloquently testify:

It is by no means obvious . . . whether a good program structure should be based on components of specific end objectives (e.g., the accomplishment of certain land reclamation targets), on the principle of cost separation (identifying as a program any activity the costs of which can be readily segregated), on the separation of means and ends (is education a means or an end in a situation such as skill-retraining courses for workers displaced by automation?), or on some artificially designed pattern that draws from all these and other classification criteria.[62]

Just what categories constitute the most useful programs and program elements is far from obvious.... If one puts all educational activities into a broad package of educational programs, he cannot simultaneously include school lunch programs or physical education activities in a Health Program, or include defense educational activi-

[58] Alan Dean, quoted in D. Novick, *ibid.*, p. 311.
[59] R. N. McKean and N. Anshen in D. Novick, *ibid.,* pp. 286-87. The authors say that this aspect of program budgeting is part of the general view adopted in the book as a whole.
[60] Arthur Smithies in *ibid.,* p. 45.
[61] A look at the classic work by Luther Gulick and Lyndall Urwick, *Papers on the Science of Administration* (New York, Columbia University Press, 1937), reveals considerable similarity between their suggested bases of organization and ways of conceptualizing programs.
[62] M. Anshen in D. Novick, *op. cit.,* pp. 19-20.

ties (such as the military academies) in the Defense Program.... In short, precisely how to achieve a rational and useful structure for a program budget is not yet evident.[63]

In much current discussion it seems to be taken for granted that transportation is a natural program category. But that conclusion is by no means obvious.[64]

A first question one might ask is whether, given their nature, health activities merit a separate, independent status in a program budget. The question arises because these activities often are constituents of, or inputs into, other activities whose purpose or goal orientation is the dominating one. Outlays by the Department of Defense for hospital care, for example, though they assist in maintaining the health of one segment of the population, are undertaken on behalf of national defense, and the latter is their justification.[65]

The difficulties with the program concept are illustrated in the space program. A first glance suggests that space projects are ideally suited for program budgeting because they appear as physical systems designed to accomplish different missions. Actually, there is a remarkable degree of interdependence between different missions and objectives—pride, scientific research, space exploration, military uses, etc.—so that it is impossible to apportion costs on a proper basis. Consider the problem of a rocket developed for one mission and useful for others. To apportion costs to each new mission is purely arbitrary. To allocate the cost to the first mission and regard the rocket as a free good for all subsequent missions is ludicrous. The only remotely reasonable alternative—making a separate program out of the rocket itself—does violence to the concept of programs as end products. The difficulty is compounded because the facilities that have multiple uses like boosters and tracking networks tend to be very expensive compared to the items that are specific to a particular mission.[66] Simple concepts of programs evaporate upon inspection.

Political realities lie behind the failure to devise principles for defining programs. As Melvin Anshen puts it, "The central issue is, of course, nothing less than the definition of the ultimate objectives of the Federal government as they are realized through operational decisions." The arrangement of the programs inevitably affects the specific actions taken to implement them. "Set in this framework," Anshen continues, "the designation of a schedule of programs may be described as building a bridge between a matter of political philosophy (what is government for?) and...assigning scarce resources among alternative governmental objectives."[67]

Because program budgeting is a form of systems analysis (and uses a form of cost-benefit analysis), the conditions that hinder or facilitate its use have largely been covered in the previous sections. The simpler the problem, the fewer the interdependencies, the greater the ability to measure the consequences of alternatives on a common scale, the more costs and benefits that are valued in the market place, the better the chances of making effective use of programs. Let us

---

[63] G. A. Steiner in *ibid.,* p. 356.

[64] A. Smithies in *ibid.,* p. 41.

[65] Marvin Frankel in *ibid.,* pp. 219-220. I have forborne citing the author who promises exciting discussion of the objectives of American education and ends up with fascinating program categories like primary, secondary, and tertiary education.

[66] See the excellent chapter by M. A. Margolis and S. M. Barro, *ibid.,* pp. 120-145.

[67] *Ibid.,* p. 18.

take transportation to illustrate some of the conditions in a specific case.

Investments in transportation are highly interdependent with one another (planes versus cars versus trains versus barges, etc.) and with decisions regarding the regional location of industry and the movements of population. In view of the powerful effects of transportation investment on regional employment, income, and competition with other modes of transport, it becomes necessary to take these factors into account. The partial equilibrium model of efficiency in the narrow sense becomes inappropriate and a general equilibrium model of the economy must be used. The combination of aggregative models at the economy-wide level and inter-region and inter-industry that this approach requires is staggering. It is precisely the limited and partial character of cost-effectiveness analyses, taking so much for granted and eliminating so many variables, that make them easy to work for empirical purposes. Furthermore, designing a large-scale transportation system involves so close a mixture of political and economic considerations that it is not possible to disentangle them. The Interstate Highway Program, for example, involved complex bargaining among Federal, State, and local governments and reconciliation of many conflicting interests. The development of certain "backward" regions, facilitating the movement of defense supplies, redistribution of income, creating countervailing power against certain monopolies, not to mention the political needs of public officials, were all involved. While cost-utility exercises might help with small segments of the problem, J. R. Meyer concludes that, "Given the complexity of the political and economic decisions involved, and the emphasis on designing a geographically consistent system, it probably would be difficult to improve on the congressional process as a means of developing such a program in an orderly and systematic way."[68]

On one condition for effective use—reorganization of the Federal government to centralize authority for wide-ranging programs—proponents of program budgeting are markedly ambivalent. The problem is that responsibility for programs is now scattered throughout the whole Federal establishment and decentralized to State and local authorities as well. In the field of health, for example, expenditures are distributed among at least twelve agencies and six departments outside of Health, Education, and Welfare. A far greater number of organizations are concerned with American activities abroad, with natural resources and with education. The multiple jurisdictions and overlapping responsibilities do violence to the concept of comprehensive and consistent programs. It "causes one to doubt," Marvin Frankel writes, "whether there can exist in the administrative echelons the kind of overall perspective that would seem indispensable if Federal health resources are to be rationally allocated."[69] To G. A. Steiner it is evident that "The present 'chest of drawers' type of organization cannot for long be comparable with program budgeting."[70] W. Z. Hirsch declares that "if we are to have effective program budgeting of natural resources activities, we shall have to provide for new institutional arrangements."[71] Yet the inevitable resistance to wholesale reorganization would be so great that, if it were deemed essential, it might well doom the enterprise. Hence, the hope is expressed that translation grids or

[68] J. R. Meyer in *ibid.*, p. 170. This paragraph is based on my interpretation of his work.
[69] M. Frankel, *ibid.*, p. 237.
[70] *Ibid.*, p. 348.
[71] *Ibid.*, p. 280.

crossover networks could be used to convert program budget decisions back into the usual budget categories in the usual agencies. That is what is done in Defense, but that Department has the advantage of having most of the activities it is concerned with under the Secretary's jurisdiction. Some program analysts believe that this solution will not do.

Recognizing that a conversion scheme is technically feasible, Anshen is aware that there are "deeply frustrating" issues to be resolved. "The heart of the problem is the fact that the program budget in operation should not be a mere statistical game. Great strategic importance will attach to both the definition of program structure and content and the establishment of specific program objectives (including magnitude, timing, and cost)."[72] The implications of program budgeting, however, go far beyond specific policies. It will be useful to distinguish between policy politics (which policy will be adopted?), partisan politics (which political party will win office?), and system politics (how will decision structures be set up?). Program budgeting is manifestly concerned with policy politics, and not much with partisan politics, although it could have important consequences for issues that divide the nation's parties. My contention is that the thrust of program budgeting makes it an integral part of system politics.

As presently conceived, program budgeting contains an extreme centralizing bias. Power is to be centralized in the Presidency (through the Budget Bureau) at the national level, in superdepartments rather than bureaus within the executive branch, and in the Federal government as a whole instead of State or local governments. Note how W. Z. Hirsch assumes the desirability of national dominance when he writes: "These methods of analysis can guide Federal officials in the responsibility of bringing local education decisions into closer harmony with national objectives."[73] G. A. Steiner observes that comprehensiveness may be affected by unrestricted Federal grants-in-aid to the states because "such a plan would remove a substantial part of Federal expenditures from a program budgeting system of the Federal government."[74] Should there be reluctance on the part of State and local officials to employ the new tools, Anshen states "… the Federal government may employ familiar incentives to accelerate this progress."[75] Summing it up, Hirsch says that it appears doubtful that a natural resources program budget would have much impact without a good deal of centralization."[76]

Within the great Federal organizations designed to encompass the widest ramifications of basic objectives, there would have to be strong executives. Cutting across the sub-units of the organization, as is the case in the Department of Defense, the program budget could only be put together by the top executive. A more useful tool for increasing his power to control decisions vis-a-vis his subordinates would be hard to find.[77]

Would large-scale program budgeting benefit the Chief Executive? Presi-

---

[72] *Ibid.,* pp. 358-59.

[73] *Ibid.,* p. 206.

[74] *Ibid.,* p. 347.

[75] *Ibid.,* p. 365.

[76] *Ibid.,* p. 280.

[77] See my comments to this effect in *The Politics of the Budgetary Process* (Boston, 1964), p. 140. For discussion of some political consequences of program budgeting, see pp. 135-142.

dent Johnson's support of program budgeting could in part stem from his desire to appear frugal and also be directed at increasing his control of the executive branch by centralizing decisions in the Bureau of the Budget. In the case of foreign affairs, it is not at all clear whether it would be preferable to emphasize country teams, with the budget made by the State Department to encompass activities of the other Federal agencies abroad, or to let Commerce, Agriculture, Defense, and other agencies include their foreign activities in their own budgets. Program budgeting will unleash great struggles of this kind in Washington. An especially intriguing possibility is that the Bureau of the Budget might prefer to let the various agencies compete, with the Bureau coordinating (that is, controlling) these activities through a comprehensive foreign affairs program devised only at the Presidential level.

Yet it is not entirely clear that Presidents would welcome all the implications of program budgeting. It is well and good to talk about long-range planning; it is another thing to tie a President's hands by committing him in advance for five years of expenditures. Looking ahead is fine but not if it means that a President cannot negate the most extensive planning efforts on grounds that seem sufficient to him.[78] He may wish to trade some program budgeting for some political support.

In any event, that all decisions ought to be made by the most central person in the most centralized body capable of grabbing hold of them is difficult to justify on scientific grounds. We see what has happened. First pure efficiency was converted to mixed efficiency. Then limited efficiency became unlimited. Yet the qualifications of efficiency experts or political systems analysis are not evident.[79]

We would be in a much stronger position to predict the consequences of program budgeting if we knew (a) how far toward a genuine program budget the Defense Department has gone and (b) whether the program budget has fulfilled its promise. To the best of my knowledge, not a single study of this important experiment was undertaken (or at least published) before the deci-

---

[78] See William H. Brown and Charles E. Gilbert, *Planning Municipal Investment: A Case Study of Philadelphia* (Philadelphia, University of Pennsylvania Press, 1961), for an excellent discussion of the desire of elected officials to remain free to shift their commitments.

[79] It may be said that I have failed to distinguish sufficiently between planning, programming, and budgeting. Planning is an orientation that looks ahead by extending costs and benefits or units of effectiveness a number of years into the future. Programming is a general procedure of systems analysis employing cost-effectiveness studies. In this view program budgeting is a mere mechanical transportation of the results of high level systems studies into convenient storage in the budgetary format. No doubt systems studies could be done without converting the results into the form of a program budget. This approach may have a lot to be said for it and it appears that it is the one that is generally followed in the Department of Defense in its presentations to Congress. But if the systems studies guide decisions as to the allocation of resources, and the studies are maintained according to particular program categories and are further legitimatized by being given status in the budget, it seems most unlikely that programming will be separated from budgeting. One is never sure whether too much or too little is being claimed for program budgeting. If all that program budgeting amounts to is a simple translation of previous systems studies into some convenient form of accounting, it hardly seems that this phenomenon is worth so much fuss. If the program catagories in the budget system are meaningful, then they must be much more than a mere translation of previously arrived at decisions. In this case, I think that it is not my task to enlighten the proponents of program budgeting, but it is their task to make themselves clear to others.

sion was made to spread it around the land. On the surface, only two of the nine program categories used in the Defense Department appear to be genuine programs in the sense of pointing to end purposes or objectives. Although strategic retaliation and continental defense appear to be distinct programs, it is difficult to separate them conceptually; my guess is that they are, in fact, considered together. The third category—general purpose forces—is presumably designed to deal with (hopefully) limited war anywhere in the world. According to Arthur Smithies, "The threat is not clearly defined and neither are the requirements for meeting it. Clearly this program is of a very different character from the other two and does not lend itself as readily to analysis in terms either of its components or of its specific contribution to defense objectives."[80]

What about the program called airlift and sealift? These activities support the general purpose forces. Research and development is carried on presumably to serve other defense objectives, and the same is true for the reserve forces.

No doubt the elements that make up the programs comprise the real action focus of the budget, but these may look less elegant when spread into thousands of elements than they do in nine neat rows. When one hears that hundreds of program elements are up for decision at one time,[81] he is entitled to some skepticism about how much genuine analysis can go into all of them. Part of the argument for program budgeting was that by thinking ahead and working all year around it would be possible to consider changes as they came up and avoid the usual last minute funk. Both Hitch[82] and Novick[83] (the RAND Corporation expert on defense budgeting) report, however, that this has not worked out. The services hesitate to submit changes piecemeal, and the Secretary wants to see what he is getting into before he acts. The vaunted five year plans are still in force but their efficacy in determining yearly decisions remains to be established.

One good operational test would be to know whether the Department's systems analysts actually use the figures from the five year plans in their work or whether they go to the services for the real stuff. Another test would be whether or not the later years of the five year projections turn out to have any future significance, or whether the battle is really over the next year that is to be scooped out as part of the budget. From a distance, it appears that the services have to work much harder to justify what they are doing. Since McNamara's office must approve changes in defense programs, and he can insist on documentation, he is in a strong position to improve thinking at the lower levels. The intensity of conflict within the Defense Department may not have changed, but it may be that the disputants are or will in the future be likely to shout at a much more sophisticated level. How much this is due to McNamara himself, to his insistence on quantitative estimates, or to the analytic advantages of a program budget cannot be determined now. It is clear

---

[80] A. Smithies in Novick, *op. cit.*, p. 37.

[81] See U.S. House Appropriations Committee Subcommittee on Department of Defense Appropriations for Fiscal 1965, 88th Congress, 2nd Session, IV, p. 133. McNamara asserted that some 652 "subject issues" had been submitted to him for the fiscal 1965 budget.

[82] Charles Hitch, *Decision-Making for Defense* (Berkeley, University of California Press, 1965).

[83] Novick, *op. cit,.* p. 100.

that a program budget, of which he alone is master, has helped impose his will on the Defense Department.

It should also be said that there are many notable differences between decision-making in defense and domestic policy that would render suspect the transmission of procedures from one realm to the other. The greater organizational unity of Defense, the immensely large amounts of money at stake, the extraordinarily greater risks involved, the inability to share more than minimal values with opponents, the vastly different array of interests and perceptions of the proper roles of the participants, are but a few of the factors involved.

The Armed Services and Appropriations Committees in the defense area, for example, are normally most reluctant to substitute their judgment on defense for that of the President and the Secretary of the Department. They do not conceive it to be their role to make day to day defense policy, and they are apparently unwilling to take on the burden of decision. They therefore accept a budget presentation based on cavernous program categories even though these are so arranged that it is impossible to make a decision on the basis of them. If they were to ask for and to receive the discussion of alternative actions contained in the much smaller program elements on which McNamara bases his decisions, they would be in a position to take the Department of Defense away from its Secretary.

There is no reason whatsoever to believe that a similar restraint would be shown by committees that deal with domestic policies. It is at least possible that the peculiar planning, programming, and budgeting system adopted in Defense could not be repeated elsewhere in the Federal establishment.

POLITICAL RATIONALITY

Political rationality is the fundamental kind of reason, because it deals with the preservation and improvement of decision structures, and decision structures are the source of all decisions. Unless a decision structure exists, no reasoning and no decisions are possible…. There can be no conflict between political rationality and… technical, legal, social, or economic rationality, because the solution of political problems makes possible an attack on any other problem, while a serious political deficiency can prevent or undo all other problem solving…. Nonpolitical decisions are reached by considering a problem in its own terms, and by evaluating proposals according to how well they solve the problem. The best available proposal should be accepted regardless of who makes it or who opposes it, and a faulty proposal should be rejected or improved no matter who makes it. Compromise is always irrational; the rational procedure is to determine which proposal is the best, and to accept it. In a political decision, on the other hand, action never is based on the merits of a proposal but always on who makes it and who opposes it. Action should be designed to avoid complete identification with any proposal and any point of view, no matter how good or how popular it might be. The best available proposal should never be accepted just because it is best; it should be deferred, objected to, discussed, until major opposition disappears. Compromise is always a rational procedure, even when the compromise is between a good and a bad proposal.[84]

We are witnessing the beginning of significant advances in the art and

---

[84] Paul Diesing, *Reason in Society* (Urbana, 1962), pp. 198, 203-204, 231-32.

science of economizing. Having given up the norm of comprehensiveness, economizers are able to join quantitative analysis with aids to calculation of the kind described by Lindblom in his strategy of disjointed incrementalism.[85]

Various devices are employed to simplify calculations. Important values are omitted entirely; others are left to different authorities to whose care they have been entrusted. Here, sensitivity analysis represents an advance because it provides an empirical basis to justify neglect of some values. Means and ends are hopelessly intertwined. The real choice is between rival policies that encapsulate somewhat different mixes of means and ends. Analysis proceeds incrementally by successive limited approximations. It is serial and remedial as successive attacks are made on problems. Rather than waiting upon experience in the real world, the analyst tries various moves in his model and runs them through to see if they work. When all else fails, the analyst may try an integrative solution reconciling a variety of values to some degree, though meeting none of them completely. He is always ready to settle for the second or third best, provided only that it is better than the going policy. Constrained by diverse limiting assumptions, weakened by deficiencies in technique, rarely able to provide unambiguous measures, the systems, cost-benefit, and program analysis is nonetheless getting better at calculating in the realm of efficiency. Alas, he is an imperialist at heart.

In the literature discussed above there appears several times the proposition that "the program budget is a neutral tool. It has no politics."[86] In truth, the program budget is suffused with policy politics, makes up a small part of President Johnson's partisan politics, and tends towards system politics. How could men account for so foolish a statement? It must be that they who make it identify program budgeting with something good and beautiful, and politics with another thing bad and ugly. McKean and Anshen speak of politics in terms of "pressure and expedient adjustments," "haphazard acts . . .unresponsive to a planned analysis of the needs of efficient decision design." From the political structure they expect only "resistance and opposition, corresponding to the familiar human disposition to protect established seats of power and procedures made honorable by the mere facts of existence and custom."[87] In other places we hear of "vested interests," "wasteful duplication," "special interest groups," and the "Parkinson syndrome."[88]

Not so long ago less sophisticated advocates of reform ignored the political realm. Now they denigrate it. And, since there must be a structure for decision, it is smuggled in as a mere adjunct of achieving efficiency. Who is to blame if the economic tail wags the political dog? It seems unfair to blame the evangelical economizer for spreading the gospel of efficiency. If economic efficiency turns out to be the one true religion, maybe it is because its prophets could so easily conquer.

It is hard to find men who take up the cause of political rationality, who plead the case for political man, and who are primarily concerned with the laws that enable the political machinery to keep working. One is driven to a philosopher like Paul Diesing to find the case for the political:

---

[85] Braybrooke and Lindblom, *op. cit.* See also Lindblom, *The Intelligence of Democracy* (New York, 1965).

[86] M. Anshen in D. Novick, *op. cit.,* p. 370.

[87] *Ibid.,* p. 289.

[88] *Ibid.,* p. 359.

...the political problem is always basic and prior to the others....This means that any suggested course of action must be evaluated first by its effects on the political structure. A course of action which corrects economic or social deficiencies but increases political difficulties must be rejected, while an action which contributes to political improvement is desirable even if it is not entirely sound from an economic or social standpoint.[89]

There is hardly a political scientist who would claim half as much. The desire to invent decision structures to facilitate the achievement of economic efficiency does not suggest a full appreciation of their proper role by students of politics.

A major task of the political system is to specify goals or objectives. It is impermissible to treat goals as if they were known in advance. "Goals" may well be the product of interaction among key participants rather than some "*deus ex machina*" or (to use Bentley's term) some "spook" which posits values in advance of our knowledge of them. Certainly, the operational objectives of the Corps of Engineers in the Water Resources field could hardly be described in terms of developing rivers and harbors.

Once the political process becomes a focus of attention, it is evident that the principal participants may not be clear about their goals. What we call goals or objectives may, in large part, be operationally determined by the policies we can agree upon. The mixtures of values found in complex policies may have to be taken in packages, so that policies may determine goals at least as much as general objectives determine policies. In a political situation, then, the need for support assumes central importance. Not simply the economic, but the political costs and benefits turn out to be crucial.

A first attempt to specify what is meant by political costs may bring closer an understanding of the range of requirements for political rationality.[90] Exchange costs are incurred by a political leader when he needs the support of other people to get a policy adopted. He has to pay for this assistance by using up resources in the form of favors, (patronage, logrolling) or coercive moves (threats or acts to veto or remove from office). By supporting a policy and influencing others to do the same, a politician antagonizes some people and may suffer their retaliation. If these hostility costs mount, they may turn into reelection costs—actions that decrease his chances (or those of his friends) of being elected or re-elected to office. Election costs, in turn, may become policy costs through inability to command the necessary formal powers to accomplish the desired policy objectives.

In the manner of Neustadt, we may also talk about reputation costs, i.e., not only loss of popularity with segments of the electorate, but also loss of esteem and effectiveness with other participants in the political system and loss or ability to secure policies other than the one immediately under consideration. Those who continually urge a President to go all out—that is, use all his resources on a wide range of issues—rarely stop to consider that the price of success in one area of policy may be defeat in another. If he loses popularity with the electorate, as President Truman did, Congress may destroy almost the whole of his domestic program. If he cracks down on the steel industry, as President Kennedy did, he may find himself constrained to lean over backwards in

---

[89]   Paul Diesing, *op. cit.,* p. 228.
[90]   I am indebted to John Harsanyi for suggestions about political rationality.

the future to avoid unremitting hostility from the business community.

A major consequence of incurring exchange and hostility costs may be undesirable power-redistribution effects. The process of getting a policy adopted or implemented may increase the power of various individuals, organizations and social groups, which later will be used against the political leader. The power of some participants may be weakened so that the political leader is unable to enjoy their protection.

The legitimacy of the political system may be threatened by costs that involve the weakening of customary political restraints. Politicians who try to suppress opposition, or who practice election frauds, may find similar tactics being used against them. The choice of a highly controversial policy may raise the costs of civic discord. Although the people involved may not hate the political leader, the fact that they hate each other may lead to consequences contrary to his desires.

The literature of economics usually treats organizations and institutions as if they were costless entities. The standard procedure is to consider rival alternatives (in consideration of price policy or other criteria), calculate the differences in cost and achievement among them, and show that one is more or less efficient than another. This typical way of thinking is sometimes misspecified. If the costs of pursuing a policy are strictly economic and can be calculated directly in the market place, then the procedure should work well. But if the costs include getting one or another organization to change its policies or procedures, then these costs must also be taken into account.[91] Perhaps there are legal, psychological, or other impediments that make it either impossible or difficult for the required changes to be made. Or the changes may require great effort and result in incurring a variety of other costs. In considering a range of alternatives, one is measuring not only efficiency but also the cost of change.

Studies based on efficiency criteria are much needed and increasingly useful. My quarrel is not with them as such, at all. I have been concerned that a single value, however important, could triumph over other values without explicit consideration being given these others. I would feel much better if political rationality were being pursued with the same vigor and capability as is economic efficiency. In that case I would have fewer qualms about extending efficiency studies into the decision-making apparatus.

My purpose has not been to accuse economizers of doing what comes naturally. Rather, I have sought to emphasize that economic rationality, however laudable in its own sphere, ought not to swallow up political rationality—but will do so, if political rationality continues to lack trained and adept defenders.

---

[91] In the field of defense policy, political factors are taken into account to the extent that the studies concentrate on the design of feasible alternatives. In the choice of overseas basing, for example, the question of feasibility in relation to treaties and friendly or unfriendly relationships with other countries is considered. Thus it seems permissible to take into account political considerations originating outside of the country, where differences of opinions and preferences among nations are to some extent accepted as legitimate, but apparently not differences internal to the American policy.

Part 6

The Science of Management and Organization

As we saw in the previous section, the initial attempts to articulate a practical science of administration, and public administration in particular, did not produce much that was substantive or useful. As a description of the responsibilities of a head of an agency or bureau, the acronym PODSCORB was helpful in about the same way as being told to plan ahead, or "THINK," when what one needs is advice or direction about how to perform a task. When students of administration did try to introduce more specifically recommendatory principles, such as organizing the physical layout of an office by task or function, the result was maxims that have the status of "proverbs". The advice pertained to some situations but not to others. Herbert Simon's critique of this approach towards a science of administration is devastating. One may, of course, still assert that there is some value in learning that there are indeed many, often contradictory, maxims that may be thought to bear on a situation; and that this point should be demonstrated carefully with reference to real life situations rather than merely being stated abstractly. But just this much would make for a strange sort of education. One can easily imagine and sympathize with the frustration of a student of administration upon hearing one's professor preface still another demonstration with the announcement, "Now here is another principle that does not always apply...."

The forgoing criticism, however, is bootless against that most rigorous movement which was dubbed a "science of management" and followed the direction set by the redoubtable Frederick W. Taylor. Taylor starts from the notion that, given any task, there must be *some* mode of performing it that would be most efficient. Therefore, the task of the manager is to find out just what that "one best way" is. To discover that would require the careful study of "time and motion." Taylor understood that the best way to perform a task would vary with each particular situation. He was interested in teaching managers not how to do tasks, nor how to organize the efforts of others to do tasks, but rather how to determine the best way of organizing and doing. Moreover, Taylor wanted to show that this task of determining the one best way in any particular situation is indeed something that *can* be done and *has to* be done for the sake of efficiency. For this, and nothing else, is the all too easily overlooked prerogative and responsibility of management. Taylor's presentation of the science of management is as much hortatory as it is demonstrative, since the hardest and most important step is in changing the attitude of managers to accept the real burden of their position. The selection from Taylor's *Scientific Management* reproduced here shows this clearly.

Essentially, what Taylor recommended is the application of the principle of the division of labor to the relationship between manager and subordinate, and in that way rationalizing and justifying that relationship. The concern is not only for efficiency but also for justice; indeed these are two sides of the same coin. Taylor expressed a genuine emotional hostility towards management exercising prerogatives, and claiming rewards, based on no real contribution to the purpose of the organization. He hated the injustice of a situation where management stupidly tries to encourage or threaten subordinates into doing their best, when it was in fact the managers' responsibility to know *how* the subordinates might do so and to direct them. Unless that pertained, any share of the proceeds that management might claim would be unjust—an exploitation in the opprobrious sense of the term. It is this side of Taylorism that makes it refreshing, and probably more than refreshing, today, for it helps expel the moral confusion in today's atmosphere where clear prerogatives of management are compromised and confused in favor of shared responsibility and cooperative decision-making. Taylor can still help guard against the danger of a soft egalitarianism and humanism that can operate at the expense of justice among the members of an organization, since such justice in truth depends upon and practically reduces to the principle of one person/one job.

When Leonard White confessed that he believed public administration still to be an "art" but that he attached importance to its tendency in the direction of becoming a "science," it was almost certainly Taylorism that he had in mind. Why, though, did White not think that Taylor had actually achieved a science? In White's own day this question might have been answered cautiously and tentatively by saying that it would be best to wait and consider the results, the payoff, of much further experience with time and motion study. Today, however, Taylorism has been with us long enough to allow for more seasoned assessment of it. Taylor's detractors, no longer facing a movement in full power and youthful enthusiasm, may now reflect more comprehensively on its fundamental limitations.

There may be said to be two fundamental problems with Taylor's "science of management." First, on its own terms the determination of the "one best way" can reach a definite conclusion if *given* a task. But this really begs a question, which in the practical life of an organization may likely turn out to be the most vexing question. Just what *is* the task? Is some particular operation, such as typing, a task; or is it a fragment of a task—and if so which one? Or is typing many tasks? One may think of a task as an operation that is intended to achieve some purpose; but the vagaries that attend any attempt to explicate an organization's purpose, or purposes, are by now commonplace. Here, again, the arguments of Herbert Simon are relevant.

The second problem with Taylorism is related to the one just mentioned. Whatever we might take to be a task, or posit as a task, it is presumably something that is to be performed by a human being. This is a presumption; but it is not logically necessary, and therein lies the problem. That is, once the task has been set, the subsequent application of the logic of the division of labor tends towards a breaking down of the task into elements so simple that they can be performed mechanically, by a servo-mechanism for example, or a pigeon. If human beings are to remain employed in an organization governed by such logic, it would seem that they would have to be treated more or less as machines. Would a world governed entirely by Taylor's principles be thoroughly dehumanized? Would it lead to a horror in which people would be reduced to maximally efficient parts of a production system—to which we would have to add that they also be maximally efficient in consumption? To be sure, nothing like this was Taylor's intention; but how can he avoid the conclusion? For fundamentally, Taylor's "science of management" is really only the application of the disposition of a production engineer to the question of the structure of the organization itself. It thus begins by abstracting from, in a word, humanity, and ends up recommending its elimination, so far as possible. For is that not what the subordinate loses when relieved of the need or responsibility to know how or why one is told what to do, that being the task of the manager? [1]

The thought that there is a fundamental opposition between "humanity" and the rigorous application of Taylor's science of management is at the root of the so-called "human-relations" movement in administration and management programs, which is dominant today. With "human relations" that opposition is interpreted not as something that poses a threat to humanity, but rather as something that prevents a fully rational science of management from ever becoming fully manifest. Human beings are simply too recalcitrantly messy to be governed in the way that Taylorism requires; i.e. as willing to accept directives from managers even without understanding their rationale, in return for a greater remunerative share of such proceeds as induced one to become a member of the organization in the first place. The selection here by F. J. Roethlisberger and William J. Dickson outlines the thinking that began with the now-famous experiments at Western Electric's Hawthorne plant. There, in a controlled study of the effects of various changes in the physical conditions of the workplace on productivity, it was discovered that some subjects liked being studied as part of an experiment; and that their productivity increased with *any* change in their physical conditions, since they knew that it was all part of the game! Researchers were forced to conclude that at the very least this "subjective" factor was significant along with such "objective" things as the quality of light or the color of the walls. Moreover, it was found that the subjects' feeling of having a significant role in a scientific experiment seemed to be effective even independently of any material reward. The discovery of this "human element" meant that workers might be expected to work more productively, and for less reward, in a condition where they were induced to feel good about themselves and their contribution.

---

[1]   A hard-charging rationalizer might object at this point and exclaim, "But what then? Are we to oppose all technological improvement in production for fear of the same consequence—that man may be reduced to being an 'appendage' to his machines? Or if not, just where should we stop our technological advances? Surely it's good to 'eliminate,' if you will, the need for human beings from toil, so far as possible. Or do you think you see a higher level of humanity than today's among peasant farmers and shepherds? I am for technology as I am for everything that enhances human power. Let it be used for ends that are good, and it is good." In response to this it must be confessed that it is not easy to imagine how human agency might come to master and limit technological development *as such*. Still, to hold that more powerful tools are always better, provided only that they are used well, presumes that human beings can find their happiness—their life's meaning—in the exercise of the freedom that, one hopes at best, will be purchased for them by those tools. It is to presume that most human beings do not necessarily find their happiness *in* their work. But is this not precisely the *question*?

Was the human relations movement in fact any more than an emendation of Taylor? This question arises because it could be argued that the psychological needs that the human relations researchers claimed to have discovered are just that, i.e. needs, which are like our animal need for food, rest, etc. and which Taylor sought to understand and satisfy for the sake of productivity. The matter can indeed be looked at in this light. And yet, to abstract in this way from the distinctively subjective character of the needs identified by human relations research is also to abstract from the fraud and chicanery necessarily involved in ministering to them. An example is the phenomenon of flattery. We may like it—we may even need it, however troubling that thought might be—and yet to employ flattery as a way of rewarding subordinates is to heighten and exploit the subordinate's lack of understanding of the actual value of the contribution he or she makes to the product. One can easily see how such techniques can be employed to fob off employees' reasonable demands to be paid according to the value of their product, thus undermining the reciprocity which allows the relationship between the individual and the organization to be rational from both points of view.[2] As was stated, this rationality is the essence of Taylorism. To be sure, Taylor does sanction the use of flattery, as is obvious from reading his account of the scientific manager's manner of speaking to the employee, Schmidt. But this is a concession to Schmidt's psychological limitations and is necessary to motivate him to increase his productivity so as to be worth a greater share of the proceeds, and, presumably, to receive them. The flattery is not itself confused with the reward. The contemporary human-relations movement tends to stress the utility of soft measures towards subordinates, and in this way wears a garb of the virtue of humanity. Taylorism is in contrast rather tough. This contrast, though, does not go to the heart of the difference between the two camps, and neither is it sufficient to conclude that human relations occupies the moral high ground.

The currency of the human-relations movement, with all its numerous branches, derives from the fact that it began as, and still bears the marks of, a movement of opposition, animated by a concern for a vague sort of humanism that was felt to be lacking or even threatened by Taylor's somewhat tougher rationalism. In some cases, for example "Total Quality Management," it is hard to see anything of more substance than some slogans adding up to the somewhat wishful thought that it is good for an organization's productivity if everyone has pride in and is dedicated to the "quality" of the product. In the case of more ambitious versions, such as the academically fashionable theories "Y" and "Z", we are told that organizations are more likely to prove successful when collective or cooperative decision-making displaces more traditional vertical authoritarian structures. To be sure, there is a certain common sense here, but no more than that. An indication of the weakness of the theories referred to here is their amazing reliance on the work of the psychologist Herbert Maslow and his theory of the hierarchy of human needs. As is well known, Maslow argued that only when such basic needs as those for food and physical security were met did humans move on to seek the satisfaction of higher needs. The highest is a need for what he termed "Self-realization, Fulfillment." It should be obvious by now, if it was not always so, that the terms

---

2   To be very explicit, for the "payment" spoken of here to be "according to product" it has to be according to the same measure by which the product is measured. That means, for commercial organizations, money.

"Self-realization/ Fulfillment" are devoid of content. Not the least of the problems for human relations is the open question of whether the "self," or some selves, may be realizable only at the expense of the organization.[3]

Ultimately, the notion that a better understanding of the psychological needs of the members of an organization, and catering to such, would be good for the organization is only a *presumption* of "human-relations" and the psychology upon which it depends. It is noteworthy that this presumption has a long history. Aristotle had held that human beings tend by nature to belong to a variety of forms of organization insofar as these are necessary to the satisfaction of their natural needs, or goods. However, this way of thinking entails that among the various forms of organization the political community stands out as supreme and supremely authoritative; and this is because it exists for the sake of the most complete, sovereign good. It also follows from this that a well constituted political community is one where rule is exercised for the good of the political community, rather than simply at its expense. This common good is the common life of virtue and happiness in which the members each have their own share. So, is it the case that contemporary organization theory actually has an affinity with Aristotle? Does it point back beyond the classical liberalism that treats of man, *qua* man, as an individual and renew our interest in pre-modern thought? There is a partial truth in this suggestion, worthy of more sustained reflection. For the present it is important to note that the big difference between Aristotle's way of thinking and all forms of modern organization theory is the set of consequences of modern social science's commitment to the fact/value distinction. From a modern perspective, there is an embarrassment in Aristotle's serious treatment of the notion of a common good, the human concern for which is the ground of his argument in favor of the primacy of the political organization over all others, as well as his distinction between the good as versus bad forms of common life. Aristotle would hold, or rather does hold, that there cannot be a comprehensive theory of organization that does not identify and concentrate on what is in fact the comprehensive organization—the political community. For modern thinkers, and of course post-modern ones, this looks like arbitrary prejudice.

---

[3] In chapters two and three of his book, *Complex Organizations,* Charles Perrow has undertaken a searching critique of the human relations movement, challenging its theoretical foundations and exposing the remarkable thinness of the research which is generally cited as evidence in its behalf. It is the best review and criticism in the literature. Having said that, one also owes it to Perrow to acknowledge that his own critique of human relations is a radical one. That is, he cites human relations as countering "the extreme rationality of scientific management with a romantic rationality…wherein all sorts of needs are posited…." as satisfiable within the organization. Perrow doubts whether even this degree of rationality is an actual feature of human organization, since such "needs" as the human relations theorists speak of are themselves *constructed* out of the roles we play in organizations, and perhaps other accidents. Perrow, therefore, joins other "post-modern" thinkers in calling for a deconstruction of such constructs. Having gone this far, it should also be noted that Perrow's explicit recognition of the social construction of the "reality" of human psychology culminates in his calling for human beings to take charge of that process of construction more deliberately (cf. his chapter eight, especially the final three pages). In this, it seems to me that Perrow all but joins hands with the traditional mode of thinking, whereby "organization theory" would merge and transform itself into political philosophy.

Is there a way of holding on to the fact/value distinction while at the same time treating of organizations as good, in some sense, for individuals? One may well doubt it. And yet, this was the miracle that seemed to have been performed by Chester Barnard, in his widely influential book *The Functions of the Executive*, first published in 1938. For Barnard, individuals become and remain members of organizations not because through them they can attain a share of the good *of* the organization. The end or purpose of the organization is only marginally or incidentally significant. Rather, organization *itself* is good. Its benefit to human life is that it saves us from what otherwise would be a completely directionless freedom. Organizations are the things that make demands of us; they require sacrifice and the government of our otherwise mindless impulses. A human being who is a member of no organization would be like one in prison—not the prison of too narrow confinement, but rather one of the complete absence of confinement. The isolated human being inhabits a prison whose boundaries are infinitely distant in all directions, and hence one in which no significant movement would be possible. Against this danger any organization, even, say, a commercial one, provides a salvation, provided it be sufficiently demanding. One could say that Barnard conflates the good with the common; and since this allows him a formal indifference to the purpose that the organization espouses or serves, the posture of neutrality towards "values" is preserved.

The great sociologist Max Weber is sometimes linked to the more rationalistic side of modern organizational theory, as represented in this volume by the likes of Frederick W. Taylor and Herbert Simon. There is some truth to this linkage; the thoughts are kindred but the lineage is not direct. However, in the case of the softer, "psychological" side of the field, as represented in all the branches of the human relations movement, the work of Chester Barnard is clearly seminal. It is hard to imagine the movement without him. The section from Barnard's book that is reproduced here, along with Charles Perrow's summary and criticism, should help the reader get to the bottom of the modern human relations approach to organization theory and, therewith, the study of administration.

SCIENTIFIC MANAGEMENT

Frederick W. Taylor

[From Frederick Winslow Taylor, *Scientific Management*, (New York: Harper and Row, Publishers, 1911), pp. 30-48, 57-60.]

The writer has found that there are three questions uppermost in the minds of men when they become interested in scientific management.

First. Wherein do the principles of scientific management differ essentially from those of ordinary management?

Second. Why are better results attained under scientific management than under the other types?

Third. Is not the most important problem that of getting the right man at the head of the company? And if you have the right man cannot the choice of the type of management be safely left to him?

One of the principal objects of the following pages will be to give a satisfactory answer to these questions. . . .

Before starting to illustrate the principles of scientific management, or "task management" as it is briefly called, it seems desirable to outline what the writer believes will be recognized as the best type of management which is in common use. This is done so that the great difference between the best of the ordinary management and scientific management may be fully appreciated.

In an industrial establishment which employs say from 500 to 1000 workmen, there will be found in many cases at least twenty to thirty different trades. The workmen in each of these trades have had their knowledge handed down to them by word of mouth, through the many years in which their trade has been developed from the primitive condition, in which our far-distant ancestors each one practiced the rudiments of many different trades, to the present state of great and growing subdivision of labor, in which each man specializes upon some comparatively small class of work.

The ingenuity of each generation has developed quicker and better methods for doing every element of the work in every trade. Thus the methods which are now in use may in a broad sense be said to be an evolution representing the survival of the fittest and best of the ideas which have been developed since the starting of each trade. However, while this is true in a broad sense, only those who are intimately acquainted with each of these trades are fully aware of the fact that in hardly any element of any trade is there uniformity in the methods which are used. Instead of having only one way which is generally accepted as a standard, there are in daily use, say, fifty or a hundred different ways of doing each element of the work. And a little thought will make it clear that this must inevitably be the case, since our methods have been handed down from man to man by word of mouth, or have, in most cases, been almost unconsciously learned through personal observation. Practically in no instances have they been codified or systematically analyzed or described. The ingenuity and experience of each generation—of each decade, even, have without doubt handed over better methods to the next. This mass of rule-of-thumb or traditional knowledge may be said to be the principal asset or possession of every tradesman. Now, in the best of the ordinary types of management, the managers recognize frankly the fact that the 500 or 1000 workmen, included in the twenty to thirty trades, who are under them, possess this mass of traditional knowledge, a large part of which is not in the possession of the management. The management, of course, includes foremen and superintendents, who themselves have been in most cases first-class workers at their trades. And yet these foremen and superintendents know, better than any one else, that their own knowledge and personal skill falls far short of the combined knowledge and dexterity of all the workmen under them. The most experienced managers, therefore, frankly place before their workmen the problem of doing the work in the best and most economical way. They recognize the task before them as that of inducing each workman to use his best endeavors, his hardest work, all his traditional knowledge, his skill, his ingenuity, and his good-will—in a word, his "initiative," so as to yield the largest possible return to his employer. The problem before the management, then, may be briefly said to be that of obtaining the best *initiative* of every workman. And the writer uses the word "initiative" in its broadest sense, to cover all of the good qualities sought for from the men.

On the other hand, no intelligent manager would hope to obtain in any full measure the initiative of his workmen unless he felt that he was giving them something more than they usually receive from their employers. Only those among the readers of this paper who have been managers or who have worked themselves at a trade realize how far the average workman falls short of giving his employer his full initiative. It is well within the mark to state that in nineteen out of twenty industrial establishments the workmen believe it to be directly against their interests to give their employers their best initiative, and that instead of working hard to do the largest possible amount of work and the best quality of work for their employers, they deliberately work as slowly as they dare while they at the same time try to make those over them believe that they are working fast.[4]

The writer repeats, therefore, that in order to have any hope of obtaining the initiative of his workmen the manager must give some *special incentive* to his men beyond that which is given to the average of the trade. This incentive can be given in several different ways, as for example, the hope of rapid promotion or advancement; higher wages, either in the form of generous piece-work prices or of a premium or bonus of some kind for good and rapid work; shorter hours of labor; better surroundings and working conditions than are ordinarily given, etc., and, above all, this special incentive should be accompanied by that personal consideration for, and friendly contact with, his workmen which comes only from a genuine and kindly interest in the welfare of these under him. It is only by giving a special inducement or "incentive" of this kind that the employer can hope even approximately to get the "initiative" of his workmen. Under the ordinary type of management the necessity for offering the workman a special inducement has come to be so generally recognized that a large proportion of those most interested in the subject look upon the adoption of some one of the modern schemes for payment (such as piece work, the premium plan, or the bonus plan, for instance) as practically the whole system of management. Under scientific management, however, the particular pay system which is adopted is merely one of the subordinate elements.

Broadly speaking, then, the best type of management in ordinary use may be defined as management in which the workmen give their best *initiative* and in return receive some *special incentive* from their employers. This type of management will be referred to as the management of "*initiative and incentive*" in contradistinction to scientific management, or task management, with which it is to be compared.

The writer hopes that the management of "initiative and incentive" will be recognized as representing the best type in ordinary use, and in fact he believes that it will be hard to persuade the average manager that anything better exists in the whole field than this type. The task which the writer has before him, then, is the difficult one of trying to prove in a thoroughly convincing way that there is another type of management which is not only better but overwhelmingly better than the management of "initiative and incentive."

The universal prejudice in favor of the management of "initiative and

---

[4]   The writer has tried to make the reason for this unfortunate state of things clear in a paper entitled "Shop Management," read before the American Society of Mechanical Engineers.

incentive" is so strong that no mere theoretical advantages which can be pointed out will be likely to convince the average manager that any other system is better. It will be upon a series of practical illustrations of the actual working of the two systems that the writer will depend in his efforts to prove that scientific management is so greatly superior to other types. Certain elementary principles, a certain philosophy, will however be recognized as the essence of that which is being illustrated in all of the practical examples which will be given. And the broad principles in which the scientific system differs from the ordinary or "rule-of-thumb" system are so simple in their nature that it seems desirable to describe them before starting with the illustrations.

Under the old type of management success depends almost entirely upon getting the "initiative" of the workmen, and it is indeed a rare case in which this initiative is really attained. Under scientific management the "initiative" of the workmen (that is, their hard work, their good-will, and their ingenuity) is obtained with absolute uniformity and to a greater extent than is possible under the old system; and in addition to this improvement on the part of the men, the managers assume new burdens, new duties, and responsibilities never dreamed of in the past. The managers assume, for instance, the burden of gathering together all of the traditional knowledge which in the past has been possessed by the workmen and then of classifying, tabulating, and reducing this knowledge to rules, laws, and formulae which are immensely helpful to the workmen in doing their daily work. In addition to developing a *science* in this way, the management take on three other types of duties which involve new and heavy burdens for themselves.

These new duties are grouped under four heads:

First. They develop a science for each element of a man's work, which replaces the old rule-of-thumb method.

Second. They scientifically select and then train, teach, and develop the workman, whereas in the past he chose his own work and trained himself as best he could.

Third. They heartily cooperate with the men so as to insure all of the work being done in accordance with the principles of the science which has been developed.

Fourth. There is an almost equal division of the work and the responsibility between the management and the workmen. The management take over all work for which they are better fitted than the workmen, while in the past almost all of the work and the greater part of the responsibility were thrown upon the men.

It is this combination of the initiative of the workmen, coupled with the new types of work done by the management, that makes scientific management so much more efficient than the old plan.

Three of these elements exist in many cases, under the management of "initiative and incentive," in a small and rudimentary way, but they are, under this management, of minor importance, whereas under scientific management they form the very essence of the whole system.

The fourth of these elements, "an almost equal division of the responsibility between the management and the workmen," requires further explanation. The philosophy of the management of "initiative and incentive" makes it necessary for each workman to bear almost the entire responsibility for the general plan as well as for each detail of his work, and in many cases for his implements as well. In addition to this he must do all of the actual physical labor. The development of a science, on the other hand, involves the establishment of many rules, laws, and formulae which replace the judgment of the individual workmen and which can be effectively used only after having been systematically recorded, indexed, etc. The practical use of scientific data also calls for a room in which to keep the books, records,[5] etc., and a desk for the planner to work at. Thus all of the planning which under the old system was done by the workman, as a result of his personal experience, must of necessity under the new system be done by the management in accordance with the laws of the science; because even if the workman was well suited to the development and use of scientific data, it would be physically impossible for him to work at his machine and at a desk at the same time. It is also clear that in most cases one type of man is needed to plan ahead and an entirely different type to execute the work.

The man in the planning room, whose specialty under scientific management is planning ahead, invariably finds that the work can be done better and more economically by a subdivision of the labor; each act of each mechanic, for example, should be preceded by various preparatory acts done by other men. And all of this involves, as we have said, "an almost equal division of the responsibility and the work between the management and the workman."

To summarize: Under the management of "initiative and incentive" practically the whole problem is "up to the workman," while under scientific management fully one-half of the problem is "up to the management."

Perhaps the most prominent single element in modern scientific management is the task idea. The work of every workman is fully planned out by the management at least one day in advance, and each man receives in most cases complete written instructions, describing in detail the task which he is to accomplish, as well as the means to be used in doing the work. And the work planned in advance in this way constitutes as task which is to be solved, as explained above, not by the workman alone, but in almost all cases by the joint effort of the workman and the management. This task specifies not only what is to be done but how it is to be done and the exact time allowed for doing it. And whenever the workman succeeds in doing his task right, and within the time limit specified, he receives an addition of from 30 per cent to 100 per cent to his ordinary wages. These tasks are carefully planned, so that both good and careful work are called for in their performance, but it should be distinctly understood that in no case is the workman called upon to work at a pace which would be injurious to his health. The task is always so regulated that the man who is well suited to his job will thrive while working at this rate during a long term of years and grow happier and more prosperous, instead of being overworked. Scientific management consists very largely in preparing for and carrying out these tasks.

The writer is fully aware that to perhaps most of the readers of this paper the four elements which differentiate the new management from the old

---

[5]   For example, the records containing the data used under scientific management in an ordinary machine-shop fill thousands of pages.

will at first appear to be merely high-sounding phrases; and he would again repeat that he has no idea of convincing the reader of their value merely through announcing their existence. His hope of carrying conviction rests upon demonstrating the tremendous force and effect of these four elements through a series of practical illustrations. It will be shown, first, that they can be applied absolutely to all classes of work, from the most elementary to the most intricate; and second, that when they are applied, the results must of necessity be overwhelmingly greater than those which it is possible to attain under the management of initiative and incentive.

The first illustration is that of handling pig iron, and this work is chosen because it is typical of perhaps the crudest and most elementary form of labor which is performed by man. This work is done by men with no other implements than their hands. The pig-iron handler stoops down, picks up a pig weighing about 92 pounds, walks for a few feet or yards and then drops it on to the ground or upon a pile. This work is so crude and elementary in its nature that the writer firmly believes that it would be possible to train an intelligent gorilla so as to become a more efficient pig-iron handler than any man can be. Yet it will be shown that the science of handling pig iron is so great and amounts to so much that it is impossible for the man who is best suited to this type of work to understand the principles of this science, or even to work in accordance with these principles without the aid of a man better educated then he is. And the further illustrations to be given will make it clear that in almost all of the mechanic arts the science which underlies each workman's act is so great and amounts to so much that the workman who is best suited actually to do the work is incapable (either through lack of education or through insufficient mental capacity) of understanding this science. This is announced as a general principle, the truth of which will become apparent as one illustration after another is given. After showing these four elements in the handling of pig iron, several illustrations will be given of their application to different kinds of work in the field of the mechanic arts, at intervals in a rising scale, beginning with the simplest and ending with the more intricate forms of labor.

One of the first pieces of work undertaken by us, when the writer started to introduce scientific management into the Bethlehem Steel Company, was to handle pig iron on task work. The opening of the Spanish War found some 80,000 tons of pig iron placed in small piles in an open field adjoining the works. Prices for pig iron had been so low that it could not be sold at a profit, and it therefore had been stored. With the opening of the Spanish War the price of pig iron rose, and this large accumulation of iron was sold. This gave us a good opportunity to show the workmen, as well as the owners and managers of the works, on a fairly large scale the advantages of task work over the old-fashioned day work and piece work, in doing a very elementary class of work.

The Bethlehem Steel Company had five blast furnaces, the product of which had been handled by a pig-iron gang for many years. This gang, at this time, consisted of about seventy-five men. They were good, average pig-iron handlers, were under an excellent foreman who himself had been a pig-iron handler, and the work was done, on the whole, about as fast and as cheaply as it was anywhere else at that time.

A railroad switch was run out into the field, right along the edge of the piles of pig iron. An inclined plank was placed against the side of a car, and each man picked up from his pile a pig of iron weighing about 92 pounds, walked up the inclined plank and dropped it on the end of the car.

We found that this gang were loading on the average about 12.5 long tons per man per day. We were surprised to find, after studying the matter, that a first-class pig-iron handler ought to handle between 47 and 48 long tons per day, instead of 12.5 tons, at which rate the work was then being done. And it was further our duty to see that this work was done without bringing on a strike among the men, without any quarrel with the men, and to see that the men were happier and better contented when loading at the new rate of 47 tons than they were when loading at the old rate of 12.5 tons.

Our first step was the scientific selection of the workman. In dealing with workmen under this type of management, it is an inflexible rule to talk to and deal with only one man at a time, since each workman has his own special abilities and limitations, and since we are not dealing with men in masses, but are trying to develop each individual man to his highest state of efficiency and prosperity. Our first step was to find the proper workman to begin with. We therefore carefully watched and studied these seventy-five men for three or four days, at the end of which time we had picked out four men who appeared to be physically able to handle pig iron at the rate of 47 tons per day. A careful study was then made of each of these men. We looked up their history as far back as practicable and thorough inquiries were made as to the character, habits, and the ambition of each of them. Finally, we selected one from among the four as the most likely man to start with. He was a little Pennsylvania Dutchman who had been observed to trot back home for a mile or so after his work in the evening about as fresh as he was when he came trotting down to work in the morning. We found that upon wages of $1.15 a day he had succeeded in buying a small plot of ground, and that he was engaged in putting up the walls of a little house for himself in the morning before starting to work and at night after leaving. He also had the reputation of being exceedingly "close," that is, of placing a very high value on a dollar. As one man whom we talked to about him said, "a penny looks about the size of a cart-wheel to him." This man we will call Schmidt.

The task before us, then, narrowed itself down to getting Schmidt to handle 47 tons of pig iron per day and making him glad to do it. This was done as follows. Schmidt was called out from among the gang of pig-iron handlers and talked to somewhat in this way:

"Schmidt, are you a high-priced man?"

"Vell, I don't know vat you mean."

"Oh yes, you do. What I want to know is whether you are a high-priced man or not."

"Vell, I don't know vat you mean."

"Oh, come now, you answer my questions. What I want to find out is whether you are a high-priced man or one of these cheap fellows here. What I want to find out is whether you want to earn $1.85 a day or whether you are satisfied with $1.15, just the same as all those cheap fellows are getting."

"Did I vant $1.85 a day? Vas dot a high-priced man? Vell, yes, I vas a high-priced man."

"Oh, you're aggravating me. Of course you want $1.85 a day—everyone wants it! you know perfectly well that that has very little to do with your being a high-priced man. For goodness' sake answer my questions, and don't waste any more of my time. Now come over here. You see that pile of pig iron?"

"Yes."

"You see that car?"

"Yes."

"Well, if you are a high-priced man, you will load that pig iron on that car tomorrow for $1.85. Now do wake up and answer my question. Tell me whether you are a high-priced man or not."

"Vell,—did I got $1.85 for loading dot pig iron on dot car tomorrow?"

"Yes, of course you do, and you get $1.85 for loading a pile like that every day right through the year. That is what a high-priced man does, and you know it just as well as I do."

"Vell, den, I vas a high-priced man."

"Now, hold on, hold on. You know just as well as I do that a high-priced man has to do exactly as he's told from morning till night. You have seen this man here before, haven't you?"

"No, I never saw him."

"Well, if you are a high-priced man, you will do exactly as this man tells you tomorrow, from morning till night. When he tells you to pick up a pig and walk, you pick it up and you walk, and when he tells you to sit down and rest, you sit down. You do that right straight through the day. And what's more, no back talk. Now a high-priced man does just what he's told to do, and no back talk. Do you understand that? When this man tells you to walk, you walk; when he tells you to sit down, you sit down, and you don't talk back to him. Now you come on to work here tomorrow morning and I'll know before night whether you are really a high-priced man or not."

This seems to be rather rough talk. And indeed it would be if applied to an educated mechanic, or even an intelligent laborer. With a man of the mentally sluggish type of Schmidt it is appropriate and not unkind, since it is effective in fixing his attention on the high wages which he wants and away from what, if it were called to his attention, he probably would consider impossibly hard work.

What would Schmidt's answer be if he were talked to in a manner which is usual under the management of "initiative and incentive"? say, as follows:

"Now, Schmidt, you are a first-class pig-iron handler and know your business well. You have been handling at the rate of 12.5 tons per day. I have given considerable study to handling pig iron, and feel sure that you could do a much larger day's work that you have been doing. Now don't you think that if you really tried you could handle 47 tons of pig iron per day, instead of 12.5 tons?"

What do you think Schmidt's answer would be to this?

Schmidt started to work, and all day long, and at regular intervals, was told by the man who stood over him with a watch, "Now pick up a pig and walk. Now sit down and rest. Now walk—now rest," etc. He worked when he was told to work, and rested when he was told to rest, and at half-past five in the afternoon had his 47.5 tons loaded on the car. And he practically never failed to work at this pace and do the task that was set him during the three years that the writer was at Bethlehem. And throughout this time he averaged a little more than $1.85 per day, whereas before he had never received over $1.15 per day, which was the ruling rate of wages at that time in Bethlehem.

That is, he received 60 per cent higher wages than were paid to other men who were not working on task work. One man after another was picked out and trained to handle pig iron at the rate of 47.5 tons per day until all of the pig iron was handled at this rate, and the men were receiving 60 per cent more wages than other workmen around them.

The writer has given above a brief description of three of the four elements which constitute the essence of scientific management; first, the careful selection of the workman, and, second and third, the method of first inducing and then training and helping the workman to work according to the scientific method. Nothing has as yet been said about the science of handling pig iron. The writer trusts, however, that before leaving this illustration the reader will be thoroughly convinced that there is a science of handling pig iron, and further that this science amounts to so much that the man who is suited to handle pig iron cannot possibly understand it, nor even work in accordance with the laws of this science, without the help of those who are over him.

* * * * *

The law is confined to that class of work in which the limit of a man's capacity is reached because he is tired out. It is the law of heavy laboring, corresponding to the work of the cart horse, rather than that of the trotter. Practically all such work consists of a heavy pull or a push on the man's arms, that is, the man's strength is exerted by either lifting or pushing something which he grasps in his hands. And the law is that for each given pull or push on the man's arms it is possible for the workman to be under load for only a definite percentage of the day. For example, when pig iron is being handled (each pig weighing 92 pounds), a first-class workman can only be under load 43 percent of the day. He must be entirely free from load during 57 percent of the day. And as the load becomes lighter, the percentage of the day under which the man can remain under load increases. So that, if the workman is handling a half pig weighing 46 pounds, he can then be under load 58 per cent of the day, and only has to rest during 42 per cent. As the weight grows lighter the man can remain under load during a larger and larger percentage of the day, until finally a load is reached which he can carry in his hands all day long without being tired out. When that point has been arrived at this law ceases to be useful as a guide to a laborer's endurance, and some other law must be found which indicates the man's capacity for work.

When a laborer is carrying a piece of pig iron weighing 92 pounds in his hands, it tires him about as much to stand still under the load as it does to walk with it, since his arm muscles are under the same severe tension whether he is moving or not. A man, however, who stands still under a load is exerting no horse-power whatever, and this accounts for the fact that no constant relation could be traded in various kinds of heavy laboring work between the foot-pounds of energy exerted and the tiring effect of the work on the man. It will also be clear that in all work of this kind it is necessary for the arms of the workman to be completely free from load (that is, for the workman to rest) at frequent intervals. Throughout the time that the man is under a heavy load the tissues of his arm muscles are in process of degeneration, and frequent periods of rest are required in order that the blood may have a chance to restore these tissues to their normal condition.

To return now to our pig-iron handlers at the Bethlehem Steel Company.

If Schmidt had been allowed to attack the pile of 47 tons of pig iron without the guidance or direction of a man who understood the art, or science, of handling pig iron, in his desire to earn his high wages he would probably have tired himself out by eleven or twelve o'clock in the day. He would have kept so steadily at work that his muscles would not have had the proper periods of rest absolutely needed for recuperation, and he would have been completely exhausted early in the day. By having a man, however, who understood this law, stand over him and direct his work, day after day, until he acquired the habit of resting at proper intervals, he was able to work at an even gait all day long without unduly tiring himself.

Now one of the very first requirements for a man who is fit to handle pig iron as a regular occupation is that he shall be so stupid and so phlegmatic that he more nearly resembles in his mental make-up the ox than any other type. The man who is mentally alert and intelligent is for this very reason entirely unsuited to what would, for him, be the grinding monotony of work of this character. Therefore the workman who is best suited to handling pig iron is unable to understand the real science of doing this class of work. He is so stupid that the word "percentage" has no meaning to him, and he must consequently be trained by a man more intelligent than himself into the habit of working in accordance with the laws of this science before he can be successful.

The writer trusts that it is now clear that even in the case of the most elementary form of labor that is known, there is a science, and that when the man best suited to this class of work has been carefully selected, when the science of doing the work has been developed, and when the carefully selected man has been trained to work in accordance with this science, the results obtained must of necessity be overwhelmingly greater than those which are possible under the plan of "initiative and incentive."

HUMAN RELATIONS

Fritz J. Roethlisberger and William J. Dickson

[From Fritz J. Roethlisberger and William J. Dickson, *Management and the Worker*, (Cambridge: Harvard University Press, 1939), pp. 551-68. Reprinted by permission of Harvard University Press and the President and Fellows of Harvard College.]

AN INDUSTRIAL ORGANIZATION AS A SOCIAL SYSTEM

We shall now attempt to state more systematically than was possible in a chronological account the results of the research and some of their implications for practice. Each stage of the research contributed to the development of a point of view in terms of which the data could be more usefully assessed. In presenting the studies, this aspect of the research program was given primary emphasis and an effort was made to show how each successive step in the research resulted in the discovery of new facts which in turn brought forth new questions and new hypotheses and assisted in the development of more adequate methods and a more adequate conceptual scheme. The point of view which gradually emerged from these studies is one from which an industrial organization is regarded as a social system. In this chapter a statement of this point of view will be made. In the next chapter various management problems which have been discussed in connection with the various research studies will be restated in terms of this new point of view. In the concluding chapter the application of the concept of an industrial concern as a social system to problems of personnel practice will be considered.

The study of the bank wiremen showed that their behavior at work could not be understood without considering the informal organization of the group and the relation of this informal organization to the total social organization of the company. The work activities of this group, together with their satisfactions and dissatisfactions, had to be viewed as manifestations of a complex pattern of interrelations. In short, the work situation of the bank wiring group had to be treated as a social system; moreover, the industrial organization of which this group was a part also had to be treated as a social system.

By "system" is meant something which must be considered as a whole because each part bears a relation of interdependence to every other part.[6] It will be the purpose of this chapter to state this conception of a social system, to specify more clearly the parts of the social system of which account has to be taken in an industrial organization, and to consider the state of equilibrium which obtains among the parts.

THE TWO MAJOR FUNCTIONS OF AN INDUSTRIAL ORGANIZATION

An industrial organization may be regarded as performing two major functions, that of producing a product and that of creating and distributing satisfactions among the individual members of the organization. The first function is ordinarily called economic. From this point of view the functioning of the concern is assessed in such terms as cost, profit, and technical efficiency. The second function, while it is readily understood, is not ordinarily designated by any generally accepted word. It is variously described as maintaining employee relations, employee good will, cooperation, etc. From this standpoint the functioning of the concern is frequently assessed in such terms as labor turnover, tenure of employment, sickness and accident rate, wages, employee attitudes, etc. The industrial concern is continually confronted, therefore, with two sets of major problems: (1) problems of external balance, and (2) problems of internal equilibrium. The problems of external balance are generally assumed to be economic; that is, problems of competition, adjusting the organization to meet changing price levels, etc. The problems of internal equilibrium are chiefly concerned with the maintenance of a kind of social organization in which individuals and groups through working together can satisfy their own desires.

Ordinarily an industrial concern is thought of primarily in terms of its success in meeting problems of external balance, or if the problems of internal equilibrium are explicitly recognized they are frequently assumed to be separate from and unrelated to the economic purpose of the enterprise. Producing an article at a profit and maintaining good employee relations are frequently regarded as antithetical propositions. The results of the studies which have been reported indicated, however, that these two sets of problems are interre-

---

6   "The interdependence of the variables in a system is one of the widest inductions from experience that we possess; or we may alternatively regard it as the definition of a system." Henderson, L. J., *Pareto's General Sociology,* Harvard University Press, 1935, p. 86.

lated and interdependent. The kind of social organization which obtains within a concern is intimately related to the effectiveness of the total organization. Likewise, the success with which the concern maintains external balance is directly related to its internal organization.

A great deal of attention has been given to the economic function of industrial organization. Scientific controls have been introduced to further the economic purposes of the concern and of the individuals within it. Much of this advance has gone on in the name of efficiency or rationalization. Nothing comparable to this advance has gone on in the development of skills and techniques for securing cooperation, that is, for getting individuals and groups of individuals working together effectively and with satisfaction to themselves. The slight advances which have been made in this area have been overshadowed by the new and powerful technological developments of modern industry.

THE TECHNICAL ORGANIZATION OF THE PLANT

In looking at an industrial organization as a social system it will first be necessary to examine the physical environment, for this is an inseparable part of any organization. The physical environment includes not only climate and weather, but also that part of the environment which is owned and used by the organization itself, namely, the physical plant, tools, machines, raw products, and so on. This latter part of the factory's physical environment is ordered and organized in a certain specified way to accomplish the task of technical production. For our purposes, therefore, it will be convenient to distinguish from the human organization this aspect of the physical environment of an industrial plant and to label it the "technical organization of the plant." This term will refer only to the logical and technical organization of material, tools, machines, and finished product, including all those physical items related to the task of technical production.

The two aspects into which an industrial plant can be roughly divided—the technical organization and the human organization—are interrelated and interdependent. The human organization is constantly molding and re-creating the technical organization either to achieve more effectively the common economic purpose or to secure more satisfaction for its members. Likewise, changes in the technical organization require an adaptation on the part of the human organization.

THE HUMAN ORGANIZATION OF THE PLANT

In the human organization we find a number of individuals working together toward a common end: the collective purpose of the total organization. Each of these individuals, however, is bringing to the work situation a different background of personal and social experiences. No two individuals are making exactly the same demands of their job. The demands a particular employee makes depend not only upon his physical needs but upon his social needs as well. These social needs and the sentiments associated with them vary with his early personal history and social conditioning as well as with the needs and sentiments of people closely associated with him both inside and outside of work.

THE INDIVIDUAL

It may be well to look more closely at the sentiments the individual is bringing to his work situation. Starting with a certain native organic endowment the child is precipitated into group life by the act of birth. The group into which the child is born is not the group in general. The child is born into a specific family. Moreover, this specific family is not a family in isolation. It is related in certain ways to other families in the community. It has a certain cultural background—a way of life, codes and routines of behavior, associated with certain beliefs and expectations. In the beginning the child brings only his organic needs to this social milieu into which he is born. Very rapidly he begins to accumulate experience. This process of accumulating experience is the process of assigning meanings to the socio-reality about him; it is the process of becoming socialized. Much of the early learning period is devoted to preparing the child to become capable of social life in its particular group. In preparing the child for social participation the immediate family group plays an important role. By the particular type of family into which the child is born he is "conditioned" to certain routines of behavior and ways of living. The early meanings he assigns to his experience are largely in terms of these codes of behavior and associated beliefs. As the child grows up and participates in groups other than the immediate family his meanings lose, although never quite entirely, their specific family form. This process of social interaction and social conditioning is never-ending and continues from birth to death. The adult's evaluation of his surroundings is determined in a good part by the system of human interrelations in which he has participated.

THE SOCIAL ORGANIZATION OF THE PLANT

However, the human organization of an industrial plant is more than a plurality of individuals, each motivated by sentiments arising from his own personal and private history and background. It is also a social organization, for the members of an industrial plant—executives, technical specialists, supervisors, factory workers, and office workers—are interacting daily with one another and from their associations certain patterns of relations are formed among them. These patterns of relations, together with the objects which symbolize them, constitute the social organization of the industrial enterprise. Most of the individuals who live among these patterns come to accept them as obvious and necessary truths and to react as they dictate. Both the kind of behavior that is expected of a person and the kind of behavior he can expect from others are prescribed by these patterns.

If one looks at a factory situation, for example, one finds individuals and groups of individuals who are associated at work acting in certain accepted and prescribed ways toward one another. There is not complete homogeneity of behavior between individuals or between one group of individuals and another, but rather there are differences of behavior expressing differences in social relationship. Some relationships fall into routine patterns, such as the relationship between superior and subordinate or between office worker and shop worker. Individuals conscious of their membership in certain groups are reacting in certain accepted ways to other individuals representing other groups. Behavior varies according to the stereotyped conceptions of relationship. The worker, for example, behaves toward his foreman in one way, toward his first-line supervisor in another way, and toward his fellow worker in still another. People holding the rank of inspector expect a certain kind of behavior from the operators—the operators from the inspectors. Now these relationships, as is well known from everyday experiences, are finely shaded and sometimes become complicated. When a person is in the presence of his supervisor alone he usually acts differently from the way he acts when his supervisor's supervisor is also present. Likewise, his supervisor acts toward him alone quite differently from the way he behaves when his own supervisor is also there. These subtle nuances of relationship are so much a part of everyday life that they are commonplace. They are taken for granted. The vast amount of social conditioning that has taken place by means of which a person maneuvers himself gracefully through the intricacies of these finely shaded social distinctions is seldom explicitly realized. Attention is paid only when a new social situation arises where the past social training of the person prevents him from making the necessary delicate interpretations of a given social signal and hence brings forth the "socially wrong" response.

In the factory, as in any social milieu, a process of social evaluation is constantly at work. From this process distinctions of "good" and "bad," "inferior" and "superior," arise. This process of evaluation is carried on with simple and ready generalizations by means of which values become attached to individuals and to groups performing certain tasks and operations. It assigns to a group of individuals performing such and such a task a particular rank in the established prestige scale. Each work group becomes a carrier of social values. In industry with its extreme diversity of occupations there are a number of such groupings. Any noticeable similarity or difference, not only in occupation but also in age, sex, and nationality, can serve as a basis of social classification, as, for example, "married women," the "old-timer," the "white-collared" or clerical worker, the "foreign element." Each of these groups, too, has its own value system.

All the patterns of interaction that arise between individuals or between different groups can be graded according to the degree of intimacy involved in the relationship. Grades of intimacy or understanding can be arranged on a scale and expressed in terms of "social distance." Social distance measures differences of sentiment and interest which separate individuals or groups from one another. Between the president of a company and the elevator operator there is considerable social distance, more for example than between the foreman and the bench worker. Social distance is to social organization what physical distance is to physical space. However, physical and social distance do not necessarily coincide. Two people may be physically near but socially distant.

Just as each employee has a particular physical location, so he has a particular social place in the total social organization. But this place is not so rigidly fixed as in a caste system. In any factory there is considerable mobility or movement. Movement can occur in two ways: the individual may pass from one occupation to another occupation higher up in the prestige scale; or the prestige scale itself may change.

It is obvious that these scales of value are never completely accepted by all the groups in the social environment. The shop worker does not quite see why the office worker, for example, should have shorter hours of work than he has. Or the new comer, whose efficiency on a particular job is about the same, but whose hourly rate is less than that of some old-timer, wonders why service should count so much. The management group, in turn, from the security of its social elevation, does not often understand what "all the fuss is about." As was indicated by many of the studies, any person who has achieved a certain rank in the prestige scale regards anything real or imaginary which tends to alter his status adversely as some thing unfair or unjust. It is apparent that any move on the part of the management may alter the existing social equilibrium to which the employee has grown accustomed and by means of which his status is defined. Immediately this disruption will be expressed in sentiments of resistance to the real or imagined alterations in the social equilibrium. From this point of view it can be seen how every item and event in the industrial environment becomes an object of a system of sentiments. According to this way of looking at things, material goods, physical events, wages, hours of work, etc., cannot be treated as things in themselves. Instead, they have to be interpreted as carriers of social value. The meanings which any person in an industrial organization assigns to the events and objects in his environment are often determined by the social situation in which the events and objects occur. The significance to an employee of a double-pedestal desk, of a particular kind of pencil, or of a handset telephone is determined by the social setting in which these objects appear. If people with double-pedestal desks supervise people with single-pedestal desks, then double-pedestal desks become symbols of status or prestige in the organization. As patterns of behavior become crystallized, every object in the environment tends to take on a particular social significance. It becomes easy to tell a person's social place in the organization by the objects which he wears and carries and which surround him. In these terms it can be seen how the introduction of a technical change may also involve for an individual or a group of individuals the loss of certain prestige symbols and, as a result, have a demoralizing effect.

From this point of view the behavior of no one person in an industrial organization, from the very top to the very bottom, can be regarded as motivated by strictly economic or logical considerations. Routine patterns of interaction involve strong sentiments. Each group in the organization manifests its own powerful sentiments. It is likely that sometimes the behavior of many staff specialists which goes under the name of "efficiency" is as much a manifestation of a very strong sentiment—the sentiment or desire to originate new combinations—as it is of anything strictly logical.

This point of view is far from the one which is frequently expressed, namely, that man is essentially an economic being carrying around with him a few noneconomic appendages. Rather, the point of view which has been expressed here is that noneconomic motives, interests, and processes, as well as economic, are fundamental in behavior in business, from the board of directors to the very last man in the organization. Man is not merely, in fact is very seldom, motivated by factors pertaining strictly to facts or logic. Sentiments are not merely things which man carries around with him as appendages. He cannot cast them off like a suit of clothes. He carries them with him wherever he goes. In business or elsewhere, he can hardly behave without expressing them. Moreover, sentiments do not exist in a social vacuum. They are the product of social behavior, of social interaction, of the fact that man lives his life as a member of different groups. Not only does man bring sentiments to the business situation because of his past experiences and conditioning outside of business, but also as a member of a specific local business organization with a particular social place in it he has certain sentiments expressing his particular relations to it.

According to this point of view, every social act in adulthood is an integrated response to both inner and outer stimuli. To each new concrete situation the adult brings his past "social conditioning." To the extent that this past social conditioning has prepared him to assimilate the new experience in the culturally accepted manner, he is said to be "adjusted." To the extent that his private or personal view of the situation is at variance with the cultural situation, the person is called "maladjusted."

THE FORMAL ORGANIZATION OF THE PLANT

The social organization of the industrial plant is in part formally organized. It is composed of a number of strata or levels which differentiate the bench-worker from the skilled mechanic, the group chief from the department chief, and so on. These levels are well defined and all the formal orders, instructions, and compensations are addressed to them. All such factors taken together make up the formal organization of the plant. It includes the systems, policies, rules, and regulations of the plant which express what the relations of one person to another are supposed to be in order to achieve effectively the task of technical production. It prescribes the relations that are supposed to obtain within the human organization and between the human organization and the technical organization. In short, the patterns of human interrelations, as defined by the systems, rules, policies, and regulations of the company, constitute the formal organization.

The formal organization of an industrial plant has two purposes: it addresses itself to the economic purposes of the total enterprise; it concerns itself also with the securing of co-operative effort. The formal organization includes all the explicitly stated systems of control introduced by the company in order to achieve the economic purposes of the total enterprise and the effective contribution of the members of the organization to those economic ends.

THE INFORMAL ORGANIZATION OF THE PLANT

All the experimental studies pointed to the fact that there is something more to the social organization than what has been formally recognized. Many of the actually existing patterns of human interaction have no representation in the formal organization at all, and others are inadequately represented by the formal organization. This fact is frequently forgotten when talking or thinking about industrial situations in general. Too often it is assumed that the organization of a company corresponds to a blueprint plan or organization chart. Actually, it never does. In the formal organization of most companies little explicit recognition is given to many social distinctions residing in the social organization. The blueprint plans of a company show the functional relations between working units, but they do not express the distinctions of social distance, movement, or equilibrium previously described. The hierarchy of prestige values which tends to make the work of men more important than the work of women, the work of clerks more important than the work at the bench, has little representation in the formal organization; nor does a blue-print plan ordinarily show the primary groups, that is, those groups enjoying daily face-to-face relations. Logical lines of horizontal and vertical coordination of functions replace the actually existing patterns of interaction between people in different social places. The formal organization cannot take account of the sentiments and values residing in the social organization by means of which individuals or groups of individuals are informally differentiated, ordered, and integrated. Individuals in their associations with one another in a factory build up personal relationships. They form into informal groups, in terms of which each person achieves a certain position or status. The nature of these informal groups is very important, as has been shown in the Relay Assembly Test Room and in the Bank Wiring Observation Room. It is well to recognize that informal organizations are not "bad," as they are sometimes assumed to be. Informal social organization exists in every plant, and can be said to be a necessary prerequisite for effective collaboration. Much collaboration exists at an informal level, and it sometimes facilitates the functioning of the formal organization. On the other hand, sometimes the informal organization develops in opposition to the formal organization. The important consideration is, therefore, the relation that exists between formal and informal organizations.

To illustrate, let us consider the Relay Assembly Test Room and the Bank Wiring Observation Room. These two studies offered an interesting contrast between two informal working groups; one situation could be characterized in almost completely opposite terms from the other. In the Relay Assembly Test Room, on the one hand, the five operators changed continuously in their rate of output up and down over the duration of the test, and yet in a curious fashion their variations in output were insensitive to many significant changes introduced during the experiment. On the other hand, in the Bank Wiring Observation Room output was being held relatively constant and there existed a hypersensitivity to change on the part of the worker, in fact, what could almost be described as an organized opposition to it.

It is interesting to note that management could draw from these studies two opposite conclusions. From the Relay Assembly Test Room experiment, they could argue that the company can do almost anything it wants in the nature of technical changes without any perceptible effect on the output of the workers. From the Bank Wiring Observation Room, they could argue equally convincingly that the company can introduce hardly any changes without meeting a pronounced opposition to them from the workers. To make this dilemma even more striking, it is only necessary to recall that the sensitivity to change in the one case occurred in the room where no experimental changes had been introduced whereas the insensitivity to change in the other case occurred in the room where the operators had been submitted to considerable experimentation. To settle this question by saying that in one case the situation was typical and in the other case atypical of ordinary shop conditions would be to beg the question, for the essential difference between the two situations would again be missed. It would ignore the social setting in which the changes occurred and the meaning which the workers themselves assigned to the changes.

Although in both cases there were certain informal arrangements not identical with the formal setup, the informal organization in one room was quite different from that in the other room, especially in its relation to the formal organization. In the case of the Relay Assembly Test Room there was a group, or informal organization, which could be characterized as a network of personal relations which had been developed in and through a particular way of working together; it was an organization which not only satisfied the wishes of its members but also worked in harmony with the aims of management. In the case of the Bank Wiring Observation Room there was an informal organization which could be characterized better as a set of practices and beliefs which its members had in common—practices and beliefs which at many points worked against the economic purposes of the company. In one case the relation between the formal and informal organization was one of compatibility; in the other case it was one of opposition. Or to put it in another way, collaboration in the Relay Assembly Test Room was at a much higher level than in the Bank Wiring Observation Room.

The difference between these two groups can be understood only by comparing the functions which their informal organizations performed for their members. The chief function of the informal group in the Bank Wiring Observation Room was to resist changes in their established routines of work or personal interrelations. This resistance to change, however, was not the chief function of the informal group in the Relay Assembly Test Room. It is true that at first the introduction of the planned changes in the test room, whether or not these changes were logically in the direction of improvement, was met with apprehension and feelings of uneasiness on the part of the operators. The girls in the beginning were never quite sure that they might not be victims of the changes.

In setting up the Relay Assembly Test Room with the object of studying the factors determining the efficiency of the worker, many of the methods and rules by means of which management tends to promote and maintain efficiency—the "bogey," not talking too much at work, etc.—were, in effect, abrogated. With the removal of this source of constraint and in a setting of heightened social significance (because many of the changes had differentiated the test room girls from the regular department and as a result had elevated the social status within the plant of each of the five girls) a new type of spontaneous social organization developed. Social conditions had been established which allowed the operators to develop their own values and objectives. The experimental conditions allowed the operators to develop openly social codes at work and these codes, unhampered by interference, gave a sustained meaning to their work. It was as if the experimenters had acted as a buffer for the operators and held their work situation steady while they developed a new type of social organization. With this change in the type of social organization there also developed a new attitude toward changes in their working environment. Toward many changes which constitute an unspecified threat in the regular work situation the operators became immune. What the Relay Assembly Test Room experiment showed was that when innovations are introduced carefully and with regard to the actual sentiments of the workers, the workers are likely to develop a spontaneous type of informal organization which will not only express more adequately their own values and significances but also is more likely to be in harmony with the aims of management.

Although all the studies of informal organization at the Hawthorne Plant were made at the employee level, it would be incorrect to assume that this phenomenon occurs only at that level. Informal organization appears at all levels, from the very bottom to the very top of the organization.[7] Informal organization at the executive level, just as at the work level, may either facilitate or impede purposive cooperation and communication. In either case, at all levels of the organization informal organizations exist as a necessary condition for collaboration. Without them, formal organization could not survive for long. Formal and informal organizations are interdependent aspects of social interaction.

THE IDEOLOGICAL ORGANIZATION OF THE PLANT

There is one aspect of social organization in an industrial plant which cuts across both the formal and informal organizations: the systems of ideas and beliefs by means of which the values residing in the total organization are expressed and the symbols around which these values are organized. Both the formal and informal organizations of a plant have systems of ideas and beliefs. Some are more capable of logical and systematic expression than others. Those of the formal organization in general are more logically explicit and articulate than those of the informal organization, but they are not for that reason more powerful in their effects than those of the informal organization. The sentiments underlying the beliefs and ideas of informal organizations are often very powerful determinants of overt behavior. Some of these systems of ideas and beliefs represent what the organization should be; that is, what the relations of people to one another should be or how people should behave. Some express the values of one part of the total organization, for each specialist tends to see the total organization from the point of view of the logic of his own specialty. Still others express the values residing in the inter-human relations of the different social groups involved.

Some of these ideas and beliefs represent more closely the actual situation than others. In all cases, however, they are abstractions from the concrete situation. In this respect they are to the concrete situation as maps are to the territories they represent.[8] And like maps these abstractions may be either misleading or useful. They may be misleading because sometimes the person using them fails to realize they are representing only one part of the total organization. Sometimes in the minds of certain individuals these abstractions tend to become divorced from the social reality and, in effect, lead an independent existence.

In their studies the investigators frequently ran into these different systems of ideas and beliefs. Although they were never made the object of systematic study, three general systems which seemed to cling together could be discerned.

The logic of cost. In the industrial plant there is a certain set of ideas and beliefs by means of which the common economic purposes of the total organization are evaluated. This we shall call the "logic of cost." Although the logic of cost is applied mostly to the technical organization, it is also sometimes applied to the human organization. When applied to the human organization

---

[7]   Barnard, C. I., The *Functions of the Executive*, Harvard University Press, 1938, pp. 223-24.

[8]   This distinction has been borrowed from Korzybski, A., *Science and Sanity*, The Science Press Printing,Co., New York, 1933.

it is frequently done under the label of "efficiency."

The word "efficiency" is used in at least five different ways, two of which are rather vague and not clearly differentiated: (a) sometimes when talking about a machine it is used in a technical sense, as the relation between output and input; (b) sometimes when talking about a manufacturing process or operation it is used to refer to relative unit cost; (c) sometimes when referring to a worker it is used to indicate a worker's production or output in relation to a certain standard of performance; (d) sometimes its reference becomes more vague and it is used as practically synonymous with "logical coordination of function"; (e) sometimes it is used in the sense of "morale" or "social integration."

We shall use the term "logic of cost" to refer only to the system of ideas and beliefs which are explicitly organized around the symbol of "cost" and are applied to the human organization from this point of view.[9] This logic represents one of the values of the formal organization: the system of ideas and beliefs which relates the human organization to the task of technical production.

The logic of efficiency. Closely associated with the logic of cost is another system of ideas and beliefs by means of which the collaborative efforts of the members of an organization are evaluated. This we shall call the "logic of efficiency."[10] This system of ideas and beliefs, which is organized around the symbol of "cooperation," represents another value of the formal organization. It is addressed primarily to the problem of how cooperation between individuals and groups of individuals can be effectively secured and is manifested in plans, such as wage payment plans, designed to promote collaboration among individuals.

A system of beliefs and ideas such as this is usually based upon certain assumptions about employee behavior. In the case of the wage payment plan in the Bank Wiring Observation Room, for example, it was assumed that the employee was a logical being and therefore could see the system, as its creators saw it, as a logical, coherent scheme which he could use to his economic advantage. It was assumed that, given the opportunity, the employee would act in such a way as to obtain the maximum of earnings consistent with his physical capacity. Carrying this basic assumption still further, it followed that the slower workers, who would interfere with the logical functioning of that system, would be disciplined by the faster workers and that daywork claims would be kept at a minimum. It was assumed that the division of labor would permit the employees to increase production through specialization. The possibility that division of labor might result in social stratification, which in turn might generate nonlogical forces that would interfere with the logical functioning of that system, was unforeseen. Practically every aspect of the wage plan followed from the basic assumption that nothing would interfere with the economic motives. It is such assumptions as these that go to make up the "logic of efficiency."

The logic of sentiments. There is another system of ideas and beliefs which we shall give the label "the logic of sentiments." It represents the values residing in the interhuman relations of the different groups within the organization. Examples of what is meant here are the arguments employees give which

---

9   According to this definition, "logic of cost" does not conform to any single one of the above uses of the word "efficiency" but conforms most closely to a combination of (b) and (c).

10   The "logic of efficiency" conforms most closely to a combination of uses (c), (d), and (e) of the word "efficiency" as given in the previous section.

center around the "right to work," "seniority", "fairness," "the living wage." This logic, as its name implies, is deeply rooted in sentiment and feeling.

Management and employee logics. At first glance it might seem that the logics of cost and efficiency are the logics of management groups, whereas the logic of sentiments is the logic of employee groups. Although in one sense this may be accurate, in another sense it is an oversimplification. All groups within the industry participate in these different logics, although some participate to a greater or less extent than others. One has only to interview a supervisor or executive to see that he has a logic of sentiments which is expressing the values residing in his personal interrelations with other supervisors or executives. Employee groups, moreover, are not unknown to apply the logic of cost.

However, it is incorrect to assume that these different logics have the same significance to different groups in an industrial plant. The logics of cost and efficiency express the values of the formal organization; the logic of sentiments expresses the values of the informal organization. To management groups and technical specialists the logics of cost and efficiency are likely to be more important than they are to employee groups. In form the logic of sentiments expressed by an executive is indistinguishable from that expressed by a worker, but in content it is quite different. As anyone knows who has had industrial experience, much time is spent in industry in debating the relative weights attaching to the logics of cost, efficiency, and sentiments when they are applied to a particular concrete situation.

A CONDITION OF EQUILIBRIUM

The parts of the industrial plant as a social system are interrelated and interdependent. Any changes in one part of the social system are accompanied by changes in other parts of the system. The parts of the system can be conceived of as being in a state of equilibrium, such that "if a small (not too great) modification different from that which will otherwise occur is impressed on the system, a reaction will at once appear tending toward the conditions that would have existed if the modification had not been impressed."[11]

Some parts of the system can change more rapidly than others. The technical organization can change more rapidly than the social organization; the formal organization can change more rapidly than the informal; the systems of beliefs and ideas can change more rapidly than the patterns of interaction and associated sentiments, of which these beliefs and ideas are an expression. In the disparity in the rates of change possible there exists a precondition for unbalance which may manifest itself in many forms.

In their studies the investigators identified two such possibilities of unbalance. One was the disparity in the rates of change possible in the technical organization, on the one hand, and the social organization, on the other. This condition was manifested in the workers' behavior by distrust and resistance to change. This resistance was expressed whenever changes were introduced too rapidly or without sufficient consideration of their social implications; in other words, whenever the workers were being asked to adjust themselves to new methods or systems which seemed to them to deprive their work of its custom-

---

[11]   For a discussion of equilibrium, see Pareto, V., *The Mind and Society*, Harcourt, Brace & Co., New York, 1935, pp. 1435-42. The quotation used above is Dr. L. J. Henderson's adaptation of Pareto's definition of equilibrium.

ary social significance. In such situations it was evident that the social codes, customs, and routines of the worker could not be accommodated to the technical innovations introduced as quickly as the innovations themselves, in the form of new machines and processes, could be made. The codes, customs, and traditions of the worker are not the product of logic but are based on deeply rooted sentiments. Not only is any alteration of the existing social organization to which the worker has grown accustomed likely to produce sentiments of resistance to the change, but too rapid interference is likely to lead to feelings of frustration and an irrational exasperation with technical change in any form.

Another possibility of unbalance lies in the relation of the ideological organization to the actual work situation. The logics of the ideological organization express only some of the values of the social organization. They frequently fail to take into account not only the feelings and sentiments of people within the plant but also the spontaneous informal social groups which form at all levels of the organization. Thus they tend to become divorced from the concrete situation and to lead an independent existence. As a result of failing to distinguish the human situation as it is from the way it is formally and logically represented to be, many human problems are stated either in terms of the perversities of human nature or in terms of logical defects in the formal organization. The facts of social organization are ignored, and consequently the result in terms of diagnosis or remedy is bound to be inadequate.

It became clear to the investigators that the limits of human collaboration are determined far more by the informal than by the formal organization of the plant. Collaboration is not wholly a matter of logical organization. It presupposes social codes, conventions, traditions, and routine or customary ways of responding to situations. Without such basic codes or conventions, effective work relations are not possible.

COOPERATION

Chester I. Barnard

[From Chester Barnard, *The Functions of the Executive*, (Cambridge: Harvard University Press, 1938), pp. 82-95, 165-71. Reprinted by permisson of Harvard University Press and the President and Fellows of Harvard College.]

THE THEORY OF FORMAL ORGANIZATION

An organization comes into being when (1) there are persons able to communicate with each other (2) who are willing to contribute action (3) to accomplish a common purpose. The elements of an organization are therefore (1) communication; (2) willingness to serve; and (3) common purpose. These elements are necessary and sufficient conditions initially, and they are found in all such organizations. The third element, purpose, is implicit in the definition. Willingness to serve, and communication, and the interdependence of the three elements in general, and their mutual dependence in specific cooperative systems, are matters of experience and observation.

For the continued existence of an organization either *effectiveness* or *effi-*

ciency is necessary;[12] and the longer the life, the more necessary both are. The vitality of organizations lies in the willingness of individuals to contribute forces to the cooperative system. This willingness requires the belief that the purpose can be carried out, a faith that diminishes to the vanishing point as it appears that it is not in fact in process of being attained. Hence, when effectiveness ceases, willingness to contribute disappears. The continuance of willingness also depends upon the satisfactions that are secured by individual contributors in the process of carrying out that purpose. If the satisfactions do not exceed the sacrifices required, willingness disappears, and the condition is one of organization inefficiency. If the satisfactions exceed the sacrifices, willingness persists, and the condition is one of efficiency of organization.

In summary, then, the initial existence of an organization depends upon a combination of these elements appropriate to the external conditions at the moment. Its survival depends upon the maintenance of an equilibrium of the system. This equilibrium is primarily internal, a matter of proportions between the elements, but it is ultimately and basically an equilibrium between the system and the total system external to it. This external system has two terms in it: first, the effectiveness of the organization, which comprises the relevance of its purpose to the environmental situation, and, second, its efficiency, which comprises the interchange between the organization and individuals. Thus the elements stated will each vary with external factors, and they are at the same time interdependent; when one is varied compensating variations must occur in the other if the system of which they are components is to remain in equilibrium, that is, is to persist or survive.

We may now appropriately consider these elements and their interrelations in some detail, having in mind the system as a whole. In later chapters we shall consider each element in greater detail with reference to its variability in dependence upon external factors, and the interrelations of the elements as determining the character of the executive functions.

I

I. Willingness to Cooperate

By definition there can be no organization without persons. However, as we have urged that it is not persons, but the services or acts or action or influences of persons, which should be treated as constituting organizations, it is clear that *willingness* of persons to contribute efforts to the cooperative system is indispensable.

There are a number of words and phrases in common use with reference to organization that reach back to the factor of individual willingness "Loyalty," "solidarity," "*esprit de corps*," "strength" of organization, are the chief. Although they are indefinite, they relate to intensity of attachment to the "cause," and are commonly understood to relate to something different from effectiveness, ability, or value of personal contributions. Thus "loyalty" is re-

---

12 Original editor's note: "An action is effective if it accomplishes its specific aim… It is efficient if it satisfies the motives of that aim, whether it is effective or not, and the process does not create offsetting dissatisfactions. We shall say that an action is inefficient if the motives are not satisfied, or offsetting dissatisfactions are incurred, even if it is effective" (*The Functions of the Executive*, p. 20).

garded as not necessarily related either to position, rank, fame, remuneration, or ability. It is vaguely recognized as an essential condition of organization.

Willingness, in the present connection, means self-abnegation, the surrender of control of personal conduct, the depersonalization of personal action. Its effect is cohesion of effort, a sticking together. Its immediate cause is the disposition necessary to "sticking together." Without this there can be no sustained personal effort as a contribution to cooperation. Activities cannot be coordinated unless there is first the disposition to make a personal act a contribution to an impersonal system of acts, one in which the individual gives up control of what he does.

The outstanding fact regarding willingness to contribute to a given specific formal organization is the indefinitely large range of variation in its intensity among individuals. If all those who may be considered potential contributors to an organization are arranged in order of willingness to serve it, the scale gradually descends from possibly intense willingness through neutral or zero willingness to intense unwillingness or opposition or hatred. The *preponderance of persons in a modern society always lies on the negative side* with reference to any particular existing or potential organization. Thus of the possible contributors only a small minority actually have a positive willingness. This is true of the largest and most comprehensive formal organizations, such as large nations, the Catholic Church, etc. Most of the persons in existing society are either indifferent to or positively opposed to any single one of them; and if the smaller organizations subordinate to these major organizations are under consideration the minority becomes of course a much smaller proportion, and usually a nearly negligible proportion, of the conceivable total.

A second fact of almost equal importance is that the willingness of any individual cannot be constant in degree. It is necessarily intermittent and fluctuating. It can scarcely be said to exist during sleep, and is obviously diminished or exhausted by weariness, discomfort, etc., a conception that was well expressed by the saying, "The spirit is willing but the flesh is weak."

A corollary of the two propositions just stated is that for any given formal organization the number of persons of positive willingness to serve, but near the neutral or zero point, is always fluctuating. I follows that the aggregate willingness of potential contributors to any formal cooperative system is unstable—a fact that is evident from the history of all formal organizations.

Willingness to cooperate, positive or negative, is the expression of the net satisfactions or dissatisfactions experienced or anticipated by each individual in comparison with those experienced or anticipated through alternative activities. These alternative opportunities may be either personal and individualistic or those afforded by other organizations. That is, willingness to cooperate is the net effect, first, of the inducements to do so in conjunction with the sacrifices involved, and then in comparison with the practically available net satisfactions afforded by alternatives. The questions to be determined, if they were matters of logical reasoning, would be, first, whether the opportunity to cooperate grants any advantage to the individual as compared with independent action; and then, if so, whether that advantage is more or less than the advantage obtainable from some other cooperative opportunity. Thus, from the viewpoint of the individual, willingness is the joint effect of personal desires and reluctances; from the viewpoint of organization it is the joint effect of objective inducements offered and burdens imposed. The measure of this net result, however, is entirely individual, personal, and subjective. Hence, organizations depend upon the motives of individuals and the inducements that satisfy them.

II. Purpose

Willingness to cooperate, except as a vague feeling of desire for association with others, cannot develop without an objective of cooperation. Unless there is such an objective it cannot be known or anticipated what specific efforts will be required of individuals, nor in many cases what satisfactions to them can be in prospect. Such an object we denominate the "purpose" of an organization. The necessity of having a purpose is axiomatic, implicit in the words "system," "coordination," "cooperation." It is something that is clearly evident in many observed systems of cooperation, although it is often not formulated in words, and sometimes cannot be so formulated. In such cases what is observed is the direction or the effect of the activities, from which purpose may be inferred.

A purpose does not incite cooperative activity unless it is accepted by those whose efforts will constitute the organization. Hence there is initially something like simultaneity in the acceptance of a purpose and willingness to cooperate.

It is important at this point to make clear that every cooperative purpose has in view of each cooperative person two aspects which we call (a) the cooperative and (b) the subjective aspect, respectively.

(a) When the viewing of the purpose is an *act of cooperation*, it approximates that of detached observers from a special position of observation; this position is that of the interests of the organization; it is largely determined by organization knowledge, but is personally interpreted. For example, if five men are cooperating to move a stone from A to B, the moving of the stone is a different thing in the organization view of each of the five men involved. Note, however, that what moving the stone means to each man personally is not here in question, but what he thinks it means to the organization *as a whole*. This includes the significance of his own effort as an element in cooperation, and that of all others; but it is not at all a matter of satisfying a personal motive.

When the purpose is a physical result of simple character, the difference between the purpose as objectively viewed by a detached observer and the purpose as viewed by each person cooperating *as an act of cooperation* is ordinarily not large or important, and the different cooperative views of the persons cooperating are correspondingly similar. Even in such cases the attentive observer will detect differences that result in disputes, errors of action, etc., even though no *personal* interest is implicated. But when the purpose is less tangible—for example in religious cooperation—the difference between objective purpose and purpose as cooperatively viewed by each person is often seen as ultimately to result in disruption.

We may say, then, that a purpose can serve as an element of a cooperative system only so long as the participants do not recognize that there are serious divergences of their understanding of that purpose as the object of cooperation. If in fact there is important difference between the aspects of the purpose as objectively and as cooperatively viewed, the divergences become quickly evident when the purpose is concrete, tangible, physical; but when the purpose is general, intangible, and of sentimental character, the divergences can be very wide and yet not be recognized. Hence an objective purpose that can serve as the basis for a cooperative system is one that is *believed* by the contributors (or potential contributors) to it to be the determined purpose of the organization. The inculcation of belief in the real existence of a common purpose is an essential executive function. It explains much educational and so-called morale work in political, industrial, and religious organizations that is so often otherwise inexplicable.

(b) Going back to the illustration of five men moving a stone, we have noted "that what moving the stone means to each man personally is not here in question, but what he thinks it means to the *organization as a whole.*" The distinction emphasized is of first importance. It suggests the fact that every participant in an organization may be regarded as having a dual personality—an organization personality and an individual personality. Strictly speaking, an organization purpose has directly no meaning for the individual. What has meaning for him is that organization's relation to him—what burdens it imposes, what benefits it confers. In referring to the aspects of purpose as cooperatively viewed, we are alluding to the *organization* personality of individuals. In many cases the two personalties are so clearly developed that they are quite apparent. In military action individual conduct may be so dominated by organization personality that it is utterly contradictory of what personal motivation would require. It has been observed of many men that their private conduct is entirely inconsistent with official conduct, although they seem completely unaware of the fact. Often it will be observed that participants in political, patriotic, or religious organizations will accept durogatory treatment of their personal conduct, including the assertion that it is inconsistent with their organization obligations, while they will become insensed at the slightest derogation of the tenets or doctrines of their organization, even though they profess not to understand them. There are innumerable other cases, however, in which almost no organization personality may be said to exist. These are cases in which personal relationship with the cooperative system is momentary or at the margin of willingness to participate.

In other words, we have clearly to distinguish between organization purpose and individual motive. It is frequently assumed in reasoning about organizations that a common purpose and individual motive are or should be identical. With the exception noted below, this is never the case; and under modern conditions it rarely even appears to be the case. Individual motive is necessarily an internal, personal, subjective thing; common purpose is necessarily an external, impersonal, objective thing even though the individual interpretation of it is subjective. The one exception to this general rule, an important one, is that the accomplishment of an organization purpose becomes itself a source of personal satisfaction and a motive for many individuals in many organizations. It is rare, however, if ever, and then I think only in connection with family, patriotic, and religious organizations under specal conditions, that organization purpose becomes or can become the *only* or even the major individual motive.

Finally, it should be noted that, once established, organizations change their unifying purposes. They tend to perpetuate themselves; and in the effort to survive, may change the reasons for existence. I shall later make clearer that in this lies an important aspect of executive functions.

III. Communication

The possibility of accomplishing a common purpose and the existence of persons whose desires might constitute motives for contributing toward such a common purpose are the opposite poles of the system of cooperative effort. The process by which these potentialities become dynamic is that of communication. Obviously a common purpose must be commonly known, and to be known must be in some way communicated. With some exceptions, verbal communication between men is the method by which this is accomplished. Similarly, though under crude and obvious conditions not to the same extent, inducements to persons depend upon communication to them.

The method of communication centers in language, oral and written. On its crudest side, motions or actions that are of obvious meaning when observed are sufficient for communication without deliberate attempt to communicate; and signaling by various methods is an important method in much cooperative activity. On the other side, both in primitive and in highly complex civilization "observational feeling" is likewise an important aspect of communication.[13] I do not think it is generally so recognized. It is necessary because of the limitations of language and the differences in the linguistic capacities of those who use language. A very large element in special experience and training and in continuity of individual association is the ability to understand without words, not merely the situation or the conditions, but the *intention*.

The techniques of communication are an important part of any organization and are the permanent problems of many. The absence of a suitable technique of communication would eliminate the possibility of adopting some purposes as a basis for organization. Communication technique shapes the form and the internal economy of organization. This will be evident at once if one visualizes the attempt to do many things now accomplished by small organizations if each "member" spoke a different language. Similarly, many technical functions could hardly be carried on without special codes; for example, engineering of chemical work. In an exhaustive theory of organization, communication would occupy a central place, because the structure, extensiveness, and scope of organization are almost entirely determined by communication techniques....

---

[13] The phrase "observational feeling" is of my own coining. The point is not sufficiently developed, and probably has not been adequately studied by anyone. I take it to be at least in part involved in group action not incited by any "overt" or verbal communication. The cases known to me from the primitive field are those reported by W.H.R. Rivers on pp. 94-97 of his *Instinct and the Unconscious* (2nd edition, Cambridge University Press, 1924), with reference to Polynesia and Melanesia. One case is summarized by F.C. Bartlett, in *Remembering* (Cambridge University Press, 1932), at p. 297. Rivers states in substance that in some of the relatively small groups decisions are often arrived at and acted upon without having ever been formulated by anybody.

I have observed on innumerable occasions apparent unanimity of decision of equals in conferences to quit discussion without a word to that effect being spoken. Often the action is initiated apparently by someone's rising; but as this frequently occurs in such groups *without* the termination of the meeting, more than mere rising is involved. "Observational feeling," I think, avoids the notion of anything being "occult."

II

I. Effectiveness of Cooperation

The continuance of an organization depends upon its ability to carry out its purpose. This clearly depends jointly upon the appropriateness of its action and upon the conditions of the environment. In other words, effectiveness is primarily a matter of technological processes. This is quite obvious in ordinary cases of purpose to accomplish a physical objective, such as building a bridge. When the objective is non-physical, as is the case with religious and social organizations, it is not so obvious.

It should be noted that a paradox is involved in this matter. An organization must disintegrate if it cannot accomplish its purpose. It also destroys itself by accomplishing its purpose. A very large number of successful organizations come into being and then disappear for this reason. Hence most continuous organizations require adoption of new purposes. This is concealed from everyday recognition by the practice of generalizing a complex series of specific purposes under one term, stated to be "*the* purpose" of this organization. This is strikingly true in the case of governmental and public utility organizations when the purpose is stated to be a particular kind of service through a period of years. A manufacturing organization is said to exist to make, say, shoes; this is its "purpose." But it is evident that not making shoes in general but making specific shoes from day to day is its series of purposes. This process of generalization, however, provides in advance for the approximate definition of new purposes automatically—so automatically that the generalization is normally substituted in our minds for the concrete performances that are the real purposes. Failure to be effective is, then, a real cause of disintegration; but failure to provide for the decisions resulting in the adoption of new purposes would have the same result. Hence the generalization of purpose which can only be defined concretely by day-to-day events is a vital aspect of permanent organization.

II. Organization Efficiency

It has already been stated that "efficiency" as conceived in this treatise is not used in the specialized and limited sense of ordinary industrial practice or in the restricted sense applicable to technological processes. So-called "practical" efficiency has little meaning, for example, as applied to many organizations such as religious organizations.

Efficiency of effort in the fundamental sense with which we are here concerned is efficiency relative to the securing of necessary personal contributions to the cooperative system. The life of the organization depends upon its ability to secure and maintain the personal contributions of energy (including the transfer of control of materials or money equivalent) necessary to effect its purposes. This ability is a composite of perhaps many efficiencies and inefficiencies in the narrow senses of these words, and it is often the case that inefficiency in some respect can be treated as the cause of total failure, in the sense that if corrected success would then be possible. But certainly in most organizations—social, political, national, religious—nothing but the absolute test of survival is significant objectively; there is no basis for comparison of the efficiencies of separate aspects.

…The emphasis now is on the view that efficiency of organization is its capacity to offer effective inducements in sufficient quantity to maintain the equilibrium of the system. It is efficiency in this sense and not the efficiency of material productiveness which maintains the vitality of organizations. There are many organizations of great power and permanency in which the idea of productive efficiency is utterly meaningless because there is no material production. Churches, patriotic societies, scientific societies, theatrical and musical organizations, are cases where the original flow of *material* inducements is toward the organization, not from it—a flow necessary to provide resources with which to supply material inducements to the small minority who require them in such organizations.

In those cases where the primary purpose of organization is the production of material things, insufficiency with respect to nonmaterial inducements leads to the attempt to substitute material inducements for nonmaterial. Under favorable circumstances, to a limited degree, and for a limited time, this substitution may be effective. But to me, at least, it appears utterly contrary to the nature of men to be sufficiently induced by material or monetary considerations to contribute enough effort to a cooperative system to enable it to be productively efficient to the degree necessary for persistence over an extended period.

If these things are true, then even in purely economic enterprises efficiency in the offering of noneconomic inducements may be as vital as productive efficiency. Perhaps the word efficiency as applied to such noneconomic inducements as I have given for illustration will seem strange or forced. This, I think, can only be because we are accustomed to use the word in a specialized sense. The noneconomic inducements are as difficult to offer as others under many circumstances. To establish conditions under which individual pride of craft and of accomplishment can be secured without destroying the material economy of standardized production in cooperative operation is a problem in real efficiency. To maintain a character of personnel that is an attractive condition of employment involves a delicate art and much insight in the selection (and rejection) of personal services offered, whether the standard of quality be high or low. To have an organization that lends prestige and secures the loyalty of desirable persons is a complex and difficult task in efficiency—in all-round efficiency, not one-sided efficiency. It is for these reasons that good organizations—commercial, governmental, military, academic, and others—will be observed to devote great attention and sometimes great expense of money to the noneconomic inducements, because they are indispensable to fundamental efficiency, as well as to effectiveness in many cases.

The theory of organization set forth in this chapter is derived from the study of organizations which are exceedingly complex, although it is stated in terms of ideal, simple organizations. The temptation is to assume that, in the more complex organizations that we meet in our actual social life, the effect of complexity is to modify or qualify the theory. This appears not to be the case. Organization, simple or complex, is always *an impersonal system of coordinated human efforts*; always there is purpose as the coordinating and unifying principle; always there is the indispensable ability to communicate, always the necessity for personal willingness, and for effectiveness and efficiency in maintaining the integrity of purpose and the continuity of contributions. Complexity appears to modify the quality and form of these elements and of the balance between them; but fundamentally the same principles that govern simple organizations may be conceived as governing the structure of complex organizations, which are composite systems.

* * * * * *

THE THEORY OF AUTHORITY

The necessity of the assent of the individual to establish authority *for him* is inescapable. A person can and will accept a communication as authoritative only when four conditions simultaneously obtain: (a) he can and does understand the communication; (b) *at the time of his decision* he believes that it is not inconsistent with the purpose of the organization; (c) *at the time of his decision*, he believes it to be compatible with his personal interest as a whole; and (d) he is able mentally and physically to comply with it.

a) A communication that cannot be understood *can* have no authority. An order issued, for example, in a language not intelligible to the recipient is no order at all—no one would so regard it. Now, many orders are exceedingly difficult to understand. They are often necessarily stated in general terms, and the persons who issued them could not themselves apply them under many conditions. Until interpreted they have no meaning. The recipient either must disregard them or merely do anything in the hope that that is compliance.

Hence, a considerable part of administrative work consists in the interpretation and reinterpretation of orders in their application to concrete circumstances that were not or could not be taken into account initially.

b) A communication believed by the recipient to be incompatible with the purpose of the organization, as he understands it, could not be accepted. Action would be frustrated by cross purposes. The most common practical example is that involved in conflicts of orders. They are not rare. An intelligent person will deny the authority of that one which contradicts the purpose of the effort as *he* understands it. In extreme cases many individuals would be virtually paralyzed by conflicting orders. They would be literally unable to comply—for example, an employee of a water system ordered to blow up an essential pump, or soldiers ordered to shoot their own comrades. I suppose all experienced executives know that when it is necessary to issue orders that will appear to the recipients to be contrary to the main purpose, especially as exemplified in prior habitual practice, it is usually necessary and always advisable, if practicable, to explain or demonstrate why the appearance of conflict is an illusion. Otherwise the orders are likely not to be executed, or to be executed inadequately.

c) If a communication is believed to involve a burden that destroys the net advantage of connection with the organization, there would no longer remain a net inducement to the individual to contribute to it. The existence of a net inducement is the only reason for accepting *any* order as having authority. Hence, if such an order is received it must be disobeyed (evaded in the more usual cases) as utterly inconsistent with personal motives that are the basis of accepting any orders at all. Cases of voluntary resignation from all sorts of organizations are common for this sole reason. Malingering and intentional lack of dependability are the more usual methods.

d) If a person is unable to comply with an order, obviously it must be disobeyed, or, better, disregarded. To order a man who cannot swim to swim a river is a sufficient case. Such extreme cases are not frequent; but they occur.

The more usual case is to order a man to do things only a little beyond his capacity; but a little impossible is still impossible.

Naturally the reader will ask: How is it possible to secure such important and enduring cooperation as we observe if in principle and in fact the determination of authority lies with the subordinate individual? It is possible because the decisions of individuals occur under the following conditions: (a) orders that are deliberately issues in enduring organizations usually comply with the four conditions mentioned above; (b) there exists a "zone of indifference" in each individual within which orders are acceptable without conscious questioning of their authority; (c) the interests of the persons who contribute to an organization as a group result in the exercise of an influence on the subject, or on the attitude of the individual, that maintains a certain stability of this zone of indifference.

There is no principle of executive conduct better established on good organizations than that orders will not be issued that cannot or will not be obeyed. Executives and most persons of experience who have thought about it know that to do so destroys authority, discipline, and morale.[14] For reasons to be stated shortly, this principle cannot ordinarily be formally admitted, or at least cannot be professed. When it appears necessary to issue orders which are initially or apparently unacceptable, either careful preliminary education, or persuasive efforts, or the prior offering of effective inducements will be made, so that the issue will not be raised, the denial of authority will not occur, and orders will be obeyed. It is generally recognized that those who least understand this fact—newly appointed minor or "first line" executives—

---

[14] Barring relatively few cases, when the attitude of the individual indicates in advance likelihood of disobedience (either before or after connection with the organization), the connection is terminated or refused before the formal question arises.

It seems advisable to add a caution here against interpreting the exposition in terms of "democracy," whether in governmental, religious, or industrial organizations. The dogmatic assertion that "democracy" or "democratic methods" are (or are not) in accordance with the principles here discussed is not tenable. As will be more evident after the consideration of objective authority, the issues involved here are much too complex and subtle to be taken into account in *any* formal scheme. Under many conditions in the political, religious, and industrial fields democratic processes create artificial questions of more or less logical character, in place of the real questions, which are matters of feeling and appropriateness and of informal organization. By oversimplification of issues this may destroy objective authority. No doubt in many situations formal democratic processes may be an important element in the maintenance of authority, i.e. of organization, cohesion, but may in other situations be disruptive, and probably never could be, in themselves, sufficient. On the other hand the solidarity of some cooperative systems (General Harbord's army, for example) under many conditions may be unexcelled, though requiring formally autocratic processes.

Moreover it should never be forgotten that authority in the aggregate arises from *all* contributors to a cooperative system, and that the weighting to be attributed to the attitude of individuals varies. It is often forgotten that in industrial (or political) organizations measures which are acceptable at the bottom may be quite unacceptable to the substantial proportion of contributors who are executives, and who will no more perform their essential functions than will others, if the conditions are, to them, impossible. The point to be emphasized is that the maintenance of the contributors necessary to the endurance of an organization requires the authority of *all* essential contributors.

are often guilty of "disorganizing" their groups for this reason, as do experienced executives who lose self-control or become unbalanced by a delusion of power or for some other reason. Inexperienced persons take literally the current notions of authority and are then said "not to know how to use authority" or "to abuse authority." Their superiors often profess the same beliefs about authority in the abstract, but their successful practices are easily observed to be inconsistent with their professions.

b) The phrase "zone of indifference" may be explained as follows: If all the orders for actions reasonably practicable be arranged in the order of their acceptability to the person affected, it may be conceived that there are a number which are clearly unacceptable, that is, which certainly will not be obeyed; there is another group somewhat more or less on the neutral line, that is, either barely acceptable or barely unacceptable; and a third group unquestionable acceptable. This last group lies within the "zone of indifference." The person affected will accept orders lying within this zone and is relatively indifferent as to what the order is so far as the question of authority is concerned. Such an order lies within the range that in a general way was anticipated at time of undertaking the connection with the organization. For example, if a soldier enlists, whether voluntarily or not, in an army in which the men are ordinarily moved about within a certain broad region, it is a matter of indifference whether the order be to go to A or B, C or D, and so on; and goings to A, B, C, D, etc., are in the zone of indifference.

The zone of indifference will be wider or narrower depending upon the degree to which the inducements exceed the burdens and sacrifices which determine the individual's adhesion to the organization. It follows that the range of orders that will be accepted will be very limited among those who are barely induced to contribute to the system.

c) Since the efficiency of organization is affected by the degree to which individuals assent to orders, denying the authority of an organization communication is a threat to the interests of all individuals who derive a net advantage from their connection with the organization, unless the orders are unacceptable to them also. Accordingly, at any given time there is among most of the contributors an active personal interest in the maintenance of the authority of all orders which to them are within the zone of indifference. The maintenance of this interest is largely a function of informal organization. Its expression goes under the names of "public opinion," "organization opinion," "feeling in the ranks," "group attitude," etc. Thus the common sense of the community informally arrived at affects the attitude of individuals, and makes them, as individuals, loth to question authority that is within or near the zone of indifference. The formal statement of this common sense is the fiction that authority comes down from above, from the general to the particular. This fiction merely establishes a presumption among individuals in favor of the acceptability of orders from superiors, enabling them to avoid making issues of such orders without incurring sense of personal subserviency or a loss of personal or individual status with their fellows.

Thus the contributors are willing to maintain the authority of communication because, where care is taken to see that only acceptable communications in general are issued, most of them fall within the zone of personal indifference; and because communal sense influences the motives of most contributors most of the time. The practical instrument of this sense is the fiction of superior authority, which makes it possible normally to treat a personal question impersonally.

The fiction[15] of superior authority is necessary for two main reasons:

1) It is the process by which the individual delegates upward, or to the organization, responsibility for what is an organization decision—an action which is depersonalized by the fact of its coordinate character. This means that if an instruction is disregarded, an executive's risk of being wrong must be accepted, a risk that the individual cannot and usually will not take unless in fact his position is at least as good as that of another with respect to correct appraisal of the relevant situation. Most persons are disposed to grant authority because they dislike the personal responsibility which they otherwise accept, especially when they are not in a good position to accept it. The practical difficulties in the operation of organization seldom lie in the excessive desire of individuals to assume responsibility for the organization action of themselves or others, but rather lie in the reluctance to take responsibility for their own actions in organization.

2) The fiction gives impersonal notice that what is at stake is the good of the organization. If objective authority is flouted for arbitrary or merely temperamental reasons, if, in other words, there is deliberate attempt to twist an organization requirement to personal advantage, rather than properly to safeguard a substantial personal interest, then there is a deliberate attack on the organization itself. To remain outside an organization is not necessarily to be more than not friendly or not interested. To fail in an obligation intentionally is an act of hostility. This no organization can permit; and it must respond with punitive action if it can, even to the point of incarcerating or executing the culprit. This is rather generally the case where a person has agreed in advance in general what he will do. Leaving an organization in the lurch is not often tolerable.

CLASSICAL MANAGEMENT THEORY

Charles Perrow

[From Charles Perrow, *Complex Organizations*, (New York: McGraw-Hill, Inc., 1986), pp. 52-76. Reprinted with permission of the author and publisher. The page and chapter references in parentheses within the body of this chapter are Professor Perrow's. They refer to Reinhard Bendix's book *Work and Authority in Industry* (New York: Wiley, 1956).]

Max Weber's actual writings on bureaucracy did not reach either social scientists or those concerned with business administration in the United States until the 1940s. The material was not translated, and there was not much social science interest in the matter. Meanwhile, a theory of industrial and business management was being developed by practicing managers and professors in the growing business schools of the United States, drawing at times upon some influential European authors such as Henry Fayol. We will not discuss this body of literature, which is referred to as classical management theory or, sometimes,

---

[15]   The word "fiction" is used because from the standpoint of logical construction it merely explains overt acts. Either as a superior officer or as a subordinate, however, I know of nothing that I actually regard as more "real" than "authority."

as the literature of the scientific management school; it is well summarized by Joseph Massie.[16] Two points need mentioning, however, since this school of thought is scorned by social scientists today. First, though the classical theory was derided for presenting "principles" that were really only proverbs,[17] all the resources of organizational research and theory today have not managed to substitute better principles (or proverbs) for those ridiculed. We have more now, but they are no more scientific or useful than the classical ones. Second, the principles, which amount to pious directives to "plan ahead," pay attention to coordination, refrain from wasting executive time on established routine functions and instead to deal with the exceptional cases that come up, served management very well. As obvious as "plan ahead" sounds, it took a lot of saying back in the 1920s, for business rarely did any planning.[18] (Today the injunctions parade under the name of "Management by Objectives," and in more mathematical terms, PERT.) It was also quite a struggle to separate the chief executive (often the founder or his relative) from routine affairs—to get him to delegate authority and deal only with the exceptions. It still is. Finally, a successful and durable business of management consulting and an endless series of successful books rest on the basic principles of the classical management school. These principles have worked and are still working, for they addressed themselves to very real problems of management, problems more pressing for managers than those discussed by social science.

The problems advanced by social scientists have been primarily the problems of human relations in an authoritarian setting. The how, when, and why of these concerns form one of the most fascinating stories in the field of organizational analysis and industrial sociology. Why did management to some extent, and social science to an overwhelming extent, become so preoccupied with human relations in the workplace, with treating the worker well and trying to construct a nonauthoritarian environment in an authoritarian setting? Reinhard Bendix, in a fascinating book on the topic of management's justification for ruling in a variety of countries and times, provides the answer for the United States in one of his chapters.[19] His account is the indispensable background for the dominant strand of organizational theory today. I have summarized it here.

FROM SURVIVAL OF THE FITTEST TO COOPERATION IN SIXTY YEARS

Classical management theorists, and Weber himself, had little to say about workers in industry or nonsalaried personnel in government. It was not until workers forced themselves on the consciousness of management by developing unions, or until a scarcity of labor occurred (due in part to the end of massive immigration), that those concerned with either organizational theory or principles of management practice began to include the worker within their

---

[16] Joseph Massie, "*Management Theory*," in *The Handbook of Organizations*, ed. James March (Chicago: Rand McNally, 1965), pp. 387-422.

[17] See the slashing criticism by Herbert Simon in his *Administrative Behavior*, 3rd ed. (New York Free Press, 1976).

[18] For an account of how little they did and how much shock was required to force planning, see Harold Wilensky, "Intelligence in Industry," *Annals, American Academy of Social Science* 388 (March 1970): 46-58.

[19] Reinhard Bendix, *Work and Authority in Industry* (New York: Wiley, 1956).

purview. Workers had been simply another resource, like the machines that began to replace them in increasing numbers. They were docile, without effective organization, needed jobs, and were remarkably content to suffer extensive hardships in the workplace and in the marketplace. Extensive, lasting unionization did not appear in the United States until the 1910s, in contrast to other industrializing countries where it began to develop fifty years earlier.

In this country, there was a special problem facing management—namely, ideology. On the one hand, democracy stressed liberty and equality for all. On the other hand, large masses of workers and nonsalaried personnel had to submit to apparently arbitrary authority, backed up by local and national police forces and legal power, for ten to twelve hours a day, six days a week. Their right to combine into organizations of their own was severely limited or simply prohibited. How, asks Bendix, could entrepreneurs justify the "privilege of voluntary action and association for themselves, while imposing upon all subordinates the duty of obedience and the obligation to serve their employers to the best of their ability?" (*xxi*) This is the most crucial question a social science of organizations could ask, yet it has rarely been raised by students of organizations.

Social Darwinism

Bendix picks up the story in the 1880s when the United States was lagging behind Britain, Germany, and France in industrialization. From about 1880 to 1910 "the United States underwent the most rapid economic expansion of any industrialized country for a comparable period of time." (254) The rapid expansion was accompanied by ruthless treatment of workers; the United States lagged far behind Britain in social reforms and unionization. Perhaps for this reason, the doctrine of Social Darwinism—the theory of survival of the fittest applied to social life rather than to animals—found more ready reception here than in Britain. Success and riches were regarded both as signs of progress for the nation, to be honored and cherished, and as the reward for those who had proved themselves in the struggle for survival. The struggle was a human battle; the "captains of industry" were better fighters than most of us, wrote sociologist C. R. Henderson in the *American Journal of Sociology* in 1896. (256) They fought on "the battlefield where the 'struggle for existence' is defining the industrially 'fittest to survive.'" Some saw success as the sign of virtue in the Christian mission of business enterprise ("What is the true conception of life but divine ownership and human administration?" asked a man of God); (257) some were more ruthless, stressing the role that the "lowest passions of mankind" played in human progress, since civilization would not advance if such evils were always avoided. But all agreed that success entitled a man to command; failure indicated the lack of the requisite personal qualities. And success was only for the few in the struggle for existence. "Many a man is entirely incapable of assuming responsibility," wrote N.C. Fowler in *The Boy, How to Help Him Succeed* in 1902. "He is a success as the led, but not as the leader. He lacks the courage of willingness to assume responsibility and the ability of handling others." (259)

For those who failed the test, so much the worse; they would be weeded out. Elbert Hubbard, whose book *A Message to Garcia* was extremely popular at the turn of the century, made the message clear (the title refers to a lieutenant who carried an important message to General Garcia in Cuba in spite of overwhelming odds.):

> We have recently been hearing much maudlin sympathy expressed for the "downtrodden denizen of the sweatshop" and the "homeless wanderer searching for the honest employment," and with it all often go many hard words for the men in power.

> Nothing is said about the employer who grows old before his time in a vain attempt to get frowsy ne'er-do-wells to do intelligent work; and has long patient striving with "help" that does nothing but loaf when his back is turned. In every store and factory there is a constant weeding-out process going on. No matter how good times are, this sorting continues, only if times are hard and work is scarce, the sorting is done finer—but out, and forever out, the incompetent and unworthy go. It is the survival of the fittest. Self-interest prompts every employer to keep the best—those who can carry a message to Garcia. (264-265)

(Modernize the language and we have this ever popular message in the mathematical equations of that branch of modern economics called "agency theory".)

But what if success eluded you? What was needed to ensure it? One answer was provided by the New Thought Movement of the late nineteenth and early twentieth centuries, designed to appeal to the ever hopeful and providing a more civilized explanation than the law of the jungle. The answer was mental power—the power of positive thinking. (It is still very much with us, providing hope for their failure.) According to the author of *Thought Force in Business*, "Business success is due to certain qualities of mind. Anything is ours, if you only want it hard enough. Just think of that. *Anything!* Try it. Try it in earnest and you will succeed. It is the operation of a mighty law." (260) The book titles tell the story: every backyard, even the lowliest, is strewn with *Acres of Diamonds* if you will only gather them. Just learn about *Your Forces and How to Use Them*; it is the key to *Mastery of Fate*, and *The Culture of Courage*. By 1925 Orison Sweet Marden had sold some 3 million copies of his various books, and unfortunate babies were named after him. One 1894 title: *Pushing to the Front*, or *Success Under Difficulties*.

The ethic was an individual one and the message for workers was clear. It was not circumstances, the chance of birth, opportunities provided by wealth and education, nor even luck that guided your fate; it was failure to try. But at least it was not that they were biologically unfit, as in Social Darwinism. The New Thought Movement did not directly challenge Social Darwinism, however, and one even finds the two in an uneasy blend.

The Collective Response of Unions

Meanwhile, workers were constructing their own explanations for the inequities of power and treasure in industry. In 1897 American trade unions had 487,000 members; seven years later they had 2,072,700. This enormous increase was accompanied by considerable violence on both sides, in the true form of the struggle for survival. But, in management's hands, the doctrine had not meant that workers too could struggle for existence; *that* would not serve society. As the president of the National Association of Manufacturers said in 1903:

> Organized labor knows but one law and that is the law of physical force—the law of the Huns and the Vandals, the law for the savage.

All its purposes are accomplished either by actual force or by the treat of force.... It is, in all essential features, a mob power knowing no master except its own will. Its history is stained with blood and ruin.... It extends its tactics of coercion and intimidation over all classes, dictating to the press and to the politicians and strangling independence of thought and American manhood. (266)

One of the objections to labor unions was that they represented collective action, not reflecting individual strength or individual will power. But that objection soon was overtaken by events, for employers found they could not fight trade unions individually; regardless of the ethic of individual responsibility, they had to band together. They had cooperated before with regard to problems of markets and government, but never to solve a problem within their own firms. Management's response was the "right to work" philosophy of the early part of the century—the "open shop" (no union) movement. Bendix analyzes the situation as follows:

The rising tide of trade unionism forced American employers to acknowledge, however implicitly, that their own individual authority in the enterprise no longer sufficed. It is necessary to appreciate the novelty of this theme. American businessmen and industrialists were the recognized elite of society. Their great wealth was accepted as a well-earned reward for their outstanding fitness in the struggle for survival. And when these ideas were applied to the relations between capital and labor, the workers were merely admonished to struggle for survival on the terms acceptable to their employers. Yet at this pinnacle of their social recognition, American businessmen were challenged by the trade unions. And they were challenged in the employer's central activity, the management of his "own" plant, where his authority was supposedly absolute. It is not surprising that the ideology of the open shop, the employers' response to this challenge, came to embody all the sacred symbols by which their own fortunes could be identified with the foundation for the social order. (276)

One of the important consequences of the challenge was that the nature of the employers' authority was in doubt. If it had been absolute, there would have been no labor problem; the offending worker would have been dismissed. If a labor problem was admitted, authority was not adequate to deal with it; otherwise, the problem would not have existed. The sad fact was that authority was being questioned by the unions. One article compared the machine tool with the "human machine" and found the latter regretfully lacking. The machine tool was "never obstinate, perverse, discouraged," and if something went wrong it could be corrected. "If the human machine could be controlled by the set rules that govern machine tool operation, the world would be a much different place."

But since it could not, and because labor had become a problem, this tended "to eat the heart out of the glorification of success," as Bendix puts it. A change in ideology was in the making, and a 1910 article admitted that it was not only hard work and the goal of success that mattered, but the employee should also gain the "confidence, respect, and cooperation of his employer." (271-274) This was significant because it recognized that the employer could prescribe the conditions of success or failure; it was not just a question of hard work, jungle laws, or positive thinking.

Enter Science

Even more destructive of the Social Darwinist struggle for survival as an ideology of management was the rise of "Scientific Management," founded by Frederick W. Taylor early in the twentieth century. Briefly, the goal of Scientific Management was to analyze jobs very carefully into their smallest aspects, scrutinize the capabilities of the human machine just as carefully, and then fit the two together to achieve the greatest economy. Job techniques would be redesigned to make maximum use of human abilities; humans would be trained to perform the jobs optimally.

It is difficult to think of this as a breakthrough for several reasons. Most important, it took skills from the hands of the workers and gave them to engineers, decreasing the owners' dependency upon workers. As mentioned earlier in this chapter, under the prevalent inside contracting system, workers were responsible for many technological innovations, and through the contractor they presumably reaped some of the rewards. Now, under the deskilling program of Taylor, they found their wages reduced and their ranks split into finely graded distinctions that helped crush collective action. Deskilling labor saved costs. This was the crucial benefit to the owners (which Bendix hardly deals with). In terms of justification of authority, Taylorism had three advantages for management. First, it applied research (stopwatch clocking of the smallest movements) to work, rather than letting tradition guide it or letting each work group set its pace. Time-study specialists and industrial engineers continue this work today in most sophisticated factories. Second, it made some bow, at least, to the interests of the workers, arguing that such research permitted management to explore the possibilities for the workers' development, allowing them to advance to the highest level that their natural abilities would allow. In this view the struggle for survival is irrelevant if everyone works up to his or her own abilities; positive thinking will not affect the outcome of scientific research.

Third, this theory suggested that it is *cooperation* between labor and capital that brings success. In Taylor's view, this was the most important message, for it should take the eyes of labor and management off the *division* of the surplus (higher wages or higher profits) and instead turn them toward the problem of increasing the *size* of the surplus; in this fashion there could be both higher wages and higher profits. Indeed, under this enlightened system there would be no need for unions. Bendix argues that it meant the end of arbitrary power on the part of the management; science would decide. The personal exercise of authority would cease. It hasn't, and whatever science exists is not neutral but pro-management. But Bendix is correct that the image of the employer was transformed in the process. "From a man whose success in the world made him the natural leader of the industrial order, he had become a leader of men whose success depended in part upon a science which would place each man in 'the highest class of work for which his natural abilities fit him.'" (280)

Employers, however, did not at first embrace the ideology of Taylorism, even though deskilling, bureaucratization, and control were proceeding apace. For one thing, Taylorism "questioned their good judgement and superior ability which had been the subject of public celebration for many years." (280) It reduced their discretion, placing it in the hands of technicians; it implied that management's failure to utilize the skills of workers was the reason for workers' inefficiencies and restiveness. Indeed, Congress conducted hearings on Taylorism, so lively was the debate and so suspicious were employers. But the effect was to break the hold of the old ideologies. Indeed, the ideal of cooperation appeared to many to be a more useful ideological underpinning than Social Darwinism. It was apparent that sheer initiative or a fighting spirit was not appropriate in increasingly large, complex, bureaucratized firms. Also, the union movement, while subsiding after World War I, was a permanent fixture, and employers would have to fight its expansion and its encroachments on managerial prerogatives with more subtle ideological weapons— even as they continued to use violence. Company unions (plantwide organizations of workers set up and controlled by management) were established, and welfare schemes were introduced to counter social unrest and the threat of socialism. Management as a class became separate from ownership, and by 1920 there were three partners, not just two—capitalist, managers, and labor. Workers now were not expected to emulate their superiors and achieve success, but to accept the modest rewards and inherent satisfactions of good work. By 1928, conversely, a management journal urged: "Treat workers as human beings. Show your interest in their personal success and welfare." (294)

The Responsibility to Lead

By 1935 a completely new note was sounding, one that was to figure heavily in the more theoretical works of two grandparents of present-day organizational theorists, Elton Mayo and Chester Barnard: "People are tractable, docile, gullible, uncritical—and wanting to be led. But far more than this is deeply true of them. They want to feel united, tied, bound to something, some cause, bigger than they, commanding them yet worthy of them, summoning them to significance in living." (296) This observation is, of course, an ancient justification for leadership (and especially totalitarianism), but it signified a clean break from the previous ideologies. Workers would realize fulfillment through working hard to maximize the profit of owners; large-scale, hierarchical industrial organizations were plainly good for people. Left to themselves, people are not of much use; in organizations they can be "summoned to significance in living." This was a far cry from the beliefs of a century earlier, when to work in a large organization was to be a "wage slave."

One implication of the changing emphasis was that employers were now enjoined to do something about or for the workers. Bendix notes:

As long as they had regarded success itself as the sign of virtue and of superior qualities, no further justification of industrial leadership had been necessary. The counterpart of this belief had been that failure was the sign of vice and of incapacity. And since success and failure resulted from the struggle for survival, it was beyond the reach of human interference. Now employers and managers proposed to do something about workers who failed to produce efficiently and to cooperate fully. Apparently they were no longer satisfied to regard such failure as the unavoidable outcome of the competitive struggle. Instead they would investigate the causes of failure and prevent their recurrence by the development of appropriate managerial policies. The qualities of leadership needed for this purpose were necessarily different from, and less self-evident than, those required for success in the struggle for survival. Among American employers the superiority of industrial leaders was as unquestioned as ever, but it had become the subject of discussion as well as of celebration. (298).

This meant that, as stated in *American Management Review* in 1924, "the study of the employee's mind alone will not solve, and often confuses, the problem. The mind of management is also an integral part of human relationships in industry." (299)

Along with the increasing responsibility of management for the character of the workplace went a change in the qualities managers were expected to have in order to succeed. In the mid-nineteenth century, those qualities were "industry, arrangement, calculation, prudence, punctuality, and perseverance." These are the moral traits of a person acting alone. They do not deal with interpersonal relations, leadership, or even competence. But industry was not very complex at the time, and such things as prudence and punctuality perhaps needed emphasis and may have even been decisive. A list from the year 1918 provides a dramatic contrast: intelligence, ability, enthusiasm, honesty, and fairness. Ten years later the lists had gone even farther: the leader should be worthy of his authority, eager to acquire new information, willing to learn from subordinates, anxious to see them develop, able to take criticism and acknowledge mistakes. Furthermore, these qualities were not inherited but could be developed through training. (301) That managers might submit to training in itself shows how great the change was. This last list, emphasizing leadership, interpersonal relations, and competence, would do very nicely today, sixty years later, and could be duplicated in a casual reading of management journals.

It was in such an environment that Dale Carnegie's *Public Speaking and Influencing Men in Business* could flourish. (It was later titled *How to Win Friends and Influence People*, suggesting a more universalistic application.) Emphasizing will power but also manipulative techniques that induce the cooperation of subordinates, Dale Carnegie Institutes have become a permanent fixture among the services available to business and are still widely used. The 1926 volume became the "official text" of many progressive organizations, such as American Telephone and Telegraph (AT&T), and management associations. As with the leadership list, the concerns were interpersonal relations and the handling of people.

Persuasion and Cooperation

The next major change in the ideologies of management was the assertion of the basic identity of the nature of managers and workers, even though the one, naturally, had developed some aspects of their nature more fully than the other. This came about with the social philosophy of Elton Mayo as applied to industrial cooperation. Unlike Taylor, Mayo broke with the tradition of regarding each worker as a wage-maximizing individual in isolation. He attacked what he called the "rabble hypothesis" of economic theory that was being used in industry and that still guides much of economics. There were three tenets to that hypothesis, said Mayo, and he took exception to all three: society consisted of unorganized individuals—discrete atoms rather than natural social groups; each individual acts according to calculations of his or her own self-interest, rather than being swayed by group norms; and each individual thinks logically, rather than being swayed by emotions and sentiments.

It was a brilliant criticism, heralding much modern organization theory. Today we emphasize the group context of behavior and the way in which context shapes the individual's goals, which are not solely self-interested. And by denying that behavior is always logical or rational, Mayo anticipated the powerful influence of Herbert Simon's notion of bounded (limited) rationality. But as we shall see in Chapter 7, economists who now study the internal processes of organizations still expound a modified version of the "rabble hypothesis" that Mayo assailed.

Mayo's alternative is not as full developed as today's social psychological and sociological theories of organizational processes; it strikes one as quite romantic and primitive in its conceptualization. But as an alternative to the theories of the 1920s and 1930s it was dramatic. (The best summary is his 1945 book *The Social Problems of an Industrial Civilization.*) He emphasized the desire to be in good standing with one's fellows, the role of emotions, and the instincts of human associations. Economic self-interest was the exception rather than the rule. This held for all people, whether owners, managers, or workers. They must all cooperate if civilization were to survive. But, almost inevitably, the distinction between workers and others crept back in Mayo's writing. The administrative elite of owners and mangers had more capacity to engage in logical thinking and calculation than the workers. It was a capacity born of the necessity of guiding complex organizations. Therefore, the elite had a greater responsibility for providing an organizational environment in which employees could fulfill their "eager humankind desire for cooperative activity." (315) People found themselves in organizations.

After analyzing the functioning of the most extensive human relations programs in the 1950s, Bendix concludes that Mayo's contribution found only limited acceptance in managerial practices but that its influence upon management ideology was pervasive. (319) A new vocabulary of motives was constructed out of his view of humankind as preeminently social and cooperative; it would offer new justifications for management authority and worker obedience.

Mayo's philosophy was severely criticized by many social scientists. His statements about "spontaneous" cooperation and his longing for a medieval past where each person knew his or her place in a cooperative endeavor made him an easy target, especially in the late 1930s and the 1940s, when labor's chances of gaining power in industry rested not on spontaneous cooperation but on the legitimization of industrial conflict through collective bargaining and strikes. Mayo's critics felt that his view of cooperation was espoused at the expense of labor and on the terms of management and other legitimate and exploitative segments of society.

Summary

The ideologies of management had gone from Social Darwinism to social cooperation in about half a century. For example, the explanation for employee failure or problems with employees run from biological unfitness to incorrect handling. The changes in ideology, of course, went hand in hand with the changes in the structure and technology of industry. As it became more bureaucratized, large, and mechanized, interpersonal problems loomed larger and those of the sheer force of will, inventiveness, or effort declined. As responsibility for costly machinery and breakdowns in assembly lines became greater, even deskilled workers needed to be retained because of their experience, and specialized craft jobs grew. As immigration dried up and capital investments increased (making work stoppages more costly for management), unionization became a more potent weapon. Attitudes of the public and public officials also changed, of course, making Social Darwinism a less acceptable explanation.[20]

The new ideologies of management, however, rested not on fixed qualities of managers or the system; instead they stressed things that management had to *do*, such as discovering a common purpose or making a deliberate effort to structure a cooperative system. The eager desire for cooperation was there; it was up to management to give it rein. At the same time as this ideology was born, the instruments for its expression were being created in the business schools and social science departments of the nation. Workers could be studied not only by time and motion engineers, but by psychologists, social psychologists, and sociologists. The vast amount of empirical work undertaken by these academicians in industrial (and military) studies was eventually to culminate in our present-day theories of organizations. The first to construct the theoretical outlines of the major theory of organizations existing today was the businessman Chester Barnard.

BARNARD'S COMPANY TOWN

When Barnard was writing *The Functions of the Executive*[21] in the late 1930s, hardly anything around qualified as an academic theory of organizations in the United States. As Bendix indicated,[22] there was a growing emphasis on the cooperative nature of business enterprises—a vague and uncomfortable ideology that capital, management, and labor somehow had to unite for the good of all. From the Social Darwinism of the late 19th century, management ideology had moved through a number of doctrines that progressively weakened

---

[20]   For a good general survey of the social problems of the Industrial Revolution and the conflicting schools of thought, see Part 1 of Harold L. Wilensky and Charles N. Lebeaux, *Industrial Society and Social Welfare*, rev. ed. (New York: Free Press, 1965). Wilensky's introduction to this edition is as pertinent as it was twenty years ago. It includes, for example, material on the lack of support for working women. This subject should become explosive in the 1980s, but since the feminist movement has sadly given low priority to the problem of child-rearing while women work full time and instead has emphasized equal rights, the injustice may continue. "Why can't a woman be like a man?" asks Henry Higgins in George Bernard Shaw's *Pygmalion*. She can, say the feminists, but as the careful surveys of Alfred Kahn and Sheila Kamerman show—for example, Kamerman, Kahn, and Paul Kingston, *Maternity Policies and Working Women* (New York: Columbia University Press, 1983)—and as Sylvia Ann Hewlett brilliantly analyzes in her *Paper Tigers* (New York: Morrow, 1985), she will have a very hard time in the United States if she tries to both work full-time and bear and rear children. Yet about 40 percent of women have to try. Women have entered the labor force in large numbers with several strikes against them. First, because of household and child-caring duties that men generally refuse to share, they have no time to spend on union-organizing activity, at a time when unions are declining and seeking to preserve the gains for the elite workers in high-wage industries. Second, employment growth is limited overwhelmingly to low-skilled jobs in low-paid service industries. Third, today's conservative political environment emphasizes individualism and free markets, while working women need protective legislation because of their dual burden. Finally, the feminist movement is also unresponsive to women's dual burden. In Europe, women's jobs are protected, maternity benefits are provided, careers are not interrupted, day care is provided, and the individual burden of child rearing is shared with the whole society.

[21]   Chester Barnard, *The Functions of the Executive* (Cambridge, Mass.: Harvard University Press, 1938).

[22]   Bendix, *Work and Authority in Industry*, Chapter 5

management's justification for authoritarian rule and led management to the uneasy position that it had a responsibility to join hands with labor in a common enterprise. Classical management theory was hardly adequate as a theory of organizations, since it relied on "plan ahead" proverbs and assumed that management was there to control the enterprise, divide the work rationally, pay minimum wages to ensure profit, and take advantage of a large and dependent labor market. It did not speak to the issues of unionism and industrial unrest. The Weberian model of bureaucracy would have been adequate by the management theorist. But this had not even been translated from the German by the 1930s and it would only begin to have an impact upon organizational theory at the end of the next decade. Besides, it was inconsistent with the growing concern with cooperation. The sweeping generalizations of Elton Mayo, offering a medieval order in the midst of rapidly changing and expanding industrial civilization, were not appropriate. Parts of Mayo as well as classical management theory could be used, of course, but there was no coherent unified theory to encompass the new view of organizations.

The void was filled by Barnard's 1938 volume. This enormously influential and remarkable book contains within it the seeds of three distinct trends of organizational theory that were to dominate the field for the next three decades. One was the institutional school as represented by Philip Selznick…; another was the decision-making school as represented by Herbert Simon…; the third was the human relations school…. The leading theorists of these schools freely acknowledged their debt to Barnard. It would not be much of an exaggeration to say that the field of organizational theory is dominated by Max Weber and Chester Barnard, each presenting different models, and that the followers of Barnard hold numerical superiority. All those simplified, dramatic dichotomies—such as mechanical systems versus organic systems; production-centered versus employee-centered organizations; rigid, inflexible versus adaptive, responsive organizations; and authoritarian versus democratic organizations—stem from the contrast of the Weberian and the Barnardian models.[23]

The Barnardian model went beyond the pious statements that labor and management should cooperate and that cooperations would reduce conflict or raise productivity. Barnard was the first to insist, at length, that organizations *by their very nature* are cooperative systems and cannot fail to be so.

In a sense this is true. People do cooperate with one another in organizations, or in any enduring social group for that matter. In organizations, the cooperation goes beyond formal rules, is not precisely calculated to conform to the amount of wages or salary, is frequently spontaneous and generous, and, by and large, is in the interests of the goals of the organization. But, in the Weberian view, this is hardly the essence of organizations, since people are basically constrained to cooperate because of hierarchy of authority, separation of office and person, and so on. As we say today, these are "structural" sources of cooperation, and creating the best structure for a particular organization is difficult and never fully realized. For Barnard, however, cooperation

---

23   Terence K. Hopkins "Bureaucratic Authority: The Convergence of Weber and Barnard," in Amitai Etzioni, *Complex Organizations* (New York: Holt, Rinehart & Winston, 1962), pp. 159-167, attempts to reconcile the two but himself comes to the conclusion that only on the most general level—organizations are both coordinated and imperative systems—is this really possible.

is the essence of organizations. He emphasized cooperation almost to the exclusion of such things as conflict, imperative coordination, and financial inducements. His position is somewhat extreme, but because it underlies so much of organizational theory today, the remainder of this chapter will be devoted to rather close criticism of it.

To read Barnard today is a chore, and I do not recommend it except for historical analysis. Barnard knew he was breaking new ground, and as a careful executive (he was president of New Jersey Bell Telephone Company, a part of the Bell Telephone System that breeds and honors careful executives), he may have felt compelled to examine and classify every lump of soil in tedious detail. The first sixty-one pages of his book consist of an attempt to ground his work in some kind of theory of human interaction, complete with epistemological discussions; this section is most notable for the endless presentation of categories on categories and the relentless analysis of workers moving a stone. Yet to unravel this semiphilosophical treatise is to gain an insight into a basic posture of a good part of organizational theory.

The Setting

Barnard was confronted with a difficult problem. The United States was only beginning to cope with the Great Depression; it did not know that a war around the corner would increase productivity as twentieth-century capitalism itself had not. The prospects were grim indeed around 1936 and 1937, when Barnard was writing. Throughout the 1930s social unrest had been high, and the legitimacy of established organizations was being questioned. Radical ideologies were strong among the intelligentsia, and direct and often violent action was apparent among the working classes. Yet to respond to this perilous situation with an authoritarian model harking back to the days of Social Darwinism was not appropriate for a subtle and highly intelligent social philosopher in those years.

The Bell System, that until recently giant web of organizations, was one of the first to adopt the principle of treating workers decently and considering them as partners in a triumvirate of capital, management, and labor. The president of AT&T wrote in a business journal in 1926 of the cooperative nature of the company and its obligations to investors, employees, and patrons. In testimony before the Federal Communications Commission in 1936, he re-emphasized this and said that his loyalties were divided as equally as possible among the three parties. The question was raised as to whether labor was not bearing the brunt of the Depression rather than the investors, thus making the partnership hardly equal, since throughout the Depression AT&T had managed to adhere to the principle of the $9 dividend on each share of stock while the number of employees had been reduced by nearly 40 percent.[24] As president of a subsidiary of AT&T, Barnard was of course aware of such issues. In fact, in an earlier position he had performed an essentially political role in dealing with the federal government.[25] Given these kinds of challenges, the

---

[24] The reduction in workers had begun before the Depression hit AT&T and could not be accounted for by the level of business that the firm had. At the end of 1937 it was doing more business than in 1929, but it still had about 30 percent fewer employees. Part of this was due to technological change, but a good part of it was due to the "speed-up" on the production line. See discussions in N.R. Danielian, AT&T, *The Story of Industrial Conquest* (New York: Vanguard Press, 1939), pp. 220-221.

[25] Ibid., pp. 259,260,270.

state of the nation in the mid-1930s, and the state of organization theory, what was Barnard's response?

The Moral Organization

First, organizations per se had to be defended and even sanctified. It is significant that the opening sentence of Barnard's book reads as follows: "With all the thought that has been turned upon the unrest of the present day in the literature of social reform, one finds practically no reference to formal organization as the concrete social process by which social action is largely accomplished.[26] That formal organizations were largely responsible for the Depression and the social unrest is, of course, not mentioned. Rather, belief in the power of individual action is alluded to as a basic cause of the trouble. Organizations, Barnard tells us, cannot fail to have a moral purpose. Society itself finds its form, its "structure and process," through formal organizations. The only goal of business, he says, can be service. It is not profit nor power nor political ideology and certainly not personal gain. The common purpose of an organization must always be a moral purpose, and to inculcate this moral purpose into the very fiber of the organization and its members is the only meaningful task of the executive.

This view is important; it is not a mere publicity handout by a corporation executive. Years later a similar position was set forth by one of the three or four leading organizational theorists, Philip Selznick, in his book *Leadership in Administration*, though Selznick wrote in far more sophisticated terms. The idea that power can exist or survive only if it is legitimate, which is found in the writings of Talcott Parsons,[27] represents a similar view. If organizations exist and have power, that power must be legitimized by society and therefore given the mantle of morality. To question this would be to question the very "structure and process" of modern society.

Why were organizations moral for Barnard? Not simply because of the key role of the executive inculcating moral purpose, though that is important, but because organizations are cooperative systems. People cooperate in organizations. They join organizations voluntarily. They cooperate toward a goal, the goal of the organization. Therefore, the goal must be a common goal, a goal of all participants. Such a goal could not fail to be moral, because morality emerges from cooperative endeavors. Society could not exist without cooperation, and the clearest form of cooperation may be seen in organizations. Thus, in this view, if people cooperate in the pursuit of common goals, there can be no problem with the output of organizations; they must be moral institutions.

The Organization and the Individual

There are a number of thorny problems with Barnard's view. First, if the emphasis is on the collectivity—the organization or the cooperative *system*—how does one handle the individual? Barnard was worried about philosophies that emphasized the individual and his or her decisions or acts, since morality was a collective phenomenon. It is the Bell System that counted, not President Gifford of AT&T or President Barnard of New Jersey Bell. But how do you separate the individual from the organization? How can you talk about

---

[26] Barnard, *The Functions of the Executive*, p. 1.

[27] Talcott Parsons, *Structure and Process in Modern Societies* (New York: Free Press, 1960), p. 121.

organizations without talking about individuals? This is a basic and enduring problem for all organizational theory. The "field" theory of Kurt Lewin, developed after Barnard's book was published, drew its strength from Lewin's attempt to discuss fields of forces rather than individuals. The interminable debate in the 1940s and 1950s over the old question of whether the group was more than the sum of its parts, and the almost inevitable but shaky answer of yes, is a similar illustration of this ontological problem. The current faddish term "synergism," indicating that something unique emerges from the interaction of discrete inputs of energy, is a reaffirmation of the reality (and superiority) of the collective character of a system. The persistent and unsatisfactory debate over whether there are such things as organizational goals, when only individuals would appear to be goal-directed sources of energy,[28] is another manifestation.

Barnard was the first, I believe, to confront this problem systematically and head-on in terms of formal organizations (through Emile Durkheim had done so for groups or society in general). It was essential for Barnard's ideology that the group win out. Therefore, he defined organizations as "nonpersonal." They do not consist of persons, or things such as machinery, or ideas such as technology, or even what he vaguely referred to as "social situations." Instead, the organization consists of "forces." These are emitted by persons, but persons themselves are not, strictly speaking, members of the organization. They are part of the environment of the organization, part of a larger cooperative system that included the organization. He insists throughout the book that organizational actions are nonpersonal in character; even executive decisions do not reflect personal choice. It is because the activities of humans are *coordinated* to make a *system* "that their significant aspects are nonpersonal."[29]

This is an awkward position to hold, and even though Barnard does maintain it throughout the book, he is forced to distinguish between the organizational aspects of people and the personal aspects. He suggests "that every participant in an organization may be regarded as having a dual personality—an organization personality and an individual personality."[30] This is somewhat similar to the concept of an organizational "office," but the difference is important. The concept of office or social position pertains to prescribed duties and responsibilities. The person holds or "fills" the office. But he or she does not, except in exaggerated cases which are subjects of ridicule and humor, *become* the office, nor is the office an equivalent (except in exaggerated cases) of a personality. For Barnard, the identification is much stronger; the organizational personality is all-pervasive for the person acting as a member of an organization. For the five men moving a stone, he notes, it is not important what this means to each man personally once they have agreed to cooperate; what is important is what each thinks it means to the organization as a whole.[31] The extreme situation is, for Barnard, the best illustration for the concept: "In military action, individual conduct may be so dominated by organization personality that it is utterly contradictory of what personal motivation

---

[28]   For a statement of this, see Herbert A. Simon, "On the Concept of Organizational Goal," *Administrative Science Quarterly* 9 (June 1964): 1-22.

[29]   Barnard, *Functions of the Executive*, p. 77.

[30]   Ibid., p. 88.

[31]   Ibid.

would require."[32]

This position allows Barnard not only to reify the organization (something that all organization theorists are forced to do to some extent) but to minimize the importance of personal choice. The executive makes decisions and thus chooses among alternatives, but these do not reflect personal choice. These actions are nonpersonal in character because the executive is part of a system of "consciously coordinated activities or forces of two or more persons,"[33] which is Barnard's definition of a formal organization. This allows him to speak contemptuously of "the exaggeration in some connections of the power and of the meaning of personal choice." The "connections" undoubtedly referred to some of the radical ideologies that were circulating during the Depression. These exaggerations of the power and meaning of personal choice, Barnard says, are "vicious roots, not merely of misunderstanding but of false and abortive effort."[34] True and productive effort will be performed through organizations.

The consequences of extolling the organization over the person are clear when we examine Barnard's insistence that organizations are superior to individuals. Organizations are rational; individuals are not. Or, in Barnard's terms, logicality emerges from the interaction of organizational personalities or the field of forces given off by people. Persons themselves, or individual actions, are likely to be nonlogical in character. Thus, one cannot define organizations as consisting of people, for then they would be nonlogical and by implication nonrational. He speaks of the "superlative degree to which logical processes *must* and *can* characterize organization action as contrasted with individual action."[35] Logic is not a characteristic of the individual but only of the coordinated relationship of individuals acting in terms of their organizational personality. Only in organization can we have the "deliberate adoption of means and ends" since this is the "essence of formal organization."[36]

This view is held by many organizational theorists. But the solution of Weber and classical management theorists is to see in the organization a means of controlling individuals in the interests of the goals of the leasers of the organization. The organization is more rational than the individuals because order is imposed on members by those who control the organization, and the order is in the interests of goals or purposes established and guarded by those in charge. It is rationality only in the *leaders'* terms. For Barnard, the organization is more rational than the thing that extracts from individual behavior the logic based on common goals and willing cooperation. The duality that pervades Weber is that of the ruler and the ruled; the duality that pervades Barnard is that of the organizational personality and the individual personality.[37]

---

32 Ibid.

33 Ibid., p. 73.

34 Ibid., p. 15.

35 Ibid., p. 186. (Italics added.)

36 Ibid.

37 Only in some forms of conflict theory of organizations is the matter of rationality handled in such a way as to avoid these two positions. If different sets of actors are rationally pursuing different interests and goals, the question of organizational rationality is moot. It is the value, for example, of Erving Goffman's iconoclastic work on mental hospitals that he insists that presumably irrational patients, ruled over by rational staff members, are indeed quite rational in their perceptions and interests. The staff members, in the patients' view, appear quite irrational. In emphasizing this,

THE PROCESSES OF ORGANIZATION

Executive Decision Making

How, then, do organizations actually function? First, there is the key role of executive decision making. Not only are leaders supposed to inculcate moral purpose into every member of the organization, but their main activity is to make the key, or, as Selznick put it years later, the "critical" decisions. As obvious as this may seem today, it was not so clear forty years ago. The role of the executive in the literature of that time was analyzed in much more general, vague, and moralistic terms. Barnard was groping his way toward an essentially behavioral analysis of leadership by singling out the importance of rational analysis of alternatives and selection of the best one. He felt that the direction an organization takes hangs on one or two major decisions made by an executive in a year. Possibly what Barnard had in mind were such things as Eddie Rickenbacker's decision, while he was president of Eastern Airlines, to emphasize cost reduction while competitive airlines were emphasizing customer comforts and expansion of service. Rickenbacker's decision made a lot of money for Eastern for a number of years, but it proved to be the wrong one as the competitors overtook the company.[38] Sewell Avery's decision to sit on millions in Montgomery Ward cash and securities in anticipation of a post-World War II depression and to stick with small stores gave Sears a permanent lead, since the latter expanded by building large suburban stores as quickly as possible. And the decision of General William Westmoreland to engage in search-and-destroy activities in Vietnam, seeking out the enemy wherever he might be, was a critical executive decision that was reversed by his replacement, General Creighton Abrams. Barnard not only saw the significance of such key decisions but he saw the need to analyze executive behavior in these terms, rather than merely in moralistic ones.

Indoctrination

Despite his analysis of executive decision making, Barnard could not see the organization as the shadow of one person. He believed that all people must share the goals that the key decisions both reflect and shape. But if organizations are cooperative systems with all people working toward a common goal, how does one explain the fact that there is conflict in organizations, recalcitrance on the part of some members, lack of cooperation, and so forth? Barnard does admit that sometimes the ends of the person and the ends of the organization are not the same; indeed, he grants, they may be in opposition. He indicates that such opposition is most likely to occur among the lower-ranking participants in an organization. When faced with such opposition, the answer is not to buy off the opponents with inducements of higher wages, nor to threaten them with loss of employment, nor to let them participate in changing the goals of the organization. The answer is indoctrination.

Goffman tends to describe the hospital as irrational as an organization, but it is in reality only ineffectual. See Erving Goffman *Asylums* (New York: Doubleday, 1961); and Charles Perrow, "Hospitals: Technology, Structure, and Goals," in *The Handbook of Organizations*, ed. James March, pp. 910-971.

[38] For this and other examples of critical decisions as to goals, see Charles Perrow, *Organizational Analysis: A Sociological View* (Belmont, California: Wadsworth, 1970), Chapter 5.

When common purposes do not exist, the answer is to manufacture them. "The most important inherent difficulty in the operation of cooperative systems" is "the necessity for indoctrinating those at the lower levels with general purposes...."[39] This may actually involve deception:

> We may say, then, that a purpose can serve as an element of a cooperative system only so long as the participants do not recognize that there are serious divergences of their understanding of that purpose as the object of cooperation. . . . Hence, an objective purpose that can serve as the basis for a cooperative system is one that is *believed* by the contributors (or potential contributors) to it to be the determined purpose of the organization. The inculcation of belief in the real existence of a common purpose is an essential executive function.[40]

Thus we have an inconsistency. Organizations consist of forces generated by people acting in concert to achieve common goals, but it turns out that the goals are not indeed always shared or common. And it is even difficult to identify goals that all would hold in common with the leaders once the leaders' aims are understood. So propaganda and indoctrination are necessary. The leaders apparently set the goals and then try to make sure that they are commonly held.

Inducements and Contributions

Another idea that does not fit with Barnard's cooperative view is that of the balance between "inducements and contributions." Only in recent years has it become fashionable to conceive of organizations as systems with inputs and outputs. Barnard was way ahead of his time when he did so on 1938. Each individual makes an input to the organization (a contribution) and receives some part of the output (an inducement). Work and loyalty are contributions. Wages, prestige, and the like are inducements. If there is an excess of inducements over contributions—if people do not give enough for what they get—the organization will fail. If the two are in balance, the organization will survive and will be in equilibrium.

The distinction between contributions and inducements was utilized extensively by Herbert Simon in his work ten years later.[41] Neither Simon nor Barnard, however, deals with the situation in which contributions exceed inducements. This accounts for profits. Presumably, it is in the interest of the organization, and certainly was in the interest of the Bell Telephone System during Barnard's reign, to make sure that people give more than they receive. Otherwise, the organization could not prosper, grow, and gather power. It is on precisely this analysis that unions make their case for a bigger share of the profits in the form of wage increases. There are other problems with the contributions-inducements theory. It is hard to escape the impression that it is obvious and tautological. If a worker leaves an organization, we say that the balance was upset for her; if she does not, it was not upset. But was it wages that caused her to leave, or other job opportunities, or dissatisfaction with the common purpose, or excess travel time, or the weather in part of the country,

---

[39] Barnard, *Functions of the Executive*, p. 233.
[40] Ibid., p. 87.
[41] Herbert Simon, *Administrative Behavior*, 3rd. Ed. (New York: Free Press, 1976): and James G. March and Herbert A. Simon, *Organizations* (New York: Wiley, 1958).

or what? The theory does not tell us; presumably, something must have happened, but this is hardly enlightening.

There is a more serious problem. Why would the employees have to make elaborate calculations of inducements and contributions if the crux of the matter were cooperation in a *common purpose*? The inducements-contributions theory rests more easily with Weber or with the classical management school than with the cooperative school. (The human relations theorists have emphasized cooperation and neglected the inducements-contributions idea; Simon does just the reverse.) However, Barnard appears to minimize this contradiction by listing eight inducements,[42] only one of which is material in character. The other seven include such terms as "the condition of communion" and "associational attractiveness." Furthermore, he repeatedly denies that material inducements are very important to organizations. Thus, the calculations of inducements and contributions can be made in terms of whether employees rank the making of cars, butter, and guns as important common goals or not. One might well wonder whether Barnard seriously believed that the employees' acceptance of the purpose of General Motors, whether that might be profit, producing cars, or whatever, was "essential" for all members. Is such a purpose an important inducement? However, much of organizational theory, especially as encompassed in the human relations approach, appears to share his view.

It is essential to Barnard's view of organizations that the importance of economic incentives be consistently played down. It is striking to find him repeatedly asserting, during the Depression, "the almost negligible" role of material incentives "beyond the level of the bare physiological necessities."[43] He seems to be saying that workers will work for the wage that will just keep them alive, and they will derive their real satisfaction from such things as the condition of communion. Even the bare physiological necessities, this corporation president and major organizational theorist continues, "are so limited that they are satisfied with small quantities." Though the Depression is not mentioned in this book (social unrest is), in another volume Barnard notes that the food allowance for a person on relief was 6 cents a meal. Nevertheless, it is "wholesale general persuasion in the form of salesmanship and advertising" that has persuaded employees that money is important.[44] (He does not note that it is organizations that advertise; that would suggest an immoral output.) The logical organization is separated from the nonlogical environment as well as from the nonlogical individual.

Authority

A plain fact about organizations is that the people at the top have a lot more authority than those at the bottom. Authority to give orders, fire, fine, and otherwise control individuals is an essential part of organizations. This presents something of a problem for those who believe in a cooperative system. Barnard's solution, widely cited and firmly embraced by many theorists, is that authority comes from the bottom. The subordinate makes a decision to grant authority to the person above him or her. If a subordinate does not accept the legitimacy of

---

[42]   Barnard, *Functions of the Executive*, p. 142.

[43]   Ibid., p. 143.

[44]   Ibid., p. 144.

an order, the person giving it has no authority.[45] The idea is an old one, probably extending back to the Greeks. Barnard himself quotes Roberto Michels, a friend of Max Weber, to the effect that even when authority rests on physical force, and is accepted because of fear of force, it is still *accepted*. Weber made much the same point but he stated it as a limiting case, noting that there is always an irreducible element of voluntary compliance in an authoritarian relationship. But what was a limiting case for Weber is the basic nature of the phenomenon for Barnard. Barnard quotes a "notable business executive" who had been an army officer in world War I to the effect that the army is the "greatest of all democracies" because when the order to move forward is given, it is the enlisted man who has to decide on his own to accept that order.[46]

Barnard also speaks of the "fiction of the superior authority," but it is hardly a fiction if one can be fired for disobeying orders or shot for not moving ahead on orders. And organizations do fire people, Barnard admits, but he prefers to refer to voluntary resignation or to "terminating the connection" when the "attitude of the individual indicates in advance likelihood of disobedience."[47] Indeed, he says at one point that "to fail in an obligation intentionally is an act of hostility. This no organization can permit; and it must respond with punitive action if it can, even to the point of incarcerating or executing the culprit."[48] There is no "fiction" involved in these exercises of superior authority. But to define authority differently would be to weaken the emphasis on cooperation. If organizations are primarily or even exclusively cooperative in nature, there is no room for a definition of authority that includes imposed rules and coercion as important aspects.[49]

Informal Groups

One of the most celebrated discussions in Barnard's work is that of the role of informal groups within organizations. Weber and the classical management theorist were, of course, aware of informal relations in organizations, but they saw them as problems to be overcome in the interest of complete control. It was the merit of Barnard's discussion that he saw the functional aspects of informal groups. Such groups are necessary, so to speak, to "oil the wheels" of the formal organization, to provide understanding and motivation in those areas where the formal organization is deficient. Barnard notes that they are responsible for establishing attitudes, understandings, customs, habits, and institutions. They are necessary to the operation of the formal or-

---

45 Ibid., pp. 163-164.
46 Ibid., p. 164. This view of authority is not consistent with Barnard's concept of the "organizational personality." As noted earlier, he uses heroic military behavior to illustrate the predominance of the organizational personality. The person who decides on his own to move forward is using his organizational personality. Since the organizational personality can be based on indoctrination or propaganda, authority can be a top-down phenomenon. In the present example, authority is considered a bottom-up phenomenon.
47 Ibid., pp. 166-167.
48 Ibid., p. 171.
49 For Weber, authority in bureaucracies was rational-legal authority, a type of domination based on legally enacted, rational rules that were held to be legitimate by all members. The rules were either agreed on or imposed. The fact that member accepted the legitimacy of the authority in no way altered the facts that rules could be imposed and that coercion lay behind them.

ganization as a means of communication, of cohesion, and of protecting the integrity of the individual.

To Barnard's discredit, however, he completely neglected the possibility of negative aspects of informal relations. This had been extensively documented in the Hawthorne study, with which he was familiar.[50] For F. J. Roethlisberger and W. J. Dickson, the informal organization could and did have disruptive and dysfunctional aspects, such as setting standards for what was considered a fair day's output that were below those of management, or supporting systematic rule violation. But Barnard denied that the informal organization could have common purposes; for him, the purpose, such as they were, were only personal.[51] This would make agreements on a fair day's production, arrived at among workers and policed by them, fall into the category of unorganized activity. Why would this be important for Barnard? Because for him, only the formal organization can be rational. Informal organizations are not; they "correspond to the unconscious or nonintellectual actions and habits of individuals," whereas formal organizations corresponds "to their reasoned and calculated actions and policies."[52] Barnard comes close here to joining Roethlisberger and Dickson in their assumption that management behavior is mainly rational and workers' behavior nonrational.

The Fulminating Executive

Finally, as we have noted, the executive is the key to the organization of society. It is he or she who bears the moral freight of organizations in society. True, all personnel are important in an organization. "The work of cooperation is not the work of leadership, but of organization as a whole." Cooperation is an attribute of organizations, for the force is given off by all. But, Barnard continues:

> These structures do not remain in existence, they usually do not come into being, the vitality is lacking, there is no enduring cooperation, without the creation of faith, the catalyst by which the living system of human effort is enabled to continue its incessant interchanges of energies and satisfactions. Cooperation, not leadership, is the creative process; but leadership is the indispensable fulminator of its forces.[53]

Of course, for such a superhuman leader, material incentives are irrelevant. The most important single contribution required of the executive is loyalty, or "domination by the organization personality."[54] But since this is also the least susceptible to tangible inducements, material incentives play an "incidental and superficial role" in the case of the executive. One wonders why, then, their salaries are high. The functionalist Barnard tells us. In a statement altogether remarkable, especially in 1938, he says that income becomes significant enough to be "an important secondary factor to individuals [top executives] in many cases, because prestige and official responsibilities impose heavy burdens on them." But, he adds, even though they need material

---

[50]   F.J. Roethlisberger and William J. Dickson, *Management and the Worker* (Cambridge, Mass.: Harvard University Press, 1947).

[51]   Barnard, *Functions of the Executive*, p. 115.

[52]   Ibid., p. 116.

[53]   Ibid., p. 259.

[54]   Ibid., p. 220.

incentives to meet the burdens of prestige, these incentives are still not only insufficient but are "often abortive."[55]

THE THEORY IN PRACTICE

Barnard was an operating executive. He knew organizations thoroughly. He spent his working life in the telephone company, and he rose to one of its highest positions. He was a man who, unlike most social scientists, could "tell it like it is"; could give the illuminating example or detail; could use his own experience to convince us of the merit of his model. Illustrations from experience or from events recorded by others do not prove anything about a theory but, in the absence of empirical research, the quality of examples and illustrations is important. If, as in Barnard's book, one finds simple illustrations (workers rolling a stone or, in his longest one, five men engaged in woodcutting) coexisting with complex and subtle theory, one is likely to ask which should be believed. Theory illuminates the real world; examples lend cogency to untested theory.

There are practically no illustrations in his book of actual organizations functioning in a situation. In fact, only three references to the telephone company occur. Two of them are trivial and incidental (all the decisions that go into moving a telephone pole, and the height of switchboards). The third is an account of a telephone operator so devoted to her ill mother that she took an inferior post in an isolated area so that, while working, she might watch the house she shared with the mother. The house burned down one day, but despite her commitment to her mother, she stayed at the switchboard, watching it burn. Her "organizational personality" won out. Says Barnard, "She showed extraordinary 'moral courage,' we would say, in conforming to a code of her organization—the *moral* necessity of uninterrupted service."[56]

Aside from this curious example, real-life organizations with their conflicts, multiple goals, cliques, and ambiguities are absent from this book. The answer, I believe, lies in Barnard's determination to purge the organization of unseemly, nonmoral, or nonlogical human behavior and to uphold the cooperative model.

Fortunately, in another volume of essays, Barnard has given us a concrete example of organizational behavior and particularly of his own behavior. He first wrote it up for a seminar at the Harvard Business School.[57]

Barnard in Action

For eighteen months at the beginning of the Great Depression, Barnard was the Director of Emergency Relief in New Jersey, and then in 1935 he served as chairman of the Relief Council in Trenton, where there had been especially severe problems of unemployment and relief administration. Here, indeed,

---

55 Ibid., p. 221.
56 Ibid., p. 269.
57 The Bell System has had a long and cozy relationship with the Harvard Business School. N.R. Danielian describes the company's overtures to professors who teach—and infuence—public utility law and regulation, and the thinly disguised propaganda addresses by executives of the company that are given at the school at the suggestion of the company. (See Danielian, *AT&T*, pp. 297-302.) Barnard himself spent a good deal of time at Harvard talking with L. J. Henderson and others.

was a nonroutine situation and an obvious clash of interests. In fact, one key meeting between Barnard and a delegation of workers was abruptly terminated when a large crowd of over 2,000 demonstrators, supporting the workers, was broken up by the police. A second meeting was scheduled and took place; the purpose was to hear the grievances of the unemployed. Barnard rejected their demand to meet with the whole Relief council and instead insisted that only he and eight of the workers' representatives meet. Barnard analyzed the situation for a seminar in sociology conducted by L. J. Henderson and later published the analysis in a collection of papers.[58]

He stressed that the complaints of the workers, to which he listened for two hours, were, with few exceptions, "either trivial or related to past history no longer relevant to the existing conditions. As a whole, they were utterly inadequate to explain or justify the organization of the relief recipients, their mass meeting, or the time and effort of the representatives, some of whom could certainly have employed themselves to better advantage materially in the endeavor to obtain jobs or create places for themselves."[59] Rather than attempting to make real complaints about relief provisions during a period of severe unemployment in an industrial city, "what these men wanted was opportunity for self-expression and recognition. . . .To have dismissed the grievances as trivial, however, would have been to destroy the opportunity that was literally more important to these personalities than more or less food for themselves or families."[60] So much for one view of the realities of the situation, more or less food. Really at stake were nonlogical sentiments; why else would they not be out looking for work? Indeed, the problem with relief was obvious; it was not the well-to-do and those who ran the state and city who were opposed to higher payments. (Barnard agreed the payments of 6 cents per meal per person were "insufficient.")[61] "The well-to-do," he told the workers' committee, "have lost plenty and are grumbling much about taxes and this or that, and lots of them have lost their nerve. But they're not the people who are opposed to you. . . .The people who are most opposed to you and whom you and I must pay most attention to are those nearest you—those just one jump ahead of the bread line."[62] This made the problem one of educating the marginally employed, not deficit spending or higher taxes for the well-off and moderately well-off (such as those with large holdings of telephone stock, which continued to pay its $9 dividend). Education, of course, would take time.

Unimpeded by nonlogical sentiments, Barnard drove his point home. "What ought to be done either in the way of correction of faults or increases of allowances, I will do if I can, because they ought to be done." Then, pounding the table for emphasis, he continued: "But one thing I want to make clear. I'll be god-dammed if I will do anything for you on the basis that you ought to have it just because you want it, or because you organize mass meetings, or what you will. I'll do my best to do what ought to be done, but I won't give you a nickel on any other basis." He would decide what "ought to be done."

---

[58] Chester Barnard, *Organization and Management* (Cambridge, Mass.: Harvard University Press, 1948), pp. 51-79.

[59] Ibid., p. 71.

[60] Ibid.

[61] Ibid., pp. 72.

[62] Ibid., pp. 74-75.

He added that his position was "based more on your own interest than on anything else. For the kind of behavior which you have been exhibiting is alienating from you the very people upon whom you or I depend to get the money for relief, and I assure you there are many who object to giving it now."[63] So much for cooperation. They were wrong in their method—the would get satisfaction only on Barnard's terms and not theirs—and they were wrong about the source of the difficulty. After another hour's discussion, they left, leaving it all in Barnard's hands. "As I look back on it, I do not think I had ever before made a purely personal accomplishment the equal of this," said Barnard.[64] Presumably Mayo would have applauded too. Characteristically, Barnard never indicated what decision he took about what should be done; it was simply not relevant. This little cameo, concrete and descriptive, of actual organization behavior and organizational problems bears little resemblance to the cooperative systems analyzed in his classic volume. Once again, we find Barnard violating his cooperative model when the realities of organizational life must be considered.

---

[63] Ibid., pp. 73-74.
[64] Ibid., p. 75.